Every totalitarian claim gradually isolates itself because it excludes so many people as defectors, fallen, lost, apostates, hypocrites, heretics, and so forth. The totalitarian manouvres himself in a corner, no matter how large his original following. (His reign of terror becomes even more terrible as he continues to justify the transgression of human rights and mass executions on religious or rational grounds.)

—C. G. Jung

'The most dangerous of all forms of oppression are laws and restrictions forcibly imposed on people in the name of religion. This is what the Monks, through collaboration with the ruling classes, did with the people in the name of religion. This is the most dangerous of all impositions, because that which is not from God is thrust upon the people to enslave and suppress them and prevent them from evolving, depriving them of the right to protest, criticise and be free. These very chains and shackles are the ones which the Prophet (Muhammad) came to destroy. Islam is an invitation to peace and freedom. Let us keep aside opportunism, group interests, forcible imposition of ideas and, God forbid, dictatorship under the cover of religion. (Let us) raise our voices with the toiling, oppressed, and deprived masses. Islam as we know it, the Islam which originates from the Quran and the traditions of the Prophet, does not restrict freedom. Any group that wants to restrict people's freedom, (the freedom) to criticise, protest, discuss and debate, does not comprehend Islam.

"Islam is the religion of freedom. Its goal is people's liberation. If a religion aims at liberating people from all forms of bondage, it cannot itself be made a chain for keeping people in bondage... The reactionaries are trying to distort the concept of freedom by equating it with a decadent version (used by) the bourgeoisie in the West, in order to enslave the masses. In the name of religion, (they wish to) further the interests of their own class by enslaving people in exploitive chains."

—Excerpted from Ayatollah Taleqani's last Friday Prayer Sermon, (Khutba), Tehran, September 1979. Quoted in Mardi-ez-Tabar-e-Nur (A Man from the Abode of Light). Anjuman-e-Touhidi-e-Resalat. Tehran. 1979. PP. 10-18).

Iran's Islamic Revolution
Suroosh Irfani

DEDICATION

Dedicated to those who carve out the path of liberation with their blood and transmit the glow of consciousness to others during the nights of oppression, who lie buried en masse and unknown in unmarked graves, locked up in torture chambers, rotting in secret dungeons, or forced into exile by the usurping oppressors of the times.

Iran's Islamic Revolution:
Popular Liberation or Religious Dictatorship?

Suroosh Irfani

Zed Books Ltd., 57 Caledonian Road, London N1 9BU.

Iran's Islamic Revolution: Popular Liberation or Religious Dictatorship? was first published by Zed Books Ltd., 57 Caledonian Road, London N1 9BU in 1983.

Copyright © Suroosh Irfani, 1983

Cover design by Jacque Solomons
Printed by The Pitman Press, Bath, U.K.

All rights reserved

> **British Library Cataloguing in Publication Data**
>
> Irfani, Suroosh
> Iran's Islamic revolution
> 1. Iran – Politics and government – 1979-
> I. Title
> 955'.053   DS318.8
>
> ISBN 0-86232-157-3
> ISBN 0-86232-158-1 Pbk

U.S. Distributor
Biblio Distribution Center, 81 Adams Drive, Totowa, New Jersey 07512.

Contents

Preface	ix
Introduction	1
1. Unfurling the Islamic Revolution	19
Syed Jamal-ud-Din 'Afghani'	19
The Tobacco Concession	22
Afghani, Iqbal, Shariati and the Progressive Islamic Movement	32
2. The Constitutional Revolution (1905–9)	44
A Short-lived People's Victory	47
3. The Jungle Revolution	50
Mirza Kuchak Khan	51
Kuchak Khan and the Soviet Union	54
End of the Jungle Revolution	61
4. Mossadeq's National Movement	67
The Movement in Retrospect	75
5. Khomeini and the June Uprising of 1963	79
Khomeini's Emergence as a National Religious Leader	79
6. Mujahideen-e-Khalq	89
Causes for Failure of People's Movement in Iran (1906–1963)	92
Guerrilla Operations	94
Shariati's Views on Religion	98
7. Ali Shariati: Teacher of Revolution	116
Methodology of the Prophet	121
Shariati and Mujahideen-e-Khalq: The Search for Models	126
8. Taleqani and the Revolution	138
9. The Islamic Revolution I	149
Torture, Political Prisoners, and Revolution	153
The Revolution for Freedom	160

10. Islamic Revolution II: January 1978–February 1979	166
11. The Runaway Revolution	182
The Hostage Crisis	191
12. Elections in the Islamic Republic	198
13. The University and the Islamic Republic	204
The 'Cultural Revolution'	205
14. Women and Religious Minorities in the Islamic Republic	211
15. Progressive Muslims and the Islamic Republic	214
The Fall of President Banisadr	221
From the Martyr's Mind: Defence Speeches, Biographies, and Poetry of Resistance	232
Appendix One	233
Appendix Two	261
Postscript	264

Preface

The realisation that over the years, Islam's dynamic and assimilative spirit has been made victim of the expediency and dogma of the professional clergy and the ruling classes makes it necessary to draw a line between the dynamic spirit of Islam and the static dogma imposed in the name of Islam by 'men of the religious bazaar'.

Dr. Ali Shariati who provided the intellectual dimension for Iran's Revolution has lucidly stated this problem in one of his opening lectures on Islamology. He said: 'Which Islam do we have in mind when we speak of an Islamic ideology? It is difficult for me to explain what I wish to say ... because when I speak about Islam, I must use words and terms which, ... have lost their meaning. This is why I am compelled to continuously explain in order to identify the Islam I am speaking of: it is the Islam of justice and leadership, not of leaders, classes and aristocracy, it is the Islam of freedom, awareness, and movement, not the Islam of bondage, stagnation, and ignorance, it is the Islam of a *mujahid* (holy warrior), not that of a *rouhani* (clergyman). In short, the Islam I have in mind is one which leads to holy battle for shaping society, for scientific *ijtehad*, (principle of reconstruction and renewal in Islamic thought) and for illuminating belief. It is not the Islam of imitation, prejudice, and resignation. Therefore, in speaking about Islam, the major problem stems from the fact that the general impression people have about Islam (a reactionary weapon wielded by the decadent ruling classes) acts as a deterrent to its reintroduction in the Muslim society. Hence, it is no easy task to speak about the uncomprehended spirit and the forgotten contents of Islam. What I wish and hope for, is a return to Islam and its acceptance as an ideology. As an ideology, Islam can be grasped and applied through a scientific, analytical, and comparative understanding of its basic principles'.*

The present volume deals with the development of the progressive Islamic movement, in the context of Iranian history both at the strategic and the intellectual levels, spanning the period from Syed Jamal-ud-Din Afghani in the last quarter of the 19th Century to

---

* Shariati, A., Islamshinasi. p.95.

Mujahideen-e-Khalq and Dr. Shariati in the mid seventies of the 20th Century.

Lahore, May, 1982.

S.I.

Introduction

KHASHM, meaning *rage*, was the code word Muslim activists used for their struggle against the Pahlavi dictatorship, climaxing in the Islamic Revolution of 1978. Quite appropriately, the word expressed the rage of a nation against a dictatorship that sustained itself through intimidation, torture, imprisonment and the execution of its political opponents. The word was formed by putting together the first letters of the three forces in the Islamic spectrum that brought about the Revolution — Khomeini, Shariati, and *Mujahideen-e-Khalq*.

Of the three forces, Khomeini represents the politicised Shia clergy[1] which has exercised a major influence in the affairs of the State ever since the mass conversion of a Sunni Iran to Shiism in the 16th Century under Safavi rule. Khomeini's main accomplishment was to successfully place the struggle against the Pahlavi dictatorship in an anti-imperialist framework and give the struggle religious sanctity by invoking his position as a *Marja-e-Taqlid* (literally: Source of Imitation), one of the highest religious ranks possible in the informal hierarchy of Shia Islam. In so doing, Khomeini consciously followed the anti-imperialist approach of Syed Jamal-ud-Din Afghani,[2] the 19th Century Muslim revolutionary who believed that by emphasizing the social and political dimensions of Islam and mobilizing the Muslim masses it was possible to forge an Islamic Front for confronting the forces of despotism and colonialism in Muslim lands. Shariati and the *Mujahideen-e-Khalq*, in pursuing the ideological direction implicit in Afghani's anti-imperialist movement, were able to develop a revolutionary Islamic ideology to form the basis for a progressive Islamic movement. This movement is progressive not only because of its anti-imperialist and anti-exploitive direction, nor because it has developed independently of the traditional Islam of formalist *Ulama* and the dogma of theological schools, but also because of its dynamic approach to Islam and the Quran.

The central ideological concern of the progressive Islamic movement is to redefine Islam in the light of modern knowledge and scientific advancement — a task and a challenge which requires the Muslim intellectual to 'rethink the whole system of Islam without breaking away with the past'.[3] As Iqbal has pointed out, it was Syed Jamal-ud-

1

Din Afghani who 'fully realised the importance and immensity of this task',[4] because of his 'deep insight into the inner meaning of the history of Muslim thought and life, his broad vision and wide experiences'.[5] By generating a new wave of consciousness in Islamic thought, Afghani became 'the living link between the past and the future,'[6] and the nucleus for progressive Islamic movements of the future.

Furthermore Iqbal believes that had the 'indefatigable' Afghani devoted his undivided energy solely for systematizing Islam as a system of belief and conduct in a contemporary light 'the world of Islam would be on much more solid ground today'.[7] In other words, Afghani was the first Muslim revolutionary who sensed that in order to bring Islam to the forefront of Muslim life and in the mainstream of the Muslim peoples struggle for liberation and identity, it was necessary to reconstruct Islam according to the extant level of consciousness, channelling the creative life impulse of pristine Islam in a progressive direction. The object of Afghani's movement was the reform of Muslim religion by invoking its original spirit and replacing the antiquated system of Islamic jurisprudence (*fiqh*) by new and enlightened laws. Where consideration for the common good and the demands of the times were to have, if necessary 'preference to the literal text of the revelation'.[8] The movement also rejected the hairsplitting of the *fuqaha*, the Islamic jurists.[9]

While Afghani remained 'a revolutionary who aimed at forcible upheaval',[10] Sheikh Abdu, the disciple and intellectual expounder of Afghani's ideas, held that no political revolution could occur without a gradual transformation in mentality and change in attitude and consciousness of the people. 90 years later, these two approaches were blended together with the emergence of Shariati and the *Mujahideen-e-Khalq*. Afghani and Sheikh Abdu can also be credited for creating the Islamic Revolutions' 'French connection' when in 1883, they were forced to seek political asylum in France, having been hounded out of Muslim countries by reactionary rulers and formalist clergymen. The two founded an Islamic Society in Paris and published the first international Islamic journal called *Urwat-ul-Wuthqa*, meaning the indissoluble link, a reference to the Quran. The journal, which soon was banned in Muslim countries under colonialist control, is believed to have profoundly influenced the development of Muslim nationalism in the East.[11] The 'French connection' established by Afghani set the trend for Muslim revolutionaries to seek asylum in Paris for the struggle against reaction and despotism in Muslim lands. It continues to this day. This connection was reactivated by Shariati during his student years in Paris in the 1960s where he studied Islamic history under Louis Massignon a Professor at College de France. A few years later, in October 1978 and during his final months of exile, Khomeini sought refuge at Neuphle Le Chateau near Paris to lead the Islamic Revolution. With the arrival in Paris of *Mujahideen-e-Khalq* leaders and other progressive Muslim revolutionaries in the summer of 1981 in the wake of the Khomeini regime's crack down against its political opponents, the 'French connection' of Islamic forces came back in full circle. Today it represents a continuation of the progressive Islamic movement against imperialism, despotism and religious reaction which began with Syed Jamalud Din Afghani a century ago.

While the extroverted Afghani remained the initiator of the Progressive Islamic Movement, and Sheikh Abdu preserved the spirit of this movement through his writings, the first systematic attempt at lending this movement an ideological framework at a modern intellectual level was made by Iqbal. As early as 1929 Iqbal had outlined the ideological direction for a progressive Islam with his lectures on the 'Reconstruction of Religious Thought in Islam'. In these lectures delivered at the Madras Muslim Association in 1929, Iqbal held that the spirit of Islam was so broad that with the exception of atheistic ideas it had assimilated all the creative and progressive ideas of the surrounding peoples and given them its own peculiar direction of development. The primary source of the law of Islam was the Quran, but it was not a legal code. Its main purpose, according to Iqbal, was to awaken in man the higher consciousness of his relation with God and the Universe. With its dynamic outlook, the Quran could not be inimical to the idea of evolution. The teaching of the Quran that life was a process of progressive creative movement necessitated that each generation guided, but unhampered, by the work of its predecessor should be permitted to solve its own problems through *ijtihad* — the principle of movement in the structure of Islam.[12] In these lectures, Iqbal also drew attention to the social significance of *touhid* — belief in the Unity of God and the need for translating this belief into working principles in human organization. The extension of the idea of social *touhid* was taken up by Khalifa Abdul Hakim[13] in Pakistan during the early 50s and by the revolutionary school of progressive Islamic thought in Iran during the 60s and early 70s. The object of social application of *touhid* was to point out the classless conception of society in Islam and its vision for creating a well harmonized humanity based on 'equality, solidarity and freedom'.[14] The State in Islam was a theocracy in this sense alone, and 'not in the sense that it be headed by a representative of God on earth who could always screen his despotic will behind his supposed infallibility'.[15]

Leadership of Social and Political Movements in Shia and Sunni Societies

The ideological framework for a progressive Islamic movement in Iran did not materialize until after the second half of this century. Reasons for this can be attributed to the special position and influence the *Ulama* enjoy in the Shia community, giving them power not only to control religious expression but also to influence the affairs of the

State. The power and influence which the clergy wields in religious, political, and social matters in Iran far surpasses that of their counterparts in Sunni societies. This is borne out by the fact that during the past hundred years in Iran the clergy has played an important role in the major popular movements against despotism and colonialism. While at one stage in these movements this role has been constructive, at other stages it has become regressive and has positively contributed to the destruction and neutralization of these movements. Moreover, it would be totally fallacious to assume that the Iranian clergy has at all times opposed the establishment and sided with popular movements against monarchical absolutism. Indeed the clergy has played a fundamental and decisive role in perpetuating the oppressive monarchical dynasties in Iran after the Shia rulers of the Safavi dynasty took control of a Sunni Iran in the 16th Century. However, within the folds of the clergy, there has always remained a tiny stream of radical Islam embodied in a small group of religious scholars who rose in opposition to the establishment in terms of religious belief.

Shiism in Iran

The implantation of Shiism in Iran owes itself to two external factors, the Safavi dynasty and the Shia clergy imported from Arab countries.[16] Being a dynasty of Turkic origins, the Safavi monarchs recruited a large number of their followers from outside Iran, mainly from Turkic nomads, Syria, and the Southern Caucasus. For political reasons, the Safavis manufactured a false geneology for themselves that linked them to Imam Musa Kazim, the seventh Shia Imam. Then they decided to convert the Sunni majority to Shiism, by force, if necessary.[17] However, the major problem the Safavi faced in implementing their policy was the non-availability of Shia scholars in the country. This problem was however solved when the Safavi rulers began importing Shia scholars from various Arab countries to help them in their undertaking. The flow of Shia *Ulama* to Iran under the protection of Safavi rulers accounts for the second external factor responsible for the conversion of Iran to Shiism. Given that the *Ulama* were dependent on royal patronage for their presence in Iran, they were initially obedient and loyal servants of the state. The practice of the *Ulama* prostrating themselves before the Safavi monarchs remains a documented fact.[18] It was during the Qajar dynasty (1795–1924) that the antagonism between the monarchs and the *Ulama* began to surface. The *Ulama*, who had grown considerably in number, could be divided into two main groups. The first, by far the larger, consisted of ordinary *mullas* who instructed rural children in religious matters. In return for their services, they received free board and lodging and a government stipend amounting to one *toman* (12 cents) per year.[19] The second group, consisting of a smaller number of religious scholars, was engaged in teaching and academic research in secluded seminaries without any direct contact with the people. The transformation in the economic and political power of the clergy, as we understand it today, is a recent phenomena having a history of not more than a century and a half behind it. The clergy secured this power following a series of crises in the wake of Iran's military defeat by Russia in 1828, the expansion of Iran's political and economic relations with the West, the emergence of a merchant bourgeoisie, and the suppression of peasant and urban movements triggered by the crisis in agriculture.[20] These developments, coupled with the migration of a large number of people to neighbouring countries, gradually generated a general discontent which took the form of peasant movements expressed in a religious context. Religious belief in consonance with the exigencies of the times and marking a departure from the passivity and inertia which the traditional belief structure had instilled among the people, was freely taking shape. An example of these reformist, even revolutionary movements is the *Sheikhiyeh* movement which then led to the more powerful *Bahai* movement in 1850. These movements laid a great emphasis on the role of the individual and his responsibility for changing oppressive social conditions. The *Sheikhiyeh* doctrine argued against the renunciation of individual initiative and social striving which was largely responsible for the social and spiritual stasis of the Iranian society because people were made to believe that only the appearance of Mehdi, the hidden Imam, at some unknown point in history would rescue them from tyranny and oppression, and usher in the era of justice and bliss in human society. The *Sheikhiyeh* emphasised that until the time Imam Mehdi reappeared, man was irrevocably in need of applying his own thought and judgment to the problems that faced him. In each period of time, and according to the changing conditions and new challenges, it was necessary that leaders should emerge from among the people in order to liberate them from oppression and injustice. Justice, then, was to be established in this very world through the struggle of the people and their leaders, who would rise from among the peasants, the craftsmen, and the scholars.[21] At about this time, the general discontent among the Iranian masses had developed into a powerful movement against the king, both in cities and rural areas. This movement, which had taken the form of armed resistance in several parts of the country, reached a stage where many peasants refused to pay taxes to the landowners and the State land was seized by the peasants and houses of feudal lords were set on fire. In the cities, the impoverished masses armed themselves with anything they could get, and attacked government offices and prisons. An attempt was also made on the life of the king. For the first time in Iranian history, the slogan for democracy was getting into circulation.[22] Although this movement was in no way directly linked to the *Bahais*—most people had never seen the Bab, religious leader of the *Bahis*, or heard him speak — by attributing it to the '*Bahai* heretics', the establishment enlisted the support of the clergy to crush the movement. The monarchy and the clergy thus joined hands in order to protect their mutual interests. By sharing economic and political power with the clergy, the monarchy succeeded in deploying religion as its instrument of suppression. A massive, ruthless massacre of the people was thus effectively accomplished by the clergy and monarchy in the name of protecting Islam against 'apostates'. It was during this period that the Qajar dynasty began bestowing lavish favours on the clergy. Vast tracts of land, often entire villages, were handed over to various clergymen, who legitimized their hold on the booty and preserved it for their descendents by calling their land holdings 'endowment'. In addition, the direct custody and supervision of all mosques was passed over to the clerical leadership. To further strengthen the bond between the clergy and the monarchy, intermarriages between the two were encouraged. The *Imam Jumma* of Tehran, (leader of congregational prayers in Tehran) married to one of the King's daughters, was among the clerical leaders who gave religious sanction to kill anyone suspected of harbouring anti-establishment sentiments. His *fatwa* read: 'Anyone who becomes suspicious of anyone else (of being a *Bahai*), anyone who discerns polytheistic thoughts in anyone else, has the right to freely kill that person in public'.[23] An unestimated number of innocent people, rebels, freedom fighters, and members of the intelligentsia were massacred by attributing to them the term *'Bahai'* and accusing them of blasphemy and heresy. Mirza Aqa Khan Kirmani, a religious scholar who sought refuge abroad during these massacres wrote: 'The *mullas* today consider the spilling of blood, a bliss (for themselves). Whipping, stoning human beings to death, and cutting off the head are considered to be religiously lawful. This has led to the situation where people have begun mutilating to shreds the bodies of their countrymen, fellow citizens, and fellows in faith. The oppression of the *mullas* and the Islamic jurists is no less than the oppression of the Monarchy'.[24] Sheikh Zanjani, another clergyman from the tiny minority of clerical dissidents wrote in his memoirs: 'Today in Iran, the terms 'Bahai' *(Babi)* and *"Kafir"* (infidel) have given the pretext to the *mullas* (to do whatever they please). The *mullas* are using these terms for robbing the merchants, shopkeepers, and peasants, and seizing their property and wealth (after killing them). Anyone who protests is physically liquidated by being branded 'infidel'. The people of Iran hate the students of theology and the *mullas* more than the policemen'.[25] After the suppression and slaughter the clergy had sponsored, its members were obsessed by the fear that any movement for freedom and reform would be antithetical to their interests. Thus, in 1884, when the issue for a free press and independent newspapers was first raised in the country, Hajj Mulla Ali, a clerical leader of Tehran, warned the Prime Minister in a letter, which partly read: 'Freedom, this most despicable of words, is good and beautiful in appearance only. In essence it is entirely defective and imperfect. It is against all the edicts and principles of the Sultan, the religious scholars, and eminent men of authority. It is against the interests and objectives of the government and dynastic rule to allow anyone to say whatever one pleases because there is freedom'.[26]

The collaboration between the clerical leaders, who had become part and parcel of the land owning bourgeoisie, and the Qajar Kings was to continue right up to 1924, when the Qajar dynasty was formally demolished. It was primarily under pressure from the clerical leaders in Qom that Reza Khan, the country's new strongman, who proposed to turn Iran into a Republic and become its first President, had to forego his plans and declare himself Reza Shah by founding the Pahlavi dynasty in 1925. The clerical support for the Pahlavi dynasty thus continued for another half a century. The clergy played a crucial role in overthrowing Mossadeq's government, the only legal government in Iranian history, and reinstating the Shah on the throne through the CIA sponsored *coup d'état* in 1953. The support of the clerical leaders for the monarchy amounted to the automatic enlistment of support on the part of the rank and file of the clergy with its petty bourgeoisie affiliations. It was this reactionary role of the overwhelming majority of the clergy that Dr. Shariati had in mind when he drew the dividing line between two forms of Shiism — what he called Safavi Shiism and Alavi Shiism. The former was the Shiism of the Establishment erected by the 'cancerous web of the compromising men of the religious bazaar'. It was the 'Black Shiism' of reaction promoted by the monarchy. From its very inception in Iran, Safavi Shiism had violated the very spirit of Shia thought by resorting to violence against the Sunnis.[27] Shariati therefore discarded the entirety of this dimension of Shia heritage in Iran, which he believed to be a distortion of Alavi Shiism, the Shiism of Ali. This was the true, authentic Shiism, the 'Red Shiism' of revolution which had existed eternally 'in contrast and in opposition to the Safavi Shiism'.[28] Thus, as a historical phenomenon, Shariati viewed religion as appearing in two distinct and contradictory ways — either as an instrument in the hands of the ruling class for the control and exploitation of the society, or as a means of struggle for establishment of a just society.[29] It is the perennial presence of religious spirit in the latter sense among a small number of religious scholars that has enabled them to play a crucial role in various social and political movements in Iran's recent history. At some stage in the movement, this handful of religious scholars have been able to drag the bulk of the clergy into the swelling tide of the movement and its leadership, even though the final outcome of these movements have been on the whole rather inconclusive.

The above aspect of the clergy's role in Shia society contrasts with the Sunni society, where popular movements have been generally led by secular and progressive Muslims, notwithstanding the persistent opposition of the majority of Sunni *Ulama*.

Sunni Clergy and Socio-Political Change

Several examples support the above argument regarding the generally regressive nature of the Sunni clergy with respect to social, political, and economic changes. To begin with, it may be recalled that Western educated and enlightened Muslims with a progressive outlook like Mohammad Ali Jinnah and Iqbal were the political and spiritual leaders of the Indian Muslim's movement for a separate homeland that led to the creation of Pakistan in 1947. Jinnah and Iqbal had succeeded in mobilizing the people and leading this movement despite the opposition of Sunni *Ulama* represented by the *Jamiat-e-Ulama-e-Hind* and *Jamaat-e-Islami*. Twenty-three years after the creation of Pakistan, it was Zulfiqar Ali Bhutto's socialist Peoples Party that swept the polls in 1970 in the first general elections ever held in the country, despite the massive propaganda against the 'Un-Islamic' Bhutto by the *Jamaat-e-Islami* and other formalist *Ulama*. The huge majority by which the Peoples Party won the elections conclusively demonstrated the fact that the clergy had completely failed in thrusting on the people its self-generated image portraying it as the sole custodian of Islam. In Sunni Algeria, it was the socialist National Liberation Front that won independence for Algeria after ten years of popular armed struggle against the French colonialists in 1962, while Indonesia won its national independence under the secular and nationalist Sukarno, as the Sunni Turkey had done under Kamal Ataturk. Also, Egypt got rid of its decadent monarchical system by socialist army officers, and Muammar Gadafi liberated Libya from the medieval rule of King Idrees by following Gamal Abdul Nasser's footsteps. A current example that may well be cited in some detail is the ongoing struggle of the Muslims in the southern Philippines for an independent Islamic state under the leadership of the Moro National Liberation Front (MNLF). Launched against the imperialist-backed regime of Ferdinand Marcos in 1969, the MNLF is a guerrilla movement fighting for secession of the southern Philippines, land of the Moros, the name by which Muslims in the southern Philippines are generally known. There are plenty of historical, political, and economic realities that have given legitimacy to the Moro struggle for an independent or at least autonomous Islamic State. For example, the Moro's colonial experience under both the Spanish and American colonialists differed from the rest of the Christian Filipinos in that the Muslims fought the colonizers at every stage of their encroachment. Except after America colonized the Philippines islands at the turn of this century, Moroland was never governed with the rest of the Philippines. After America gained control of the islands, several ideas for the colonization of the vast and rich Muslim Moroland were considered. It was proposed as a land for American negroes, Texan farmers and Jews, before the decision to settle it with Christian Filipinos from the northern islands began to be implemented. This was thought necessary for exploiting the vast farmland and natural resources of the region, rich in timber, mineral, and marine resources. With the escalation in settlement of Christian Filipinos in Muslim areas, Muslims, who constituted 98% of the population in the southern islands in 1900, became a minority of 40% by 1970.[30] The Muslims, a persecuted minority during the years of American colonization, were refused fair treatment even by the new masters in Manila after the Philippines gained independence in 1949. As a result, the exploitation of Muslim areas has gone on unabated and continues to this day. The Muslim region provides for 60% of the Philippines' timber, 56% of its corn, half of its coconut and fish, much of its rice, rubber, fruit and livestock, and all the important minerals such as zinc, iron ore, copper, gold, and nickel. Yet the standard of living of Muslims has been the lowest in the Philippines. To give one example of disparity, it was calculated in 1973 that Muslim islands averaged 20 km of road per 100,000 people against nearly 400 km per 100,000 in the Philippines non-Muslim provinces.[31] When these political and economic arguments were expressed in the framework of the demand for a just Islamic State in the southern Philippines by the MNLF, they triggered an enthusiastic response among the Muslim masses. Muslim leaders — all non-clerical—concluded that in a Philippines dominated by American corporate interests and politicians unsympathetic to the plight of the Moro Muslims, Islam would become a ritual religion and the area would remain backward and endlessly exploited by the Manila government. With the launching of the Moro stuggle for national liberation, Islam has emerged as the most pronounced aspect of Moro identity and the standard bearer of the Moro Revolution. However, the Marcos regime seems to have succeeded in enlisting the support of the Sunni *Ulama* in its propaganda to discredit the Moro National Liberation Front as Un-Islamic and a communist inspired Marxist movement. In a recent interview, Nur Misuari, Chairman of the MNLF observed that the colonial powers had always used Islam and the Muslims 'to destroy exactly what the Muslim people are fighting for'.[32] Marcos, Misuari claimed, was acting in the same way as the colonialists had done, for he believed that by using the *Ulama* against the MNLF, he could destroy the Moro struggle. 'The *Ulama* are not contributing to the solution (of the Moro problem)', according to the MNLF Chairman. 'They are making the problem more complicated and prolonging the suffering of the masses in the South'.[33] Misuari acknowledges the fact that the *Ulama* constitute 'an important sector' in the Moro society. But if the *Ulama* continued to allow themselves to be used against the MNLF by the Marcos regime, 'then no solution would be forthcoming.' For the moment, however, the Moro National Liberation Front continues to be the central force in the struggle of the Philippines Muslims for a separate homeland. The use of Leftist terminology by MNLF leaders and their learning from the history and experience of other revolutionary movements has not altered the Islamic orientation of the movement. Nor has the campaign of the *Ulama*—Marcos Front against the Moro Liberation struggle shaken the confidence of the masses which constitute the movement's backbone.

Clearly then, both in Shia Iran and Sunni countries, Islam has remained the major force for politicizing and mobilizing the masses, and in terms of which people have sought social, economic and political emancipation. However the difference between the Sunni and Shia societies lies in that whereas in the former, people have generally rallied under a non-clerical leadership notwithstanding the *fatwas* of the Sunni *Ulama* to do the contrary, in the Shia society like Iran, the clergy has played a crucial role in determining the course and outcome of a popular movement.

Sunni Islam and Shia Islam

In order to understand the essentially differing roles of Shia and Sunni clergy within their respective communities in the context of popular movements, it is necessary to comprehend the difference between Shia and Sunni Islam. Both Shia and Sunni Muslims believe in Divine Unity (*touhid*), The Prophet Mohammad, and the Quran. However, the major politically significant difference between them lies in the principle of *imamat* or leadership. Shiism believes that the leadership of the community was the exclusive prerogative of the Prophet himself. In their view, Ali, the Prophet's son-in-law, should have succeeded him as willed by the Prophet. The Sunnis, however, believe that 'the Prophet formed an Islamic society based on the Quran, the revealed book of Islam, and thus completed his mission'.[34] Therefore according to Sunnis, after the Prophet it was up to the people to elect a leader on the basis of their own judgement.[35] The Sunnis believe that if the Prophet wanted to nominate anyone for the leadership of the Muslims, he would have made his choice clear without leaving the least shade of doubt. For just as the Prophet was obliged to announce and teach the verses of the Quran clearly and in a way so that there could be no confusion, it was his duty 'to show the same care and clarity in announcing the successor if indeed one had been so decreed by God, in order to prevent any conspiracies, rejection, or misinterpretation',[36] that might occur subsequently. Sunnis also point out that if God had revealed to the Prophet to write an official decree clarifying the matter of succession, he would have written such a statement under any circumstances. He could not have overlooked doing so just because this or that person protested or argued against it.[37] But since God had not commissioned the Prophet to announce Ali as his successor, the Prophet did not do so and it was left to the people to elect the successor. After the Prophet's death, all the Muslims (the Emigrants who migrated with the Prophet from Mecca to Medina as well as the Helpers, citizens of Medina) gathered in Saqifeh to elect the caliph as the leader of the Islamic State and they elected Abu Bakr.

But the argument of Shiism goes like this: 'The succession to the Prophet differs from a political successor. The Prophet did not just have a political position, as to lead us to claim that he did not have the right to appoint a successor and people should elect the one who is to govern them. For the Prophet as a leader, master, and teacher was not appointed by the people so that this successor should also be selected by them. The Prophet was appointed by God. The fact of the matter is that the station of Prophethood is not a popularly elective office. It is not a power which people give to a person. Thus, a Prophet is not an elected individual. It is for this reason that his mission and the continuity of his movement must be put into the hands of a successor who is qualified for the same type of leadership and mission as the Prophet himself'.[38]

Since Shias believe that Ali was selected by the Prophet as his successor, they follow a line of religious leadership emanating from Ali. There are twelve heirs or successors called Imams, in this lineage. The Twelfth Imam, the Imam Mehdi, is believed to have disappeared and gone into occultation. He is known as the 'Hidden Imam' who continues his existence on a non-earthly plane. The Shia school of thought in Islam holds that legitimate authority rests with the Imam only. If the sole legitimate successor of the Prophet is no longer on the earthly plane, that means any worldly power that claims to exercise authority must be illegitimate, unless it can demonstrate in a clear and undisputed fashion that it exercises rule on behalf of the absent Imam.[39]

This is where the Grand Ayatollahs *(Ayatollah-Ol-Ozmas)* step in. A Grand Ayatollah is a *Mujtahid,* one who forms his own independent opinion on religious matters through his own discretion. During the period when the Hidden Imam remains concealed, there are *Mujtahids* who have to guide the faithful as his agents in religious matters.[40] Those who follow the *Mujtahid* are known as *Muqalid* (imitators), for they accept the saying of another without knowledge of its basis. The sayings and actions of the Grand Ayatollahs may be taken as authoritative by his followers with faith in their correctness and without investigating the reasons.[41] A *Mujtahid* who has reached the highest level of Islamic learning and is known for his piety, and commands a following among people, attains the highest religious position in Shiism when he becomes a *Marja-e-Taqlid* (Source of imitation). A *Mujtahid* who is a *Marja-e-Taqlid* is called a Grand Ayatollah. Generally at any given time, there are a few Grand Ayatollahs who, on behalf of the Hidden Imam, have assumed the burden of interpreting Islam. With today's Grand Ayatollahs, of which Khomeini is one, standing in for the Hidden Imam until his reappearance as a saviour, it follows that the responsibilities of leadership fall on their shoulders. There are today less than a dozen Grand Ayatollahs[42] and about 50 Ayatollahs.[43] The difference between a Grand Ayatollah and an ordinary

Ayatollah is significant. While both are *Mujtahids*, only the Grand Ayatollah is a Source of Imitation and has followers. Next in the descending order of the religious hierarchy come the *Hujat-ulIslams* (Manifestation of Islam) who are about five thousand in number. A *Hujat-ul-Isalm* is also a *Mujtahid*, but unlike the Ayatollah, he has not written a *resalah* (an *epistle*) and has not specialized in any branch yet. In scholastic terms these titles have little meaning. Many scholars who enjoy a high reputation and who have contributed significantly to the learning of Islam do not have the religious titles that others with lesser knowledge of Islam hold.[44] Further down this pyramidal hierarchy are tens of thousands of *tallabe*, live-in students committed to full time religious studies at a *hoze* (Religious School), and *Pishnamaz*, a prayer leader in some mosque or village. However, it is only the *Marja-e-Taqlid* composed of the inner council of Grand Ayatollahs whose religious decrees are obeyed unquestioned. Each Grand Ayatollah is recognised as having reached the highest level of Islamic learning. Their opinion on everything is generally accepted by their followers as emanating indirectly from God[45] and the Hidden Imam.

The concentration of religious power in an organized and yet informal clerical structure in Shiism has vested the clergy with much influence enabling it to play a significant role in all popular political and social movements in Iran's history. Moreover, until very recently, religious matters had remained almost the exclusive monopoly of the clergy in Iran. Although during the first quarter of this century the progressive outlook of Ayatollah Na'eini and Ayatollah Modaress had penetrated beyond the concerns of the traditional clerical folds, the *Ulama's* total control on religious matters militated against the 'emergence of figures who were fully devoted to Islam but came from a different intellectual and social background than the *Ulama*.'[46] This is the reason why a modern Islamic thinker such as Iqbal in the Indo-Pakistan subcontinent or the modernist thinkers of the Arab world had not emerged in Iran.[47] However, after 1960 an Islamic development in thought and expression that in many ways could be linked to Afghani and Iqbal, and that was distinct from the traditional concerns of the Shia *Ulama*, began emerging. At the political-reformist level, this Islamic development could be seen in the Liberation Movement founded by Western educated 'moderate' Muslims like Mehdi Bazargaan. And at the revolutionary level, it could be seen in the progressive Islamic ideology being developed by Ayatollah Taleqani, Dr. Ali Shariati and the *Mujahideen-e-Khalq*.

The present work is an attempt at presenting the progressive Islamic movement, in the process of crystalizing in the crucible of Iranian history, spanning the period from the Tobacco Movement in 1890 to the Islamic Revolution in 1978–79.

Chapterwise Summary of Contents

As the progressive Islamic movement in Iran can be traced back to Syed Jamal-ud-Din Afghani and his attempts at articulating Islam as a mobilizatory ideology of the Muslim masses against despotism and colonialism, the present volume opens with a chapter on Syed Jamal-ud-Din and his role in the Tobacco Movement (1892-94). This uprising of the Iranian people against the ruling Shah of the time was sparked off when the latter handed over all affairs pertaining to the cultivation and marketing of Iran's tobacco to the British. The tobacco uprising marked the first partially successful attempt by the Muslim masses at launching a unified movement under the banner of Islam against internal despotism and the forces of colonialism, with the clergy in the forefront. By seeking a reinterpretation of Islamic thought and stressing its social and political aspects, Syed Jamal-ud-Din aimed at using Islam as a weapon against oppression, exploitation, and injustice. It was his belief that given the right direction, the clergy could be made to play a constructive and positive role in mobilizing the masses. It is in this respect that the 'Tobacco Movement' of the 1890s is considered a prototype for the Islamic Revolution in 1978.

Although Syed Jamal had followers all over the Muslim world, it was in Iran 'where his views and his political agitation had both an immediate and a long range effect'.[48] His influence continued to grow beyond the Tobacco Movement, finding expresssion in the Constitutional Revolution (1905-09). Because of the role the intelligentsia played in this movement its objectives were more clearly defined than those of the Tobacco Movement. Directed against the absolute power of the monarch, the Constitutional Revolution sought to strip the Shah of his absolute power by investing the State authority with a freely elected Parliament. Insofar as the Constitutional Revolution is a logical sequel to the unfinished uprising during the Tobacco Crisis, Chapter two takes a brief look at this movement.

Chapter three deals with Mirza Kuchak Khan and his Jungle Revolution (1914-21). It was the policy of the Pahlavi dynasty to veil, even distort, the historical importance of this Muslim revolutionary who was the first to attempt a protracted struggle for liberating Iran from the reactionary monarchical system and oppressive colonialism through guerrilla warfare. To further shroud Kuchak Khan's revolution in a maze of ambiguity, both British and American historians have played upon Kuchak Khan's cooperation with the Russians following the Bolshevik Revolution in 1917, portraying Iran's national and Islamic hero as a 'Communist puppet'. Even Russian historians have been reluctant to acknowledge Kuchak Khan's role as the first progressive revolutionary in contemporary Islamic history, accusing him of conspiracy with the 'imperialists and Iranian reactionaries'.[49] Perhaps this verdict of Russian historians is motivated by their need to justify the shifts in Lenin's policy in respect of Kuchak Khan's Jungle Revolution. Lenin had initially supported Kuchak Khan but after 'communist hardliners' in the Jungle Revolution carried out their *coup d'état* against Kuchak Khan, the Soviet Union renounced the latter to favour the breakaway group of her own proteges. The events that followed the *coup* against Kuchak Khan's leadership facilitated the disruption of the Jungle Revolution and the emergence of Reza Shah to power in 1921. This paved the way for a repressive dynasty that was to last for over half a century. Brought to power by the British, Reza Shah remained the unchallenged strongman of Iran until he was exiled after the Second World War by the Allies and replaced by his son, Mohammad Reza Pahlavi.

It was not until 1951 that the Iranians, getting weary of the absolute control the British imperialists exercised on their natural resources, rose up to support Mossadeq, their Prime Minister, in a national movement directed against Western imperialists and the corrupt Monarchy. Chapter four deals with Mossadeq and his movement, which ended when the CIA, in collusion with the Iranian generals and religious leaders, ousted Mossadeq from power and reinstated the Shah in 1953.

Chapter five deals with the agitation against the Shah's regime in June, 1963. Following the success of the 1953 *coup,* America had gained a strong foothold in Iran. The ease with which America was consolidating its position in Iran was deeply resented by the people. For example, while Iranians were being subjected to increasing oppression and curtailment of civil and political liberties by SAVAK, the Shah's secret police and torture machine, Americans in Iran had been granted immunity from Iranian law. As a consequence of this bill passed by the rubber stamp Parliament, any legal matter in which an American serving in Iran found himself involved was to be settled by American courts and not in Iran. It was this 'capitulation' to U.S. imperialism and Khomeini's scathing criticism of it that triggered the 'June Uprising', reaching its climax with the arrest of Ayatollah Khomeini by the Government. The uprising was crushed within a few days, and Khomeini was exiled to Najaf, the Shia religious centre in Iraq.

Chapter six deals with the aftermath of the 'June Uprising'. Although the mood of despair generated by the brutal massacre of the masses during the 'June Uprising' had forced the majority of activists campaigning against the Shah to renounce their opposition, it did not prevent the younger and the more deeply committed revolutionaries from arriving at the realisation that armed struggle was the only recourse for resisting the dictatorship. The mid-sixties saw the emergence of two guerrilla groups, the *Mujahideen-e-Khalq* (Islamic) and the *Fedayeen-e-Khalq* (Marxist-Leninist). Drawing their members mainly from the educational institutions and the professional middle class, these young guerrillas, often from amongst the most outstanding of students, embarked upon a daring battle against the regime. During seven years of armed struggle, from 1971 to the breakout of the Revolution in 1978, these revolutionary organizations lost over three hundred members to the Shah's firing squads, SAVAK's torture, and skirmishes with the Shah's security forces. Although both the *Fedayeen-e-Khalq* and the *Mujahideen-e-Khalq* had an incontrovertible role in accelerating the revolutionary process, this chapter deals with the role of the *Mujahideen* only, owing to the special significance of this organization in the Progressive Islamic Movement and the Islamic Revolution. It was not only the first but also the only guerrilla organization subscribing to a progressive Islamic ideology to have operated against the Shah's regime with a well planned strategy. The vicissitudes suffered by this organization due to the blows from SAVAK, the formalist clergy, as well as from the 'pseudo left opportunists' from within the organization call for a discussion of this organization in some detail.

Chapter seven deals with the role of Dr. Ali Shariati, the revolutionary Islamic ideologue responsible for the crystalization of the new Islamic consciousness and the cultural revolution in Islam. With the advent of Shariati, Islamic terms like *hajj* (pilgrimage), *jehad* (sacred striving in a permanent revolution) and *shahadat* (martyrdom), having remained locked within a texture of words, surged into life adding a revolutionary impetus to their meaning. Shariati's revolutionary reinterpretation of Islam charged the people, particularly the young, with renewed courage, commitment, responsibility and awareness. For them, accountability to God was inseparable from social action and fighting for the liberation of the people. By reintroducing people to revolutionary Islam, in theory as well as in practice, Shariati and the *Mujahideen-e-Khalq* broke the barrier of fear, silence, and despair that had frozen the possibility of any initiative among the people, particularly among the religiously oriented Muslim youth.

Chapter eight discusses the role of Ayatollah Taleqani, the 'unorthodox *mulla*' who took progressive Islam not only to theological centres, but also to the University in the 1950s and was the first teacher of the *Mujahideen-e-Khalq*. Despite his advanced age and fragile health, the legacy of the three decades he spent in the Shah's prisons or in exile, Taleqani actually directed and led the Islamic Revolution inside Iran. Thus, while Khomeini remained the leader of the Revolution and issued his statements and guidelines from abroad, Taleqani, after the people won his release from prison in October 1978, became the nucleus of the Revolution within the country. It was Taleqani, who, defying the Martial Law of General Azhari's regime, invited the people to observe *Ashura,* a day of religious mourning, by marching in the streets. Taleqani himself led the procession of over one and a half million Iranians along the Capital's main thoroughfare. The march marked a turning point in the peoples' revolution and in the hitherto traditional meaning of the *Ashura* procession. The international Press called the march a vote of no confidence against the Shah.

Chapter nine discusses the Islamic Revolution and some of the major forces that shaped the development of events leading to the Revolution. The role of social, political, and economic forces has been briefly discussed. This chapter also discusses the central role which political prisoners played in spurring on the Revolution. Freedom for political prisoners was among the main demands during the period of mass mobilization. Also of fundamental importance in generating the intense hatred against the Pahlavi regime which eventually led to its destruction, was the regime's use of torture against its political opponents. This too, has been discussed in some detail. Chapter nine also discusses the role of the University in the struggle of the Iranian people for freedom. After the CIA *coup* in 1953, the University remained the only 'Fort of Resistance' against the regime. When Richard Nixon arrived in Tehran to negotiate oil concessions for American companies shortly after the 1953 *coup*, Tehran University became the venue for anti-Shah and anti-American demonstrations. The Shah ordered his troops to silence the students. As a result, para troopers from the Imperial Army invaded the University and opened fire on students killing three and wounding many. 16 *Azar* (7 December 1953), the day the students were gunned down on campus, became a symbol of student resistance in the years to come. The University played a pivotal role in the Revolution, serving as a secret recruiting centre for the two revolutionary organizations, the *Mujahideen* and *Fedayeen*. After Taleqani and Shariati brought Islam to the University, it was the students and the junior teachers who translated these revolutionary ideas into social action by forming the *Mujahideen-e-Khalq* organization.

The ground work having been done by all these forces over the long years of struggle, only a spark was needed to ignite a full scale people's uprising. Also necessary was the leadership of someone who could give cohesion to the masses and enlist their trust, particularly among the lower classes and the illiterate. And just as the Shah had deified himself and his dynasty to justify his autocratic rule, likewise he needed to be countered by a deified 'weapon' that was decidedly against oppression and injustice. Given these circumstance, it was in keeping with the Iranian tradition for Ayatollah Khomeini, the Grand Ayatollah and the leading Source of Imitation *(Marja-e-Taqlid)* for millions of Shia Muslims in Iran, to rise to the challenge. He became the unifying symbol for the most remarkable mass movement in history, by assuming its leadership. Given this leadership, the anti-imperialist Islamic Revolution surged forward to attain its first objective by overthrowing the monarchy. The events which made up the Islamic Revolution are discussed in Chapter ten.

Chapters eleven to fifteen deal with some of the major events following the creation of an Islamic Republic and briefly examine the nature of the ongoing struggle in Iran.

The section on Poetry of Resistance and Defense Speeches consists of translations of poems and defence speeches by *Mujahideen-e-Khalq* revolutionaries who were executed by the Pahlavi regime during the 70s.

Notes

1. Prior to the Revolution, Khomeini represented only a tiny minority of those clergymen who were actively opposed to the Shah's regime. While the overwhelming majority of the clergy were neutral or non-committal, many prominent religious leaders actually defended the monarchy. It was only after the popular movement against the Pahlavi dictatorship was well underway that the bulk of the clergy was also drawn into the movement.
2. Ayatollah Motahari, *Piramon-e-Enqilab-e-Islami.* (About Islamic Revolution), Sadra Publications, Tehran, 1979.
3. Iqbal, M., *The Reconstruction of Religious Thought in Islam.* Sheikh Mohammad Ashraf, Lahore, 1976, p.97.
4. Ibid.
5. Ibid.
6. Ibid.
7. Ibid.
8. *A Shorter Encyclopaedia of Islam.* Leiden: E. J. Brill, p.406.
9. Ibid.
10. Ibid.
11. Ibid.
12. Iqbal, M., 'The Principle of Movement in the Structure of Islam', sixth lecture in the series *Reconstruction of Religious Thought in Islam.* Quoted in *Life of Iqbal,* Vol.II, Ferozsons, Lahore, 1978, p.115.
13. Hakim, K. A., *Islamic Ideology,* Institute of Islamic Culture, Lahore, 1950.
14. Iqbal, M., *The Reconstruction of Religious Thought in Islam,* Sheikh Mohammad Ashraf, Lahore, 1977, p.154.
15. Ibid.
16. Algar, H., 'Iran and Shiism' in, *The Islamic Revolution in Iran,* Kalim Siddiqui, (ed), The Muslim Institute and the Open Press. London, 1980.
17. Ibid.
18. Ibid., p.4.
19. Homa Nateq, *Ruhaniyet va Azadi ha e Demokratik,* (The Clergy and Democratic Freedom), *Jahan,* No.3, 6 March 1982 p.6-9.
20. Ibid.
21. Ibid.
22. Ibid.
23. Ibid., p.8.
24. Ibid.

25. Ibid.
26. Ibid.
27. Algar, H., 'Islam As Ideology — The Thoughts of Ali Shariati', in *The Islamic Revolution In Iran* (Kalim Siddiqui, ed). The Muslim Institute — Open Press, London, 1980. p.42.
28. Ibid.
29. Ibid.
30. Philippines File, *Arabia; The Islamic World Review* No.11, July, 1982, p. 24–35.
31. Ibid.
32. Ibid.
33. Ibid.
34. Shariati, A., *Selection and/or Election (Vesayat va Showra)*. Shariati Foundation — Hamdami publishers, Tehran, 1979, p.4.
35. Ibid.
36. Ibid., p.2.
37. Ibid.
38. Ibid., p.2-3.
39. Algar, H., 'Iran and Shiism'. In, *The Islamic Revolution in Iran*, ed. Kalim Siddiqui, The Muslim Institute, London, 1980, p.2.
40. *A Shorter Encyclopaedia of Islam*, Leiden: E.J. Brill.
41. Ibid.
42. As pointed out by the Grand Ayatollah Qomi (*Ettela'at*, No. 16095, 11 March 1980), there are about 'ten or eleven' Grand Ayatollahs in the Shia world to-day. With the death of the Grand Ayatollah Mahalatti in recent months, the number of Grand Ayatollahs does not appear to be more than ten.
43. Abrahimian, E., *Structural Causes of the Iranian Revolution*. MERIP Reports, No.87, May, 1980.
44. 'What is an Ayatollah?' In, *The Iranian*, Vol. 1, No.5, July 25, 1979.
45. Ibid.
46. Algar, H., 'Islam as Ideology — The Thoughts of Ali Shariati'. In, *The Islamic Revolution in Iran*, (Kalim Siddiqui, ed.) The Muslim Institute, London, 1980, p.36.
47. Ibid.
48. McDaniel, R.A., *The Shuster Mission and the Persian Constitutional Revolution*, Bibliothica Islamica, Minneapolis 1974, p.49-50.
49. *Tarikh-e-Iran* (History of Iran). Translated into Persian by K. Kashavarzi. Pooyesh Publications, Tehran, 1980. This book, authored by a panel of half a dozen Russian historians, was first published by Moscow University in 1977. Henceforth called *Tarikh-e-Iran*.

1. Unfurling the Islamic Revolution

Syed Jamal-ud-Din 'Afghani'

Iran's anti-imperialist Islamic Revolution which brought the Persian monarchy to its doom in 1979 was a consummatory sequel to the unfinished popular movements that had sporadically shaken the thrones of the Persian Shahs for the past 90 years. Going back to Syed Jamal-ud-Din Assadabadi, better known as 'Afghani', the first Muslim revolutionary to develop 'an Islamic response to imperialism',[1] these popular movements expressed the yearning of the oppressed Muslim masses to rid themselves from a dual hegemony — the internal despotism of the ruling tyrants and the external exploitation of their colonialist masters. Syed Jamal-ud-Din's was a progressive Islamic movement because he sensed the necessity for redefining Islam in the light of modern knowledge and scientific advancement, with the object of making the revolutionary Islamic spirit accessible as a weapon against imperialism, despotism, and reaction. Afghani's entire life was a struggle to check and challenge the unrestrained power of oriental despots and the increasing political and military presence of the West in Muslim countries. This he attempted to accomplish by emphasising the social and political aspects of Islam and reinterpreting traditional Islamic ideas in terms of the exigencies of the times.

Living during the second half of the 19th Century, Syed Jamal-ud-Din rejected both the static-traditional views of Islam as well as the tendency of the Muslim intelligentsia and leaders to blindly follow the West. Instead, Afghani emphasized the social and pragmatic values, like political activism and the freer use of human reason.[2] He also endeavoured to build up the military power of Islamic States and strove for political unity among them. 'By seeking these values within the Islamic tradition instead of borrowing them from the West, Syed Jamal was able to obtain an influence on religious Muslims not possible for those who simply apprehended Western ideas.'[3]

Thus Syed Jamal-ud-Din Afghani pioneered that school of thought in the Muslim world which, while rejecting the orthodox dogmatic Islam on the one hand and the imitation of Western socio-political models on the other, regards Islamic dynamism — the rethinking of Islamic principles in terms of existing social, political and economic exigencies — as the surest way for making the liberating message of the Holy Quran a living reality for living Muslims. Because of his progressive views, Afghani was expelled by the reactionary rulers of Muslim countries and exiled by clergymen who considered his presence a threat to their own religious monopoly and position. For example, in 1873, he was expelled from Turkey, at the instigation of Sheikh-ul-Islam Fehmi, the leading clergyman in Istanbul. Afghani had delivered a series of lectures on religion and science at the newly established University at Istanbul. The content of these lectures was declared to be Un-Islamic and against the Prophet of Islam by the Sheikh-ul-Islam of Istanbul, who demanded Afghani's deportation. But it was clear that the more urgent reason for the clergymen's wrath and chagrin was Afghani's growing popularity among Turkey's intelligentsia.

Unity of Religion and Politics

Syed Jamal had noted that Muslim rulers had made religion subservient to politics for perpetuating their personal power and dynastic control in Muslim lands. For example, in the Sunni world, 'the Khalifa and the ruler considered himself to be the *Ulul Amr* (meaning, though not quite literally, the divinely authorised). Obedience to him was considered to be incumbent from a religious point of view'.[4] The unity of religion and politics that Syed Jamal advocated did not allow political oppression to give itself religious sanctity. 'On the contrary, it meant that the Muslim masses should count it a religious duty to participate in politics.'[5] Afghani believed that the unity of politics and religion was indispensable for effectively fighting the two evils of internal despotism and foreign colonialism. Through his publications and lectures, the Syed endeavoured to convince Muslims that Islam, as a school of thought and an ideology could deliver Muslims from the despotism of the indigenous ruling class and foreign colonialism. He pointed out that Islam is a religion of science, action, and endeavour, and a faith of striving and struggle. 'A religion of reconstruction and of fight against corruption.'[6]

Syed Jamal-ul-Din's call for Muslim unity was primarily meant for liberating them from the imperialists' yoke, and not for forging Muslim cohesion in terms of a Caliphate or under the exclusive rule of the *Ulama*. His summons to Muslims for social action were based on the Quranic verse 'Allah changeth not the conditions of a people until they first change that which is in their hearts'.[7] Moreover, this call was addressed to all Muslims, and the choice of allies sought by the Syed in his mission was purely tactical.[8]

Afghani's Views on Shia and Sunni Clergy

Through his intimate association with Shia and Sunni societies, Syed Jamal-ud-Din had 'well sensed the differences and dissimilarities between the Shia clergy and the Sunni clergy'.[9] According to Ayatollah

Motahari, Afghani had observed that 'the Sunni clergy is not independent and a native faction, and cannot be counted on as a significant power capable of challenging the forces of oppression and colonialism.'[10] The reason being that the Sunni clergy had been attached to governments and rulers who had through the centuries introduced themselves to the people under the title of *Ulul Amr*. 'That is why in Sunni society, he never went after the *Ulama*, but directly to the people'.[11] As a result of this observation, Afghani concluded that 'the Sunni religious scholars could not be utilized as a base in the struggle against opression and colonialism, for they enjoyed no ascendency and were similar to other classes of the masses.'[12] But the Shia clergy was not like this. It had an independent status and was financially autonomous, for it was directly supported by the Shia masses. Knowing this Syed Jamal homed in on the *Ulama* in Shia society to inject them with social and political awareness and to mobilize them as the base for fighting oppression and colonialism.[13] In Sunni societies, he went directly to the masses or modernist reformers. In Iran, Syed Jamal's policy in regard to the Shia clergy was very effective both in the Tobacco Movement (1890) and the Constitution Movement (1906) which marked a confluence of the struggle by Iranian modernists, reformers and the clergy for curtailing the absolute power of the monarchy. However, it needs to be pointed out that whereas Ayatollah Motahari's views on the role of the clergy in Sunni societies appear to be supported by historical developments in several Sunni societies during this century, the wholesale endorsement of the Shia clergy *per se* as anti-establishment and revolutionary is to grossly distort history because the role of Shia clergy in perpetrating the rule of Shia dynasties in Iran is an indisputable fact. As pointed out earlier, within Shiism there has been a dichotomy between a Shiism of the Establishment and a Shiism of Resistance. While the clergy as a class has always supported the establishment — an irrevocable consequence of its symbiotic relationship with the monarchical system—it has not been able to curb the tendency among the few radical religious scholars to side with the impoverished masses in their struggle against the tyranny of the establishment. It was by tapping and channelizing this tendency among the small number of religious scholars that the reformist intelligentsia generated the Tobacco Movement. The clergy as a class became identified with this movement well after the movement had swelled to a national uprising. Thus, even though the clergy on its own had not initiated the Tobacco Movement, it assumed the Movement's leadership after the reformists succeeded in mobilizing some of its members, well realizing the clergy's influence on the predominantly Muslim masses.

It was in this sense that widely travelled Afghani was familiar with the psychology of the Islamic society, of the factors which influenced it, and of the forces that could impel its social evolution. It was during his visit to India in 1855 and 'his contacts with Indian Muslims under British rule that Afghani first developed his lifelong hatred of the British'.[14] And by the time of 'his first appearance in Afghanistan in 1866, Afghani was a champion of Muslim struggle against British imperialist encroachments and a violent critic of British rule over Muslims'.[15] Afghani returned to Iran during the 1880s after having spent well over a decade as an itinerant activist in Istanbul, Cairo, London, Paris, Moscow, St Petersburg, and other cities in the West and the East. In Paris, Syed Jamal founded an international Islamic society[16] with the help of his brilliant disciple, Sheikh Mohammad Abdu, expelled from Egypt for his progressive Islamic views. Sheikh Abdu was to become the most effective and well known exponent of Afghani's Islamic approach. In 1883 the Sheikh and Afghani founded a society in Paris called *Urwat-ul-Wuthqa,* meaning 'the indisoluble link', a reference to the Quran as the common bond among Muslims. The society also published the first international Islamic journal by the same name which profoundly influenced Muslim intellectuals,[17] so much so that the journal was banned in India and in other Muslim countries. At the time Syed Jamal-ud-Din arrived in Iran, Nasir-ud-Din Shah, the reigning Qajar King, had converted Iran into a concession area for foreign powers, with British colonialists in firm control of the nation's resources. The climax of this concession granting trend to Western powers and Tsarist Russia in return for loans which were mainly used for the Shah's extravagant life style and frequent foreign trips, was reached with the 'Tobacco Concession'.

The Tobacco Concession

Granted to the British in March 1890, this concession gave the Shah an annual purse of £15,000, in return for which the Shah handed over the complete control of the production, purchase, sale, and export of Iranian tobacco to the British Rege company. Besides giving the British access to all Government facilities in towns and villages and the cheap labour of local peasants, the 'Tobacco Concession' also gave the British company the rights for importing all the equipment it needed, even arms and ammunition that it thought necessary, without the supervision of the Iranian Government.[18]

The Government kept the Tobacco Concession deal secret, being well aware that people would resent it and for good reasons: tobacco directly affected the livelihood of a large number of the masses since it was widely grown in the country and many people were involved in selling it in the local market as well as exporting it. Adding to the explosiveness of the situation was the resentment, on grounds of religion, that an item of daily use was being handled by infidels.[19] 'The flames were also fanned by the growing discontent over the sale of Iran's resources to unbelievers and over increasing misrule of exploitation by the governing classes, who were backed up by England and Russia'.[20] It was for Syed Jamal-ud-Din to focus the discontent simmering in the Iranian society upon Nasir-ud-Din Shah, the ruling tyrant who had been in power for fifty years.

Masterminding an Uprising
Syed Jamal organized the Muslim reformers and modernizers and urged them to develop tactics of agitation against the Shah by using 'the religiously motivated anti-foreign feeling of the *Ulama* and the masses'.[21] Syed Jamal-ud-Din had given up on those *Ulama* whose asphyxiating grip on the Quran and didactic interpretations had become a major cause for the misery, material and moral degradation of the people. He was convinced that a revolutionary and genuine religious scholar, aware and capable of critical thinking and creative insight, unlike those *Ulama* who read religious texts without thinking from dawn to dusk, could become the nation's saviour.[22] But the majority of *Ulama*, the Syed observed, 'were incapable of even looking after their own household, not to speak of running a Government'.[23]

Syed Jamal's campaign against the despotic Shah was based on a simple premise – from the Islamic point of view, monarchy and absolute rule by one individual amounted to the usurpation of people's rights. Thus, attributing the pathetic state of the Iranian masses to the oppression and injustice of their rulers, Syed Jamal-ud-Din directed his campaign against the person of the Shah on grounds that he had sold Iran to foreign powers, raising his well known slogan 'Down with the Monarchy'.[24] Under instructions of the British Mission in Iran, the Shah ordered Syed Jamal-ud-Din to leave Tehran, a city whose people were becoming increasingly fascinated by the ideas of the charismatic Syed Jamal, a magnificent orator. The Syed sought refuge at Shahabdul Azim, a shrine near Tehran, from the relative security of which he continued his campaign against the Shah.

As the Syed's criticism and condemnation of the monarchy became more virulent, the circle of people flocking to his meetings began increasing at a rate far beyond the Shah's anticipation. This so infuriated and disturbed the Shah that he violated the sanctity of the shrine by sending in his troops to arrest Syed Jamal-ud-Din. The latter was harshly treated by the Shah's soldiers, before being sent on a long and harassed ride into exile. For the next year or two, London was to be the home of Syed Jamal. Arriving in London in 1891, Syed Jamal continued his role in the Tobacco Movement by shipping critical articles and propaganda to Iran,[25] where his followers were actively engaged in stirring up people's sentiments against the British, circulating opposition bulletins and sending letters to Government officials criticising them for supporting the Shah. Excerpt from one letter addressed to a Shah's aide reads: 'How could you appear before the Prophet while you have caused such oppression on his followers?... These few pounds of tobacco which were produced with labour and which a few men with trouble used to export in order to obtain a piece of bread, have been coveted and they have been granted to the infidels and forbidden to the followers of the Prophet'.[26] At the same time, the *mullas* 'were preaching against the sale of Iran to infidels and there was already the beginning of the peculiar alliance between the religious and the radical parties which was to continue so effectively throughout the Tobacco Movement and beyond'.[27]

Actively engaged in stirring up agitation against Nasir-ud-Din Shah who was being portrayed as a tool of British imperialism, Syed Jamal's followers became a direct extension of his ideas, a fact documented in a letter of the British Charge d' affaires in Tehran at the time. Commenting on the arrest of Mirza Ali Reza, a disciple of Syed Jamal, the letter addressed to the British Foreign Office in London reads: 'His (Mirza Ali Reza's) secret correspondence proved him to be one of Syed Jamal's chief agents, and to be his mouthpiece in propagating the belief that England is an oppressive ruler by whom the natives of India were cruelly used, and it is to Russia that Persians should look for assistance and protection. These occurrences have caused a good deal of excitement more especially as they have taken place during the month of Ramazan'.[28] Also reported in the letter were the 'two distinct and opposing causes for these disturbances', namely, the modernist reformers and the traditional *mullas*. While the former were trying to expose 'the tyrannical and corrupt form of Government' which the monarchy had imposed upon the people, 'the fanatical *mullas* were preaching everywhere against the surrender of the Faithful into the hands of the infidels'. The *mullas* were warning the masses, the letter noted, that trade of all kinds, mines, banks, tobacco, and roads, had been sold to the Europeans 'who will gradually obtain corn land and even Mussallman women'.[29] The *Ulama's* concern was shared by the merchants of the bazaar, but for different reasons — giving the tobacco monopoly to the British would have adversely affected the tobacco merchants, for they were expected to 'sell and buy at prices arbitrarily fixed by a foreign company',[30] a proposition they deeply resented. As for the *Ulama*, they were becoming increasingly concerned at the increasing number of foreign representatives and personnel for the British company arriving in Iran. 'The appearance of a large number of non-Muslim foreigners working for the tobacco corporation was one of the most important reasons for the agitation — their dominating presence was resented, especially by the *Ulama*'.[31] Thus, cooperation between the *Ulama* and merchants was not only based upon their opposition to foreign domination, but also on the social position of each in Iranian society. 'They represented two powers, largely independent of the State: that of economic enterprise and that of religious direction. The sanctuary offered by the Mosque and the residence of the *Ulama* provided an ultimate refuge from the oppression of the State; and the closure of the bazaar, and with it the temporary paralysis of urban life, gave the merchants a powerful instrument of pressure'.[32] This peculiar alliance between the merchant class and the *Ulama* was to be activated again during the Constitutional Revolution (1905—9) and the Islamic Revolution (1978—79).

The Tobacco Uprising
Following the public declaration of the Tobacco Concession, the resentment of the masses that had been building up against the oppressive regime of Nasir-ud-Din Shah and the exploitation by foreign colonialists reached its ignition point. Mass demonstrations broke out against the tobacco concessions, first in Shiraz, the provincial capital of a tobacco growing area, and then in the whole country. In Shiraz, people assembled outside the city's gate and refused entry to the representatives of the British Company. In Isfahan, a leading tobacco merchant publicly burnt his huge tobacco stock rather than submit to the 'disgrace' of selling it at a price fixed by the British.[33] As for Tehran, when the people learned that the Shah had ordered the expulsion of Mirza Hasan Ashtiani, the leading religious figure within the country and an outspoken critic of the Shah, the city exploded with protest demonstrations. For the first time in Iran's history, women joined the front ranks of street processions and raised slogans against the Shah and his Court.[34] 'Tehran had never witnessed such demonstrations,' noted a local historian, 'the people marched on the Masjid-e-Shah (the city's central mosque) whereupon the *Imam Jumma* of the mosque, (who was a supporter of the Government) rose to the pulpit to dissuade the people from marching on, threatening the people even pleading with them to turn back. But, instead, the furious people dragged down the *Imam* from the pulpit in a barrage of insults, abuse and slogans. Rioting women beat up two of the Sultan's representatives until they were senseless. A man lunged with a sword at no less a person of the royal family than the Regent. . . People broke the doors and windows of Government buildings and attacked the Regent's residence where they were fired upon by the soldiers. But it appeared as if the people were indifferent to death.' 'It seems that these people,' continues the observer, 'had been waiting for such an opportunity for years. The problem of "tobacco concessions" is a mere excuse. The actual aim and intention of the people is to undo the monarchy. Their real purpose is to fight the Sultan.'[35] It should be, however, noted that at this point in the people's movement against the Shah, none of the Ayatollahs — the men of religious eminence — had issued a *fatwa* in support of the people's demand for annullment of the Tobacco Concession. It was at this time that Syed Jamal wrote his historic letter to Mirza Hasan Shirazi, the Grand Ayatollah and the highest Shia religious authority of the time *(Marja-i-Taqlid)* who was residing in Samara, a small town in Iraq. Syed Jamal comprehended that the readiness which had blossomed

among the people to sacrifice their lives in fighting against oppression and injustice would wither away if a person of authority, whose leadership was unequivocally acceptable to the people did not emerge as a focal point for lending cohesion and direction to the swelling tide of the movement. The Syed was well aware of the fact that since conditions were ripe for a revolution, the revolutionary symbols of struggle in Islam could lend an indisputable and invincible justification to the people's uprising. Given the characteristic cultural and religious context of the Iranian society, all that the people's uprising needed for a final forward thrust against the Shah's regime was the impetus of religious sanctity, which, at the time, only a person of Mirza Hasan Shirazi's stature could give by issuing an anti-Shah *fatwa* (religious declaration).

A Fatwa From Samara?

A *fatwa* did indeed appear imposing religious sanctions against the use of tobacco by Muslims as long as tobacco was the monopoly of a British Company. People spared no time in attributing the *fatwa* to Mirza Hassan Shirazi, the Grand Ayatollah in Samara, because it reflected the objective reality of the people's struggle against a despotic monarchy and provided it with religious legitimacy. Following the appearance of the *fatwa*, the entire state administration became paralysed. 'Overnight, people broke their smoking pipes and *hookas* as a mark of solidarity with the *fatwa*. All activity that had anything to do with tobacco came to an abrupt halt. It was after this successful boycott and the non-violent resistance against the British tobacco company that Gandhi launched the passive resistance campaign against the British, and boycotted the use of British products throughout India.'[36] Militants, however, were not satisfied with this *fatwa*. They began circulating leaflets, falsely attributing to the Grand Ayatollah a more militant *fatwa* stating that if the tobacco concession were not rescinded within 48 hours people would launch a *Jehad* (religiously sanctioned warfare) against the monarchy.[37] Again, because this statement reflected the true nature of the people's struggle and aspirations in a religiously legitimate framework, and regardless of the fact that it was falsely attributed to the Grand Ayatollah, the statement 'gained immediate circulation in the city and was discussed with such seriousness and certainty that the people of Tehran procured arms for themselves the same day'.[38] Realizing that if the movement were to continue it would lead to the loss of his crown, the Shah rescinded the tobacco concession.

As it was known that Syed Jamal-ud-Din Afghani had written a letter to the Grand Ayatollah Shirazi urging him to issue a *fatwa* to support the people's struggle, it became a matter of common belief that Afghani was the one who influenced the Grand Ayatollah or whoever issued the *fatwa* in his name, to declare that the use of tobacco was tantamount to war against God and the Hidden Imam. In his long epistle[39] to the Grand Ayatollah, Syed Jamal, in keeping with the traditions of the times, first lauded the status of the Grand Ayatollah and his person, and then drew his attention to the responsibility that he owed the Muslim masses because of the political power his supreme position in the religious hierarchy had vested him with. The Syed analyzed the situation in Iran, the decadent system of the Shah's establishment, and the numerous pacts the Shah had concluded with foreign powers in the areas of mines, highways, tobacco, and banks — concessions which literally amounted to the 'sale of Iran to foreign powers'. The letter also drew the Grand Ayatollah's attention to the fact that the oppressive monarchy had plundered the masses and given rise to poverty, decadence, and corruption in the country. Afghani then warned the Grand Ayatollah that any further delay on his part in supporting the people by lending their struggle religious legitimacy would endanger the country and defeat the movement. He therefore urged the religious leader to issue a *fatwa* declaring that the people should not support the Shah who was the enemy of God and the people.

Regardless of whether this letter was instrumental in the appearance of the controversial *fatwa*, it reflects Afghani's comprehension of historical reality, his understanding of the importance of the clergy's *fatwa* among the illiterate masses, his sensitivity to the society's objective conditions, and his belief in mobilizing the oppressed and dissatisfied masses into a movement powered by their cultural values and religious belief.

As for the controversy about whether the *fatwa* prohibiting the use of tobacco was issued by the Ayatollah Shirazi in Samara or forged in Tehran in order not to let down the people, it began from the moment the *fatwa* appeared and continues to this day. According to Hamid Algar, Professor of history at Berkley University, the confusion surrounding the origin of the *fatwa* is in a large part attributable to the regime of Nasir-ud-Din Shah, who hoped thereby to reduce its effect.[40] Despite this confusion, people attributed the *fatwa* to Ayatollah Shirazi because, as the sole *Marja-e-Taqlid*, the highest rank in the Shia religious hierarchy, Shirazi could demand the obedience of all believers and ensure the totality of the *fatwa's* effect. However, Professor Algar concedes that it is not clear whether the wording of the *fatwa* was by the Grand Ayatollah Shirazi, or whether it was issued by others in his name. It is possible that among the powers delegated by Mirza Hassan Shirazi to his representative in Tehran was included 'that of issuing in his name, at an appropriate moment, a *fatwa* prohibiting the use of tobacco'.[41] More recently, Homa Nateq, Professor of History at Tehran University and a onetime colleague of Dr. Ali Shariati during their student years at Sorbonne University in Paris, has pointed out that the *fatwa* attributed to Ayatollah Shirazi was indeed a forgery. It was forged by the merchant class who were severely affected by the tobacco concession. Professor Nateq who did her doctoral dissertation on Syed Jamal-ud-Din Afghani, states that many clergymen who were actually involved in the tobacco movement and participated in the struggle, such as Sheikh Hassan Kerbalie, afterwards openly admitted[42] that the *fatwa* had been a forgery. It was forged by the desperate tobacco merchants who were severely affected by the tobacco concession and felt betrayed by the silence of the clerical leadership. During the build up of the tobacco movement, the lack of support on the part of the clerical leaders had become so embarrassing that the exasperated merchants began condemning the *mujtahids,* learned religious scholars, openly for not rejecting the tobacco concession from the religious perspective.[43] This is evident in the 'night letters', the secretly circulated bulletins that began appearing at the time, which criticized the clergy for staying away from the movement and supporting the Shah. One such letter, addressed to the clergy partly reads: 'You have become *mullas* with the money of the people. The expenses for your studies were borne by the labours of the shopkeepers, traders, and farmers. People did not suffer deprivation so that you should become owners and rulers. Why then don't you walk in step with the people?'[44] Another night letter ridiculed the clergymen by pointing out that while the clergy was always lying in wait to spill anyone's blood on petty issues, it was now 'selling our nation to aliens without the least bit of compunction'.[45] Under these circumstances, when a *fatwa* prohibiting the use of tobacco did finally appear, few among the masses could afford to be skeptical about its origin. Regardless of whether it was genuine or spurious, it had given religious legitimacy to the people's struggle and brought them to the brink of a general armed uprising against the monarchical establishment. The Shah, therefore, had no other option but to rescind the tobacco concession and get the word circulated that he had done so because of his respect for the clerical leadership. Through this appeasing gesture, the Shah succeeded in winning over the clergy to his side, and put an end to the tobacco crisis.

The Price of Victory
People rejoiced at what they thought to be their victory, unaware of the fact that British colonialists had forced the Shah to pay £500,000 in damages for abrogating the Tobacco Concession. Since the Government did not have that kind of money, it found itself compelled to borrow the money from the British owned Imperial Bank of Iran at 6% interest.[46] This was the first loan the British imposed upon the Iranians, the repayment of which by the toiling masses induced an embittered observer to comment: 'The sources for repayment of this money are the poor peasants, those struck by poverty, and the wretched. Because the money plundered by the King, Viziers, Khans and the aristocracy never comes out of their pockets once it ends up there'.[47]

Thus, although the people had achieved an apparent victory insofar as their vocal demand for abrogation of the Tobacco Concession had been met, this victory fell far short of any genuine achievement on the part of the people; because the demand for abrogation of the tobacco concession had implied, in the first instance, the desire for terminating all the pacts imposed by the colonialists, as well as the monarchy itself. Moreover, the cancellation of the concession did nothing to prevent the British from continuing their plunder of the people and looting their national resources.[48] Also, the clergy had failed to comprehend its special potential for changing the conditions of society to the people's advantage. This failure of the clergy mainly rested with its traditionally conservative, even closed, outlook, and its superficial views of social, historical, and religious issues, which were often beyond the grasp of the majority of clerical minds. An expression of the clergy's limited outlook is reflected in the fact that it was only concerned with the 'abrogation' of the Tobacco Concession and supported the people as long as the Shah had not announced its cancellation. Thus, when the Shah announced the cancellation of the concession, the clergy concluded that its mission had been accomplished and the battle won. It was no longer concerned with the consequences of the cancellation, regardless of the fact that the conditions which the British had imposed on Iran to compensate for the treaty's cancellation were more humiliating and exploitive than the concession itself.[49]

The Syed Writes Again

Syed Jamal-ud-Din was by no means pleased with the King's tactical submission to the people's demands expressed in his announcement that the Tobacco Concession was to be rescinded. Afghani's own assessment of the situation, based on reports[50] that were reaching him from Iran, showed that the masses, as well as many among the top ranking officers in the Shah's own army, resented the premature end which the tobacco movement had suffered owing to the clergy's compromise with the Shah once the people had demonstrated their power and scored an initial victory. We find Syed Jamal-ud-Din, agonized in his exile in London at these developments, writing to religious leaders warning them not to think that victory had been achieved and their task accomplished. The Shah's bowing down, the Syed warned, was only a temporary affair arising from his weakened position vis a vis the clerics and the people. The Shah, he pointed out in his letter, was planning retaliatory action. Behind the facade of submission to the clergy, brutal reprisals were being designed that could endanger the existence of the clergy itself.[51] Syed Jamal-ud-Din then informed the religious leaders of the intelligence reports his supporters had sent him, to the effect that the Shah was recruiting foreign mercenaries for commanding the units of his army, for he did not trust his own Iranian commanders. The Syed then urged the *Ulama* to issue a *fatwa* instructing the people not to comply with the Shah's rule any more and to defy him openly.

The Syed believed that the *fatwa* supporting the tobacco movement had been a decisive factor in demonstrating to the Shah and the world at large, the power of Islam and of the clergy in focussing the attention of the masses against a particular target. It had invested the clergy with a grave responsibility which it could not afford to overlook owing to expediency. The Syed's letter, therefore, was an admonition, a plea and a warning that urged the clergy to take action against the Shah. Part of Syed Jamal-ud-Din's second letter to Ayatollah Mirza Hasan Shirazi and other religious leaders reads: 'By your decision (to issue the *fatwa* against the use of tobacco) 0 leaders of religion! you magnified Islam. . . So that the foreigners realised it was not possible to stand against your power. . . They realised that you are the fortress of the nation, and the affairs of the nation are in your hands. But the grave trouble is this, that this criminal apostate (the Shah, in order to vindicate his defeat in the Tobacco Movement) is exiling the *Ulama* from the provinces. He has realised it is not possible for his orders to be implemented except by the compliance of the army officers. But the army officers are not opposed to the *Ulama* or wish them evil. So the Shah has decided to get his military officers from abroad. It is for this reason that he has made Kent and his like Chief of Police and Commander of the Cossack Brigade. That culprit and his friends are trying to get military commanders from a foreign country. The Europeans have understood that now is the time for them to become owners of Iran without any war or battle. They have realised that the *Ulama* who defended Islam and the domain of religion are losing their power and their influence is waning. . . Anyone who thinks that ousting the Shah from power is not possible without troops, guns, and bombs, has thought in vain. For that is not so. Because a faith and a belief has penetrated the people's mind and settled in their hearts that opposition to the *Ulama* is opposition to God. O followers of Koran! If you apply God's decree to this usurper, this unjust tyrant, if you declare that by the authority of God, obedience to this man is *haram* (religiously unlawful) he will be dethroned without any war and bloodshed. . . God has shown to you a manifestation of the power He has bestowed upon you (in the Tobacco Movement). Those who lacked firm faith before this event (the *fatwa* prohibiting the use of tobacco) and doubted the power and influence of your words gained faith. The Muslim nation, on hearing a single word from you became united to crush their Pharaoh. Other countries were also amazed by this power, the influence of your word, and the speed with which this Order (the *fatwa*) took effect. And the *kafirs* (infidels) were dazed. This is a power which God has given you so that with this you may guard the faith and Islam. In that case, is it worthy of you that you should abandon religion and hestitate to help mankind despite all this power? Do not hesitate to remove this man from power — a man who has usurped power, whose only work is debauchery and licence, and whose only order is for perpetuating oppression. A man, who after sucking the blood of the Muslims and crushing the bones of the poor and the downtrodden, and making the nation indigent... is intent upon handing over the country which has been a source of honour for Islam and a bastion for religion, to foreigners... I once again repeat – the Ministers, the Commanders, the Army, the People, even the sons of the Oppressor – are all awaiting your order. They are waiting to hear a single word from you to pull this Pharaoh down from the throne and relieve the people of God from his harm'.[52] That the contents of Syed Jamal's letter were based on facts which the Shah had strictly guarded but which the Syed's supporters within the regime, presumably army officers perturbed by the growing influence of British officers in the army, had passed on to him, is confirmed in the official communications of the British embassy in Tehran. A letter written on the situation in Iran in 1892 by the British Ambassador to the British Foreign Minister reads: 'Syed Jamal-ud-Din has addressed a letter to the *Ulama* in Iran in which he has directly insulted and severely attacked the monarchy.... The Shah is extremely angered and disturbed by Syed Jamal's accusations. He is frightened of the damaging results his (Syed Jamal's) writings may create in Iran. The greater part of the Shah's anger is due to the reason that Syed Jamal has revealed certain facts about the current situation in Iran which don't leave the least bit of doubt....'[53] Unfortunately for Syed Jamal and his followers, his plea was not heeded and the clerics in positions of religious leadership preferred to remain silent in favour of the *status quo*. Moreover, since the Tobacco Movement had enhanced their stature and influence, perhaps they preferred not to take too seriously Syed Jamal's foresight and the information he was furnishing. 'Above all, they failed to provide any real answer to the manifold problems – political, social, economic – facing Iran in the second half of the 19th Century. *Ijtihad* was on the whole used narrowly, in a strictly legalistic sense, its genuine potentialities, much wanted by a few reformers, were seldom activated with honesty and perceptiveness.[54] Any attempt or wish to 'reshape the norms of political life and the basis of the State was foreign to the *Ulama* in Qajar Iran. Thus it was that the forces of renewal passed them by'.[55]

Despite its obvious failures, the Tobacco Movement retains its special place in the history of Islamic Movements. It was the first popular movement emanating from the people who had unified solidly under the symbolic leadership of the clergy. Given a religious sanction, the movement succeeded in demolishing the foundation Britain was laying for a British Raj in Iran on the pattern of the East India Company.

However, Afghani's influence on the Muslim intelligentsia continued to grow and he unfurled a movement that is progressive because it represents an attempt for people's liberation and 'opens a common front with all Third World countries that face the world capitalist system'.[56] However, the primary shortcoming of Afghani's approach was that while emanating from his powerful personality, the movement was channelled mainly towards rulers and men of power. By influencing these men, Afghani hoped to bring about the desired changes in Muslim societies. In other words, Afghani struggled to change the destiny of the oppressed and exploited Muslim masses by changing their rulers. Towards the end of his life, he realised that his life's mission would have been more meaningful had he focussed all his energies on giving social and political consciousness to the masses and mobilising them directly instead of attempting to reach them by persuading and influencing those in political or religious authority.

The failure of his dream for Islamic solidarity and reform is voiced in one of his last letters, part of which reads: 'Would that I had sown all the seeds of my ideas in the receptive ground of the people's thought. Well would it have been had I not wasted this fruitful and beneficent seed of mine in the brackish and sterile soil of that effete sovereignty. For what I sowed in that soil never grew, and what I planted in that brackish earth perished away. During all this time, none of my well-intentioned consels sank into the ears of the rulers of the East, whose selfishness and ignorance prevented them from accepting my words.'[57] Moreover, Syed Jamal was now convinced, even though near the end of his life, that changing one man at the top for another could not have helped to bring about fundamental social and political changes for ameliorating the conditions of the masses. What was really needed, as Afghani now comprehended, was the complete destruction of the existing social structure, which offered nothing but suffering to the masses, before a new and just system could evolve.

These twilight thoughts of Syed Jamal-ud-Din Afghani which are unacceptable to many *Ulama* professing to be followers of Afghani's movement, have been expressed by him in the following words, his last advice to the Muslims: 'The stream of renovation flows quickly towards the East. The edifice of despotic governments totters to its fall. Strive so far as you can to destroy the foundations of this despotism, not to pluck up and cast out its individual agents. Strive so far as you can to abolish those practices that stand between you and your happiness and prosperity. Do not content yourself to annihilate those who employ those practices. If you merely strive to oppose individuals, your time will be lost.'

Afghani, Iqbal, Shariati and the Progressive Islamic Movement:

The spirit of Afghani's mission and the passion that had propelled his efforts for regenerating the Muslim society was given a concrete and definite direction by Iqbal, whom Dr. Ali Shariati hailed as a 'distinguished figure in the history of human thought and a dazzling individual whom the pristine richness of Islam had presented to human society'.[58] Iqbal's importance in the progressive Islamic movement is central because he gave the 'revolutionary movement of Syed Jamal-ud-Din "ideological sustenance". He gave intellectual roots to the field of rebellion and revolt Syed Jamal-ud-Din had tilled'.[59] Clearly then, Dr. Ali Shariati, the revolutionary thinker who provided the ideological framework for Iran's Islamic Revolution by pursuing the intellectual direction Iqbal had etched considered Iqbal as 'one of the greatest Muslim personalities that Islam has presented to the world'.[60] However, it was people like Ustad Taqi Shariati, Dr. Shariati's father, Taher Ahmadzadeh, and Ayatollah Taleqani who began the first serious and concerted effort in Iran for a progressive Islamic movement in the early forties. Ustad Taqi Shariati and Ahmadzadeh revived the Islamic revolutionary struggle after Reza Shah's suppressive regime was deposed by the allies at the beginning of World War II.[61] They established the first academic centre for a progressive Islamic movement at their native city of Mashhad in 1941, calling it the Centre for Propagation of Islamic Truth *(Kanun-e-Nashr-e-Haqiqat-e-Eslami)*. A few years later, this movement was further enriched with its discovery of Iqbal and his ideas. By the early 50s Iqbal had become a well known figure among Iran's intelligentsia and educational circles. It is worth noting Mossadeq's contribution in projecting Iqbal among Iranians. As the country's Prime Minister and national hero, Mossadeq broadcast a special radio message on Iqbal Day in 1952[62] and praised him for his role in the struggle of Indian Muslims against British imperialism. The same year, *Rumi-e-Asr*,[63] the first book introducing Iqbal to Iranians in their own language, was also published and so well received that soon it went through a second printing. During the decade that followed, the complete Persian works of Iqbal had appeared in Iran[64] and his Urdu poetry was also translated into Persian as were his lectures on the Reconstruction of Religious Thought in Islam. Iqbal's ideas and approach to Islam had begun penetrating progressive religious circles and been incorporated into the ideological framework of Mehdi Bazargaan's Liberation Movement. A senior professor of Physics at Tehran University whom Mossadeq had appointed as the Chief of the nationalised oil industry in 1952, Bazargaan had formed the Liberation Movement with the help of a few Muslim intellectuals and Ayatollah Taleqani, Taher Ahmedzadeh, Dr. Yadollah Sahabi and Ustad Taqi Shariati. The Liberation Movement presented the first organised attempt for incorporating Islam as the ideological foundation for a progressive Islamic movement at the social and political level. A distinctive feature of this movement was that it had developed independently of the theological schools in Qom.

Taleqani's four-volume commentary on the Holy Quran[65] and his book on *Ownership and Islam*[66] were among the first works to deal with the social and economic implications of Islam as an ideology.

These books, along with the several research treatises written by Bazargaan, provided a theoretical ground work for an Islamic ideology in tune with scientific and contemporary developments. After his return from France in 1964 where he obtained Ph.D. in History and Sociology, Shariati gave a crucial and revolutionary dimension to the progressive Islamic Movement. He went beyond the comparative approach of Iqbal and Bazargaan which relied on scientific and philosophical developments for expounding Islamic principles. He discovered original relationships and new meaning within the Quranic context concerning social principles and social movements which he then tried to develop within the framework of a revolutionary ideology.

Shariati and the Intelligentsia in Muslim Countries

Shariati believed that the trend among the intelligentsia in Muslim countries to opt for secular or imported ideologies and relying on them for solving the problems of their society was going to be destructive in the long run, for it would not only sabotage the struggle against imperialism but would also strengthen the power of reactionary clergymen. Shariati wanted the intelligentsia which had turned away from Islam on account of its exposure to the distorted version propounded by the reactionaries, to reflect on Islam once again. For there was a crucial difference between a religion whose leading personalities had fallen on battlefields or had died in imprisonment and those religions whose proponents rotted in remote enclaves far from the social reality of their times in their individual quest for perfection. Shariati was of the opinion that both the conventional clergymen and the intelligentsia were unable to perceive the vital spirit of Islam. Both of them had a restrictive and a negative approach to Islam.[67] While he favoured a 'truly progressive clergy',[68] Shariati dismissed the obscurantist clerics who in their ignorance of the development in human thought and civilization and culture, were inveterate opponents and enemies of the Western civilization, change, novelty and innovation.[69] He also criticized those intellectuals who were 'lost in their blind imitation of the West because of the lack of courage and critical judgment.[70] By maintaining that Religion and State were unrelated, the intelligentsia in Muslim countries was falling a prey to the designs of imperialism. This contention of the intelligentsia in Muslim countries was in imitation of the intelligentsia of the West who spoke of the separation of the Church and the State.[71] According to Shariati, the dichotomy of Church vs State does not exist in Islam. Nor has there been a particular ruling class at the dawn of Islam where there was no separation of 'intellectual', 'spiritual' or 'working classes'. The devout Muslim pioneer was a worker, a preacher, a fighter, and a thinker. With the passage of time, however, a formal class of clergy emerged which has been generally biased towards maintaining the lop-sided class based social structure. By doing so, the clergy was maintaining and safeguarding its own interests. This is how religion became synonymous with being a tool for justifying the *status quo* and the existing social conditions. It became a bulwark for safeguarding the interests of a minority against the majority.[72] But such deviations from the anti-exploitive spirit of Islam did not cancel the goal of human existence and the true Islamic spirit. Shariati therefore urged the intelligentsia to pay attention to the social reality of their society through the lens of their own consciousness and culture, instead of getting carried away by the current of imported ideologies.

Expressing these ideas on the occasion of a meeting of teachers and students to commemorate Iqbal's death anniversary at the University of Mashhad in 1966, Shariati said: 'Our national culture is an Islamic culture, our social spirit is religious. I have seen how imperialism has at times used Islam as a means for its own ends, or has fought against it. I know that Islam is full of social and political currents directed against the formation of classes. It has a world view towards evolution through social struggle. In my society, Islam is the faith of the masses and a powerful social force. It is history, as well as our national culture. By nature it is progressive and constructive with its stance toward social justice and expansion of consciousness. Islam believes in the human, social, and material dignity of its adherents. If I am able to mine this grand and rich mine, if I am able to give Islamic awareness to the people who have faith in Islam, if I can open their eyes as their hearts to the dynamic and eventful history of Islam, and acquaint them with a school vibrant with awareness and consciousness of life, then I would have fulfilled my mission as an aware, enlightened and open-minded intellectual. The mission of an educator or an open-minded intellectual is nothing but this: to give national or class consciousness to a society by taking into consideration its culture, and its spiritual and national personality.'[73] As part of his insistent 'advice' to the intelligentsia, Shariati added, 'If imperialism, oppression and reaction are using religion as a weapon against the people you should disarm them and take their weapon for supporting the people. How does one disarm the enemy? By renouncing the weapon, negating its value and denying it recognition? Or by snatching it from the enemy's hands?'

'In Islamic countries, the struggle of the intelligentsia against religion is serving the purpose of reaction, imperialism, and forces opposed to the people. Because while the masses will never renounce their religion by intelligentsia's undermining of Islam, those claiming to be the custodians of Islam will be strengthened. These self-professed custodians will grow more powerful in their hold upon the masses and in their attacks against the intelligentsia, social justice, freedom and progress.'[74] Shariati therefore called upon all the intelligentsia in Muslim countries to start 'a war of liberation for rescuing Islam'[75] from the manacles of dogma, reaction, exploitation and despotism which the hypocritical leadership in Islamic States had imposed upon the oppressed Muslim masses with the connivance of the reactionary clergymen and dogmatists. Only then could the Muslims hope for a just Islamic order, once the foundations of reaction, despotism and imperialism had been demolished.

Shariati and the Obscurantist Clergy

Like Afghani and Iqbal, the progressive Islamic thinkers and reformers before him, Shariati was not spared the scathing attacks of the reactionary folds of the clergy. Many clergymen, some of them in collaboration with SAVAK but most of them because of their ignorance, hurled all sorts of accusations against Shariati. He was variously labelled 'Marxist', 'apostate', 'Wahabi', 'Sunni', 'Communist', 'imposter', — the choice for the accusative brand being determined by the accusers' own prejudices. For example, when Shariati opened a week long seminar on Iqbal at Hossienieh Irshad in 1972 where papers were read on the dynamic, anti-exploitive and anti-imperialist spirit of Islam, many *mullas* condemned Shariati in their speeches delivered from the pulpits in mosques for eulogising a Sunni Iqbal who had 'insulted' the Prophet's family. In the context of these accusations by the 'rival', Shariati wrote in his book on Iqbal: 'This tirade of propaganda against the expansion and progress of Islam as a progressive revolutionary ideology is orchestrated by a rival who finds himself rebuffed, exposed, and threatened with extinction by the true Islamic ideology'.[76] Reflecting on the strait jacket mentality of *mullas,* Shariati wrote: 'Social revolutions, changes in the infrastructure of the society and in the system of production, distribution, and consumption, negation of classes and the exploitation of 'work' by 'money', problems of international imperialism, human rights, social laws, investigation of causes of social movements and change, economic and political dependence of Islamic societies on imperialism, cultural imperialism, comprador bourgeoisie and other contemporary problems are nothing but *kufr* for these religious scholars who claim to be inheritors of the Prophet's mission. Anyone who finds himself concerned about these problems is rendered by a single stroke, an infidel, a *kafir,* a Wahabi, Communist or Christian'.[77] Shariati found it intriguing that these 'official' custodians of 'Islam' in their opposition to true Islam were supported by those forces which were openly non-religious, formally secular, or were even opposed to Islam in principle. The supporters of this diseased Islam of the reactionaries, Shariati observed, were not afraid of *touhid* as a *dogma* but were afraid of it as a world-view. As a world-view, *touhid* aimed at realizing the unity of God in human relations and social systems. 'In our Islam, *touhid* is a world-view, living and meaningful, opposed to the avaricious tendency for hoarding and aims for eradicating the disease of money-worship. It aims to efface the stigma of exploitation, consumerism, and aristocracy'.[78] Thus, the reactionary clergymen who supported the existing system of the ruling classes were not afraid of the Quran were it to be used only as a 'holy scripture'. But were it to be used as a manual for consciousness, guidance, responsibility and action, they were afraid of it. 'Our Islam is the uncompromising, blood-shedding enemy of oppression, ignorance, reaction, social stagnation, aristocracy and capitalism, and a friend of the hungry, the homeless, the victims of capital, prejudice, and injustice. It is the vanguard for liberation of the toiling, subjected, and oppressed masses (the *mostazafin*) of our age. It is the revolutionary response of the oppressed of the earth. It is a concrete and tangible representation of how to be, how to live, how to speak, how to be silent, how to fight, how to worship, how to think, how to be responsible. They are frightened of this Islam and of this faith. The progressive revolutionary religion disarms both the Pope (representing the official clergy) and Marx. Its primary objective is to uproot the palace of the Caesars!

'Whenever the spirit of *touhid* revives and its historical role is comprehended by a people, it re-embarks on its (unfinished) mission for consciousness, justice, peoples' liberation and their development and growth. But the revolutionary *jehad* and the intellectual *ijtehad* finds itself opposed by three forces:

1: 'The powerful, the hoarders and accumulators of wealth. By those who keep one hand over the head of the people (as a pretentious sign of concern for the people's welfare) and the other hand inside the people's pocket. The dining tables of these persons are colorfully laden because of the plunder and enslavement of the people.

2: 'Custodians of ancient traditons and customs, hereditary values and historical reaction, social stagnation, mental ignorance. They consider themselves to be inheritors of the Prophet, "signs of God" and "manifestation of Islam". According to Allama Naeini, the brave *mulla* who lived at the turn of the century, they are founders of religious dictatorship and religious reaction. The force represented by these reactionaries is the more lethal of all forces bent upon crushing the blooming grandeur and power of progressive Islam. These reactionaries foresee the power of *touhidi* spirit more quickly than the real enemy (the "powerful" oppressors), for the uprooting flood of change enters, first of all, their nests. The *touhidi* Prophets, Moses, Christ, and Mohammad, had also to confront the opposition of this force. For example, during the times of Mohammad, the leading religious scholars of Arabs and Jews who had been forecasting the advent of Prophet Mohammad were the first to oppose and contradict him. They were successful for a time in discrediting the holy Prophet and generating indifference and suspicion and contempt towards him because of the foothold these false men of religion enjoyed among the people, just because the people had grown accustomed to their religious views. This is a fact which has been repeated throughout history. It reveals the principle that all along in man's history, it is religion which has fought against religion. *Touhid* has been drained of its content by *touhid*. And Islam has been dealt the most lethal blows by Islam. The opposite is equally true – only religion can rescue man from the intellectual degeneration, alienation and humiliation, degradation, paralysis of will and blunting of consciousness caused by religion. This rigid, lifeless and degenerate "Islam" which has brought about such a destructive doom for the Muslim masses can be toppled and replaced only by Islam – the true Islam. In order to liberate ourselves from the pathological dominance of this false "God", we should seek help of the creative energy and the illuminating and liberating force of God. The revolutionary religion is by itself the negation of reactionary religion. Just as light dispels darkness, knowledge dispels ignorance, waking dispels sleep and movement dispels inertia, so does the true religion dispel false religion. The presence of the one is annihilation of the other.

3: 'The third force which finds itself at odds with the revolutionary resurgence of faith in the social conscience of the society is the intelligentsia opposed to religion. Since the intelligentsia finds itself threatened with losing its progressive bases of support to progressive religion, it is compelled to fight and resist progressive religion.'[79]

It was Dr. Shariati who articulated the revolutionary Islamic ideology that in its relatively tentative form had inspired people like Afghani and Iqbal but now was assimilable to a whole generation of progressive Muslims. The hundreds of inspiring lectures Shariati gave on the progressive redefinition of Islam found a vast clandestine circulation during the Pahlavi era on tape cassettes and cyclostyled pamphlets, and played a decisive role in revitalising the young generation. He equipped progressive Muslims with the Book, the Weapon, and the Balance, and exhorted them to continue the struggle for destroying the 'spider's web of imperialism, exploitation, and religious hypocrisy'.

Thus for the first time, since Syed Jamal-ud-Din Afghani unfurled the progressive Islamic Movement about a century ago, this movement was no longer confined and dependent upon a single individual or ideologue for its propagation and expansion, but had become the nucleus of a collective consciousness, as witnessed in the emergence of a generation of socially aware and spiritually oriented progressive Muslims, crystalizing in the *Mujahideen-e-Khalq* organization of progressive Islamic guerrillas. *Mujahideen-e-Khalq* strove to lend the progressive Islamic movement a dimension which they thought it had lacked in the past – organization and the strategy of scientific struggle. Their decision to operate as an urban guerrilla organization against despotism, imperialism and exploitation was a natural response to contemporary Muslim history in general, and Iranian history in particular. *Mujahideen-e-Khalq* regarded their organization as a logical and historical outcome of the developments that had spanned Iranian history since the turn of the century. The emergence of Mirza Kuchak Khan, the first Muslim revolutionary in recent history to lead a long drawn out guerrilla warfare against the despotism of Iranian monarchy and British imperialism, the failure of Mossadeq's movement in 1953 and Khomeini's uprising in June, 1963, were seen as a continuum. By linking up with Mirza Kuchak Khan's jungle revolution, the *Mujahideen-e-Khalq* embarked upon a decisive course of action which was unique as compared to other Islamic movements in that it was ideological in a creative, dynamic, and progressive sense. While Afghani, Iqbal, Shariati, Taleqani and Bazargaan had made significant contributions in identifying the theoretical direction for a progressive Islamic approach, the *Mujahideen* became the vanguard for the actualization of this Islamic approach in a practical, organizational and 'real' sense. Indeed, the founder members of the *Mujahideen* were the younger and revolutionary members of Liberation Movement which the older generation of progressive Muslims — Bazargaan, Taleqani and Ustad Taqi Shariati (Dr. Shariati's father) had founded. These young members of the Liberation Movement, after the Shah's brutal crack down on the opposition in 1963 and the effective cessation of all political activity in the country with the institution of SAVAK, had decided to embark upon guerrilla action as the only recourse for keeping the flame of resistance against despotism and imperialism alive.

Notes

1. Keddie; N.R., *An Islamic Response to Imperialism.* University of California Press, Berkley, 1965.
2. Keddie, N.R., *Sayyid Jamal ad-Din 'Al-afghani'.* University of California Press, Berkley, 1972. Henceforth to be called 'Al-afghani'.
3. Ibid., p.1.
4. Ayatollah Motahari, 'Islamic Movements During the Last 100 Years'. In, *The Message of Peace,* Vol.1, No.1, Qom, 1979, p.45.
5. Ibid.
6. Ibid., p.43.
7. Algar, H., *Religion and State in Iran.* University of California Press, Berkley, 1969, p.197.
8. Ibid.
9. Ayatollah Motahari, 'Islamic Movements During the Last 100 Years'. In, *The Message of Peace.* Qom, Rajab 13, 1399. Vol.1. No.1, p.42.
10. Ibid., p.42.
11. Ibid.
12. Ibid., Afghani's above observation would seem to be supported by the Islamic movement in the Indo-Pakistan subcontinent which culminated in the creation of a separate homeland for Muslims in India in 1947. None of the prominent leaders in the social, political, and religious awakening of the predominantly Sunni Muslims in India — Syed Ahmad Khan, Syed Ameer Ali, Allama Iq-

bal, Mohammad Ali Jinnah — were theologians or clergymen. During the several decades preceding Pakistan's birth, these men, who were reformers with progressive views, were rejected and harassed by most of the leading clergymen. Mohammad Ali Jinnah, leader of the Muslims in India was accused of hypocrisy in professing loyalty to Islam. In 1945, leader of Indian clergymen's party *(Jamiat-e-Ulamai-Hind)* invoked his religious standing and issued a religious decree *(fatwa)* forbidding Muslims from joining Jinnah's Muslim League or voting for it 'because such actions were contrary to the dictates of Islam'. He also labelled Jinnah, whom Muslims had begun calling their 'Great Leader', as the 'Great Heathen'. How effective this *fatwa* was can be judged by the results of the elections that followed, where 97% of Muslims in India voted for Jinnah's Muslim League. Further credence to Afghani's observation is provided by the first free General Elections held in Pakistan in 1970. In these elections, although majority of *Ulama* and the formalist *Jamat-e-Islami* opposed Mr. Bhutto and his socialist Pakistan People's Party, and extensively campagined against the 'irreligious', 'Un-Islamic' and 'Socialist' Bhutto, the People's Party won the elections with a decisive majority.

13. Ayatollah Motahari, *Islamic Movement During the Last 100 Year*.
14. Keddie, N.R., *An Islamic Response to Imperialism*. University of California Press, Berkley, 1968, p.11.
15. Ibid., p.12.
16. *A Shorter Encyclopaedia of Islam,* E.J. Brill Leiden, 1961.
17. Ibid.
18. Bakhshaeshi, E., *One hundred years of struggle by Progressive Clergy.* (In Persian) Qom. 1979. Henceforth to be called 'One Hundred Years'.
19. Keddie, N.R., *Al-afghani*.
20. Ibid., p.336.
21. Ibid.
22. Nateq, H., *Lecture on Syed Jamal-ud-Din Assadabadi*. Tehran University, May 1979.
23. Ibid.
24. Ibid.
25. Keddie, N.R., *Al-afghani*.
26. Ibid., p.339.
27. Ibid., p.338.
28. Ibid.
29. Ibid.
30. Algar, H., *Religion and State in Iran*. University of California Press, Berkley, 1969, p.207.
31. Ibid.
32. Ibid.
33. *One Hundred Years*.
34. Ibid.
35. Zanjani, M., *Tehrimay Tanbaku,* quoted in *One Hundred Years*, p.44—9.

36. Shariati, A., *Eqbal-Me-mar-e-Tajdid-e-bana-ye-Tafkar-e-Eslami*. (Iqbal Architect of Reconstructed Islamic thought). Tehran, p.60.
37. *One Hundred Years*.
38. Ibid., p.36. During the Iranian Revolution in 1979, while the militant revolutionaries urged Khomeini to issue a *fatwa* granting religious sanction to armed struggle against the Pahlavi dictatorship, to the very end, Khomeini refused to issue this *fatwa*. Nevertheless, a nationwide armed uprising spontaneously erupted on 9 February 1979 and proved to be the decisive factor in achieving the Revolution's first objective—destruction of the monarchy.
39. *One Hundred Years, Al-afghani*.
40. Algar, H., *Religion And State In Iran*. University of California Press, Berkley, 1969.
41. Ibid., p.211—12.
42. Homa Nateq, *Rahaniyet-va-Azadi-ha-e-Demokratik* (The Clergy and Democratic Freedom). *Jahan*, No.3, March 6, 1982. pp. 6-9.
43. Ibid.
44. Ibid.
45. Ibid.
46. Kirmani, Nazim Islam, *Tarikhay Baidar-ei-Iranian*. Quoted in *Mojahed*, Number 65, 1979, p.3.
47. *One Hundred Years*.
48. *Mojahed*. No.65, 1979.
49. Over the years, the clergy supporting and favouring the monarchical system in Iran has presented the crisis faced by Nasir-ud-Din Shah during the Tobacco Movement in a different light. An example of this point of view is provided in an extensive religious treatise published by Ayatollah Shams-ud-Din Najafi. Entitled *Goftar-e-Shieh Der Osool va Faroue*, the book has been endorsed and commended by Grand Ayatollahs both in Iran and Iraq, including Grand Ayatollah Syed Mohsin Tabatabae Hakim, the highest religious authority of the Shia world who died in 1964. Other Grand Ayatollahs who formally commended this work include Ayatollah Syed Abol-Qasem Khoi (Najaf), Ayatollah Syed Kazem Shariatmadari (Qom), Ayatollah Ahmad Khonsari (Tehran), Ayatollah Taqi Amoli (Tehran), Ayatollah Mar'ashi Najafi (Tehran), Ayatollah Sabzevari (Najaf) and Ayatollah Syed Abdulla Shirazi (Najaf).

A passage from the book specifically written to support the premise that there is no contradiction between the clergy and the monarchical system, and lavishing praise on Nasir-ud-Din Shah for his role in the Tobacco Crisis, reads: 'Because of the special favour and consideration Nasir-ud-Din Shah had for the clerical class, he did not oppose the *fatwa* of the Great Leader, Source of Religious Authority and Gracious Leader of the Clergy — (Ayatollah) Mirza Hasan Shirazi. By giving his support to the *fatwa* (issued by Mirza Hassan Shirazi prohibiting the use of tobacco) the Shah was able to neutralize the sinister plans of a foreign government and thus rescued the people of Iran from the harm of an alien government' (*Goftar-e-Shieh Dar Osool va Faroue*. Twelfth edition, Tehran, 1970. p.410).

It is also worth noting that the senior most Grand Ayatollah of the Shia world today, Ayatollah Khoi, as well as Ayatollah Mar'ashi, issued religious decrees to the effect that Dr. Shariati's works were 'perverse', 'misleading' and 'pernicious'. The 'purchase, sale, and keeping' of such books was 'not religiously permissible' according to Ayatollah Khoi's *fatwa* issued on 22 Rajab, 1398 of the Islamic Calendar (corresponding to 12 June, 1978).

50. Jamali, S., *Zindagi va Mobarezatay Syed Jamal-ud-Din Assadabadi.* (Life and struggles of Syed Jamal-ud-Din Assadabadi) Tehran, 1979.
51. Ibid.
52. Ibid., p. 100—9.
53. Ibid., p.109, 111.
54. Algar, H., *Religion and State in Iran*, p.259.
55. Ibid., p.260.
56. Ahmed Ben Bella's interview in *Arabia: The Islamic World Review,* September 1981.
57. Browne, E.G., *The Persian Revolution of 1905-1909.* Cambridge, 1910, p.28—9. Quoted by Keddie, 'An Islamic Response' p.40.
58. Shariati, A., *Maa Va Eqbal*. Hossienieh Irshad, Tehran, 1980. Henceforth called, *We And Iqbal*, p. 5—6.
59. Ibid.
60. Ibid.
61. Co-founder of Islamic Revolution Critiques Situation. *News and Views.* Vol.1, No.109, 15 December 1979. Department of Information and Publication. Ministry of Foreign Affairs of the Islamic Republic of Iran.
62. Irfani, K.A.H., *Iqbal Iranion ki Nazar Main,* (Iqbal as seen by Iranians). Iqbal Academy, 1956.
63. Irfani, K.A.H., *Rumi-e-Asr* (Rumi of the Age) Mare'fat publications, Tehran, 1952.
64. Saroosh, A., *Kuliyat* Collected Persian Verse of Iqbal. Snai Publishers, Tehran, 1963.
65. Taleqani, Syed M., *Parto-e-ez-Qoran.* (A Ray From The Quran) Enteshar, Tehran, 1969.
66. *Eslam Va Malika-yet* (Ownership and Islam), Tehran 1955.
67. Shariati, A., *Eqbal-Mamar-e-Tajdid-e-Bana-e-Tafakur-e-Eslam.* (Iqbal — Architect of Reconstructed Islamic Thought). Tehran, 1978.
68. Shariati, A., *Eqideh*. Tehran, 1979, p.36.
69. Shariati, A., *Iqbal — Architect of Reconstructed Islamic Thought*.
70. Ibid., p.83.
71. Ibid.
72. Ibid.
73. Ibid., p.77—81.
74. Ibid.
75. Shariati, A., *Takhasos*. Tasha-ye-e-Sorkh publications, Tehran,

1979, p.22.
76. Shariati, A., *We and Iqbal*. Hossienieh Irshad, Tehran, 1979, p.207.
77. Ibid.
78. Ibid. p.216-22.
79. Ibid., p.216–21.

2. The Constitutional Revolution (1905-9)

The Ulama
The distinctive feature of the Tobacco Movement was that it represented the first successful anti-imperialist mass mobilization under the clergy's leadership. Important as the role of the intelligentsia and reformists may have been in generating socio-political awareness among the *Ulama* and the people, the fact remains that the movement was led by the clergy. And once the clergy leadership had reached an accommodation with the Shah and called off the mass movement, there was little the reformists and intelligentsia could do even though they might have realised the clergy's error. This is clear in the letter Afghani wrote to the Grand Ayatollah Shirazi urging him to continue the movement against the Shah even after the latter had agreed to rescind the Tobacco Concession.

Since the social, political, and economic conditions that generated the Tobacco Movement had remained essentially unchanged, and given the continuing efforts of the reformists, modernists and intelligentsia to seek constitutional reforms along democratic lines, the general state of unrest and dissatisfaction continued to simmer on. Before long, the *Ulama* found themselves in an uneasy and temporary alliance,[1] with the reformist elements. 'The outcome of this alliance was the movement of 1905-6 culminating in the establishment of a consultative assembly'.[2]

After the apparent success of the Tobacco Movement, the influence of the *Ulama* as an opposition watchdog began to dampen, mainly because many among the *Ulama* were assimilated in the Shah's system of oppression and corruption. 'Titles and allowances were lavished upon them and their recommendations became essential for the success of any petition or request presented to the Government'.[3] Thus, not only did the *Ulama* fail to exploit their ascendency and power to dismantle the Qajar dynasty, 'It seemed that they were to become partners of the State in oppression'.[4] However, since there was no firm basis for this cooperation, the informal alliance between the *Ulama* and the State began to waver and eventually crumbled. Meanwhile, Iran's economy continued to become increasingly dependent on foreign loans mainly procured from Tsarist Russia. The *Ulama* had optimistically hoped, in their ignorance, that Nasir-ud-Din Shah would be sobered into austerity and righteousness by their demonstration of power in the Tobacco Movement. But the persistently extravagant life style of the Shah and the heavy cost that his trips to Europe on borrowed foreign loans had incurred were causing a crushing burden on the national economy. Moreover, foreign domination of Iran which had by no means ebbed, was steadily on the increase, with Tsarist Russia gaining lucrative concessions in return for the loans it was extending to the Shah for meeting the Court's expenses. Deciding that Nasir-ud-Din Shah was an incorrigible lout who had driven Iran to the depths of decadence and oppression, Mirza Kirmani, a disciple of Syed Jamal-ud-Din, planned and carried out the assassination of the despot Shah in 1896.

The elimination of Nasir-ud-Din brought his son, Muzaffer-ud-Din Shah to the throne, who promised reforms, but proved himself to be as totally fascinated by extravagant trips to Europe financed by loans from foreign powers, as his father had been. Meanwhile, modernists and reformists were beginning to manifest their serious concern for reforms by forming 'secret societies.' Their aim was to push for a constitution that would curtail the absolute power of the Sultan, and introduce a parliamentary democracy like that of constitutional monarchies of the West.

The Intelligentsia

The internal, historical context for a democratic reformist movement — the Constitutional Revolution — had already been laid by the Tobacco Movement. But what distinguished it from the Tobacco Movement was the decisive role the intelligentsia and the modernists had played in giving it logic and direction. The classical Iranian historians of the Constitutional Revolution (Ahmed Kasravi, Mehdi Malekzadeh, Yahyai Dowlatabadi, and Nizam-ul-Islam Kirmani) have all argued that the modern idea of liberty, equality and fraternity propagated by Westernized intellectuals 'awakened the sleeping public' at the end of the 19th Century and thereby led to the national resurgence of the 20th Century. It has also been argued that the arrival of Western concepts created an intellectual revolution which, in turn, produced socio-political revolution.[5]

A Protest Movement

The Constitution Revolution began as a protest movement against Ain-u-Dola, the Prime Minister, whom the people were holding responsible for the inefficiency, corruption and oppression in the country.[6] Ain-u-Dola inadvertently sparked off the protest himself when he rounded up a group of merchants accused of selling sugar at a price higher than that fixed by the Government. The Prime Minister had the merchants flogged in his office. In protest, the indignant merchants, many of whom did not even deal in sugar and yet were flogged, staged a sit-in at a mosque in Tehran. The Mosque's Imam, who was a supporter of the Prime Minister, drove out the squatters from the mosque. The protestors took sanctuary at Shah Abdul Azim, a shrine outside Tehran, where they were joined by throngs of *tullabs*, *Ulama*, and people from all walks of life. The modernists and intelligentsia through their 'secret societies' established contact with the *Ulama* leading the sit-in at Shah Abdul Azim,[7] and gave the unrest a decisive direction by floating the demand for a 'House of Justice' or *Adalat Khana*. As the number of protestors assembling at Shah Abdul Azim and the pitch of the demand for removal of the Prime Minister kept on increasing, Muzaffar-ud-Din Shah found it expedient to accept all the demands listed by the *Ulama* – modernist opposition. But the vacillating Shah's reluctance at actually implementing these demands intensified the unrest. Ain-u-Dola was still lodged as Prime Minister and his heavy–handed methods for crushing his critics continued unabated. As discontent continued to spread over the whole country, a consolidated and strengthened opposition began pressing the demand for a constitution and Parliament with the aim of stripping the King of absolute power. Once again, the ailing Mozzafar-ud-Din Shah bowed down to this demand to contain the unrest and save his throne. The people thus achieved, at least on paper, what they had been fighting for without the need to engage in a civil war. By 1906, the first Parliamentary elections in Iran's history had been held. The ailing King inaugurated the Parliament in October of the same year, and died shortly after giving his blessings to a constitution that appeared to rank among the most democratic of the times.

The Constitution Subverted

With the death of Muzaffar-ud-Din Shah in 1906, his ambitious son Mohammad Ali ascended a throne which, under the new constitution, represented only a symbolic ceremonial function. But the new Shah, it was evident, had no intention of subscribing to the constitution. He boosted his power by forming the Cossack Brigade manned by Russian mercenaries, negotiated a heavy loan with Tsarist Russia over the Parliament's shoulders for his wasteful whims, but, nevertheless, 'sent a Koran sealed with the oath that he would observe the Constitution'.[8] Finding his position strengthened, the Shah made history with a brutal show of force when his Cossack Brigade surrounded the Parliament and bombarded it as he had ordered to subdue the Constitutionalists. The leading members of the Parliament known for their reformist ideas were executed in the Royal bid for reasserting absolute authority on State administration. But the Shah's violent abrogation of a constitution which enjoyed popular support, and his drive for absolute power was challenged by the people, leading to a popular armed uprising against him. Beginning in Tabriz, capital of Azerbaijan Province in western Iran, the uprising soon engulfed the whole country and became a popular nationalist movement. The Shah defended himself against the peoples militia — the *Mujahideen* Constitutionalists — by deploying his army.

A Short-lived People's Victory

The civil war ended when *Mujahideen* from Tabriz under the leadership of Sattar Khan converged on Tehran, where they were joined by Sardar As'ad and other groups of revolutionaries from the central and northern provinces. In the confrontation that followed the *Mujahideen* put the Shah's army to rout and made their victorious entry into Tehran in 1909. Mohammad Ali Shah fled to Russia with the connivance of the Russian Legation in Tehran where he had sought refuge. The Constitutionalists appointed Ahmed Ali, the thirteen year old son of the exiled Shah as the new constitutional monarch.

However, it was not long before the gains made by the people in the Constitutional Revolution were neutralized through the combined effort of the two imperialist powers of the time and the monarchist and reactionary elements within the country.[9] Several factors worked for the success of imperialist design in de-activating the Constitution. Shortly after the conquest of Tehran, the armed revolutionary militia — the *Mujahideen* — were persuaded to disarm themselves on the grounds that the nation's objectives had been achieved, as the 'bad man' who had violated the Constitution was defeated. Moreover, since the focal objective of the Constitutional Revolution calling for the creation of a 'House of Justice' and a Consultative Assembly had been achieved, the people and many among the movement's leaders believed that their mission had been accomplished. As a result, there was no longer any rallying point or shared focus to lend continuity to the people's movement. The masses were made to believe that the flight of the tyrant Shah after the conquest of Tehran amounted to the realisation of people's aspirations. As a result, 'that same class of aristocrats from the circle of Mohammad Ali Shah and the Qajar dynasty found their way to the Parliament'.[10]

However, the major reason for the failure of the Constitutional movement and the reversion to the Old Order lay with the ambiguities which the clergymen began creating in people's minds, by questioning the religious legitimacy of the Constitution, and making this issue a major controversy. Just as the clergymen who supported the Constitutional Movement had used religious slogans in favour of the movement, after the Constitution was instituted and the Parliament installed, most clergymen began using religion to undo the Parliament and the Constitution by challenging its religious legitimacy. With the exception of a few religious scholars, the clerical class launched an all out offensive against the Parliament and the bills for social and political reforms it was working for. The writings of Sheikh Fazlullah, a virulent cleric of the time, epitomise the general sentiments of the clerical class regarding the social reforms proposed by the Parliament. Earlier, the clergy had succeeded in preventing the Constituent Assembly from giving women the right to vote. Now the clerical attacks were directed against the bills calling for complete freedom of the Press and equality of all people, whether Muslims or non-Muslims, before the law. Sheikh Fazlullah's logic for attacking these proposed reforms was as follows: 'The members of Parliament are going to pass a law that would give the Press complete freedom. This law is against Islam. It would lead to the publication of pernicious books and spread corruption and immorality. It is religiously unlawful *(haram)* to publish works of Voltaire, the Frenchman who has done nothing but insult the Prophet (Mohammad) and Islam. A free press is *haram* in Quran. They (the Constitutionalists) want freedom to spread corruption and immorality by educating women and building schools for the education of girls. They want to spend our religious funds on constructing railways and industry. They want freedom so that they can say—"all nations on earth have equal rights and should mingle with one another, and exchange each other's women". Their concept of equality would allow a Jew to fornicate with a Muslim boy. That is why they say long live freedom, long live equality, long live brotherhood and equality. Why don't they say long live Islam? long live Quran?'[11] The clerical class, with the support of the native agents of the colonialists, the local aristocracy and feudal lords, led the struggle against the Constitution and socio-political reforms by popularising the slogan, 'We want Religion, we do not want a Constitution', and, 'the Constitution and the Parliament is un-Islamic because it calls for equality of all people before the law. This means that Muslims and non-Muslims, Jews and Zoroastrians are to be treated equally'.[12] Doubts, ambiguities, and conflict generated by this controversy soon engulfed the whole nation. In creating this controversy, imperialists masterfully exploited the hatred and suspicion of the Muslim masses against the *Bahai* sect, a 19th Century offshoot of Shia Islam whose adherents were being branded as apostates. As a result, the clergy began popularising the notion that the Constitutional Revolution had been planned and initiated by the *Bahais* who wanted a liberal atmosphere for themselves in order to preach their religion without hindrance.[13] This propaganda gave the aristocracy and the monarchists justification to massacre opponents of the Qajar dynasty in the name of struggle against *Bahaism* and safeguarding Islam. With power sliding back into the hands of the conspiratorial aristocracy and the denunciation of the Constitution by clerical quarters, the interference of Tsarist Russia and Britain in Iran began to rise again.

Notes

1. Algar, H., *Religion and State in Iran*. University of California Press, Berkley, 1969, p.258.
2. Ibid.
3. Ibid.
4. Ibid., p.219.
5. Abrahimian, E., 'The Causes of the Constitutional Revolution in Iran'. *International Journal of Middle East Studies*. Vol.10, No.3, August, 1979.
6. Sykes. P., *Persia*. Oxford University Press, 1922.
7. Algar, H., *Religion and State in Iran*.
8. Sykes, P., *Persia*. Oxford University Press, 1922.
9. Afrasiabi, B., Dehqan, S., *Taleqani va Tarikh*. Tehran, 1980. Henceforth called *Taleqani and History*.
10. Ayatollah Taleqani's speech in Tehran University, Eid-ul-Fitr Khutba, 1979.
11. Homa Nateq. 'Ruhaniyet Va Azadi ha yeh Demokratik' (The Clergy and Democratic Freedom). In, *Jehan*, 13 April 1982.
12. Ibid.
13. Afrasiabi, B., and Dehqan, S., *Taleqani and History*. See Taher Ahmedzadeh, Introduction to Chapter 3, p.110-128.

3. The Jungle Revolution

Rivalry between Britain and Russia for control of Iran had been going on since the 18th Century, reaching a highpoint by the turn of the 20th Century. According to a treaty signed by Britain and Russia in 1907, these powers divided Iran into two 'zones of influence' wherein each power was allowed to further its own interests without any hindrance by the other. Britain acknowledged Iran's Northern and Central provinces as the 'Russian zone', while Russia acknowledged Iran's Southern provinces as the 'British zone'.[1] By 1914, Iran had become an objective expression of the 1907 Anglo-Russian treaty: on the one hand, the south and the south west had been occupied by British forces who had entered Iran on the pretext of protecting Britain's route to India. The presence of these forces had vastly extended British influence in Iran's internal affairs. On the other hand, northern and western areas were under the control of Tsarist Russia, whose penetration of Persia was apparently motivated by the desire for neutralizing the British presence and also for making up for Tsarist reverses suffered at the European front. But the presence of foreign troops in Iran was not limited to Britain and Russia — Turkish troops supported by Germany had stationed themselves in parts of Iran's Azerbaijan and Kurdistan provinces, ostensibly for forestalling a British-Iraqi invasion of Turkey.[2] As for the central Government of the Shah in Tehran, its power chiefly rested with the Cossack Brigade, whose 8,000 troops were commanded by Russian mercenaries. Also at the Shah's disposal was a 5,000 strong Gendarmerie manned by Swedish officers, its contingents stationed in all major cities of the country.[3] The reaction of the Iranian nationalists to the state of affairs gripping their country was turbulent and diffuse. Thus, while members of the intelligentsia were busy circulating 'night letters' secretly and printing protest articles and bulletins, others, notably the more seasoned politicians, were trying to bring together the scattered revolutionary forces in a unified front. The more militant elements, however, were out hunting for arms and ammunition.[4]

It was during these times of chaos and confusion that Mirza Kuchak Khan, a young revolutionary from the northern province of Gilan reached the conclusion that the only way to liberate Iran from foreign powers and their local proteges was through armed struggle.[5] Mirza Kuchak Khan began his armed resistance with a handful of followers in 1914 in the woodlands of northern Iran which soon became the nucleus of 'The Jungle Revolution—a popular armed insurrection that had been initially based on the nationalistic feelings of freedom fighters within a 'pan — Islamic framework'.[6] It was soon to become the most powerful guerrilla movement in Iran's history. Directed against Iran's monarchical system and the influence of Britain and Tsarist Russia in Iran, Mirza Kuchak Khan's revolution became, at its height, a grand coalition 'joining together a Religious—Socialist movement with strong nationalist overtones'.[7] A characteristic feature of Kuchak Khan's Movement was that it was 'religious' only in the sense that it was conducted by people who were simple and ordinary Muslims, with no professional religious pretensions.

Mirza Kuchak Khan

Born at Rasht, capital of the forested northern province of Gilan in 1878, he was named Younas. Incidentally, his father was known as Mirza Bozarg (the 'Big Mirza'), so the young Younas came to be called Mirza Kuchak (the 'Small Mirza').[8] Mirza Kuchak, who hailed from a peasant family, was first educated in a school at Rasht, and a few years later enrolled himself as a pupil in religious studies at a theological school in Tehran. Mirza Kuchak Khan stayed briefly at this school, but then renounced his intention of becoming a professional clergyman. Nevertheless he found himself committed to and propelled by the revolutionary and liberating spirit which he believed Islam contained, to the very end of his life. While in Tehran, Mirza Kuchak Khan became a member of *Ittehad-e-Islami*, a secret body deriving its name from the organization Syed Jamal-ud-Din had founded in Istanbul in the last years of his life.[9]

As to the beginning of the Jungle Revolution, several versions exist. All of them, however, agree that Mirza Kuchak Khan launched this movement almost singlehanded and with the barest means at his disposal. According to one account,[10] Mirza Kuchak Khan set out from Tehran for the northern jungle alone. In Gilan he was joined by four revolutionaries and together they fought their first victorious encounter against government troops.

Kuchak Khan and the Jungle revolutionaries had long hair and beards, attributed to the fact that Mirza Kuchak Khan and his comrades had sworn upon the Quran not to shave their hair until they had liberated Iran from the clutches of the monarchical system, and British and Tsarist colonialism.[11]

Mirza Kuchak Khan's World View

A devout Muslim who strictly observed daily prayers and fasted in the holy month of Ramazan, Mirza Kuchak Khan believed that none of man's actions were worth undertaking if lacking in harmony with the Divine will. The battle between Truth and Falsehood, between those, who, like the prophets of God, supported the toiling and deprived masses against the likes of Pharoahs and their class, was irrevocable and irreconcilable. In this confrontation, Mirza Kuchak Khan considered himself to be a follower of the path trod by the Prophets like Moses and Mohammad (on whom be Peace). He found himself committed to fight for the freedom and welfare of the suffering and weakened massess, 'even if such struggle involved the loss of millions of lives and millions in property'.[12]

We find Mirza Kuchak Khan expressing these views in his exchange of letters with the Russian chief of the Tehran garrison whom the Shah had acquired for his protection, from the Tsar. In his letter to Mirza Kuchak Khan, the Russian officer, on behalf of the Shah who was greatly distressed by the Jungle insurrection, offered Mirza Kuchak Khan 'a position and resources so that he would be able to spend the rest of his life with the greatest respect and prestige,'[13] if he abandoned the Jungle Movement. In this letter, the Russian had made clever allusions to the holy Quran and emphasized that the already miserable and impoverished Muslims were suffering more and more as a result of the disruption Kuchak Khan's movement had caused in the normal routine of life. The Russian lauded him as a 'perfect man' and said that it was not becoming for a man of Kuchak Khan's saintly stature to cause misery and hardship to the poor Muslim masses. The letter also noted that Mirza Kuchak Khan was 'a patriot, a wise well—wisher of Iran, and a spiritually chaste person'.[14] The chief of the Tehran garrison ended his letter by inviting Kuchak Khan to visit the Cossack Brigade as his 'dear guest'. Replying to this letter, Mirza Kuchak Khan pointed out that the Russian had used sweet seducing words to fog and blunt his reason, and his only aim was to win over Kuchak Khan's support for the hated and despised regime of the Shah, a proposition to which he could never submit. Kuchak Khan further deposed that such words and offers had been used by the British as well, who had offered him sovereignty of Iran if only he came to terms with them, but he had rejected all such gestures for he fervently believed in his sacred mission. 'It is given in the Islamic law that whenever infidels come to dominate the Islamic State, Muslims should rise up to confront them. But the British Government cries out, "We don't know what Islam and Justice mean. We only wish to enslave the weak nations and crush them in order to attain our own ends".'[15] But 'revolutions in the cause of justice were afoot in the world',[16] Kuchak Khan noted, referring to the Russian Revolution that had not yet succeeded at the time but was surging towards victory. These revolutions, Kuchak Khan said, 'were motivating us to declare that all provinces of Iran constitute a Republic based on Socialist principles, in order to rid the toiling masses from the yoke of the luxury loving class'.[17] Mirza Kuchak Khan then vowed that there was no place for compromise in his sacred struggle, even if that meant bloodshed: 'I shall keep striving to bring prosperity to my country, even if that means loss of millions of lives and millions in property. I shall answer, as Moses answered the Pharoah, and Mohammad answered Abu Jahl. The reply which the spiritual, the friends and founders of freedom give in the Court of Divine Justice for I am also one of their followers. I and my comrades, you and your followers, are treading upon two opposite paths. It is to be seen if the wise men of the future would laugh and jest on our martyred bodies or admire your victory.'[18]

Outlining Objectives for the Revolution

Mirza Kuchak Khan is known to have been a quiet, unassuming person with a charisma marked by disarming humility and simplicity.[19] He mobilised the peasants and the rural youth with his brief, simple speeches, stressing the necessity for driving out the colonial powers and their local agents, the king and the chieftans, who had plundered the wealth and degraded the Iranian honour for many years.[20] The Jungle Revolution was directed at achieving the following basic objectives: expulsion of colonial forces, effacement of injustice and the creation of security and justice equally for all, and the struggle against despotism and individual dictatorship.[21] These objectives were read out at a peasants' rally around 1916, at a time when Kuchak Khan was fighting against three forces: the troops of Tsarist Russia, the British agents and the Shah's mercenaries. The following points were read out and supported at this meeting:[22]

1. 'We have gathered here to regain our lost rights which have been trampled upon by Tsarist (Russian) agents. We must provide complete amenities of life for the toiling people.
2. 'The second, point of our 'Community' *(Jame'yet)* is that a National Government must replace the (present) Government installed by Britain and Russia (in Tehran).
3. 'All people would be equal before the law, regardless of position and rank, belief and religion.
4. 'All lands, farms, and industries, everything in the country shall belong to all. Each person is entitled to use the benefit from this (wealth) equally.'

Beginning the Revolution

The Jungle Revolutionaries began their movement by attacking the estates of big landowners and those native landlords who had opted for Russian citizenship in order to acquire large landholdings in Iran's northern provinces that were under the influence of Tsarist Russia.

This physical penetration of Russian influence was a logical consequence of the 1907 Anglo-Russian treaty, in that Russia had begun absorbing its zone of influence by protecting rich landowners and merchants and by collecting the revenue that was actually the Iranian Government's due.[23] It was for this reason that the Jungle revolutionaries had first to confront Russian troops during their initial military operations for national liberation. Each victory of the Jungle guerillas, besides raising Kuchak Khan's credibility and popularity among the masses, enriched his movement both in men and arms.[24]

By 1917, the Jungle Revolution had established itself as the major liberation movement in the country. It was led by a committee calling itself *Ittehad-e-Islami* which had declared, under the banner of Islam, Iran's independence and freedom from colonialism as its primary objective.[25]

By 1918, the Movement was consolidated in the Gilan Province, expanding to the neighbouring province of Mazandaran and other Caspian coastal areas. At the same time, the newspaper *Jungal* began appearing as the organ of *Ittehad-e-Islam* Committee.[26] Mirza Kuchak Khan had vastly expanded his camps for military training where the rural youth and peasants were trained by young Iranian instructors as well as a few German volunteers.

With the victory of the Bolsheviks in the Russian Revolution in October 1917, the Jungle Revolution gained a major boost. It was relieved on its Russian Front owing to the disarray in which Tsarist troops found themselves following the fall of the Tsar in Moscow. And it was to receive the assistance of revolutionaries who were now in power in Moscow.

Kuchak Khan and the Soviet Union

On 28 May 1920, the Russian navy invaded Anzeli, the northern Iranian city port on the Caspian. It bombarded the strongholds of the British garrison in the city, already abandoned by British forces, and took control of Anzeli. The pretext the Russians used for their invasion was not altogether unconvincing. They claimed that, under British instructions, the Iranian Government was assisting Russian counter-revolutionaries fighting the Bolsheviks. It was to protect the Bolshevik Revolution from the counter-revolutionaries who had sought refuge on the Iranian side of the border, the Russians said, that their troops had arrived in Anzeli. However, they assured the Shah's Government that the Red forces would vacate Iran after they had eliminated the counter-revolutionaries operating from Iranian soil.

The Soviet Union could not have chosen a better occasion for its invasion of Port Anzeli. At the time of invasion, Britain had decidedly become the most resented foreign power in Iran owing to its persistent domination and manipulative control of the Iranian scene. Also intensifying the people's resentment was the corruption and despotism of the Shah's regime for which Britain was held responsible. But the main factor which augured favourably for the Russians was the undeniable popularity of the October Revolution among the Iranian people. Many Iranians found themselves identifying with the Russian Revolution, for it represented the victory of the Russian people against the decadent monarchy of the Tsar, an accomplishment which for many Iranians remained a cherished dream.[27] Moreover, they considered the Soviet Union as 'the symbol of justice and equality and a staunch supporter of the weaker nations'.[28] It was within such a perspective that a few days after the landing of Red forces in Iran, leaders and representatives of different national and ideological political groups converged at Anzeli. They contacted Mirza Kuchak Khan, who was the undisputed national revolutionary leader, and discussed the desirability and necessity of Russian assistance for the revolutionary forces in Iran. Moreover, with the annihilation of the colonial regime of the Tsar, Britain was clearly the main enemy of the Iranian people. Given this context and the encouraging expectations the October Revolution had triggered among Iran's revolutionaries, Mirza Kuchak Khan accepted the Russian invitation for a meeting at Port Anzeli. By accepting this invitation, Kuchak Khan wished 'to make it clear to friends and foes that I am a friend of the Bolsheviks'.[29] He declared that he was meeting the Russians 'to strengthen our friendship with them in order to expel the British who are our enemies and who are their (the Soviet's) enemies, and the enemies of all the people of the world'.[30]

Details of negotiations between Mirza Kuchak Khan and the Russians have been recorded in the diaries of Mirza Ismail,[31] Kuchak Khan's nephew, comrade-in-arms and a close aide who remained with the Mirza to the end of the Jungle movement. According to these diaries, the Russians offered to support Mirza Kuchak Khan in gaining power in the prospective Republic of Iran, on condition that the Iranian Republic be erected along the Bolshevik blueprint. This offer Kuchak Khan rejected. The Russians then suggested that a government consisting of Jungle revolutionaries and members of *Hezb-e-Adalat* or Adalat Party, meaning Justice Party, (a party based in the Soviet Union consisting of Iranian communists who had emigrated to the USSR but had now returned to Iran) be formed. Kuchak Khan rejected this proposition as well because he believed that members of *Hezb-e-Adalat* lacked an intimate understanding of the traditions, customs, morals and sensitivities of the Iranian people. This was due to the reason that members of *Hezb-e-Adalat* had lived the greater parts of their lives in Russian towns. Hence they could not be considered qualified for running the day to day affairs of the people's revolution in Iran.[32] In other words, Mirza Kuchak Khan believed that every revolution needed a strategy and tactics that conformed with the conditions and the experiences of the society.[33] After long discussions and despite the objections of the Communist hardliners in the Russian based Adalat Party, the Russians signed a declaration with Kuchak Khan announcing 'the complete agreement of both sides' on the following points:[34]

1. The principles of Communism as applying to the immediate confiscation of land and property are not to be executed. There shall be no communist propaganda.
2. Creation of a Provisional Revolutionary Republic.
3. After Tehran has been captured and a Parliament of people's elected representatives has been formed, any form of Government which the elected representatives of the people agree upon will be installed.
4. The destiny of the Revolution will be handed over to this Government. The Russians shall not interfere in this Government.
5. Beside the Soviet troops (numbering 2,000) already present in Iran, no further troops shall enter Iran from Russia, without the permission and endorsement of the (Iranian) Government.
6. The Republic of Iran is responsible for the expenses of these Soviet troops.
7. All arms and ammunition requested from the Bolsheviks will be paid for (the Bolsheviks agreed to supply arms, but refused to receive payment).
8. The Russians should hand over to this Government the confiscated wealth of Iranian merchants residing in Russia, because this wealth belonged to Iran.
9. Handing over to the Republic of Iran (by the Soviet Government) all trade and commerce (rights and privileges acquired in the past by Tsarist Russia in Iran).

Following this agreement, a revolutionary committee consisting of the secular supporters of Kuchak Khan, his Islamic supporters, and members from the Adalat Party was formed with Kuchak Khan as its chairman. The Jungle Movement reached its height during 1920-21. In June 1920, Kuchak Khan captured Rasht and Anzeli, the major cities in the North, and declared Gilan a Socialist Republic. The Provisional Revolutionary Government and the Revolutionary Council for Defence were formed under Kuchak Khan's leadership. This Government aimed at establishing a Republic throughout Iran, abrogation of onesided and unequal treaties, protection of individual property rights of all citizens, and protection and safeguarding of Islam.[35]

As the British ambassador in Tehran would reminisce years later, the Iranian Government was helpless to cope with the Jungle Movement, and it had been Britain's guidance and direction that had preserved the collapse of the monarchy.[36] The ambassador was of the opinion that had Mirza Kuchak Khan marched upon Tehran in 1920, the capital would have fallen into his lap like a 'ripe apple'. But Kuchak Khan had misjudged his own strength and the weakness of the Central Government, and allowed the critical opportunity to slip by.[37] However, the more decisive element which prevented the Jungle Revolution from achieving total victory lay in its internal contradictions which finally rent it asunder.

The joint front of the revolutionaries led by Kuchak Khan at this time consisted of the following forces:
1. Kuchak Khan and his followers with a nationalist—Islamic orientation. Many of these belonged to the merchant class, but the majority of his followers were peasants and farmers.
2. Ehsanullah Khan, representing the section of petty bourgeoise intellectuals.
3. Khalu Qorban and the Communists supported by Kurdish militants.

This 'united front' disintegrated only a month after the Soviet Republic of Gilan was founded as differences between Kuchak Khan and the communists led to the seizure of power by the latter in a *coup d'état* that forced Kuchak Khan to withdraw to his jungle stronghold.[38]

The reasons for the aggravation of differences between the factions were much too obvious. Shortly after Kuchak Khan's agreement with the Bolsheviks, communist activists who had entered Iran with the Red Army linked up with their comrades in the Jungle Movement. They published their own Persian paper, *The Communist,* and carried on an intensive ideological propaganda campaign among the Muslim revolutionaries. All these steps, however, clearly contradicted the agreement that Kuchak Khan had signed with the Russians. Moreover, in obvious disregard of the agreement, the number of Bolsheviks entering Gilan was increasing steadily as was the interference of Red forces in support of the communist factions among the Jungle revolutionaries.[39]

As Kuchak Khan and his followers were not skilled politicians nor exposed to ideological education in a systematic and scientific manner, they had been unable to lay an adequate ideological foundation for a revolutionary Islamic movement.[40] Nor had they developed any economic strategy with clearly defined guidelines for the practical application of Islamic principles of equality and justice in the society to which they had been preaching. In other words, Mirza Kuchak Khan had not developed a revolutionary ideology rooted in Islam that could answer the tactical, economic, philosophical and political problems that were bound to arise during the course of a revolution. It was because of this that Bolsheviks of Iranian origin who had returned from Russia with their new ideology and had penetrated the ranks of the Jungle guerillas, succeeded in attracting a large number of young revolutionaries to their own worldview, having a clear edge in terms of propaganda techniques and the ability to articulate and convince. This speedy and wholesale propaganda by brilliant Bolsheviks from *Hezb-e-Adalat* had led to a deep split among the guerillas, dividing them into two groups:
1. Communist radicals under the leadership of Abu Khaf, the Russian activist, and two of Kuchak Khan's former colleagues — Ehsanullah

Khan and Khalu Qorban.
2. Muslim Socialists, Nationalist, and traditional Muslims, all adhering to Kuchak Khan's leadership.[41]

A Communist Coup

Without Kuchak Khan's knowledge, the Communist faction had requested Russia for 700 troops and two aeroplanes.[42] At this time Kuchak Khan is reported to have told Abu Khaf and Ehsanullah Khan: 'We wanted to drive out the British with your (Soviet Union's) help. Now you want to take the place of the British'.[43] That Abu Khaf, Ehsanullah Khan and Khalu Qorban, constituting the communists, were intent upon taking full control of the Jungle Revolution became all the more clear when Roskolinkov, the pro-Kuchak Khan Admiral of the Soviet fleet at Port Anzeli was recalled to Moscow. He was replaced by Madevani, whose arrival in Gilan was immediately followed by the *coup d'état* on 19 July 1920.[44] Although the plotters had planned the assassination of Mirza Kuchak Khan, one of his sympathisers had passed on the information that enabled Kuchak Khan to escape with some of his men to the forested mountains.[45]

The hardliners could not have chosen a time more suited to their purpose. A group of the Jungle revolutionaries were engaged against the British in Qazvin, a city less than a hundred miles north of Tehran, while another contingent was fighting the Shah's troops in the northern Mazandaran province. Commanders of Kuchak Khan's contingents fighting in Lushan, unaware of the events in Rasht, were summoned by the new leaders and arrested on their arrival. Many of Kuchak Khan's supporters taken by surprise by 'communist hardliners' were killed or taken prisoner. However, a large number of them succeeded in reaching Kuchak Khan's stronghold in the jungle.[46]

On 30 July 1920, the 'hardliners' led by Ehsanullah Khan set up a new revolutionary government in Rasht, composed of some members from the Central Committee of the Communist Party of Iran and Adalat Party, a few Kurdish chiefs, and a few Russian advisers. Soon after, these 'hardliners' launched a campaign to discredit Kuchak Khan's leadership. He was dubbed a 'superstitious mystic' and 'fortune teller', and accused of collaborating with the British and the reactionaries. He was also accused of embezzling the Revolution's funds.[47] The new leadership stepped up its campaign against religion in general and the Quran in particular. Cadres and political agents of the new government forcibly removed the *chador* and *hejab*, the traditional head scarf and cover used by Muslim women.[48] In Rasht, all mosques were shut down and their walls were whitewashed and were painted with the symbols and slogans of the new leadership. Many mosques were burned down and all those suspected of being supporters or sympathisers of Mirza Kuchak Khan were persecuted, tortured, or killed.[49]

A Soviet Analysis:
In their analysis of the Jungle Revolution, Soviet historians have partly blamed the Iranian Communists who at the time of Kuchak Khan's movement consisted of 'petty bourgeoise elements incapable of leadership and of dealing with the problems of a national liberation struggle.'[50] According to these historians, who apparently represent the Soviet Union's official point of view on the issue, Ehsanullah Khan and his colleagues from the Central Committee of the Communist Party of Iran had reached the conclusion that since Iran was a capitalist state, a socialist revolution was necessary. To carry out this revolution, Ehsanullah Khan's Government 'confiscated property of petty bourgeoise, small land owners, industrialists, and even peasants and small farmers in Rasht, Anzeli, and other areas of Gilan. They launched a propaganda campaign against religion, the Quran, and the clergy. They wanted that women should immediately remove the *chadors* from their head. They refused to co-operate with the national bourgeoise and Kuchak Khan'.[51] Although Ehsanullah Khan's Government had vowed to liberate the masses and eliminate private ownership, it 'not only failed to provide seeds and animals (tools and means of production) to the peasants, but in many cases it confiscated their own animals. It increased taxes on urban masses which included small merchants and small industrialists. And after taking control of Rasht and other cities, it stationed guards at the city gates to prevent the goods of peasants from freely reaching the bazaar of the city'.[52] 'This politics of extremism', continues the analysts' account, 'dismissed the credibility of Ehsanullah Khan's Government', and shortly thereafter, 'these adventurous elements' had to leave the Central Committee of the Communist Party of Iran.[53] Ehsanullah Khan was stripped of power, and Haider Amu Oghli, an Iranian communist who proved to be an ingenious activist during the constitutional revolution in 1906, became the new chairman of the Central Committee. The new committee made an analytical reassessment of the socio-economic conditions of Iran, arriving at a new thesis which outlined new tactics for the Iranian Communist Party. According to this thesis, Iran was not a capitalist society but in a transitional stage, passing from a stage characterized by tribal-feudal patriarchy to capitalism. This thesis therefore, rejected pure socialist movements under the given conditions. It argued in favour of a united front, consisting of all classes from the proletariat to the bourgeoise, for fighting against the Shah, the big feudal lords, and the imperialists. The thesis also pointed out the necessity for reaching an agreement with Mirza Kuchak Khan. Communist propaganda among the people was to be undertaken without insulting their religious feelings and a revolutionary army for fighting the imperialists and the Shah was to be organized. Following the chalking out of these guidelines, the new leadership of the Iranian Communist Party began negotiations with Kuchak Khan for setting up a joint front of all anti-

imperialist forces under Kuchak Khan's leadership. As a result, the joint front was formed in May 1921, consisting of the Jungle revolutionaries under Kuchak Khan, the communists under Haider Amu Oghli, and Ehsanullah Khan's group. Kuchak Khan became the chairman of the revolutionary committee and head of the new government of the Socialist Republic of Gilan. This government took steps for improving conditions of mass health and education. Several new schools with free education were opened, and a vast campaign for eradicating illiteracy in rural areas was undertaken. Workers and labourers, fishermen and boatmen formed their own syndicates. A mass campaign for acquainting the people with the problems posed by imperialism and the reactionary Government in Tehran, was launched from an expanding network of propaganda and information centres.[54] But this united front failed to achieve the objectives. Ehsanullah Khan, whose personal vanity had been wounded since he was ousted from the leadership of the movement, attacked Tehran to demonstrate the superiority of his faction to the other groups. Ehsanullah Khan launched this attack without adequate military preparations and in defiance to the Revolutionary Committee's opposition. As a result, his 3000 strong army was routed and Ehsanullah Khan was expelled from the Revolutionary Committee.[55]

The Final Break up

The uneasy accord between Kuchak Khan's Jungle revolutionaries and the communists ended forever when a group of Jungle revolutionaries, suspecting that the communists had plotted to assassinate Mirza Kuchak Khan during his prospective meeting with Haider Amu Oghli, the Iranian communist leader who had been Lenin's aide during the Bolshevik Revolution, attacked the site of the rendezvous and captured Haider Amu Oghli who was later killed. This incident was followed by renewed fighting between the Jungle revolutionaries and the communists. While the Shah's troops, capitalizing upon this in-fighting in the Jungle Movement were edging closer to Rasht, the Soviet Union, unknown to the communist faction of Ehsanullah Khan and Khalu Qorban, had arrived at a compromise with Britain and Tehran. Diplomatic exchanges between Tehran and Moscow made at this time indicate that the shifts in Soviet policy *vis a vis* the Jungle Revolution had been made even before Kuchak Khan's position had been weakened. It was within such a context that Rothstein, the Russian ambassador in Tehran, had assured the Shah that his Government found itself committed to its agreement with Iran and 'shall undertake with utmost sincerity the necessary steps for the speedy solution of the Gilan problem'.[56] The Shah on his part expressed his optimism that in future, 'the cordial relations between our two countries would be consolidated on a strong foundation', and that as a result of the help and arrangements made by the Soviet ambassador, 'the unfortunate affairs in Gilan would be brought to an end'.[57]

According to the Russo-Iran treaty signed in February 1921, both countries agreed neither to permit the setting up of groups or organizations opposed to the other country on their own soil, nor to assist such organizations. Russia was given the discretion to take the steps it thought necessary for safeguarding its national security in the event it perceived its boundaries threatened by the presence of the troops of a third country on Iranian soil. The political and economic compromises between Russia and Britain on one hand, and between Russia and the Shah's Government on the other, coupled with the surrender of the communist's forces controlling the Republic of Gilan to Reza Khan, the new strongman brought to power by the British in Tehran, sealed the fate of Kuchak Khan and his revolutionaries. That the Soviet Union had decided to strike a deal with Reza Shah in Tehran at the expense of the Jungle Revolution is clearly reflected in the letter[58] of the Soviet ambassador to Mirza Kuchak Khan. Defending the Russo-Iran agreement, ambassador Rothstein told Kuchak Khan that the above agreement could be taken as replacing the Jungle Revolution for it involved the best approach for stemming and reducing British influence in Iran.[59] Part of Rothstein's letter to Mirza Kuchak Khan reads: 'It was not possible for you to prevail upon the (Tehran) Government or compel it to make changes, or liberate the country from the presence and influence of the British. I repeat that this is not due to any fault of yours but is a consequence of the world situation after the (First World) war. ... in view of the fact that we, that is, the Soviet Government, consider revolutionary activities (in Iran) at this time not only useless but definitely damaging, we have altered the form of our politics, adopting an alternate strategy. Although only a few months have passed since the signing of our treaty with Iran and I have been appointed here only recently, there has been a visible progress in our policies, which indicates that British influence (in Iran) is declining, not only in the north but to some extent it seems to have been shaken even in the south as well'.[60] The Soviet ambassador also argued in favour of 'clearing Iran's northern route to Russia,' which was controlled by the Jungle revolutionaries, in order to facilitate 'normal trade relations between Russia and Iran'. Rothstein attributed the major cause for the prevalence of poverty in Iran to its inadequate trade with other countries. On these grounds, Rothstein urged Kuchak Khan to terminate his Movement, at least for the time being, leaving it for Kuchak Khan to choose between the 'rewards' his compliance would bring and the 'unpleasant' consequences of his refusal.[61]

End of the Jungle Revolution

By the 12th day of *Safar*, the year 1340 of the Islamic calendar (10

November 1921), Reza Khan—led government forces had reached the outskirts of Rasht, capital of the communist controlled Soviet Socialist Republic of Gilan. The combined forces of Ehsanullah Khan, Khalu Qorban and the Red Army decided on immediate surrender.[62] Khalu Qorban, War Minister of the Gilan Government, was deputed to negotiate the terms for surrender with Reza Khan, who was later to crown himself as Reza Shah, founder of the Pahlavi regime. Following this, Reza Khan's troops entered Rasht, where a formal ceremony was held in which Khalu Qorban, Ehsanullah Khan and other leaders swore allegiance to the Government of Iran. As a token of good will, the Shah's regime conferred military ranks on the leaders of the former Republic of Gilan. Khalu Qorban, now given the rank of a Colonel in Reza Khan's army, was made commander of the forces for liquidating Kuchak Khan and his followers who were still resisting in the jungles of the north. Ehsanullah Khan chose to sail away to Moscow with the Red Army, where later he was to write his memoirs. These events were relayed in a short news item that the Iranian Embassy in London had sent to the London *Times* on 15 November 1921. The note reads, 'Rasht and Anzeli which were under the occupation of Mirza Kuchak Khan have been taken back. Kuchak Khan's partners Khalu Qorban, Khalu Morad and their followers have surrendered to the Shah and have been granted amnesty. Kuchak Khan, many of whose soldiers and commanders have been killed, has escaped to the mountains'.[63]

In the confrontations that followed between government forces and Jungle revolutionaries, Kuchak Khan's guerrillas were offered amnesty if they surrendered. While a large number of revolutionaries abandoned the struggle, thousands, operating in small bands, each from its own stronghold and without mutual co-ordination, continued their resistance. Nearly three thousand of the guerrillas as well as the Shah's troops lost their lives in skirmishes that lasted for the next three years.[64] A number of Indian Muslims in the British army who were sent to fight the Jungle revolutionaries during the Revolution's early days, but had defected and joined Kuchak Khan, were arrested as the Revolution finally died out, and handed over to the British authorities in Tehran. These soldiers were later sent to Baghdad where they were executed by hanging.[65]

As for Mirza Kuchak Khan, he died in a snowstorm in the tortuous mountains he was trekking to reach the position of one of his guerrilla groups. One of Kuchak Khan's closest fighting companions, 'Hooshang', a German revolutionary volunteer since the earliest day of the Movement, was also killed in the snowstorm.[66] The bodies of these two were discovered by a village teahouse man, then taken away by a landlord, a bitter enemy of Mirza Kuchak Khan. The landlord cut off Kuchak Khan's head and placed it for public exhibition.[67] It was then taken by Khalu Qorban to Tehran and presented to Reza Shah. However, it is related that Reza Shah was more angered than pleased by Khalu Qorban's gesture and ordered the head to be buried in the Tehran graveyard.[68] Soon after, Khuchak Khan's head was stolen from his grave and brought back to be buried beside his body at Sulaiman Darab[69] — a village in Gilan which today throbs in the hearts of young revolutionaries in Iran as the symbol of the first Muslim freedom fighter in contemporary history whose life epitomized the fearless spirit of revolution and struggle against dictatorship, imperialism and exploitation.

The Rebirth of Mirza Kuchak Khan

Kuchak Khan was reborn as a national hero when he was rediscovered by young Muslim revolutionaries who founded the *Mujahideen-e-Khalq* organization in 1965. These progressive Muslim guerrillas, on the basis of their analysis of Iran's history, positioned their movement in a direction that was regarded as a logical continuation of the Jungle Revolution. In order to emphasize their link with Kuchak Khan, the *Mujahideen* named their first underground paper *Jangal*, which reflected their strategy and called for armed resistance against imperialism and the Shah's dictatorship. With the people's victory in the Islamic Revolution in 1979, Mirza Kuchak Khan re-emerged as the nation's revered hero, admired even by the conservative clergy whose predecessors had opposed Kuchak Khan and called him 'communist' in the turbulent years of the Jungle Revolution.[70] Interestingly enough, this posthumous adulation had been too clearly anticipated by Mirza Kuchak Khan. A letter he wrote just a few days before his death reads: 'It is a pity that the people of Iran worship the dead. They have not yet acknowledged the value of this living group (of revolutionaries). But after we have been obliterated, the day would dawn when they would realize who we were and what we desired and what we fought for ... today our enemies call us robbers and plunderers, whereas each single step we took was meant for the well-being and security of the people. We hear these accusations, and we leave the verdict to Almighty God.'[71] It is known that Kuchak Khan's followers, in keeping with his legal judgement, executed Moin-ur-Ra-aya, the man thought to be responsible for killing Haider-Umo-Ughli, the Communist leader.[72]

After putting down the Jungle Revolution, Reza Khan continued his ascendency as Iran's new strongman and became Prime Minister in 1923. Ahmad Shah, the last of the Qajar Kings, was exiled to Europe setting the stage for the declaration of a Republican form of government in Iran. For a while Reza Khan, impressed by what Kamal Ataturk was doing in Turkey for bringing his country into the mainstream of 20th Century civilization, toyed with the idea of declaring Iran a Republic. The man in the street, the middle class, the merchants, the constitutionalists and the intellectuals strongly adhered to the idea of making Iran a Republic. But these efforts were condemned by the *Ulama* in Qom. To safeguard their interests and to neutralize the possibility of the introduction of a Kemalist pattern in Iran, the *Ulama* insisted that the monarchy be retained. Reza Khan finally paid a visit to Qom in 1925 and conferred with the spiritual leaders. Afterwards he declared that all efforts for a Republic were to be stopped and all energies be directed towards reforms and independence of the country.[73] Thereafter, he became the King, founded the Pahlavi dynasty and declared his resolve to strengthen the fundamentals of religion in the country.

For the moment, it seemed, the *Ulama* had been the winners and the intelligentsia and modernists the losers. However, before long Reza Shah, who now wanted to build what he believed to be a new Iran, showed that he was determined to go his way even if that meant the ruthless suppression of any opposition or criticism. During his reign, Reza Shah became the liquidator of many of his critics including a few clergymen. Before long, he made it illegal for people to wear turbans. Any of the *Ulama* wishing to wear a turban was required to first obtain a license. Clergymen found wearing a turban without license were imprisoned, and often beaten.

Notes

1. Sykes, P., *Persia*. Oxford University Press, 1922.
2. Ismail, R., *Qiyame Jangal,* Javedan publications, Tehran, 1978. Henceforth called *Qiyame Jangal.*
3. Ibid.
4. Ibid.
5. Mirfakhrai, E., *Sardare Jangal.* Javedan publications, Tehran (2nd ed.) 1978. Henceforth called Sardare Jangal.
6. *Qiyame Jangal.*
7. Ibid., p.7,8.
8. *Sardare Jangal.*
9. *Qiyame Jangal.*
10. Ibid.
11. Ibid.
12. *Qiyame Jangal.*
13. *Qiyame Jangal.*
14. Ibid.
15. Ibid., p.123.
16. Ibid.
17. Ibid.
18. Ibid.
19. Ibid.
20. *Qahremane Jangal.* Enayat (ed.) Aref Publications. Tehran (1980). Henceforth called *Qahremane Jangal.*
21. *Sardare Jungal.*
22. *Qahremane Jangal.* p.117.
23. Sykes, P., *Persia*. Oxford University Press, 1922.

24. *Qiyame Jangal.*
25. Ibid.
26. *Sardare Jangal.*
27. *Qiyame Jangal.*
28. Ibid., p.138.
29. Ibid., p.187.
30. Ibid.
31. Mirza Ismail's diaries have been published under the title *Qiyame Jangal,* Tehran (1979).
32. *Qiyame Jangal.*
33. *Qahremane Jangal.*
34. Adopted from *Qiyame Jangal,* p.138.
35. Ibid.
36. Sykes. *History of Iran.* Vol.2.
37. Ibid.
38. *Sardare Jangal.*
39. *Qiyame Jangal.*
40. Ibid.
41. *Qiyame Jangal. Sardare Jangal.*
42. *Qahremane Jangal.*
43. Ibid., p.130.
44. Ibid.
45. *Qiyame Jangal.*
46. *Qiyame Jangal.*
47. *Qahremane Jangal.*
48. Ivanov — *Tarikhe Novine Iran* (New History of Iran). Quoted in *Qahramane Jangal.*
49. *Qahremane Jangal.*
50. *Tarikh-e-Iran* (History of Iran). Translated into Persian by K. Kashavarzi. Pooyesh Publications, Tehran, 1980. This book, authored by a panel of half a dozen Russian historians, was first published by Moscow University in 1977. Henceforth called *Tarikh-e-Iran.*
51. Ibid., p.433.
52. Ibid.
53. Ibid.
54. Ibid.
55. *Sardare Jangal.*
56. *Qahremane Jangal,* p.161.
57. Ibid., p.161.
58. *Sardare Jangal.*
59. Ibid.
60. Ibid.
61. *Qahremane Jangal.*
62. *Qiyame Jangal.*
63. *Sardare Jangal* p. 382.
64. *Qiyame Jangal.*
65. *Sardare Jangal.*
66. Ibid.
67. *Qiyame Jangal.*

68. Ibid.
69. *Sardar-e-Jangal.*
70. Ayatollah Modaress, the politically influential cleric in Iran during the first quarter of this century lauded Mirza Kuchak Khan and his fighters as 'true Muslims'. The Ayatollah found it necessary to make this statement because of the suspicion and hatred the conservative clergy was fanning against Mirza Kuchak Khan whom they had dubbed as an 'infidel communist'. More recently, Ayatollah Rafsanjani, Speaker of the Iranian Parliament and a leader of the clergy—dominated Islamic Republic Party hailed Kuchak Khan as an Islamic Revolutionary and a 'progressive cleric' who had heroically fought against foreign colonialists and dictatorship.
71. *Sardar-e-Jangal,* p.374.
72. *Qiyame Jangal.*
73. Wilbur, Donald N., *Contemporary Iran,* Fredrick and Praeger. New York (1967).

4. Mossadeq's National Movement

Reza Khan

Reza Khan, commander of the Cossack Brigade, had come to power through a *coup d'état* in 1921 supported by Britain. Britain had reasons of her own for choosing Reza Khan to become Iran's new strongman. Because of Iran's proximity to the Soviet Union, Britain was intent upon keeping Iran as a vital link in its defence chain extending from India to the Baltic.[1] In bringing Reza Khan to power, Britain had decided to shift her power base in Iran from the less certain tribal and feudal forces to a strong central government.[2] To consolidate his position, Reza Khan neutralized potential sources of threat to his authority by crushing the tribal chiefs and feudal lords. Insofar as the Soviet Union had analysed these measures by Reza Khan in the context of its specific ideological framework, it erroneously concluded Reza Khan to be progressive rather than fascist. The Soviet Union therefore decided to reach an accommodation with the Central Government in Tehran at the expense of Kuchak Khan's Jungle Revolution in northern Iran. Before long, Reza Khan, who had toyed with the idea of declaring Iran a republic and becoming its first President for over two years, proclaimed himself the new monarch and founded the Pahlavi dynasty in 1925. It is interesting to note that while the modernists and intelligentsia had thrown their weight behind the efforts for a republic, the clergy insisted on retaining the monarchical system. Thus Reza Shah mounted the throne and founded the Pahlavi dynasty with the solid support of the clergy behind him and despite the opposition by reformists and the intelligentsia. Conflict between the modernist-intelligentsia on the one hand and the clergy on the other thus plunged Iran into the iron grip of a dictatorship that was to last for half a century.

When the allies occupied Iran during the Second World War, Reza Khan, because of his support for Germany, was sent into exile and his son, the 18 year old Mohammad Reza was made the new Shah of Iran. With the exile of Reza Shah, Iran experienced considerable political respite. The new liberal atmosphere proved to be most conducive for the consolidation of democratic and nationalist organizations, thus preparing the ground work for the national struggle that was to engulf

Iran, for the nationalization of oil and the eviction of imperialists from the Iranian scene.

By the time the world entered the second half of the 20th Century, it was witness to a spate of political and social movements and transformations in different parts of the globe. The victory of the Chinese people and the movements for national sovereignty in Indonesia and the Indo-Pakistan sub-continent had transmitted their reverberations to other countries under colonial and semi-colonial subjugation in Africa and Asia. In Iran, this movement for national independence and freedom from foreign influence was epitomized by Mossadeq and the movement he led. The other political fronts in Iran of the early 50s were represented by the Tudeh Communist Party, the rightist wing of the National Front headed by Ayatollah Kashani, leading political *mulla* of the time, and the national bourgeoisie in the National Front.

The Tudeh Party

In being the best organised political group, the Tudeh enjoyed considerable support in major Iranian cities. Its membership among urban workers exceeded 25,000, and it had the support of over 400,000 workers through its syndicate affiliates.[3] The majority of university students were Tudeh Party supporters as were over six hundred army officers and twelve thousand army personnel,[4] lending the Tudeh Party formidable strength. Established along the orthodox lines of the Russian Communist Party in 1941, the Tudeh had its origin in the Communist Party of Iran which was in existence during the second decade of this century. The Tudeh Party was a staunch supporter of Russian interests in Iran and solicited enthusiastically for the transfer of Iran's dependence from Western imperialist powers to the Soviet Union. It wanted Mossadeq to accomodate Soviet interests in Iran and to give the Soviet Union concessions for Iran's northern oil reserves. The Tudeh Party argument in support of this proposition was that since the USSR was not an imperialist country, any concessions given to the Russians were directly related to the benefit of the working classes. Moreover, the Tudeh Party was prepared to compromise with the pro-British factions within Iran by recognizing British interests in the oil rich south. These views, which amounted to a restatement of the defunct Anglo-Russian treaty of 1907 which had divided Iran into British and Russian zones of influence, found their way into the columns of *Mardom,* organ of the Tudeh Party. We find Ehsan Tabari, a leading Tudeh ideologue, saying that the Tudeh was prepared to 'acknowledge British rights in the south on condition that Russians were given concessions in the north'.[5] While campaigning for presenting itself as the true representative of Iran's toiling masses, the Tudeh Party engaged in a scathing campaign against Mossadeq, branding him as 'the agent of U.S. imperialism'. As for Mossadeq, his relations with the Tudeh were, at best, ambivalent. He attacked the Tudeh Party but also tried to use its weight against the

Shah.[6] His inability to control it and Tudeh's intransigence in acknowledging Mossadeq as the national leader were among the reasons that weakened the ranks of the opposition and enabled the United States to crush Mossadeq. Opposing the Tudeh Party were the pro-Western politicians who were in favour of safeguarding Western interests in Iran and who stood for confronting the 'communist threat' with the help of the West. This political front was decisively strengthened when Ayatollah Kashani withdrew his support from Mossadeq, and paved the way for the Iranian Generals to go ahead with the CIA designed coup d'état that toppled Mossadeq from power in August 1953.

Mossadeq's Political Orientation

Mossadeq envisaged a 'free Iran' independent of both the Eastern and the Western power blocs. Such a policy, Mossadeq thought, was feasible through his strategy of 'negative confrontation' with the Super Powers. Mossadeq was of the view that reliance in any form and on any pretext on a foreign power was bound to inject the influence of that power in Iran's national affairs. Such influences infested the political scene in Iran, Mossadeq observed, making Iranian politicians willing or unwilling tools of foreign powers. By maintaining a balance between the Super Powers, Mossadeq hoped to 'cleanse the Iranian society' and its economic, political, social and cultural dimensions which had been contaminated by the influence of these foreign powers upon whom Iran was dependent.[7] In voicing these views, Mossadeq was restating the words Mirża Kuchak Khan, leader of the Jungle Revolution, had spoken to his communist comrades bent upon the wholesale 'Sovietizing' of the Revolution 30 years ago: 'For us, an alien is an alien. North and South make no difference. In balancing ourselves between them lies the only means for our salvation. It is in the light of this policy that we can enjoy our material and spiritual wealth to which we have a right like any other nation... I am an Iranian and a Muslim and I shall fight as long as I am alive, against anything that threatens Islam and Iran'.[8] In terms of its organizational support, Mossadeq's movement was based on the support of the 'National Front', a coalition of various political groups fighting for the nationalization of the oil industry. The Front enjoyed a popular base which had been further broadened with the support of Iran's traditional clergy represented by Ayatollah Kashani. The latter also enjoyed the support of the militant wing of *Fedayeen-e-Islam*, a formalist-Islamic rightist group whose aim was to physically eliminate all opposition to the traditional Islamic dogma. The 'rightists' in the National Front represented interests of those clerics, landowners and big bourgeoise who, while opposing British influence in Iran, supported America because of their anti-Communist orientation. It was after Mossadeq had refused to negotiate with America for bringing the 'Oil Crisis' to a U.S. endorsed solution that this right wing, led by Kashani, stiffened its resistance to Mossadeq and eventually renounced him,[9] to ease the way for the Generals to overthrow Mossadeq.

Mossadeq vs the West

During this two years as Prime Minister, Mossadeq won two major victories. On the domestic front, he succeeded in transferring power from the Imperial Court to the National Parliament, the *Majlis;* while on the external front, Mossadeq dealt a serious blow to imperialism by the nationalization of Iranian oil. The chief target of Mossadeq's nationalization movement was the Anglo-Iranian oil company, the bastion of British imperialism in Iran. Through this company, Britain controlled over a quarter million square miles of Iran's oil rich areas, including the world's largest oil refinery at Abadan producing 25 million tons of refined oil per year. The company also owned a fleet of over one hundred oil tankers for shipping Iran's wealth abroad and ten thousand trucks for transporting oil supplies within the country.[10] The extent to which the British imperialists plundered Iranians of their national wealth can be judged by the fact that during 1914-50, Britain had exported 324 million tons of Iranian oil, paying only $420 million to Iran as royalty, an amount which was a mere 8% of the company's net profit of 5 billion dollars.[11] Even as late as 1951, while Iran received only 18 cents per barrel for its oil, its Middle Eastern counterparts, Bahrain, Saudi Arabia and Iraq, were receiving 35, 56, and 60 cents respectively.[12] Besides, Britain was causing a serious drain on Iran's exchequer by retaining for herself colonial rights and privileges, like importing goods to Iran without payment of customs duties. For example, the amount of goods Britain had imported into Iran during 1940-51 had deprived the Iranian Government of revenues exceeding the amount of oil royalties Iran was receiving from the British.[13]

Given Britain's stakes in Iran, it was expected that any talk about nationalization of oil would elicit a severe reaction from the British. Thus, as the demand for nationalization of oil became more and more vocal with Mossadeq's emergence as the national leader, diplomatic pressures coupled with threats of military action from Britain began to increase. When Mossadeq made his historic declaration that he would expel the British from Iran, the British Foreign Secretary made it clear that his government would not tolerate the expulsion of the Anglo-Iran oil company from Iran. To show that it meant business, Britain positioned its war ships near Abadan, the city housing Iran's largest oil refinery. After the oil nationalization bill was passed by Iran's parliament, additional units of the British Navy were sent to the Gulf area. British forces took up positions on the Iran-Iraq border amidst rumours that she was going to occupy Iran's oil rich areas.[14] This interference by the British in the internal affairs of Iran further intensified the people's mobilization against Western imperialism. By May 1951, Mossadeq had appointed a committee that included Mehdi Bazargaan — who, more than a quarter of a century later would become the first Prime Minister of the Islamic Republic of Iran — to work out details for implementing the nationalization of oil. This committee created the National Iranian Oil Company to replace the British company. But Britain was not prepared to swallow these developments. It refused to recognize the annulment of the 1933 treaty with Iran which granted Britain control of Iran's oil fields. Even Truman, the American President, tried to persuade Mossadeq into re-negotiating a new treaty with Britain.

The failure of joint British-American manoeuvres to pressure Mossadeq into negotiations led to the economic blockade of Iran by the Western imperialists. It was clear why the West so desperately needed to crush Mossadeq — the movement for the nationalization of oil in Iran had not left other oil rich countries unaffected. In 1951, the year Mossadeq became Iran's Prime Minister to fight the battle for oil, the Iraqi parliament, for the first time in its history, raised the issue of nationalization of oil. Only a few months later, demonstrators in the oil rich island of Bahrain were demanding the nationalization of Bahrain's oil and the expulsion of the British and the Americans controlling the island's oil. That same year the Egyptians began demanding nationalization of the Anglo-Egyptian oil company. This demand was to climax in the movement that toppled King Farooq of Egypt, leading to the eventual nationalization of the Suez Canal by Gamal Abdul Nasser.[15] It was therefore inconceivable that the imperialists would have tolerated Iran's exit from the Western orbit, even if this exit were not intended for the benefit of the Soviet Union.

The Clergy and the Oil Crisis

Just as the imperialists and their native agents deployed the clergy to turn the Constitutional movement into a runaway scenario against *Bahaism* (the philosophy of the *Bahai* Sect) in 1909, they raised the bogey of the 'communist threat' to undermine Mossadeq's national movement in 1953. To undermine Mossadeq's national mobilization and the popular movement against colonialism, the Grand Ayatollah Brujardi, religious leader of the Shia World, and royalist members of Parliament, held a public demonstration of their support for the Pahlavi regime at Faizieh Theological School in Qom. It was declared at this meeting that since nationalization of oil violated principles of private ownership, it was, therefore, Un-Islamic.[16] Moreover, Mossadeq was openly condemned for leading the country towards communism. Shortly thereafter, the clergy's concept of anti-colonialist struggle was clarified by Ayatollah Kashani in an interview with a French newspaper. In this interview, Kashani declared that struggle against colonialism as it was going on in the country (expressed in the demand for nationalization of oil) was fruitless, 'what we should do is to call an Islamic Conference of Islamic States with the objective of fighting drug addiction, corruption and prostitution, so that our youth do not fall prey to deviant thoughts'[17] It was by employing such arguments that the clergy hoped to separate the oil nationalization issue from the people's anti-colonialist struggle. As part of his sacred struggle against colonialism Kashani ordered that acid be thrown on the faces of unveiled women working in government offices.[18] The clergy leadership and the feudal lords orchestrated their anti-Mossadeq campaign so effectively that 'people were made to believe that the coming to power of Mossadeq's National Front would be the same as the domination of Iran by communists'.[19] They preached that 'Islam was in danger' and people had to 'rise to save Islam'.[20] The clergymen associated with the imperial court used every opportunity and every unethical manoeuvre to generate doubts and ambiguities about the Tudeh Communist Party. As Taleqani, the progressive Ayatollah was to recall later,[21] during the critical days of the Nationalization Crisis, a number of pro-Shah clerics gathered at the house of Ayatollah Behbahani and spent the whole night writing forged letters on behalf of the Tudeh Party to thousands of clergymen in the country. The general content of these letters, written in red ink, and sent to clergymen all over Iran with the signature of the Tudeh Party, read: 'Very soon we shall hang you by your turbans on street poles'.[22] Also, anti-Islamic slogans were scrawled in Tehran by paid agents of imperialists and royalists to magnify the 'communist threat'.[23] As noted by Ahmadzadeh, the veteran progressive Islamic revolutionary who was released from the Shah's prison in the wake of the Islamic Revolution in 1978, the Shia world's religious leader of the time, Ayatollah-Ol-Ozma Brujardi, was swayed by the, 'Islam is in danger'[24] propaganda to the extent that as the supreme religious leader he sent an urgent cable to the Shah who had fled to Rome, urging him to come back to Iran 'for Shiism and Islam need you'.[25] The Grand Ayatollah was to send another cable to the Shah after he had been put back on the throne by CIA, cautioning him against travelling by air as the Shah's younger brother had recently lost his life in an air crash. The telegram read: 'Since you belong to Shiism and your travels are undertaken for the preservation of Shiism and the Shia, please refrain from travelling by air, lest your life be endangered'.[26]

The relationship between Mossadeq and Kashani, the leading political Ayatollah although 'intense but difficult' during the early phase of the movement, was characterized by Kashani's reluctance to accept Mossadeq's political leadership. Had Kashani, representing the *Ulama* power, and Mossadeq, representing the Nationalists and national bourgeoisie reached an understanding, Iran would have had a different history.[27] 'What Kashani did to me, what they have done to me, even Brutus would not have done to Caesar,'[28] Mossadeq is reported to have said after the Americans ousted him and brought the Shah back to power. As for Ayatollah Kashani, he was convinced that 'all that Mossadeq wished was to crush and destroy me'.[29]

Before long, Kashani, who was leading the rightist group that was becoming increasingly vocal in its criticisms of Mossadeq, withdrew his support from Mossadeq to watch and endorse the aftermath of the drama from the sidelines.

The Coup d'Etat

According to those who engineered the *coup*, Mossadeq was overthrown with the help of the clergy, the ruffians, and the Army.[30]

The blow that shattered the people's movement to bits in 1953 was not the exclusive doing of the CIA, for the internal power contenders — Kashani, the religious leaders, and the Tudeh Party — had caused a progressive corrosion in Mossadeq's leadership. Renounced by the clergy and hounded by the communists, Mossadeq made desperate attempts to maintain his position. Meanwhile, the Shah had fled to Rome. Following the Shah's exit, Tudeh supporters flooded the streets and pulled down the statues of the Shah from city squares and his portraits from government buildings. But the following day, on 19 August 1953, Tehran witnessed armed gangs of mercenaries fueled by American dollars ravaging the city. General Zahedi, a former interior minister whom Mossadeq had fired from the army after he was found implicated in an anti-Mossadeq *coup* a year earlier, was in command of the *coup d'état*. With his tanks and troops marauding Tehran's main streets, and the mercenary gangs wielding clubs, pistols and daggers in the alleys, the General and his gangs massacred hundreds of demonstrators who had poured into the streets to declare their opposition to the *coup*. Before sunset, the streets had been cleared of pro-Tudeh and pro-Mossadeq demonstrators protesting against the *coup d'état*, and Zahedi cabled the Shah to return to his throne. Mossadeq was arrested and put on trial in a military court which sentenced him to death. The sentence was later commuted to life imprisonment. Mossadeq's foreign minister, however, was executed. The entire operation had cost the CIA $390,000.[31]

Within a month of the *coup*, 7000 members of the Tudeh Party had been arrested. Six hundred army officers and 12000 army personnel who had filled Tudeh Party membership forms[32] were detected and purged. More than one hundred members and sympathizers of the Tudeh Party were executed in Qasr prison alone.[33]

Immediately after the *coup*, America gave Iran an interest free loan of $45 million, and also lifted the economic blockade that had ruined the country's economy. Iranians had already learned that the American ambassador in Tehran had told Mossadeq a day before the *coup* that America could no longer tolerate Mossadeq and his policies.[34] A couple of months later *L'Observer*, the French newspaper, was reporting that America had given 45 million dollars to General Zahedi for 'crushing the communists, preparing the conditions for the settlement of the oil issue, re-establishing diplomatic relations with Britain, and entering into military pacts with Turkey and America for safeguarding the free world'.[35]

Surprisingly enough, the Soviet Union made a gesture of appeasement to the Zahedi Government by doing what it had refused to do when Mossadeq was in power. During the economic blockade of Iran by Western imperialists, Mossadeq had on several occasions urgently pleaded with the USSR to honour the payment of her debt to Iran that ran into several million dollars. The Soviet Union, which had ignored Mossadeq's requests for the payment of the badly needed cash, made the payment after General Zahedi had become the new Prime Minister.[36]

The West Makes up its 'Losses'

A couple of months after the 1953 *coup,* Americans began negotiating with General Zahedi about forming the International Oil Consortium. This Consortium was to deal with the Iranian oil industry and the sale of its oil in the world market. In April 1954, representatives of American and British oil companies reached an agreement about forming the Consortium and for exploiting Iran's oil. The Consortium decided that the former Anglo-Iran oil company of Britain should be paid 400 million dollars in damages by Zahedi's Government for the loss of its rights in Iran following Mossadeq's nationalization policies. Also decided by the Consortium was the division of Iranian oil among its members according to an arrangement that gave the American oil companies 40%, the British another 40%, and the French and Royal-Dutch-Shell, the remaining 20%[37] of Iranian oil.

To prevent any move on the part of the Iranian people against this agreement, Zahedi's government arrested a large number of military and police officers known for their progressive views and Tudeh Party sympathies. A number of teachers involved in organizing a general strike to force the rejection of this agreement were also taken prisoner.[38] The imposition of this agreement by the Consortium on the people of Iran practically amounted to the anulment of the nationalization bill of 1951. As a result of the agreement between the Shah and the Consortium signed in 1954, the entire establishment of the Iranian oil industry, namely, oil refineries, oil pipe lines, grid stations, ports and airports fell into the hands of the Consortium. The National Iranian Oil Company became only a cover for veiling the usurpation of Iranian oil by foreign companies. In fact, the extent and scale of plunder of Iran's oil wealth increased severalfold after 1954. For example, during the first nine years of its operation in Iran, the Consortium drew more oil from Iran's oil wells than the British had done in 50 years.[39] The only discernible difference beteen the pre-nationalization and post-nationalization situation lay in that British influence was rapidly replaced by American imperialism.

A Soviet Analysis:

The Tudeh Party's role during Mossadeq's Movement has remained a subject for much discussion and analysis. The Soviet view of Tudeh's role in the oil crisis which echoes the views of the Tudeh party and its present leadership, may be summed up in the following words: 'The Tudeh Party committed major mistakes during the struggle for nationalization of oil. The basic error lay in the fact that it was unaware of the anti-imperialist nature of the national bourgeoisie and confused it with comprador bourgeoisie. Such was the Left extremism and erroneous policy which the Tudeh Party adopted with respect to the National Front and policies of Mossadeq's Government. This position of the Tudeh Party severely obstructed the creation of a single, united anti-imperialist front. Therefore, it was the inability of the Tudeh Party and the National Front to create a single front which caused Iran's national liberation movement, that had reached its peak during 1951-53, to be defeated in the end'.[40]

Soviet historians have also attributed Mossadeq's defeat to his alleged refusal to sell oil to socialist countries. Had he done so, these historians argue, the financial problems facing Mossadeq would have been considerably reduced, and it would have been possible to neutralize the effect of the economic boycott of imperialist countries.[41] These historians observe a contradiction in Mossadeq's campaign against British and U.S. imperialism. For while Mossadeq fought to liberate Iran from the imperialism of the West, he made no attempts to get closer to the socialist countries, at least to the extent of establishing trade relations and selling the unmarketed Iranian oil. However, since it is known that Mossadeq had tried to sell oil to the socialist countries but was snubbed with the response that socialist countries had sufficient oil of their own,[42] the above argument of the Soviet historians cannot be taken too seriously.

The Movement in Retrospect

It was not until January 1979, a quarter of a century after Mossadeq's fall, that the facts about the role of Ayatollah Kashani, the ambitious political *mulla*, and his personality clash with Mossadeq were to be spoken of in public. In the first mass meeting held in Iran to commemorate Mossadeq at his hometown at Ahmedabad, Ayatollah Taleqani, the progressive Ayatollah who was leading the revolution inside Iran at the time, said:[43] '(In 1953) we received a blow from within ourselves that was much harder than the blow by foreign powers ... The internal agents and spies of imperialism began sowing seeds of disintegration through their psychological games, playing upon their (Mossadeq's and Kashani's) human weaknesses. ... They cornered Ayatollah Kashani with their psychological games, (saying) that this movement is yours, — what is Mossadeq doing here? .... all power rests in your hands! These spies, who were known to us, and were known for what they were, surrounded that old man and separated him from Mossadeq..... soon the rumour spread that a plot was being hatched, that Ayatollah Kashani was supporting General Zahedi'. But the more revealing account of the intrigues and paranoia prevailing among the clerical circles that made CIA's plan for overthrowing Mossadeq successful, were brought to light only recently by General Battmannqlich, Chief of Staff of the army that carried out the military operations of the *coup* in 1953. The General, who was arrested following the Islamic Revolution, was put on trial in December 1980 for his leading role in the 1953 *coup*. During his defence, General Battmannqlich earnestly argued in defence of the role he had played 27 years ago. For him, the *coup d'état* had been 'a national and religious duty' which had been sanctified by the holy blessings of Ayatollah Kashani.[44] Excerpts from the General's statements published in the local press reads:[45] 'Because of my irrevocable belief in Islam, I had been graced with the blessings of Ayatollah-ol-Ozma Kashani. All those close to him know that I was one of his disciples and my actions had his support. During the latter part of Mossadeq's government, members of the Tudeh Party had penetrated into all spheres of national activity, and the country was at the brink of destruction. In an audience that he honoured me with, his holiness Ayatollah Kashani said to me "save the country from the evil of the Tudeyees (members of Tudeh Party)". . . Because of my close association with Ayatollah Kashani, I was to experience the wrath of Mossadeq's associates.'

General Battmannqlich recalled that a couple of months before the *coup* Ayatollah Kashani had told him, 'These Kafirs (Tudeh Party members) should be fixed up.'[46] The General related that he had told the Ayatollah there were no men at his command to enable him do this. Ayatollah Kashani, General Battmannqlich said, had reassured him, telling him to have patience as things were going to change soon. Three days before the *coup d'état,* General Battmannqlich was appointed the Army's Chief of Staff on General Zahedi's orders, a position which Battmannqlich accepted after he was assured once again of Kashani's blessings.[47]

It was because of his knowledge of these events that Ayatollah Taleqani, the 'Father of Islamic Revolution' said in one of his last speeches before his death in September, 1979, 'They (the imperialists) have always used the "cane of Communist threat" for crushing the liberation movements of our people. Did they not club our heads with it through their *coup d'état* on 18 August 1953? We should beware, we should be on guard. We should not allow (the imperialists) to crush our movement (with this cane) again.'[48]

Notes

1. Afrasiabi, B and Dehqan, S., *Taleqani and History*, p.113.
2. Ibid.
3. Halliday, F., 'The Tudeh Party in Iranian Politics.' MERIP Reports. Vol.10, No.3, 1980, p. 22–23.
4. *Enqelabe Islami,* Tehran, 4 December 1980.
5. Brier, P., Blanche, P., *Iran: Revolution in the name of God.* (Persian translation), Sahab Books, Tehran, 1979, p.235.
6. Ibid.
7. Tajik, A., 'Coup d'etat.' *Enqelabe Islami.* No. 341, Tehran, September, 1980.
8. Astawan, H. K., *Siyasat ha-e-Mo'vazan'ai Man'fi.* Vol.II, pp.74-75, Tehran 1978.
9. Brier, P. and Blanche, P., *Iran: Revolution in the Name of God.* (Persian translation). Sahab Books, Tehran, 1979.
10. *Tarikh-e-Iran.*
11. Ibid.
12. Ibid.
13. Ibid.
14. Ibid.
15. Ibid.
16. Homa Nateq, 'The Clergy And Democratic Freedom'. In *Jahan,* 13 April 1982, p.14.
17. Ibid.
18. Ibid.
19. Ahmedzadeh, T., in *Taleqani and History,* p.121.
20. Ibid.
21. Ibid.
22. Ibid., p.121.
23. Ibid., p.122.
24. Ibid.
25. Ibid.
26. Ibid.
27. Brier, P., Blanche, P., *Iran: Revolution in the name of God.* (Persian translation) Sahab Books, Tehran, 1979.
28. Ibid., p.238.
29. Ibid.
30. Roosevelt, C., *Counter Coup.* Quoted by Homa Nateq, in The Clergy And Democratic Freedom. *Jahan,* 13 April 1982.
31. Ibid.
32. *Enqelabe Islami,* 4 December 1980.
33. Brier, P., Blanche, P., *Iran: Revolution in the name of God.* Tehran, 1979.
34. *Khandaniha* 22 August 1953.
35. *L'Observer,* 1 Oct. 1953.
36. Tajik, A., 'Coup d'etat' *Enqelabe Islami.* No. 341. Tehran, September, 1980.
37. *Tarikh-e-Iran.*
38. Ibid.

39. Ibid.
40. *Tarikh-e-Iran.* p. 550.
41. Ibid.
42. Roosevelt, C., *Counter Coup.* (Persian translation). JAMA. Tehran, 1981.
43. Ayatollah Taleqani's speech at Ahmedabad, January, 1979.
44. *Enqelabe Islami,* No.416, Tehran. 4 December 1980.
45. Ibid.
46. Ibid.
47. Ibid.
48. Afrasiabi, B. and Dehqan, S., *Taleqani And History.*

5. Khomeini and the June Uprising of 1963

For almost a decade after overthrowing Mossadeq's government in 1953, the Shah ruled Iran without confronting any serious opposition. His relations with the Grand Ayatollahs of the time, including the Ayatollah Ol-Ozma Brujardi, the leading *Marja-e-Taqlid* and religious leader of the Shia world, were friendly and without friction. It was not until the death of Ayatollah Brujardi in 1962 that Khomeini, a distinguished teacher of Islamic Jurisprudence, Philosophy, and Mysticism at Qom's theological schools, was to gain recognition as the most outspoken critic of the Shah's regime. Khomeini regarded the Shah's policy of separating the Church from the State and his westernization of Iranian society as 'a plot by Imperialists and Zionists' for controlling Iran. The ultimate objective of this policy, as viewed by Khomeini, was the liquidation of the clergy and its influence upon the Iranian masses. Khomeini argued that the Shah was planning to weaken the clergy by encouraging the invasion of Iranian society by Western culture and values.[1] The Shah was a willing instrument for implementing the imperialist's plot, because 'the survival of his regime was inseparable from the continual consolidation of imperialist culture in Iran'.[2] There was little that was new about these arguments, except that Khomeini had voiced them more eloquently and had given them a revolutionary perspective by frequently using the terms 'Zionism' and 'imperialism' in his speeches. After all, many clerics had voiced more or less similar arguments when they began opposing the Constitutional Revolution in 1906 and the proposition for turning Iran into a republic in 1925, on the grounds that this would bring the country under the control of the intelligentsia and modernists, whom the formalist clerics had always viewed with deep suspicion.

Khomeini's Emergence as a National Religious Leader

In 1961, the Shah introduced some major changes in the Constitution. For the first time in history, Iranian women were given the right to vote and their social equality with men was recognized. Another constitutional amendment called for a modification in the oath taking ceremony of government officials. According to the new procedure, government officers were not required to swear specifically on the Quran but by referring to 'the heavenly book I believe in'.[3] Also affected by the constitutional changes was the former election procedure under which non-Muslim candidates were not entitled to Muslim votes.[4] The new amendments removed this restriction from non-Muslim candidates. There was much in these constitutional changes to enrage religious leaders, among them Ayatollah Khomeini. The bill calling for equal rights for men and women was viewed by Khomeini as 'a decadent trap' the Shah had laid for Iranian women to draw them to the 'swamps of corruption, prostitution, and destruction'.[5] The exclusion of the Quran from oath services for government employment was defended by the regime on grounds that it would open the way for religious minorities to join government organizations. The clergy, however, viewed it as a calculated step for de-Islamizing Iran. It was in the context of these developments that Khomeini became the source of the most scathing attacks against the regime since it was put back in power in 1953. Until the introduction of these amendments, Khomeini, like the rest of the Ayatollahs, had supported the Shah. Indeed, when the Shah initially stepped back, under the clergy's pressure, on his proposed bill giving equal rights to women during local bodies elections early in 1962, Khomeini expressed his gratitude to the Shah and declared that 'His Imperial Majesty had acted along Quranic principles,'[6] and that it was therefore incumbent upon people to obey the King, who was the 'guardian of the Constitution and independence and security of the country'.[7] However the complete sense in which Khomeini envisaged blind obedience to the ruling authority is reflected in his remark on the nature of an Islamic government headed by a 'just ruler'. 'If a just ruler orders the arrest of any person or burning down the house of another, or the extermination of a community which is detrimental to Islam and Muslims, his order is just and must be obeyed'.[8] However, the turning point in Khomeini's loyalty to the monarchy came after the Shah decided to firmly go ahead with social and economic reforms through his 'White Revolution', and after his decision to give Iranian women the right to vote and equal legal status became irrevocable. The Shah had also decided to abolish landlordism in Iran through his 'White Revolution'. These two issues laid down the ground for the June Uprising in 1963. 'Women's emancipation and women's right to vote is against the law of Islam and of the country'[9] insisted Khomeini. The Ayatollah advised the Shah to leave the 1906 Constitution alone 'until the appearance of the hidden Imam'. Till that time, argued Khomeini, no one had the right to make any changes in the Constitution. To drive home his point, Khomeini threw in his all out support for the 1906 Constitution because 'In this constitution, women have not been given the right to vote and they are not allowed to get elected'.[10]

It was therefore religiously lawful to demand that 'women be prevented from working in offices' because 'any office a woman enters would be infested with corruption'.[11] The Shah's refusal to rescind the proposed constitutional amendments made Khomeini the most unforgiving critic of the Pahlavi dynasty and the monarchy. By the end of 1962, Khomeini had embarked upon a path whose objective was to demolish a constitution that he himself had vowed no one had the right to touch 'until the appearance of the hidden Imam'.

Soldiers Invade a Theological School

On 21 March 1963, the day marking the beginning of Iranian new year, Khomeini addressed a crowd that had gathered to greet him for the new year in the Faizieh Theological School. Parts of this speech, which became Khomeini's well known New Year message to the nation read:

> 'The ruling 'apparatus' which has imposed itself on Iran has violated the sacred principles of Islam. The honour of Muslims is at stake. The ruthless regime, by making un-Islamic changes in the Constitution, wishes to disgrace and degrade the people of Iran. It is planning to endorse and implement a bill that calls for equal rights for men and women. This bill violates the fundamental principles of Islam and Quran. This means that the regime wants to take 18 years old girls for military conscription and force them into the barracks of soldiers. It wants to take away the young and chaste Muslim girls under the threat of bayonets to centres for corruption. The target of the foreigners is the Quran and the clergy. The undercover agents of foreigners are conspiring with the likes of Shah's government to annihilate the Quran and to crush the clergy. They want to degrade, imprison and destroy us, so that the Jews in America and occupied Palestine may benefit. I therefore declare this Eid (new year day) a day of mourning for the Muslim Community, so that Muslims be informed of the dangers threatening Quran and this country of the Quran. I warn this ruthless establishment, this despotic government, to step down because of its crime for violating Islamic principles and the Constitution. A government which adheres to Islamic principles and shares the sorrows of the Iranian people (should come in its place.'[12]

Enraged by this unsparing attack, the Government sent elite units of Imperial Guards to storm the Faizieh School, the venue of Khomeini's lectures in Qom. The day after Khomeini's bulletin was published, the Shah's troops invaded Faizieh and severely bashed up students, teachers, and anyone within their reach in the school compound. Over a hundred people were injured and a dozen killed during the rampage. The Shah expected that after this punishment, Khomeini would leave him alone to pursue his 'White Revolution', the programme America had designed for consolidating the Shah and 'curbing communism' through social and economic reforms. But there was little the Shah had gained by sending his troops to attack the school in Qom. Not only had he failed to intimidate Khomeini into silence, he provided him with another occasion to lash out against the monarchy. In May 1963, an adamant Khomeini issued another public bulletin in which he called for the impeachment of the Government. This was the first time in Iran's history that a Grand Ayatollah was making such a demand. In this speech, Khomeini had become even more vocal and defiant. He equated the monarchial system with the robbing and plundering of the people, and declared that the monarchy was striving to strike Islam at its roots, that wherever monarchy existed, it meant that Islam had been violated. The finality of the confrontation between Khomeini and the Shah was clearly echoed in the concluding words of this speech where Khomeini, addressing the Shah, said, 'I have now prepared my heart for the tips of your bayonets, but I shall never be prepared to bow down to your intimidation, or submit to your oppression and despotism.'[13]

The Uprising

The month of *Muharram* in the Islamic Calendar is considered as one of the sacred months, particularly by the Shia Muslims who observe it as a period of religious mourning. *Muharram* was only a month away when Khomeini made the above statements. He was now sending the *mullas* in Iran's 80,000 to 120,000 mosques his 'guidelines' regarding the social-political direction which he thought religious sermons should assume during the holy month. Khomeini's staunchest followers, only a few at the time, followed his directions and gave their speeches and sermons a political flavour. Khomeini's instructions aimed at sharpening the social awareness of the masses in a religious context: people were to be told about the 'tyrannical acts' which the '*Yazid* of the age' — the Pahlavi dynasty — was perpetrating. They were to be urged that instead of beating their breasts and flagellating their backs with chains in mournful memory of Hosein, they should rush to aid the 'contemporary' Hosein, (Khomeini) who had risen against the living *Yazid* (the Shah).[14] These instructions also called for acquainting people with the dangers of Zionism and its agents who were freely operating in Iran with the Shah's approval. Thus, the religious processions that paraded the streets of Tehran in June 1963, during the holy month of *Muharram*, had an unmistakable political flavor. Students from Tehran University led their procession to the city's densely crowded bazaar where in their speeches they hailed the struggle of the Iranian people and Khomeini's religious leadership. The students well realized Khomeini's importance for mobilizing and unifying the masses at the grass roots level in their struggle against imperialism. 'The victory of the Iranian people in their fight against imperialism and reaction is certain because of the general mobilization and awakening among the people of Iran brought about through Imam Khomeini's leadership',[15] declared a student leader in a public rally.

As for Khomeini, he made his speech on *Ashura*, 4 June — the day Imam Hosein, grandson of the Prophet Muhammad (peace be upon him), was martyred 13 centuries ago for opposing the despotic regime of the time. In this speech, Khomeini once again bitterly criticised the Shah and his regime. A few hours after his speech Khomeini was arrested. As news of his arrest spread, furious demonstrations spread all over the country. The Government immediately took action and deployed a large number of army units to quash the demonstrators. In Qom, it took the army only half a day to silence the demonstrators protesting the arrest of Ayatollah Khomeini. But in Tehran, demonstrators proved themselves to be more resilient, and it took the army three days to crush the uprising. The Shah admitted killing only 56 persons, the foreign news agencies put the figure at several hundred, while the opposition claimed that 15,000 people had been killed. The exact number of people killed will never be known, but it is clear that the scale of the demonstrations and the retaliation by the Army led to the loss of many lives.

That the Shah had prepared himself in advance for a final and unsparing crack down on his opponents is indicated by the fact that he himself courted the uprising by arresting Khomeini. Perhaps he thought it was necessary to do so to demonstrate his determination to go ahead with his reforms and his readiness to crush dissidents into silence or compromise. Only a few weeks before the June Uprising, the Shah had said, 'If it is, unfortunately, necessary to say that our Great Revolution should be tainted with the blood of a number of innocent people, that is, the Government officers (the army and police), and also the blood of a number of lost and wretched people (those opposing his regime), it cannot be helped and it shall be done.'[16] A few years later, the Shah cited the June Uprising as an expression of the 'unholy alliance' of the communists and the 'reactionary' Islamists against his regime. In his opinion, 'this riot was instigated by reactionary elements, by a person who claimed to be a *rouhani* (clergyman). But it was clear that this person had a mysterious connection with foreign agents. As we were later to find out the vagrants of the former Tudeh Party, a party which was totally against Divinity, praised this man using the title of 'Ayatollah'. The riot on June 4 was the best example of the unholy alliance between the "black reactionaries" and the "destructive red forces". This riot was undertaken with the money of a group of feudal lords who had suffered as a result of the land reforms.'[17]

This allegation of the Shah was a departure from his earlier accusations which portrayed Khomeini as an agent of President Nasser of Egypt.[18] Although the regime used this accusation right up to the Islamic Revolution in 1978, little credence was given to it by the people. For the stand of the Tudeh Party and the Soviet Union *vis-a-vis* the June Uprising was unequivocal. Following the events in Iran on 4 June 1963, Radio Moscow had commented: 'Street demonstrations were carried out today in Tehran, Mashhad and Qom by the reactionary elements in Iran who are unhappy with the reforms taking place in that country such as the land reforms, and who consider the expansion of social rights and freedom for Iranian women contrary to their desires. The leaders of the riots and the real activists were certain religious leaders.'[19] Also, *Izvestia*, the Russian daily, expressed Kremlin's position by stating that at the instigation of a group of reactionary Muslim clergymen, riots had occurred in major Iranian cities against the land reforms.[20]

However, these views from Moscow were not altogether baseless. For even though Khomeini was personally against opposing the Shah on the land issue,[21] religious leaders, motivated mainly by their opposition to the land reforms *per se*, had thrown in their support for Khomeini. It was only after Khomeini's movement against the monarchical system had gained some momentum that the clergymen who resented the bill because it threatened the large tracts of land at their disposal, found it expedient to join the movement. The slogan that these *Ulama* raised was the one closest to their hearts — opposition to land reforms. This fact did not escape the observation of a French journalist whose report on the June Uprising in *Le Monde* reads: 'It is certain that some of the *mullas* and merchants are associated with feudal lords, but it does not seem that Khomeini belongs to this group. But the fact cannot be ignored that the masses in the south of the city (Tehran's slum area), the unemployed and petty workers are singularly participating in these demostrations.'[22] After Khomeini was arrested and the uprising crushed, all the Grand Ayatollahs within Iran converged in Tehran or sent their representatives to protest Khomeini's arrest. The clergy leadership was concerned lest the regime took an 'unwise' step against Khomeini, a *Marja-e-Taqlid* (Source of Imitation) for millions of Shia Muslims. Moreover, under the Iranian law, religious leaders of Khomeini's rank were exempt from imprisonment and execution. As a result, the regime found itself compelled to transfer Khomeini to a lodging in a Tehran suburb and placed him under house detention.

Khomeini's Release

It was not until March 1964 that Khomeini was finally released and allowed to return to Qom. In the first speech he made only three days after his release to a group of students from Tehran University, Khomeini said, 'I am not of those *mullas* to sit here and take up rosary beads. I am not a Pope only to conduct a ceremony on Sundays. Those of you who are in the University should spread the word that the clergy does not support the Shah's revolution. One cannot enforce reforms under the tips of bayonets. By writing on the walls in Tehran "Khomeini is a traitor", the country cannot be reformed.'[23]

Khomeini's speeches after his release from detention became increasingly people oriented, in the sense that he began to specifically talk about the dismal economic situation of the under-privileged masses. He spoke about the indifference of the regime to the poor who were living below subsistence level in many parts of Iran, while flowers were being imported from Holland by the ruling class for their frivolous ceremonies.[24]

As the first anniversary of the June Uprising was approaching Khomeini's main preoccupation was to get the support of other religious leaders for declaring 4 June as a day of national mourning. But Khomeini succeeded in getting only two or three Ayatollahs to sign their names under his bulletin to indicate their support. The majority of Ayatollahs found it expedient not to risk signing their names under a Khomeini sponsored bulletin, a few even going to the extent of obstructing its publication.[25] This incident clearly showed that Khomeini was more of a 'lone ranger' among an estimated 80,000 to 100,000 members of the professional clerical class and that the decisive majority of religious leaders did not see Islam and the Quran as Khomeini did. As a result, Khomeini failed in mobilizing the masses and organizing a nationwide strike for observing the first anniversary of the 4 June massacre. Because of this failure, the Shah became increasingly convinced that the troubles in June 1963 were 'short-lived' because his social, economic, and political reforms had been endorsed by the Iranian nation. The great majority of religious leaders knew this and many had given him their support.[26]

The 'Capitulation' Bill

As the Shah's regime was becoming more and more dependent on the United States for implementing its policies, the presence of an ever increasing number of U.S. personnel was necessitated. The regime realized that its survival rested on the continual arrival of large numbers of U.S. advisers in all spheres of development, particularly defence. The regime was therefore prepared to accept any condition imposed by the U.S. that would accelerate the inflow of U.S. advisers. A primary condition that Iran had to meet was to ensure the immunity of Americans in Iran to Iranian law. In this context, the Shah-sponsored parliament passed a bill that granted diplomatic immunity to all U.S. servicemen and their families and personnel stationed in Iran. Under this bill, Americans who violated the law or were implicated in events requiring legal procedure could be tried only in U.S. courts. Khomeini viewed this bill as the surrender and capitulation of the Iranian nation to America.

On 26 October 1964, the day marking the forty-fifth birthday of the Shah and a national holiday for nationwide festivities, Khomeini made a speech that was to be his last in Iran for the next 15 years.

In this speech, Khomeini made a systematic exposition of the 'regime's treason' for 'selling the nation to America'. Excerpts from this speech read:

> 'I cannot express my heart's sentiments. My heart is heavy. Since the moment I have learned about the problems (ensuing from U.S. domination) of Iran, I sleep less. Iran no longer has any occasion for festivity *(Eid)*. They have turned our *Eid* into a day of mourning, yet together they (Shah and America) dance. They sold us and our independence and yet they rejoice with dance and festivities. Our honour has been crushed. Iran's greatness is destroyed. They have taken a bill to the *Majlis* which gives all American military advisers, their families, employees, their personnel and servants or anyone linked to them, immunity from (the consequences) of any crime they commit in Iran. If an American cook or servant kills your religious leader, Iran's police is not allowed to stop him from doing so. Iran's Court does not have the right to try him. The case must go to America, and there, the "masters" should decide! (The regime) knows that if the clergy has influence and power, it won't let this nation become a prisoner of America one day and of Britain another day. It won't allow Israel to monopolize the economy of Iran. If the clerics have power, they will kick this Government in the mouth and throw these members out of the Parliament. If the clergy has power, it will not allow boys and girls to wrestle in each other's embrace. It won't allow the pure daughters of the people to be in the hands of young men in schools (the male school teachers). It won't allow women to be sent to teach in boys' schools, and men be sent to teach in girls' schools and stir up corruption'.[27]

Khomeini vowed that the clergy would never allow an American puppet such as the Shah to rule Iran with such high handedness. It would 'kick him out of Iran'.

It was in this speech that Khomeini publicly declared that the regime in power in Iran was 'American'. He stressed the need for Islamic countries to be independent of super powers, adding that at the present time, U.S. imperialism was enemy number one of Muslims: 'America is worse than Britain. Britain is worse than America. Russia is worse than both. Each is worse than the other. Each is more unholy than the other. But today, we have to deal with America'.[28]

The Exile
This speech had clearly demonstrated to the regime that Khomeini would continue his criticisms as long as he was physically around. But disposing of the Ayatollah under ambiguous circumstances would have created trouble and resentment against the regime. Any steps for physi-

cally eliminating Khomeini would have shaken the support of moderate Ayatollahs and the majority of clergymen, who still supported the monarchy. It was on these grounds that the Shah decided to quietly send away Khomeini into exile.

On 4 November 1964, the night Lyndon Johnson became the President of America, Khomeini was taken into custody by SAVAK agents from his residence in Qom. The Ayatollah was directly driven to Tehran's Mehrabad airport and put on a special aircraft that took him away into exile that was to last 14 years. 'He was neither condemned, nor even judged, he was simply requested to go and exercise his incendiary eloquence elsewhere',[29] commented the ex-Shah on Khomeini's exile while he was himself in exile following the victorious return of Khomeini to Iran in 1979.

The aircraft flew Ayatollah Khomeini to Turkey, where he lived for a few months before settling down in Najaf in Iraq for the next 14 years. A few months after Khomeini was exiled, a militant group of his followers called *Fedayeen-e-Islam* assassinated Hassanali Mansur, Iran's Prime Minister, for his role in endorsing the 'Capitulation Bill'. The militants were arrested, three of them were executed and over a dozen given long prison sentences. With this, Khomeini's movement inside Iran came to a practical halt.

Clearly then until 1964, Khomeini had not succeeded in extending his influence beyond a limited section among the traditional religious masses. The situation had been further complicated by those *Ulama* who were opposing the Shah because the land reforms proposed by the 'White Revolution' affected their own interests. These developments had created a good deal of suspicion and ambiguity about the nature of Khomeini's movement in 1963. Also, Khomeini's statement that it was Un-Islamic for women to be given the right to vote had convinced the middle class, the intelligentsia and the less tradition-minded Muslims that Khomeini was a reactionary, despite his anti-imperialist utterances. As a result, not only did Khomeini fail in sustaining a mass movement against the regime, he also failed in his subsequent attempts for mass mobilization and protest strikes during the following years for observing the anniversaries of the June massacre. Many students and progressive Muslims in Bazargan's Liberation Movement had taken part in the June Uprising because of its professed anti-imperialist stance. However, another 15 years were needed for the emergence of progressive, Islamic, ideological and revolutionary forces like the *Fedayeen-e-Khalq*, Dr. Shariati, and *Mujahideen-e-Khalq* to help generate the necessary conditions for the massive movement of the Iranian people that demolished the monarchy in 1979. With Khomeini's exit from Iran and the suppression of opposition activities in any form by SAVAK, the stage was set for the emergence of guerrilla organizations. Guerrilla operations in Iran began on 19 February 1971, when 13 *Fedayeen-e-Khalq* Marxists attacked the police post in the village of Siahkal in the northern forests, about 60 kilometres from Tehran. Although all the guerrillas involved in the operation were subsequently killed, the incident inspired many radicals, Islamic as well as Marxist, to take up arms against the Pahlavi regime. Thus, the Siahkal incident marked the beginning of eight years of intense guerrilla activity.[30] As for Khomeini, his activities were limited to the statements that he made from time to time on the Iranian situation from Najaf, the Shia religious centre in Iraq where he had taken refuge.

Notes

1. Rouhani, E., *Nehzat-e-Imam Khomeini*. Tehran, 1979.
2. Ibid.
3. Ibid.
4. Ibid.
5. Ibid., p.145.
6. Homa Nateq, 'Ruhaniyet-Va-Azadi-ha-e-Demokratik.' (The Clergy And Democratic Freedom), *Jahan*, 13 April 1982, p.14.
7. Ibid.
8. Ibid.
9. Ibid.
10. Ibid.
11. Ibid.
12. Rouhani, E., *Nehzat-e-Imam Khomeini*. Tehran, 1979. p.145.
13. Ibid., p.370.
14. Ibid.
15. Ibid., p.441.
16. Ette'lat. 18 May 1963. Inaugural address to the 3rd Congress of Lions International, Tehran.
17. Pahlavi, M.R., *Engelabe Safid*. (the former Shah's book 'The White Revolution') p.45-46.
18. Rouhani, E., *Nehzat-e-Imam Khomeini*.
19. Ibid., p.514 (edited translation from the Persian).
20. Ibid., p.515.
21. Ibid., p.186.
22. *Le Monde*, Number 760, 25 July 1963. (translated from Persian), quoted in *Nehzat-e-Imam Khomeini*.
23. Ibid., p.656–59.
24. Ibid., p.656–59.
25. Ibid.
26. Pahlavi, M.R., *The Shah's Story*. Michael Joseph, London, 1980.
27. Ibid., p.716–26.
28. Ibid.
29. Pahlavi, M.R., *The Shah's Story*. Michael Joseph, London, 1980, p.77.
30. Abrahimian, E., *The Guerrilla Movement in Iran*. MERIP: Vol.10. No.3. March-April, 1979, p.3.

6. Mujahideen-e-Khalq

'They were devout disciples of the Quran. They opened the way for **Jehad** *(Islamic Revolution)'.*[1]

—*Ayatollah Taleqani*

If the CIA *coup* against Mossadeq in 1953 signalled the 'dusk' for the Iranian nation's struggle for freedom, independence, and human dignity, the tanks and guns that crushed the June Uprising ten years later ushered in the 'night' of oppression during which the Shah's despotism was to reach its bizarre climax. The immediate mood generated by the June massacare was one of apathy and despair. Many political and religious leaders displayed this mood by withdrawing from politics, while others were subdued into silence or decided it was time for co-operating with the Shah's regime and for working towards his royal dream for a 'Great Civilization'. As for the militants, they were either in prison or in exile, if not already killed. The Pahlavi dynasty, therefore, was once again wielding its authority virtually unchallenged and more brutally than it had ever done before. However, for a tiny number of young revolutionaries, within the abyss of this despair the nucleus of new hope was crystallizing. The aftermath of the June Uprising had convinced these young men whose spirits remained unbroken, that the only way in which a meaningful and effective struggle against the regime could be conducted was through armed struggle — a struggle that stemmed from a carefully chalked out strategy emanating from a concrete organizational network and was conducted within a dynamic ideological framework.[2] For these young revolutionaries, the June Uprising had marked a natural death for all forms of reformist and parliamentary struggle. The Shah's readiness to deploy his massive army for shooting down street demonstrators, the SAVAK's efficiency in liquidating opposition movements before they even got started 'compelled the Opposition, especially its younger members, to question the traditional methods of resistance — election boycott, general strikes, and street demonstrations. The 1963 bloodbath exposed the bankruptcy of these peaceful methods. After 1963,

89

militants, irrespective of their ideology, had to ask themselves the question: "What is to be done?" the answer was clear: guerrilla warfare'.[3]

At that period in history, Marxism as an ideology had proved its effectiveness in the liberation struggle of the oppressed peoples around the world. It had organized and guided many popular movements to victory on the basis of its systematic approach. It was therefore natural for the nuclei of revolutionary guerrilla movements crystalizing in Asia and Latin America to adopt this ideology for guiding their struggle. In the Iran of the mid-60s, Marxism-Leninism had been adopted by the *Fedayeen-e-Khalq*, the first underground organization to carry out guerrilla operations against the Pahlavi regime. Following the exit of the Tudeh Communist Party from the scene of struggle against the Pahlavi dictatorship, the *Fedayeen-e-Khalq* had become the most popular ideological organization among intellectuals and students. The most conscious of Iran's youth, students and intelligentsia, were joining the *Fedayeen* or supporting it to fulfil the responsibility their consciousness and social awareness, emanating from the nobler dimension of human nature, was demanding. There were plenty of social and historical reasons for the lack of enthusiasm on the part of the students and the intelligentsia for Islam and the Quran. Some of these reasons being the traditional opposition which reactionary regimes had incited against progressive religious views, and the promotion of a corrupt and decadent culture based on reactionary interpretations by the so-called custodians of religion, most of whom had endorsed the Pahlavi monarchy as 'Islamic'. The obscurantist stance adopted by many clergymen during the Constitutional Revolution and the Jungle Revolution had served to sabotage these movements. It was also well known that the clerical leaders had invoked Islam to protect the monarchical system in 1923 when Reza Khan, under reformist pressure, was planning to declare Iran a republic, and again in 1953, when the clerical leadership supported the reinstallation of the Pahlavi monarchy after it had been nearly dissolved. Thus, the social backwardness and impoverished cultural perspective of the masses had been cleverly exploited by vested interests in the secular and religious domains. As a result the Quran and Islam as presented by the formalist religious class and deployed by the ruling classes had not only failed to attract the young generation to faith, but turned them away.[4]

At this time Islam seemed to have lost ground as an inspiring ideal for generating a systematic, long-drawn struggle against imperialism, exploitation, and dictatorship, and the cream of Iran's consciousness was being skimmed by Marxism. This changed with the simultaneous emergence of two Islamic forces — Ali Shariati, the Islamic ideologist who reinterpreted Islam as a revolutionary ideology, and the *Mujahideen-e-Khalq*, progressive Islamic guerrillas. They set out to change the course of history in Iran and perhaps the Islamic world, at large. For the first time in the history of contemporary revolutionary struggle, Islam was crystallizing as a revolutionary ideology, and not as a mere emotional slogan to fuel spontaneous movements. In fact, one of the chief reasons for the weakness and failure of the June Uprising had been the non-availability of a clear and well defined Islamic ideology upon which a systematic revolutionary strategy could rest. The June Uprising, propelled by religious emotions emanating from the formalist, traditional brand of Islam of the theological schools, had lacked adequate organization for a scientific strategic struggle, as well as a link with 20th Century consciousness. As a result, Khomeini had been able to draw only a limited section of the Muslim masses and a small number of Muslim intelligentsia to support his movement. Islam had so far been used, as in other Muslim countries, as a mere slogan, and had become the monopoly of orthodox dogmatic religious scholars. It was for these reasons that traditional Islamic thought lacked the 'timelink' with the rich harvest 1400 years of evolution in human thought and consciousness had produced. It was for Ali Shariati and the *Mujahideen-e-Khalq* to begin a battle for Islam on two fronts: the liberation of Islam from the prison of lethal dogmatism, and the liberation of the oppressed people from imperialism, exploitation, and despotism. In their battle to release Islam from the shackles of medieval thought, Shariati and the *Mujahideen* picked up where Syed Jamal-ul-Din, Mirza Kuchak Khan and Iqbal had left the banner of revolutionary Islam — the former through his writings and lectures and the latter by developing their ideology through revolutionary social action.

The Organization

The *Sazeman-e-Mujahideen-e-Khalq-e-Iran* (Peoples Mujahideen Organization of Iran) was founded by five university graduates from Tehran University in 1965. Oldest among the founders was the 27 years old Mohammad Hanif-nejad, the son of a small shopkeeper born at Tabriz in a family with strong religious orientation. Even as a high school student, Hanif-nejad was involved in religious activities. Later, as a student at Tehran University Agricultural College, Hanif-nejad formed an Islamic student's association and joined Bazargaan's Liberation Movement.[5] Muhammad Hanif had taken part in the June Uprising in 1963 for which he was arrested and imprisoned for a few months. The term in prison brought him in contact with Ayatollah Taleqani, also serving a prison sentence. It was under Taleqani's guidance that Hanif-nejad made a deeper acquaintance with the Quran and was initiated into comprehending its content from a dynamic viewpoint.[6] Other founder members of the organization, Saeed Mohsen, a civil engineer from a lower middle class family, and Ali Asgher Baadizadegaan, a junior professor of Chemistry at Tehran University,[7] had also served prison terms following the June Uprising in 1963. Also among the founders was Ahmed Rezai 24, a school teacher and Islamic researcher who had joined the Liberation Movement while still a high school student. Rezai and Mohammad Hanif 'followed the Liberation Movement's footsteps in reinterpreting Islam, reaching the conclusion that true Islam stood not only against despotism, but also against capitalism, imperialism, and conservative clericalism'.[8] Ahmad Rezai was the first member of the *Mujahideen-e-Khalq* to get killed in the struggle against the regime. Two of his younger brothers, Reza Rezai, 23, and Mehdi Rezai 19, and a sister, Sadiqa Rezai 18, were also killed by SAVAK for resisting the Shah's regime.

The co-founders of the organization made an analytical study of Islamic history and the history of Iran, analysing the reasons for the failure of popular movements that had shaken Iran since the turn of the century. The *Mujahideen* used this analysis and other conclusions arrived at in a systematic, scientific manner for developing their political-military strategy against the regime. They picked up where Kuchak Khan had left the banner for an armed revolution that was progressive and Islamic and an expression of Hazrat Ali's saying, 'The road from Faith leads to action, and from action the road leads to Faith as well'.[9]

Causes for Failure of People's Movement in Iran: (1906 – 1963)

The *Mujahideen's* analysis of the causes for failure of past movements yielded them several observations and conclusions. They found that the people had never betrayed any revolutionary movement during the last 60 years of Iranian history and had not stinted from joining the movement against oppression, even to the point of sacrificing their lives whenever they had found a trustworthy leader. Thus, for example, during the civil war that broke out in the Constitutional Revolution in 1906 people had conclusively demonstrated their commitment to the revolution – they had even demonstrated their willingness to forego their food and the basic amenities of life to support the revolution. Also during the Jungle Revolution, the fighters making up Kuchak Khan's army were predominantly peasants and villagers; and in the struggle for nationalization of oil, when the economic blockade by imperialists was breaking the back of the country's economy, people whole-heartedly responded to Mossadeq's plea for financial backing, giving all their possessions, even jewellry and furniture to resist the economic blockade. The *Mujahideen* therefore disagreed with the conclusions of those analysts who attributed past failures to the lack of preparedness on the part of the people. It was not lack of readiness on the part of the masses, the *Mujahideen* argued, but absence of conducive subjective conditions and the lack of qualified leadership that had made a failure of past movements. 'As the conditions for the struggle became more and more complex, the leadership did not demonstrate the ability to adopt to the complexity of the situation'.[10] The methods and strategy of struggle employed by the leaders in the past had not been compatible with the social situation. Therefore, a main contradiction of the struggle that repeatedly ended with the people's defeat resided with the leadership; that is, the complexity of the principles and praxis of struggle versus the simple-mindedness of the leaders. The main points of the *Mujahideen's* assessment on the failure of past movements against dictatorship and imperialism in Iran can be summed up as follows:

1. In the past, the people had joined a movement with the aim of removing a 'corrupt' ruler at the top and replacing him by a 'just' ruler. These movements were, therefore, essentially of a reformist character because those leading the movements lacked a thorough understanding of the nature of their enemy. Occasionally the people succeeded in changing a minister or sending their own representatives to the Parliament. But these successes were ephemeral and never succeeded in ending the corruption and poverty prevailing in society.
2. Insofar as religion had played an important motivational role in these movements, they could be termed religious, but they were not ideological. And ideological struggle had to rest upon an adequate theoretical framework, a system of thought which could answer the needs, the problems and questions facing the people. It also had to deal comprehensively and adequately with the philosophical inquiries of those adhering to that ideology. For example, questions like 'What is Man?', 'What is Islamic Economy?', 'Who are the infidels *(kafirs)* and who are the hypocrites *(monafeqin)* under the current circumstances?' needed to be dealt with coherently and scientifically. Similarly, questions about the origin of the Universe, or the philosophy of history, required to be answered by a system of thought that claimed to be an ideology. Hence, given that the previous movements were not ideological in this sense, they were not able to answer the social problems facing contemporary man. And even though these movements were motivated by religion, they reached a dead end because they were devoid of a long term strategy and organization. Moreover, since these movements were directed only against an obvious symbol of despotism or injustice – the 'bad man' at the top – they could not have gone beyond the demand for superficial reforms, leaving the more subtle and deeper contradictions unresolved. Lacking the organizational framework of a clearly chalked out ideology, these movements carried within them an inherent weakness which corroded their capacity for obliterating despotism, exploitation, and imperialism. Furthermore, the ideological deficiency of these religious movements was one of the reasons for the indifference with which a substantial section of the intelligentsia

viewed Islam and also for their reluctance and failure to seriously Islam's revolutionary potential.[11]
3. Past struggles had failed because they lacked adequate revolutionary organization and structure. In each instance, the movement had relied entirely on one person only for its leadership. There was no leadership cadre or group that had devoted itself wholly to the struggle as its principal task, taking it, as it were, as a full time enterprise. Nor was there a group that had trained itself concerning problems and issues confronting the leadership. As a result, when the focal figure of a movement, its leader, was eliminated or removed from the scene, it marked the end of that movement, as had been the case with Kuchak Khan and Mossadeq.
4. The leadership of past movements lacked a scientific understanding of social problems, revolutionary problems, and knowledge about revolutionary resistance and struggle. As a result it could not maintain a continuous, stage by stage, comprehension of the social movement or evaluate its effectiveness, and redesign its strategy and tactics. In other words, 'revolutionary struggle (or the movement) had not been approached as a science with its own body of knowledge and its own methods. As a result, struggles in the past had not enjoyed precise strategy and policy'.[12]

Guerrilla Operations

Having arrived at the need for adopting armed struggle as the fundamental mode of resistance against the Shah's imperialist backed dictatorship, the *Mujahideen-e-Khalq* made Islam their ideological ground. They believed that their organized armed struggle was based on a correct strategy which had grown out of a realistic analysis of the prevailing social conditions.[13]

The *Mujahideen* did not begin their military operations for another six years, even though they had carefully screened and recruited over 200 members. These members were required to undergo an instructional programme in ideology that could take up to two years. During this period, the *Mujahideen* recruits studied the Quran, the *Nahjol Balagha*, the book of speeches and statements by Hazrat Ali, and Islamic history. They were also required to acquaint themselves with contemporary revolutionary experience by studying the Algerian, Cuban, Chinese, Russian and Vietnamese revolutions, and develop a critical understanding of Marxism. Next in the instructional programme was military training. Several pioneer *Mujahideen* were trained in Palestinian camps in Jordan, some of them enriching their experience by fighting alongside the Palestinians against the Royal Jordanian Army in 1971 during the 'Black September' conflict. By 1971 the *Mujahideen* organization was able to carry out one of the most successful information gathering assignments of any of the guerrilla groups operating in Iran. Under the leadership of Mahmood Asgharizadeh, the organization's information group was able to pinpoint and even take pictures of over 1300 SAVAK personnel as well as the main military and political figures of the period. It successfully carried out a series of military operations against the regime that included the bombing of the Tehran electrical works, the assassination of a U.S. military adviser to the Shah, and the Chief of Tehran police. The bombing of the car carrying General Price, the highest ranking American military man stationed in Iran, and of the building belonging to Coca Cola were also among the operations marking the first phase of the armed struggle against the regime.[14] On the day former President Nixon arrived in Tehran in 1972, the *Mujahideen* carried out several explosions in the capital.[15] The *Mujahideen* also attempted to hijack an aircraft belonging to the national flag carrier, Iran Air. SAVAK succeeded in arresting a number of *Mujahideen* following the hijacking. One of those arrested revealed information under severe torture, leading to the arrest of another 66 members of the organization.[16]

The organization received a major blow in 1972 when Shahmorad Delfani, a member of the Tudeh Party acting as undercover agent for SAVAK became friendly with one of the *Mujahideen,* whom he had met in prison. Delfani offered to help the organization in procuring arms and arranging for the illegal travel abroad of its members. Through Delfani, SAVAK was able to trace down the entire leadership cadre of the *Mujahideen* organization.[17] 11 members comprising the leadership were captured late in 1971. In the months that followed, four members were killed under torture and another five were executed by the firing squad on 25 May 1972. Iran had another six years to go before the posters of these martyrs would be hoisted in the massive demonstrations that overthrew the Shah, and before people would come to know of the last words of the *Mujahideen* founders. Blindfolded and facing the firing squad thay shouted before being executed: 'Allah-o-Akbar! Down with Imperialism! Down with the Shah!'

However, two *Muhahideen* who escaped from SAVAK's custody- Reza Rezai and Kazem Zolnavar — went underground and began rebuilding the organization. Reza was killed in a gunfight with security agents in 1973, while Kazem was captured a year later and executed with eight others in 1975.

Despite their losses, the *Mujahideen* continued to grow. They published an underground journal called *Jungle,* signifying the organization's historical link with Mirza Kuchak Khan's Jungle Revolution. The organization also sent five members to help the Dhofar rebels fighting the Shah's army which had been sent to assist Sultan Qabus of Oman.[18] Other operations included the bombing of Reza Shah's mausoleum near Tehran, the offices of the Israeli airline and British Airways, a grid station in Tabriz and the police post in a university.[19]

By the middle of 1975, the *Mujahideen* had lost 50 members to the Shah's firing squads, SAVAK's torture and in gunfights with the Shah's Police.[20] With the stepping up of their guerrilla activities, the *Mujahideen* began cooperating with *Fedayeen-e-Khalq*, the Marxist guerrillas. This included exchanging information of strategical importance and, when possible, helping members of either organization to escape from SAVAK's custody.

Islam vs. Islam

The *Mujahideen's* analysis of Islamic history brought them to the conclusion that true Islam was opposed to despotism, capitalism, colonialism and conservative clericalism.[21] But over the centuries, because of misinterpretation of the Quran by compromising, ambitious and opportunist leadership shrouding its personal motives in the guise of God and Islam, Islam had deviated from its intended path, originally directed towards creating the *touhidi* society. The combination of intellectual and philosophical aberrations in the Islamic worldview which owed their origin to Hellenistic influence, coupled with the inertia infused by escapist mysticism, had deflected the focus of the Quranic message intended for human liberation to the service of tyrannical regimes and political establishments. These regimes had used the Quran for tranquilising and anaesthetizing the masses. As a result, the most narcotic ideas and beliefs were being fed to the people in the name of the Quran and its interpretation.[22] But the *Mujahideen* believed that the content of the Quran, its intrinsic dynamic potential, was such that in the final analysis, the Quran's authentic and true message would manifest itself despite all the attempts that had been made to distort this message.[23] Thus as the *Mujahideen* saw it, Islam as it existed today had very little in common with the Islam preached and practiced by the Prophet; for today it was being used for justifying and perpetuating the vested interests of the rulers. As in the past, the contemporary Muslim leaders were using a counterfeit Islam against authentic Islam by stripping Islamic concepts of their revolutionary essence and meaning.[24] An example of this is found in the trial of Mehdi Rezai, a pioneer *Mujahideen* member arrested during a shoot—out with the Shah's secret police in 1972 and later killed under torture by SAVAK. During Mehdi's trial, the official government prosecutor ridiculed the *Mujahideen's* Islamic ideology, saying that the *Mujahideen* were misusing Islamic concepts like *jehad*. For in Islam, he said, *jehad* was to be undertaken against one's own evil and lusty nature, or against the infidels, and not against a Muslim monarch such as the Shah.[25] But for the *Mujahideen*, such ideological sophistry was nothing new because throughout the ages, class systems had attempted to pervert the content of revolutionary terminology, draining it of its true meaning in order to neutralize its effectiveness in society. As a result, the likes of the Shah of Iran and other despots had presented themselves as patrons of Islam, calling themselves *Zello'allah* (the shadow of God), and *Khalifato Allah* (God's representative on earth).[26] Such deviations in Islam had been anticipated by true Muslim revolutionaries. For example, Hazrat Ali, the Companion of the Prophet, had stated that deviations in comprehending and interpreting the Quran would occur in the years to come to such an extent that the Quran would appear to be stripped of its dynamic essence. 'There will be a time when nothing will be left of Islam but a name, nor anything of Quran but the letters on the page'.[27] The *Mujahideen* regarded the state of Islam in the present era as an objective and clear reflection of Hazrat Ali's forecasts. The most revolutionary terms had been warped and put to the service of class systems regardless of the fact that the popular revolutions of the past had been carried out by God's Prophets in different stages of history, with the sole objective of freeing the toiling and exploited masses and for establishing their rule. The *Mujahideen* saw a parallel between the Prophets' movement and the struggle of contemporary Muslim revolutionaries for people's liberation. Since the darkest days of slavery and ignorance, the Prophets had struggled for the rule of the people and for leading the most deprived and oppressed classes (the *mostazafin*) to the earth's leadership. Following Divine Will, the Prophets had urged people to rise and actively strive for realizing the concepts of equity *(qest)* in their society. The Quran had expressed this mission in these terms: 'We sent the Prophets with clear proofs, accompanied by the Book and the Balance, so that the people would rise up to bring equity. (*Al-Hadid:* 25)'. But the path of these movements had been blocked by the enemies of God and the people for they were frightened of the wide support the Prophets enjoyed among the masses. And in order to eliminate this popular support which threatened the rulers' interests, the rulers would kill or enslave the sympathizers of the Prophets or resort to trickery and propaganda for sowing suspicion in the hearts of the people about the Prophets and isolating them. During the present times, in Iran as in other Muslim countries, reactionary regimes who relied on the imperialists for their sustenance and on the obscurantist clergy for their religious legitimacy, were using a similar strategy for crushing those revolutionary Muslims who were rising to activate the Islamic principles of social justice. In the name of Islam, these regimes were suffocating the very voices that preached the true message of Islam.[28] It was therefore to be expected that the *Mujahideen's jehad*, their sacred armed struggle against such regimes, would be countered by the oppressors in power, be it the imperialist backed regime of the Shah and his Court's *mullas* or the monopolistic professional *mulla* who felt his religious bazaar was threatened with extinction with the emergence of the true and liberating religious spirit.

Shariati's Views on Religion

That such confrontations between the true spirit of religion and its farcical facade raised by the various interest groups in society was nothing new was well understood by Ali Shariati. In his lectures and articles, Shariati repeatedly pointed out that throughout history, ideological battles had always been battles of religion against religion. 'When the Abrahamic Prophets, who were shepherds chosen from among the masses, rebelled and urged the people to rise against the inhuman exploitive system in their society, they found themselves confronting an enemy hidden under the self-sanctified guise of religion. Therefore, the greatest obstacle that had stood in the way of the Prophets' movement happened to be religion'.[29] The *Mujahideen* were in tune with these views being voiced by Shariati, for their own independent analysis of history had brought them to a similar conclusion. However it was Shariati who elaborated this theme in a wider theoretical context. As Shariati saw it, religion was essentially 'an innate aspect of human nature, the innate dimension that is intended to propel man towards freedom, consciousness, and creativity'.[30] However, in actual fact, religion had become something else. Placed in the historical context, religion had shown itself to be 'the enemy of man's quest for freedom, consciousness, and creativity'[31] and a main hurdle in man's social and spiritual growth and evolution. One of the main skills of the enemies of humanity, according to Shariati, was to distort the divinely dynamic and creative function of religion. Thus religion, which could have liberated man from the limited frame-work of his routine, day by day biological and animal existence to prepare him for progress and transcendental experience, had been made a narcotizing element and a means for justifying the status quo of the stagnant social system.[32] The false men of religion succeeded in doing so by confining religion to the Hereafter *(akherat)*. In this sense, 'only when you lay your head in your grave would religion be of any use to you'.[33] If that were true, says Shariati, then how could religion be of use to us on this side of the grave. If earthly life was separated from the 'whole life', which included the 'Hereafter', religion would cease to act as the trigger to activate man into any responsible action.[34] Shariati bewailed that people had been killed for religion and many had been crucified over conflicting interpretations of religion. 'People have been sacrificed for religion and to the different interpretations of religion. Throughout history the love for power, material wealth, dynastic rule and hypocrisy has been justified as religion. The masses were made to degrade themselves in the name of religion. And all along, the element which exhorted people towards awareness, freedom, and rebellion against these inhuman systems was also religion.'[35]

Shariati emphasized that Islam as preached and practiced by the Prophet represented the greatest revolution the world had witnessed.

The object of Prophet Mohammad's mission was to purge human society from the *shirk* (polytheism) of class, race, and other man made discriminations and weave a society of equality and brotherhood. But with the passage of time, those in positions of power had deviated from the revolutionary spirit of Islam and proceeded, instead, to consolidate their dynastic rule. This was how not long after the death of the Prophet Mohammad (peace be upon him) and contrary to the teachings of Islam, Muawiya, Governor of Syria, laid the foundation for the dynastic rule of his family by nominating his own son, Yazid, as Caliph. This dynastic rule was perpetuated after Yazid had slain the grandson of Prophet Mohammad and other potential contenders who might have threatened Yazid's power. As a result those who were originally opposed to the revolution that Islam created had become heirs to this revolutionary movement and its message. They steered this revolution in the direction that suited their racial, national, and dynastic interests.

The battle of religion against religion, therefore, was not to end. As long as the oppressors and the oppressed, the exploiters and the exploited, the *mostakbarin* and the *mostazafin* existed, there would be two opposing religions: the religion of *shirk* (polytheism) for upholding the vested interests of the ruling 'elite' and for perpetuating the hold of 'gods' of deceit, race, class, power and wealth in society, and the religion of *touhid* for obliterating these manifestations of *shirk* in society separating man from man, and in consequence, separating man from God.[36] The *Mujahideen*, therefore, were engaged in the archetypal battle between *touhid* and *shirk,* between belief in Allah, the Transcendent One, and belief in man made gods. On the one hand, belief in *shirk* was expressing itself in the class system and in all other manifestations stemming from the satanic conviction 'I am superior to you'.[37] On the other hand, belief in *touhid* was destined to lead mankind towards its goal — a society, classless and integrated in Divine Unity, reflecting the Unity of God in the unity of mankind.

Mujahideen's Response to the Regime's Accusations

Naturally, then, the Islam which fueled the *Mujahideen's* ideology was opposed to that Islam wherein the Shah who had conferred upon himself the titles of 'King of Kings' *(Shahenshah)* and 'Light of the Aryans' *(Arya Mahr)*, 'Protector of Aryan's Light', was considered a defender of the Shia faith and a devout Muslim. The Shah's regime, which claimed to be the custodian of Islam, was campaigning through the media and the clergy supporting it that the *Mujahideen* were 'Marxist terrorists' and 'apostates' and thus the shedding of their blood was a religious duty. On their part, the *Mujahideen* tried to counter the Shah's propaganda by issuing a statement[38] in which they systematically evaluated and responded to the regimes accusations. The *Mujahideen* pointed out in this statement that the 'tricks and treachery' the Shah was using in his attempts at presenting himself as the guardian of the

Islamic faith were exactly those which his predecessors in religious pretention and treachery — Yazid and his tribe, the usurping murderers of the grandson of the Prophet of Islam and his household — had used 13 centuries ago. These treacherous 'Muslims', the *Mujahideen* noted, had violated Islamic teachings and had transformed the Islamic Caliphate into a type of monarchy similar to that in ancient Persia and Rome, a development which was totally alien to Islam. The *Mujahideen* accused the Shah of verbally proclaiming Islam while he was donating petroleum to the Zionists, who were using it in their jets for bombing Palestinian Muslims. The Shah was carrying out the suppression and massacre of his opponents while indulging in wasteful celebrations and an opulent life-style. 'He claims to be a Muslim, yet celebrates his self-coronation by inviting guests from all parts of the world and serving them 50 year old imported French champagne.'[39] The statement recalled that although he claimed to be a Muslim, the Shah had exiled Muslim leaders like Ayatollah Khomeini, tortured to death progressive Muslim revolutionaries, and harassed, imprisoned and exiled Ayatollah Taleqani for cooperating with the *Mujahideen* and the Liberation Movement. Excerpt from this statement reads: 'Which Islam is it that the Shah refers to? Is it not the Islam, of Imperialism? The counterfeit "Islam" of imperialism is carefully spoon-fed to Muslim countries, and results in their colonization, with the imperialists ultimately in control of the economics, education, and culture of the Muslim countries. According to this "Islam of Imperialism", Islam is made for the next world only and has nothing to do with the life of this world... The Imperialist's brand of Islam dictates that Islamic nations be their colonies and allows them to loot all the wealth, resources, and productivity of Muslim nations. But the Islam of the Prophet Mohammad (on whom be peace) is the only true Islam. Its revolutionary spirit is not compatible with, or comparable to, the (present) weakness and spinelessness of the Muslims. The Islam which Prophet Mohammad brought would never provide land to Zionists for them to cultivate and produce food for their armies aiding them to kill the oppressed and impoverished Palestinian masses. Under the Islam taught by Prophet Mohammad, the treacherous Shah and his exploitive guests would not serve themselves 50-year old French champagne. The Islam which the Prophet Mohammad brought is revolutionary and it is for precisely this reason that the Iranian Muslims are joining the revolution. The Shah is afraid of the new wave of Islamic cultural revolution, a wave that is adhered to and propagated by none other than the *Mujahideen-e-Khalq*. We have not brought with us a new religion. Islam, from its beginning, has been progressive and revolutionary, and has fought against oppression. We are revolting today, as Islam has always done, to break down the obstacles that are blocking the path of man and society towards perfection. The Shah is frightened from this wave of Muslim awakening. He is frightened of a revolutionary Islam. He attempts to discredit such a movement and cries out: "A revolutionary cannot be a Muslim. One must be either a Muslim or a revolutionary!" (According to the Shah's logic) a person who participates in any guerrilla activity must, therefore, be a non-believer; one who is both a revolutionary and a Muslim must be a liar and an apostate by the regime's standards.

'The truth is that a true Muslim can be nothing but a revolutionary. If the battle against oppression and immorality is Un-Islamic, if the battle against the supporters and servants of imperialists is Un-Islamic, if the battle against corruption is Un-Islamic, if a desire for freedom is Un-Islamic, if the battle against the exploitation of the people is Un-Islamic, then we and the rest of the Iranian people confess to being Un-Islamic.

'Furthermore, if sucking the blood of hardworking people and plundering the production of farmers and labourers and profiteering from the people's essential needs is Islamic, if placing the country's fate and its people in the hands of American and Zionist spies and military advisers is Islamic, if possession of castles and luxurious mansions, and private airplanes, while the people are starving to death in masses, is Islamic, if making farmers homeless, and gunning down students and labourers is Islamic, if torturing political prisoners and arresting and torturing the mothers, fathers, wives, children, sisters and brothers of fugitive revolutionaries is Islamic, if plundering the vast resources of oil, arranging the most wasteful celebrations in history (the Shah's self-coronation and celebrations marking 2500 years of monarchy in Iran that is estimated to have cost the State treasury a hundred million dollars) spending millions of dollars from the treasury of our destitute people for the pleasure of a bunch of treacherous international criminals is Islamic, then we, alongside all the Iranian people confess to being non-Muslims, and we wish to clearly state that only the Shah and his servants and supporters in his Pharoanic rule can be Muslims. It is a great honour for us to be recognized by the treacherous regime of the Shah as his enemy. This indicates that our essence is contradictory to the nature of his blood-shedding regime. (Ours) is a sacred war and an answer to God's Commandment: "Why should you not fight in the cause of God and in the cause of those who being weak are ill-treated and oppressed? Men, women, and children who cry, will our Lord rescue us from this town, whose people are oppressors, and raise up for us, one who will help?" ' (The Quran, 4:75).

Demolishing the Myth of the Regime's Invincibility

By consciously embarking upon a path that entailed nothing but death *(shahadat)* and medieval tortures at the hands of SAVAK in the event of arrest, the *Mujahideen* demolished the myth of the Pahlavi regime's invincibility. Their movement began to seep the spirit of hope, courage, and militant resistance among the young. Because the *Mujahideen's* operations against the regime stemmed from an ideology that rested on belief in Divine Unity and the worldview emanating from it, the *Mujahideen* attracted the serious attention of Muslim youth and intelligentsia. It is for this reason that 'the value of their *jehad* in shaping the development of the subjective correlates of the Islamic Revolution remains an indisputable fact'.[40] By presenting Islam as a revolutionary ideology capable of meeting the strategic and tactical needs of organized revolutionary struggle, the *Mujahideen* reintroduced Islam as a weapon against imperialism, exploitation, and despotism which they regarded as the main obstacles on the path of man's social and spiritual evolution. Drawing their inspiration from religious and historical figures like Hazrat Ali, Mirza Kuchak Khan, and also their own martyred members such as Mehdi Rezai and Fatima Amini, the *Mujahideen* surged ahead as a political – social force accelerating the cultural revolution within Islam. Progressive Islam thus became a challenge to Marxist movements in Iran, particularly among the students and intelligentsia. The *Fedayeen-e-Khalq*, the Marxist-Leninist guerrilla organization, had strongly influenced the intelligentsia and the university, making the latter a clandestine centre for militant recruits. However the *Mujahideen's* ideology enjoyed a cultural and emotional background that had already acquired an intellectual dimension with the Liberation Movement which was being extended along revolutionary lines by Ali Shariati. Consequently the *Mujahideen's* movement received a firm forward thrust. It was the *Mujahideen's* rapidly growing popularity among Iranian students and the progressive intelligentsia, both inside the country and abroad, which perturbed not only the Pahlavi regime, but the conservative clergy as well. The regime had not succeeded, despite the use of all the means at its disposal, in liquidating the *Mujahideen*. To destroy the sympathy and support that the *Mujahideen* had mustered, the regime's propaganda against *Mujahideen* branded them variously as 'communists', 'apostates', 'terrorists' and 'Islamic Marxists'. In presenting itself as the true custodian of the Islamic faith, the Pahlavi regime was supported by the majority of the clergy. A group of clergymen even issued a religious decree *(fatwa)*, declaring that the *Mujahideen* were not Muslims.[41] For the *Mujahideen*, these accusations marked an anticipated tactic in the perennial battle of religion against religion. Their answer to the combined smear campaign of the Shah, the clergymen supporting his regime, and the formalist-dogmatic clergy read: 'For many years, the hypocritical and fraudulent clerics of the court have been proclaiming that the Shah is the shadow of God. (They have been) inviting people to obey the Shah as their true religious leader . . . . the perfidious Shah claims to be closer to God than anyone else and has claimed many times that he has been supported and protected by Hazrat Abbas and Imam Mahdi. For a long time, reactionaries and imperialists have continued their rule by disrupting revolutionary struggle. They were able to do this, primarily, by taking advantage of the people, many of whom are unaware of the basic principles of Islam, by bribing and buying off those who hide themselves under a religious cloak and then using them for hypocritically accusing the revolutionaries of blasphemy. With such diversions, the imperialists have attempted to separate the people's revolution from the vanguard revolutionaries."[42]

The statement also pointed to the profound effect which the *Mujahideen* with their emphasis on the 'revolutionary foundations of pristine Islam' had had on the Iranian society. To combat this, the *Mujahideen* said, the Shah was doing all he could to create a gulf of suspicion between the revolutionaries and the people. Although the Shah claimed that the people and the *Mujahideen* were mutual enemies, he was afraid to reveal 'the names of the revolutionary martyrs, the date of their trials, and the place of their executions'. The *Mujahideen* contended that the Shah was 'even afraid of the corpses of these innocent martyrs', and refused to return them to their families 'because he fears their graves will become sacred shrines for the oppressed people'. Because of this, when the regime wanted to shed the blood of the revolutionaries, it first introduced the revolutionaries as 'irreligious criminals and non-Muslims'. This was because the Shah was 'more frightened of the *Mujahideen's* Islamic ideology and of the revolutionary impact of Islam, of tomorrow, when the revolution was destined to spread', than he was of the *Mujahideen* themselves. It was therefore, 'clear that the Shah was determined to destroy the *mujahid* and his ideology through deception or by force, if not both'. Thus, the motives of the regime 'for the foolish and meaningless propaganda in the newspapers and the radio, which publicize their nonsensical accusations of us as "Islamic Marxists", "apostates", "terrorists", "saboteurs", "thieves", and "traitors", was clear'.

Problems Facing Progressive Islamic Movements: The Marxist *Coup d'etat* and the 'Pseudo Left Opportunist Deviation: The *Mujahideen* were dealt a severe blow by the Shah's regime when Shahmorad Delfani, a former communist operating as a secret agent for SAVAK penetrated their ranks. As a result, in September 1971 SAVAK displayed its total command of the lessons it had received under Israeli and American Intelligence specialists by netting nearly two hundred *Mujahideen*, including all the co-founders of the organization. This blow reduced the active membership of the organization by as much as 90%. The loss in members was, however, compensated within a couple of years as more youngsters joined the organization. Recruitment of new members in larger numbers meant the relaxing of some of their own stringent selection principles. The most lethal blow that nearly destroyed the organization came in 1975, not due to any ingenuity of SAVAK but owing to the ideological split in the leadership cadre of *Mujahideen* - between those who had turned to Marxism and insisted upon converting *Mujahideen* into a Marxist-Leninist organization, and those who confronted the Marxists by adhering to the Islamic ideology of the organization. The rift deepened when the Marxists, who had gained the upper hand in the central committee of the organization as a result of imprisonment, death, or execution of the original leadership cadres, began a purge of their Islamic opponents and issued a bulletin in which they declared that since Islam as an ideology would have failed to answer the problems facing the revolution, the organization had adopted the Marxist-Leninist ideology. The bulletin's publication was preceded by the expulsion of all those *Mujahideen* who refused to acquiesce to the new leadership and its new ideology. The extent of the violence associated with the Marxists take-over is reflected in the murder of the surviving Islamic members of the leadership cadres by the Marxists, among them Sharif Vaqafi. In what turned out to be perhaps the most bizarre occurrence in the history of political organizations in Iran, Taqi Shahram, the Marxist who masterminded the *coup*, and his comrades rounded up Sharif Vaqafi in a Tehran street and shot him in cold blood. Then they threw his bullet riddled body in a well on the outskirts of Tehran after burning it to erase possible clues of the event. But the regime discovered Sharif Vaqafi's half burnt body and soon after captured a number of Marxist *Mujahideen* to get a first hand picture of the in-fighting in the organization it had so fervently sought to liquidate.

People's reaction to these events was one of incredulity. The common assumption was that SAVAK had planted its own men in the *Mujahideen* organization to destroy it ideologically from within. However, the publication of the Marxists' bulletin in which the 'Marxist *Mujahideen*' confirmed that over 50% of Islamic *Mujahideen* had been purged or eliminated 'as a result of the evolution of the Organization from Islam to Marxism',[43] left little room for attributing the grisly event to SAVAK. Parts of the Marxists' bulletin giving analytical justification for their deeds read:[44] 'Islam, because of its belief in God, prophethood and the day of judgement cannot be ranked with the progressive social forces or be taken as a harbinger of the final victory of the toiling masses over the class system of exploitation, and for the actual establishment of the *touhidi* society characterized by the absence of oppression and classes (which the Shia Muslims envision in the unified society and single *Umma* of the Mehdi). Therefore, *touhidi* society which represents the complete effacement of exploitation and oppression is not a belief which can be practically and objectively achieved in Islam. At a point Islam abandons the toiling masses and heads for capitalism, Therefore by their adherence to Islam, the *Mujahideen-e-Khalq* are claiming to represent the contradictory poles of Islam and the toiling masses, God as well as Revolution. These poles, in being contradictory, would ultimately split at a point during the growth of this irreconcilable contradiction (within the organization), so that half the organization will steer to the left, towards the toiling masses, that is, Marxism. While the other half is predestined to adopt a deeper religious colour and steer to the Right. The separation of progressive Marxists from the *Mujahideen-e-Khalq* organization has left behind (only) the reactionaries in the organization.' Rejecting the Marxists analysis, the *Mujahideen*, who were now regrouping themselves and rebuilding their organization after the split, argued that if some members of the Islamic organization had changed their ideology, they could have left the organization to continue along their new ideological line as an independent group or by merging into existing Marxist groups, instead of taking up arms against the Islamic members and slaughtering them in a bid for annihilating the Islamic character of the organization. 'No one had blocked the way for a split were it based upon principles'.[45] Moreover, argued the *Mujahideen*, the *coup d'état* by the 'opportunists' was incompatible with Marxism itself, for it was in no way contrary to the aspirations of Marxist revolutionaries to support and strengthen a decidedly progressive organization such as the *Mujahideen*.[46] Even with their one dimensional materialistic perception which described the *Mujahideen* as a 'petty bourgeoise organization', these Marxist members of the organization should have accepted the sanctity and right for existence of the *Mujahideen* as an Islamic organization. They should have viewed all adventurism, opportunism, and deviations aiming at disintegrating the (Islamic) nucleus of this organization as a treachery to the entire struggle of the people for liberation'.[47] On their part, the Marxist members while justifying the take-over of the central committee of the *Mujahideen-e-Khalq* organization reasoned that they could violate the commonly accepted and acknowledged principles and regulations of the organization because they had evolved to what they perceived to be a 'more substantial and evolved ideology'.[48]

The Muslim *Mujahideen* refuted the arguments tabled by the Marxist members, whom they termed as 'pseudo Left opportunists', both from the Marxist as well as Islamic ideological premises. As the *Mujahideen* saw it, the justifications and arguments of the 'opportunists' were 'ideologically weak and rationally infantile' for they lacked scientific and rational credibility. 'If any member of a guerrilla organization begins to believe that his own individual point of view and conviction is more evolved and developed than the overall ideological foundation of the rganization, and on the basis of this belief feels that he is justified to do as he pleases with other members of the organization, then, no scientific and rational rules and principles would be left for constituting the common ground for members of an organization. In that case everyone in the organization would consider it permissible for himself to commit any crime he pleases.'[49]

The *Mujahideen* argued that even if it were to be accepted that the leftist opportunists had arrived at a more evolved ideology, even then they had no right 'to violate and trample upon the historical rights of other ideological groups and progressive and revolutionary organizations. Because absolute evolution in our world always manifests itself and follows its course through relatively evolved organizations'.[50] Therefore, if the leftist opportunists were to accept that the *Mujahideen-e-Khalq* organization with its *touhidi* worldview was not counter—revolutionary and reactionary, and accepted its right to participate in social struggle, 'they should not have chosen to remain in the organization after they had revoked the organization's ideology'. Because after they had renounced and rejected the ideology of the organization, 'they could no longer be considered its members'. They should have left the organization to those who remained loyal to its ideology. 'Instead of trying to take control of the *Mujahideen-e-Khalq*, they should have formed their own organization and directed their criticism against us from their own ideological platform'.[51] The *Mujahideen* noted that the history of revolutionary struggle was replete with divisions, splits and schisms that were principled. Likewise, the Left opportunists should have made a principled exit. In that case, the *Mujahideen* said that they would have continued to regard the breakaway Leftists as a principled anti-imperialist force in the unified struggle of the progressive forces against the Shah. But instead of adopting a solution based on principle, 'they chose an opportunistic solution that led to betrayal and treachery'.[52] The *Mujahideen* further said that leaving aside the 'fascistic and vicious methods the Pseudo Marxists adopted', they did not condemn them for becoming Marxists. 'We hold the position that there is no compulsion in religion'.[53] The issue was simply of an opportunistic, even 'un-Marxist' approach which the breakaway Leftists had adopted in relation to the *Mujahideen-e-Khalq* organization. The *Mujahideen* rounded off their analysis by repeating that if in an organization a person, group or movement found itself disagreeing in principle with the strategy and ideology of the organization, there was no other option for it than to split off from the original organization in a principled manner.

It had been predicted by the breakaway Marxists, as well as several Muslim intellectuals, that as a result of this ideological conflict, the *Mujahideen-e-Khalq* would swerve to the Right and begin regarding all the Marxist groups as their principal contradiction and enemy. However, the *Mujahideen* confirmed that the split had not caused any change in their main contradiction. 'The basic contradiction in our society is the contradiction between the people and imperialism. Therefore, our main enemy is the Pahlavi regime, the imperialist's puppet and its imperialist supporters'.[54] The necessary condition for a successful struggle against 'Left opportunism' therefore lay precisely in an increasingly relentless and decisive struggle against the Shah's regime, so as to positively demonstrate the fallacy of the prediction of a swerve to the Right in the *Mujahideen-e-Khalq's* strategy.[55]

The *Mujahideen* were aware that there was no point in concentrating their energies through word and action against the opportunists. 'Only struggle and revolutionary action against imperialism and its puppet regime is the index for determining the authenticity, genuineness, and validity of our ideology *vis a vis* the Leftist opportunists. Our firm adherence to our principled anti-imperialist position, as in the past, ideologically, strategically and politically, is the response most valid for generating the necessary conditions for negating opportunism and lending credence to our ideological truth.'[56]

The Islamic *Mujahideen* were not the only force which regarded the opportunistic development and its bloody bid for taking control of the organization as an act of treason. The *Fedayeen-e-Khalq* as well as other progressive revolutionary forces like Dr. Ali Shariati, condemned the *coup d'état*. The in-fighting between the Pseudo Leftists and *Mujahideen* did not cease with the separation of the Marxist and Islamic factions. 'We continued to receive blows to our military and organizational structure right up to the early part of 1977 in working out the opportunist problem,'[57] the *Mujahideen* recount. 'Not only were several of our finest brothers martyred, but our organization came close to disintegrating on at least two occasions.'[58]

A year after the *coup* by the 'Pseudo Left opportunists', the *Mujahideen* had reorganized themselves sufficiently well to confirm their presence on the scene of struggle as a progressive Islamic force. They issued a statement reaffirming the aims of their organization and declared their position in the following points:[59]

1. Our ideology is Islam. It emanates from the *touhidi* worldview which directs the society through revolutionary strategy and methods towards the complete effacement of exploitation and the establishment of *Nizam-e-Touhidi* (unitarian system based on conscious awareness of Divine Unity). Therefore, under all historical conditions, our ideology relies and rests upon the (*mostazafin*) the most deprived and the most progressive forces among social classes. Therefore, the *Mujahid-e-Khalq* (People's Crusader) in the light of his Islamic ideology is distinguished by his characteristics which are directed against imperialism, reaction, and exploitation, and which necessitate an armed strategy under the present conditions.

2. The 'Pseudo Left Opportunist' development has not caused any change in our basic contradiction. The (Shah's) regime and its imperialist supporters remain our main enemy.

3. No Muslim element or organization should contact or cooperate with these Pseudo Left Opportunists.

4. We shall fight this Pseudo Left Opportunistic development so that it either returns to the correct line or becomes redundant and isolated. Our fight is a political struggle, with (political) methods directed at exposing this deviation (and its irrationality). We condemn employing reactionary methods like murder, cooperation with the

police, betrayal, and getting help from the regime (which the 'opportunist Left' was using against *Mujahideen*) in our struggle against the opportunist Left deviation.
5. We make a distinction between these opportunists and other Marxists, unless the latter endorse and support these opportunists.
6. We respect all forces fighting against imperialism, reaction, and exploitation, and we make use of their scientific achievements and revolutionary experience.
7. This opportunist Left development has prematurely brought about a Rightist reactionary development which at the present stage (of the struggle of progressive Muslims) is the real internal danger threatening all those forces who are fighting under the banner of Islam. We are combating this (reactionary development), which has begun by opposing the revolutionary forces, in particular the *Mujahideen*. But later in its development, by rejecting armed conflict and resorting to compromise, compliance and eventual withdrawal from the people's front, (this reactionary development would opt for changing the basic contradiction in the people's struggle against imperialism). This opportunist Pseudo Left development has led to development of reactionary features amidst the progressive Islamic forces.[60]

The conservative clergy, which had been opposed to the *Mujahideen* from the start blamed the *Mujahideen* for having established their organization as a bridge for leading Muslims to Marxism. According to these elements, the reasons for the breakup of the organization and for turning of some of its members to Marxism had to be sought in the ideological teachings of the organization. For these clergymen, *Mujahideen's* teaching had been 'deviationist' from the outset. The *Mujahideen* saw this campaign by the formalist clergy as a concerted effort to discredit their standing as a popular Islamic organization. In their instructional programme for new members after the *coup* by the Pseudo Marxists, the *Mujahideen* explained that the reason some members became Marxists was the effect of their renunciation of the ideological teachings and programme of the organization, their inadequate exposure to the original instructional programme and their opposition to the ideological content of the organization.[61] The turning of some members to Marxism had not been caused by the 'deviationist' ideological content of the *Mujahideen*, but because the Pseudo Marxists had turned away from these teachings and were unable to 'grasp the real teachings of the *Mujahideen*'.[62]

While the in-fighting between the Islamic and Marxist *Mujahideen* was going on, neither of these factions had ceased its operations against the regime. 'The activities of the Islamic *Mujahideen* included a bank robbery in Isfahan (for financing the organization), a bomb attack on the Israeli Cultural Centre in Tehran, and a strike in Aryamehr University (later renamed Sharif Vaqafi University) to commemorate the fourth anniversary of the execution of their founders. The activities of the

Marxist *Mujahideen* included the bombing of ITT offices and the assassination of two American military advisers. By early 1976, the two *Mujahideen* factions had suffered such heavy losses that they began to reconsider their tactics. The Islamic *Mujahideen* stepped up their campus activities — circulated their own and Shariati's publications, and established contact with the Islamic Student Association in North America and Western Europe. Meanwhile, the Marxist *Mujahideen* intensified their labour activities, called for the establishment of a new working class party, started a paper called *Qiyam-i-Kargar* (Workers' Revolt), and formed links with Maoists heading the confederation of Iranian students in Western Europe. It also entered negotiations with the *Fedayeen-e-Khalq* (Marxist-Leninist guerrillas) to merge the two organizations, but soon broke off the talks on the grounds that the latter remained tied to its 'Guevarist ideas', and refused to denounce Soviet 'Social imperialism'. For its part, the *Fedayeen* accused the Marxist *Mujahideen* of 'blindly accepting Maoism', and backed off from merging with an organization that had shed the blood of the Islamic *Mujahideen* and openly denounced Islam as a 'petty bourgeois ideology'.[63]

While critical analysis of the 'Marxists Coup' continues to be made by various revolutionary groups, its scientific analysis remains an important topic in the instructional programme for members of *Mujahideen-e-Khalq* as well as in university circles and ideological seminars. The spiritual character in the *Mujahideen's* evaluation of the Left opportunists who nearly destroyed their organization is unmistakable: 'The extent to which the Marxist opportunists had overlooked the reality of the *Mujahideen* and the reality of Islam, they had wronged their own spirit and violated their own psyche.'[64] They shall pay severe retribution for their action, 'not only in the dimension of existence that extends beyond our present life, but in this world and in front of the people as well. Because in the *touhidi* worldview, a worldview stemming from consciousness of a Transcendent Divine Unity, every whit of virtue and every whit of evil are taken into consideration.'[65]

As for the *Mujahideen's* current position on Marxists in general, it is not their policy to make a wholesale condemnation of all Marxists, without placing a distinction between the dedicated and committed elements and the opportunist Pseudo Leftists - unless, of course, the former support and endorse the views of the latter. The *Mujahideen* see their policy in consonance with the progressive spirit of their Islamic ideology, for in the final analysis, 'it is for Allah to judge between those who differ'. As the Quran says, 'Everyone acts according to his manners; but your Lord best knows who is best guided in the path ... Allah will judge between them on the day of resurrection ... and We have not appointed you a keeper over them, and you are not placed in charge of them' c.f. the Quran 17:84, 22:17, 6:108).

The breakaway Marxist *Mujahideen* who now call themselves the 'Organization of Fighters for the Liberation of the Working Classes'

(Paikar), still maintain that their emergence was inevitable, being the consequence of contradictions originally inherent in the *Mujahideen* organization. The *Paikar* members therefore consider their own group as more progressive than the *Mujahideen*, owing to their belief that they represent the more evolved stage in the history of the original organization.

Reasons for the Marxists Coup

While literature dealing with the analysis of the 1975 events in the *Mujahideen* organization continues to increase and will remain an issue for analysis for a long time to come, the *Mujahideen* have pointed out some organizational weaknesses which could have contributed to the bloody split of 1975. The *Mujahideen* say that their concern for making up their losses in membership which they suffered in 1972 when SAVAK netted nearly 200 of their members had made them less exacting in their selection standards. New members had been recruited, sometimes without dwelling upon an adequate assessment of their worldview and orientation towards religion and Islam. Moreover after the blow by SAVAK in 1972, the *Mujahideen* had given priority to military action rather than ideological education, a development which was not in keeping with the original instructional procedure laid down by the organization which required new members to spend several months undergoing ideological education before embarking upon military operations. For example, the first 18 member group of *Mujahideen* experienced ideological and organizational study and training for three years before starting military operations.[66] Thus, many of the *Mujahideen* members who were recruited after 1972 were not ideologically as clear as their predecessor. As a result, a large number of them, primarily those who belonged to Tehran, changed over to Marxism. This contention of the *Mujahideen* about ideological weakness in many of their new members after 1972 seems to be supported by the arguments the Marxists used against Islam in their bulletin on ideological issues. One of the reasons cited by the Marxists as a weaknesses in Islam was the complete submission required to the all powerful God.[67] Such an attitude, argued the Marxists, stripped the individual of personal initiative and the desire to fight oppression in society. It is clear that in their arguments against Islam, the Marxist opportunists were stuck with the classical views of Western Marxists who regarded all religion as the 'opium of the masses'. Views which were, no doubt, correct insofar as they stemmed from a study of Western civilization — a civilization that had been condemned to experience its darkest era and go through its 'dark ages' at a time when the power of the Christian Church was at its height. But this inverse relationship between the power of religion and the progress of civilization was unknown to Islam. Contrary to the Christian civilization, Islamic civilization had touched new heights during the period true Islam was alive, when the Islamic spirit permeated the Muslim society, and the power of a liberating religious spirit had propelled knowledge into new avenues of scientific discovery. But by the turn of the 20th Century, when Islam as Islam had ceased to exist, and the Quranic message had been lost to Muslims due to their fossilized worldview, inert doctrine and dogma, the Muslim world was going through its 'dark ages' — being a passive, helpless slave of the colonialists.

Furthermore, the understanding of Islam by 'Marxist Opportunists' was too superficial to be cognizant of the existential accountability and individual responsibility that a dynamic belief in the Hereafter involved (the continuation of life after death, hence accountability for one's actions). The Quran had clearly declared the sanctity of human choice and responsibility in the words, 'Each soul is a hostage of his own deeds' (17:13). As for the Marxists argument that belief in an all powerful God would strip the individual of personal initiative for fighting oppression, far from injecting passivity among its followers, the Quran exhorts the believers to fight oppression as a religious duty. Even if the oppressed were weaker than their oppressors they should put up a fight for they would be assisted by the Divine Will directing the evolution of man and society. (22:39)

The experiences which the *Mujahideen-e-Khalq* have undergone since the inception of their organization reflect a comprehensive picture of the complex problems which a revolutionary Islamic ideology in the field of social and political action is likely to confront. Broadly speaking, the forces to which any progressive Islamic movement that strives for building a society 'based on Islam as it has been, and not on what it has become' is vulnerable, may be classified into two categories: Left opportunism and one dimensionalism in the name of scientism, and Right fanaticism and fascism in the name of religion.

Notes

1. Ayatollah Taleqani's statement on the seventh anniversary of execution of *Mujahideen* founders, 25 May 1979.
2. *Sharh-e-Tasis Va Vaqae-e-Sazman-e-Mujahideen-e-Khalq-e-Iran*, (History of Events and Formation of Peoples Mujahideen Organization). Henceforth called *Sharh-e-Tasis*.
3. Abrahimian, E., *The Guerrilla Movement in Iran (1963–1977)* Middle East Research and Information Project March/April, 1980, p.4.
4. *Mojahed* No.2, February 1980, p.17.
5. Abrahimian, E., *The Guerrilla Movement in Iran*. MERIP, Vol. 10, March-April, 1980.
6. Afrasiabi, B. and Dehqani, S., *Taleqani and History*.
7. Abrahimian, E., *The Guerrilla Movement in Iran*.

8. Ibid., p.9.
9. *Enqelabe Islami*, No. 422, 1981.
10. *Mojahed*, Vol. 6, June 1980, p. 20.
11. The inability of the obscurantist clergy at transforming Islam from a dogma into a dynamic revolutionary ideology, indeed their failure to comprehend this necessity and their opposition to any progressive Muslim thinker (like Syed Jamal-ud-Din or Iqbal) who sought to draw the Muslim's attention to this problem, was a major factor for alienating the intellectuals and the educated from Islam. Through this unconscious strategy, the traditional formalist clergy had been remarkably successful in perpetuating its monopoly on Islam, to Islam's detriment.
12. *Mojahed*, Vol. 6, June 1980, p.20.
13. *Sharh-e-Tasis*.
14. *Sharh-e-Tasis*.
15. Brier, P. and Blanche, P., *Iran: Revolution in the name of God*. (Persian translation). Sahab publications, Tehran 1979, p.
16. Abrahimian, E., *The Guerrilla Movement in Iran*. MERIP, Vol. 10. March-April, 1980.
17. *Sharh-e-Tasis*.
18. Abrahimian, E., *The Guerrilla Movement in Iran*. MERIP, Vol. 10, March-April 1980.
19. *Sharh-e-Tasis*. Brier, P. and Blanche, P., *Iran-Revolution in the name of God*.
20. *Mojahed*, May 1980.
21. Ibid.
22. *Mojahed*, May, 1980.
23. That opportunist Muslim rulers exploited religion to generate a sense of passivity among Muslims in the name of Fatalism has been pointed out by Iqbal in the *Reconstruction of Religious Thought in Islam*, pp.110–111. 'God was conceived as the last line in the chain of causation and consequently the real author of all that happens in the Universe. The practical materialism of the opportunist Ommayud rulers needed a peg on which to hang their misdeeds at Kerbala and to secure the fruits of Amir Muawiya's revolt against the possibilities of a popular rebellion. Mabad is reported to have said to Hasan of Basra that the Ommayuds killed Muslims and attributed their acts to the decrees of God. "These enemies of God," replied Hasan, "are liars". Thus arose, inspite of protest by Muslim divines, a morally degrading fatalism and the constitutional theory known as the 'accomplished fact' in order to support vested interests. This is not at all surprising. In our own times, philosophers have furnished a kind of intellectual justification for the finality of the present capitalistic structure of society. The same thing appears to have happened to Islam.'
24. *Mojahed*, June, 1980.
25. Tape recording of the 'Defence Speech of Mehdi Razaie', retrieved from the archives of SAVAK after the Islamic Revolution and published by the *Mujahideen* organization, 1979.

26. *Mojahed*, June, 1980.
27. Ibid.
28. *The Statement of the People's Mujahideen Organization of Iran in Response to Recent Accusations of the Iranian Regime.* (English Translation, 1977).
29. Shariati, A., *Niyaz-ha-e-Insan-e-Imroz* (The Needs of the Contemporary Man) Hossieniel Irshad, Tehran, (1978), p.69.
30. Ibid.
31. Ibid.
32. Ibid.
33. Ibid.
34. Ibid.
35. Shariati, A., *Mazhab-aley-hey-Mazhab.* (Religion vs. Religion).
36. Shariati, A., *Touhid Va Shirk* (Monotheism and Polytheism).
37. In the Islamic tradition, the intransigence of Satan in submitting to Adam in defiance to God's command is attributed to Satan's pride which caused him to invoke his 'superior origins'. Satan justified his refusal with the argument that since God created him out of fire while Adam was created of dust, he was superior to Adam. This issue has been dealt with by the Quran in the following words: 'And when we said to the angels, make obeisance to Adam, they did obeisance, but Satan did not, he refused and he was proud, and he was one of the unbelievers' (2:34). As pointed out by Khalifa Abdul Hakim, one of the proponents of the dynamic school of Islamic thought and by other progressive Islamic thinkers, including Shariati, Adam does not refer to an historical individual. In a general sense, Adam means humanity. (The Quran, 7: 10, 11; 38: 71, 72). The goal for Adam as the archetypal Man or humanity, is to evolve towards perfection by actualizing the attributes of God in human organization and to establish a *touhidi* society wherein mankind attains unity on the basis of equity, brotherhood, and freedom. This is how Divine Unity would be manifested on the material plane and in human organization — in the unity of mankind as a single community. However, in evolving towards this ideal, Satan's position 'I am superior to you because of my origin, that is, because of my superior class, race, etc.' is the main hurdle facing Adam's evolution towards perfection. According to Shariati, it is in man that the battle between his higher nature and his baser side (Satan) takes place. The objective correlates of this subjective hurdle in the evolution of man and society at this stage in human history, according to *Mujahideen-e-Khalq*, is represented by imperialism. Since Islam does not accept any compromise with falsehood, the battle against falsehood (i.e., against all anti-evolutionary hurdles) should be carried out to the final end. It was in this context that Mohammad Hanifnejad, a founder of the *Mujahideen* organization said: 'If we do not make an armed confrontation with Imperialism and its pernicious, world devouring characteristics, we must resign ourselves and surrender to its enslavement'. (*Mojahed*, April, 1980). Inciden-

tally, Khomeini's recurrent references to America as 'The Great Satan' *(Shaitan-e-Bozorg)* provides a restatement of this premise.
38. *The Statement of the People's Mojahideen Organization of Iran in Response to Recent Accusations of the Iranian Regime.* (English translation), 1977.
39. Ibid.
40. Special Bulletin of the Militant Muslims' Movement *(Jombesh-e-Muslamanan-e-Mobarez)*. Tehran, May, 1979.
41. *Sharh-e-Tasis.*
42. *The Statememt of the People's Mujahideen Organization of Iran in Response to Recent Accusations of the Iranian Regime.* (English translation, 1977).
43. An academic analysis of the statement of 'Pseudo leftist opportunists', published by *Mujahideen Khalq Organization*, Tehran, 1978, p. 22-23.
44. Ibid.
45. Ibid.
46. Ibid.
47. Ibid.
48. *Sharh-e-Tasis,* p. 16-17.
49. *Sharh-e-Tasis,* p. 16-17.
50. Ibid.
51. Ibid.
52. Ibid.
53. Ibid.
54. Ibid. p.34—35.
55. Ibid.
56. Ibid.
57. *Mojahed,* 11 February 1980, p.13.
58. Ibid.
59. *An Academic study of the Pseudo Left Bulletin.* Peoples Mujahideen Organization of Iran, 1979, p. 1—3.
60. That the Mujahideen's above analysis and prediction was correct was confirmed by events that followed the Islamic Revolution. After taking control of power, the clergymen dominated Islamic Republic Party pursued an internal policy which stemmed from the premise that the main contradiction facing it and its Islam was the *Mujahideen-e-Khalq.* Just weeks after the Shah was overthrown, IRP zealots began openly preaching in public meetings all over the country against the *Mujahideen,* whom they termed as 'hypocrites' and 'apostates'. Slogans declaring 'Even the Shah is acceptable to us but not Rajavi (*Mujahideen-e-Khalq* leader) began appearing in city streets confirming that the formalist obscurantist clergymen regarded *Mujahideen* as their main enemy, and not imperialism or even the monarchy.
61. *Rahnamud-ha-e-dar bar-e-ye-talimat va kar-e-talimati-e-Mujahideen.* (Some guidelines about the teachings of *Mujahideen-e-Khalq* Organization, 1978, p.19.
62. Ibid.
63. Abrahimian, E., *The Guerrilla Movement in Iran.* MERIP Vol.

      10. March-April, 1980, p.12.
64. *An Academic Analysis of the Pseudo Left Opportunists*, p.140.
65. Ibid.
66. Only two members, Masud Rajavi, 34, and Musa Khiabani 33, from this group survived to see the regime of the Shah overthrown. Arrested in 1973, they were serving life sentences in the Shah's prisons, but the rising tide of the people's movement won them their release in January, 1979.
67. Dr. Tavanian Fard's interview, *Ettela'at-e-Haftegi*, Number 2000, August 1980.

7. Ali Shariati: Teacher of the Revolution

Dr. Ali Shariati
Our Martyred Teacher
The Fearless one
By God he was daring
Beginning our awakening
through struggle
against imperialism
May his memory
and name
live for ever
May his soul
remain joyous.[1]

Shariati was everywhere during the Islamic Revolution. All over Iran, the streets and alleys, lamp posts, shop windows, doors and walls of houses—even tree trunks—revealed the Revolution personified in two faces-the stern countenance of Ayatollah Khomeini, and complementing it, the cheerful face of the clean-shaven Ali Shariati. 80% of revolutionary literature that began flooding the sidewalks in makeshift bookstalls from central Tehran to the remotest corner of the country was Shariati's. The circulation of his books and tapes of his speeches ran into millions during the six months it took for the revolutionary process to climax in the general armed uprising on 11 February 1979. No particular group or organization could have projected Shariati at such a mass and generalized level. He had become the spontaneous, collective expression of the progressive revolutionary consciousness that characterized the Revolution through the collective enthusiasm of people, particularly the students. One could say that Ali Shariati, the revolutionary Islamic thinker, historian and sociologist, had mined the mind of Iran with the regenerated spirit of Islam that exploded to yield the Islamic Revolution.

As Shariati saw it, a revolution had a purpose, however diffusely defined, and a history, however little understood. Like other natural and human phenomena, revolutions were governed by *Sunnat-e-illahi-*

laws devised by the Creator for ordering and evolving the Universe. One such law which is considered to be central to revolutions and has been frequently quoted by Islamic scholars, since Syed Jamal-ud-Din Afghani drew their attention to it over a century ago, says that the condition of a people will not change unless they first change themselves inwardly (the Quran, *Ar-Rad:* 11). That is, inner transformation precedes social transformation. In other words, the revolution within the individual precedes the revolution in society. The foundation and the infra-structure of Iran's Islamic Revolution, according to Ayatollah Taleqani, the man who led the Revolution inside Iran, was the inner transformation Dr. Shariati had undergone.[2] As a result of this inner transformation, Ali Shariati redefined Islam as a revolutionary ideology readily assimilable by the consciousness of a generation at the threshold of the 21st Century. Shariati transmitted this revolutionary consciousness to others through hundreds of lectures and millions of tape recordings of his speeches, as well as his books and pamphlets, that had achieved a wide clandestine circulation even before he died in 1977 at the age of 44. In sharing with others his revolutionary insights into the Quran and the Islam his inner odyssey had unfurled, Shariati was obstructed not only by SAVAK's persecution machinery, but also by the equally insidious enemy within the folds of Islam, the obscurantist clergy, whom Taleqani described as being 'more Catholic than the Pope' and 'dangerous'.[3]

Contemporaneous with his return from Paris in 1964 where he had gone to study History and Sociology, the Liberation Movement in Iran had undergone a qualitative change. After June 1963, the need for a revolutionary course of action had made itself felt among the radical elements in the progressive Islamic movement, both inside Iran and abroad. Shariati was among those student activists abroad who had outgrown the reformist framework of the Liberation Movement and had reached the conclusion that a grass roots struggle against imperialism and dictatorship necessitated both ideological and armed struggle.[4] He had already begun the task of formulating the theoretical foundation for a progressive Islamic Revolution when he was returning to Iran. From 1964 until his death in 1977, Shariati remained an untiring revolutionary ideologue consumed by the mission to bring Islam to the forefront of the struggle for national, individual, political and economic liberation in Muslim societies in general and Iran in particular. If Islam could be presented as it really was, that is, as a revolutionary ideology, it would not only draw the young generation who had grown indifferent to the ritualistic dogma of a formalist religion to itself, but transform them into revolutionary elements who would be prepared to give all they had, including their lives, in the struggle against imperialism and despotism. For as Shariati saw it, the contradiction between the progressive spirit of Islam and imperialism was fundamental and irreconcilable: 'The battle between Truth and Oppression is irreconcilable because of the fundamental differences and contradictions in their objectives. Islam has a similar stand against imperialism. Each is bent upon rooting out the other because of the basic contradictions in their principles, aspirations, and objectives. Islam is concerned with the liberation, freedom, and perfection of man, with harmony and justice, whereas imperialism is concerned with the exploitation of man and nations, trampling upon people's rights, obliterating man by changing him into a consumerist pig, a political slave or exploited worker. Therefore, the contradiction between Islam and imperialism is a contradiction in principle.'[5]

Shariati was born in December 1933 at Mazinan, a small village in the lap of Kavir desert in Khorassan province. His father, Ustad Taqi Shariati was an eminent Islamic scholar (*mujtahid*) and founder of the Centre for Propagation of Islamic Truth at Mashhad. Like his father, Shariati was well aware of the limitations of his environment, the restrictive outlook of people, and the traditional forms that surrounded him. For him, the static, traditional forms moulding the psychology, perception, and outlook of people were simply 'a point of departure for a creative leap forward.'[6] This creative life impulse did not allow Shariati to be restricted and contained within his environment. He was determined to subject the traditional forms and practices to his own purpose instead of being subjected by them.[7]

In 1956, Shariati enrolled as an undergraduate student at Mashhad University in the Faculty of Letters, and embarked upon the two-front battle he was to wage throughout his life. On the one hand, it was a battle against 'extreme traditionalists who had spun a web around themselves, separated Islam from society, retreated into a corner of the mosque and the *madrassa,* and often reacted negatively to any kind of intellectual movement within society. They had covered the brilliant truths of Islam with a dark veil behind which they themselves also hid'.[8] On the other hand Shariati had to fight the 'rootless and imitative intellectuals who had made the "new scholasticism" their stronghold'.[9]

As Shariati saw it, both the traditional formalist clergy and the alienated, rootless intellectuals 'had severed their relations with society and the masses, and humbly bowed their heads before the manifestations of corruption and decadence of the modern age'.[10] As for himself, he could not remain silent or passively accept the negative equilibrium that dominated his society.

The French Years

In 1958 Shariati won a State scholarship for graduate studies abroad. He joined the University of Paris and for the next five years he studied history of religion and sociology. His academic and social concern was dominated by a constant search for a sociology that would be able to interpret and analyse, irrespective of the status and development of capitalist society or communist system, 'the realities of the life of those people whose subjection to imperialism had been approved even by the European communists'.[11] It was in France where the most significant influence which seems to have triggered the inner transformation in Shariati began taking shape. This happened in 1960 when he began working under the supervision of Professor Louis Massignon, the renowned French Orientalist, as a research assistant. It is clear from Shariati's autobiographical writings that his path toward spiritual illumination began to unfold after he met Massignon and worked with him on Islamic issues until the Professor's death in 1962. The overflowing spiritual ecstasy with which Shariati mentions Massignon in his writings is all too familiar to those acquainted with the nature of relationship between the spiritual novice and his guide on the inner path of self-discovery. 'Massignon was the greatest Islamic scholar of the age', observes Shariati in *Kavir,* his autobiographical writings. 'The beauty of his spirit and the grandeur of his rich feelings had a greater impact on me than his scientific and intellectual genius. He was great in the real sense of the word. He irrigated my soul and filled (the emptiness) of my heart.'[12] Shortly before his own life was terminated by SAVAK in an apartment near London in 1977, Shariati wrote, 'I cannot imagine what my life would have been had I not known Massignon. Without him, what an impoverished soul, a shrivelled heart, a mundane mind, and a stupid world-view I would have had. His heart now throbs in my breast.'[13]

Besides Massignon, who opened the way for Shariati's inner illumination and spiritual transformation, Sartre and Gurwitsch, who was at one time Lenin and Trotsky's comrade, left a lasting impression on the formative mind of Shariati who acknowledges the influence of his French teachers with the words, 'My reverential salutations to Gurwitsch and Sartre', both of whom Shariati knew personally, 'they taught me how to think.'[14]

During his student years in France, Shariati was actively involved in the Iranian student's resistance against the Pahlavi dictatorship. As one of the founders of the Liberation Movement outside Iran, Shariati began publishing with a group of Iranian nationalists one of the most widely read Persian-language journals in Europe[15] called *Iran-e-Azad* (Free Iran). He was also associated with the National Liberation Front fighting for Algerian independence and the Palestine Revolution. Believing that revolutionary ideas harvested through the revolutionary experience of popular and anti-imperialist movements around the world could be instructive for Iranian revolutionaries, Shariati translated into Persian some of the works of African revolutionary writers like Franz Fanon, Umar Uzgan, and a number of non-Muslim writers. Moreover, he was beginning to realise the necessity for armed struggle for overthrowing the dictatorial regime in Iran. 'There is no doubt that the ruling establishment (in Iran) can be destroyed only through, or at least with the help of, a revolutionary organization. The point is, where and how this revolutionary course of action is to begin?'[16] A few years later Shariati found the answer to his question when the fedayeen and *Mujahideen-e-Khalq* began guerrilla operations against the Pahlavi dictatorship.

Return to Iran
In 1964 Shariati returned to Iran with his wife and two children. He was arrested at the border and directly driven to prison. Six months later he was released but prevented from teaching at universities. This did not frustrate Shariati who took up teaching in a rural high school near his provincial hometown. Then in 1966, Shariati was offered the position of assistant professor at Mashhad University. But the phenomenal popularity of Shariati's courses in History of Religion led to the termination of his employment. This break with the establishment marked the beginning of the most productive period in Shariati's life. He helped in founding Hossienieh Irshad Research Centre at Tehran in 1967. During the six years that followed he was intensely involved in teaching and writing activities offering courses and public lectures on *Islamshinasi* (Islamology) to students enrolled at the Centre. In these lectures, Shariati redefined Islam in the light of modern consciousness and brought his students in contact with the development in human consciousness that had taken place over the centuries to the present.

These courses had become so popular that Hossienieh Irshad began drawing students from other parts of the country in addition to those in Tehran, so much so that for the summer session in 1973, six thousand students had enrolled for Shariati's Islamic courses.[17] Deciding that it could no longer allow Shariati to continue generating waves of revolutionary consciousness in society, the regime decided to close down Hossienieh Irshad. Preceding the Centre's closure, the SAVAK-orchestrated campaign against Shariati calling him 'Islamic Marxist', 'apostate' and *'Bahai'* was intensified and aided by the formalist clergymen. From the pulpit of their mosques, these clergymen began issuing *fatwa* (religious decree) that Shariati's works were 'un-Islamic', and that he was an 'infidel', 'Sunni', 'Wahabi' and a 'hypocrite' — the choice of the accusative term being determined by the accuser's own prejudices. As a result, in September 1973, Hossienieh Irshad, which the obscurantist *mullas* had begun calling *Kafiristan*[18] (land of infidels) was forced into closure. The regime had also ordered Shariati's arrest who had gone into hiding. For almost a year, SAVAK was unable to track down Shariati. Then it took Shariati's ageing father, Ustad Taqi Shariati hostage and put him in prison. The move forced Shariati to surrender himself to the regime in order to get his ailing father released. From November 1974 to March 1975 Shariati was placed in solitary confinement and subjected to torture. The regime was prepared to release him if he promised to keep silent and ceased propagating Islam as a revolutionary ideology. Shariati's refusal to compromise would have led to his death were it not for the popular protest and international pressure on the Shah's regime urging Shariati's release. The Algerian leaders, it is commonly believed, played a crucial role in persuading the Shah to release Shariati who had worked for the Algerian revolution during his student years in Paris. As a result, Shariati was released in March 1975, but prevented from writing and meeting people owing to SAVAK's continuous harrassment, restrictions and pressure. In order to continue his struggle against the regime, Shariati decided to leave Iran secretly. On 16 May 1977, he escaped to Britain, and took up residence in an apartment near London. On 19 June 1977, Shariati was found dead on the floor of his apartment, a deed which people spared no time in attributing to SAVAK. The Shah's regime made every effort to project the impression that it had nothing to do with Shariati's sudden death. An official press handout even lauded the services of the 'prominent Islamic scholar' and regretted his demise. However, these measures did not prevent campus unrest and student protest from developing both inside Iran and abroad. Hundreds of Muslim activists converged in London to attend memorial services for Dr. Shariati, following which his body was airlifted to Syria and buried beside the tomb of Hazrat Zainab, the grand-daughter of Prophet Mohammad and Imam Hosein's sister.[19]

Methodology of the Prophet

To bring Islam to the forefront of socio-political struggle in an ideological framework, and to inject it as a dynamic force in the life of the individual and society, Shariati suggests using the method that he believed the Prophet Mohammad had used for effecting social change and inner transformation among people. This method was different and distinct from other approaches — the conservative, the revolutionary, and the reformist. For Shariati, conservatism was a method used by formalists and guardians of traditions. It was employed by those who sought to preserve the outworn customs and superstitions in a society because they believed themselves to be the society's guardians.[20] The conservative clings to the outmoded customs of the past because 'his logic tells him that if we changed the customs of the past, it is as if we have separated the root from the tree'.[21] For the conservative, therefore, social relationships that had become enmeshed into customs and the existing social structure were sacred vestiges of the society. Opposed to conservatism was revolutionarism which viewed the retention of outdated customs and relationships as tantamount to social stagnation. For the revolutionary, it was necessary to make a sudden break with the forms, customs and relationships which had become chains clamped to the body and spirit of the people. The supposedly middle way between the above two approaches was reformism with its emphasis on changing social conditions gradually. But such an approach was not feasible in practice, because the long period of time required by the reformist approach allowed internal and external enemies to gain strength and destroy the objectives reformists hoped to attain through gradual change.

The method of the Prophet, however, was different from the above three methods — he kept the form of a custom, but changed its meaning in a revolutionary way. 'The Prophet preserves the form, the container of a custom which has deep roots in society and to which people have gotten used to from generation to generation, but he changes the contents. He changes the spirit, direction and practical application of this custom in a revolutionary, decisive and immediate manner.'[22] Shariati thought that the Prophet's method had the positive characteristics of all the other methods. Among the many examples Shariati cited to illustrate the Prophet's method was *hajj*, the annual pilgrimage to Mecca. Before Prophet Mohammad, the circumambulation of Kaaba was a glorified form of idol worship loaded with ancestor worship and superstitions. While the Arabs performed the pilgrimage for idol worship, they believed that Abraham, the Friend of God had built Kaaba, the house where they kept their idols. According to Shariati, it was revealed to the Prophet of Islam to take the form of the *hajj* ritual and change it into 'the largest, most beautiful, and deepest rite founded upon the Unity of God and the oneness of mankind'.[23] Through his revolutionary approach which retained the mould and form of the ritual but revolutionized its meaning, the Prophet, according to Shariati, took the rite of the pilgrimage of idol worshipping tribes and changed it into a custom 'completely contrary to and opposite of, its original use'.[24] This was a revolutionary leap, marking a shift in consciousness and in the way one apprehended things. As a result of this method, the Arab people did not have to undergo the anguish of having to dispense with historically rooted and emotionally valued traditions and rituals. Rather, 'they sensed the revival and truth and cleansing of their eternal customs'.[25] They could, thus, easily move from idol worship to the other end of the spectrum: Unity. Although this method was more sudden and unexpected than any cultural or intellectual revolution, society was not aware of the fact that the building and foundations of its idol worship had been torn down. 'This leap, this social method found within the traditions of the Prophet is a revolution within a custom which preserves the outer form but changes the content.'[26] Shariati believed that the Prophet's method was the only method which the clear minded intelligentsia could effectively use for bringing about change and transformation in the modern Muslims and their society. 'It is with this method that one can reach revolutionary goals without forcibly bearing all the consequences of a revolution and without opposing the basis of faith and ancient social values.'[27] The great advantage of this method was that through applying it, one did not remove oneself from the people. Being a firm believer in traditions of his culture, Shariati realised that it was not possible to inject ideas from other cultures which had no organic roots. By applying the methodology of the Prophet in his own society, Shariati was able to redefine 'the basis of the belief of his people as well as his society's perception of itself'.[28]

Following the Prophet's method, Shariati attributed to *hajj* a symbolic significance with social and political implications, in a contemporary idiom. As Shariati saw it, *hajj* was a magnificent ritual for tuning man's consciousness to the frequency of a permanent revolution, and for propelling man and society on the evolutionary path of growth towards perfection. There was a definite social and political component to *hajj* in addition to its spiritual significance. For instance, the ritual that required the pilgrims to hit three idols with stones during a stage in *hajj* was viewed by Shariati as having a crucial symbolic significance for the present. He saw these three idols as Capitalism, Despotism, and Religious Hypocrisy. *Hajj* was an objective expression of oneness and unity of mankind, of a classless and harmonised humanity striving together toward sublime value. The challange for the Muslim was to translate the *touhid* subjectivly experienced during *hajj* into working principles and objective realities in one's life and society by keeping constantly in mind the significance of the experience and renewing it through recollection of God 'Who created you from a single soul'. (The Quran, IV:1) *Hajj* was an exercise where one trained oneself in the Abrahamic tradition to become the destroyer of reactionary forms and outmoded relationships in one's society. When standing at Abraham's position *(Maqam-e-Ibrahim,* a stage during *hajj)* 'you promise God that you will fight to save people from being burned by the fire of oppression, ignorance and reaction. During the battle for people's liberation *(jehad)* throw yourself in fire to save other people. Live the way Abraham did and be the architect of the Kaaba of faith in your times. Help people to step out from the swamps of stagnated and useless lives. Awaken them from their stupor so that they refuse to suffer oppression in the darkness of ignorance.' To strive truly in the way of God and the way of the people, one had first to achieve *taqva,* that is, 'train oneself in becoming a responsible rebel by becoming genuinely involved in the problems of the people'.[29] For it was not possible to achieve *taqva* 'by becoming a monk and isolating oneself from people'.[30] However, it was no easy task to become a *mujahid,* a striver in the path of God and the people, without facing immense hardships and staggering odds: 'The way of righteousness, the road toward Allah may never be approached without practicing devotion, self-denial, transpersonal generosity *(isaar),* captivity, torture, exile, pain, endless danger, even the firing squad. This is how one may walk with the people and step in the direction to approach Allah.'[31]

Shariati applied the Prophet's methodology to the problems of society, history, and man's growth and development, thereby developing a sociology, a philosophy of history, and anthropology (or evolutionary psychology) in the Islamic tradition. The foundation of all this work rests on *touhid* (Divine Unity) as a worldview. For Shariati, belief in *touhid* has its social, material, and human implications. It lays down the infrastructure for the unity of mankind, for the integration of social classes, and for the unity of creation in the Universe. Applied to the social plane, the simple logic of *touhid* is that if God is one, humanity must become one to reflect the Unity of God in the unity of mankind. Shariati's conception of man, society and history is evolutionary, dynamic, and dialectical. He views man as a combination of opposites and a dialectical being. The contradiction between the two poles within him — his lowly, animal and base tendencies and his quest for sublime values, for transcending his situation and urging him towards absolute perfection (God), creates the permanent evolutionary oscillation in man. Thus man is torn between the two forces within him pulling him in opposite directions, towards baseness (mud) and towards Absolute Perfection (God). Because of his dual nature, man is subject to a certain form of deterministic evolutionary movement. God is Absolute Will and Consciousness. Man is a manifestation of God's Will and is continuously evolving towards God. Religion is a means for this evolutionary movement, not an end in itself. As for History, it is the story of man's becoming. Whereas Man is born of the inner battle between 'mud and spirit' and 'Satan and God' in Adam, History begins with the battle between Cain and Abel. The war within Adam is subjective, that between Cain and Abel is objective. History, like man, is a dialectical movement. The contradiction in history begins when Cain (representing private ownership and the agricultural system) kills Abel (representing the age of primitive communism). Abel, the herdsman, is killed by Cain, the landlord. With this, the age of common ownership of sources of production in nature (the age of hunting and pastoralism), and the spirit of brotherhood and true faith, is destroyed. It is replaced by the age of agriculture, private ownership, religious hypocrisy and violation of other people's rights. Before the struggle between Cain and Abel began, private and monopolistic ownership of natural resources, for instance, of water and earth was non—existent. Everything was equally available to everyone.[32]

Shariati's concept of Sociology is also derived from the Quran and other Islamic sources. As he views it, only two forms of societies are possible — the society based upon *touhid*, belief in Divine Unity, and the society based upon *shirk*, ascribing partners to God (polytheism). Opposed to *touhid* as a worldview is the worldview based upon *shirk*. A leitmotif in Shariati's works stresses the point that the difference between the two worldviews *(touhid* vs *shirk)* is no simple difference — for the battle of history is the war between these worldviews. Throughout history, religion in various forms of *shirk* has justified social *shirk*, i.e., divisions in the society, whether economic, moral, or racial. Whereas *touhid*, throughout history, has been fighting against the worldview of *shirk* and the social divisions and hierarchies born of this worldview. The battle of history, therefore, is the battle of religion against religion. Shariati believes that the 19th Century intellectuals were right in their belief that religion had played a narcotizing role, for they had seen religion to have always been used as a tool by the ruling classes for justifying their oppression and exploitation of the people. But these intellectuals, Shariati noted, had failed to distinguish between the worldview of *shirk* and the worldview of *touhid,* an error in which modern intellectuals were persisting to this day.[33]

Ideological Commitment and Social Action

According to Shariati, Islam brought the greatest revolution in the social and spiritual history of man by changing the direction of religious energy from the 'hereafter' to the 'here' and 'now' Through a thematic analysis of Quranic chapters, Shariati demonstrated that the dominant theme accounting for three quarters of the Quran dealt with society and life, natural and material phenomena, and thought, reflection and belief. Furthermore, only two of the 114 chapters in the Quran dealt with religious rituals.[34] Social commitment, consciousness, and choice were therefore central to the individual's role in Islam. The Quran was a continuum between people and God, enjoining that service to people was service to God. Man's evolutionary growth and the development of his personality was possible only through social struggle. By withdrawing from life it was possible to make a philosopher, poet, or an ascetic, but not a Muslim. Hence Shariati's insistent message that to become a true Muslim, one must direct all one's energy, will, and blood to the path of growth and evolution of human society by fighting against oppression, exploitation, and ignorance of the masses. In the socially aware and conscientious individual, ideological commitment was an expression of this intrinsic sense of responsibility and yearning for higher values. Given this inner tendency and universal urge, the Muslim youth on the path of awareness had to face a peculiar dilemma. Having rejected the stagnant facade of a formalist Islam, the youth had two choices: either to opt for modernism by incorporating the consumer oriented model of Western capitalism in their imperialist-backed society, or to accept Marxism with its materialistic philosophical basis. Neither of these options could really serve the interest of Muslims. Moreover, both imperialism and Marxism would not countenance the emergence of Islam as a progressive revolutionary ideology though for entirely different reasons. Imperialism was opposed to revolutionary Islam because it feared losing its markets and its exploitive control of Muslim societies. Whereas Marxism could oppose revolutionary Islam for fear of losing its ideological basis among revolutionary forces in a predominantly Muslim Third World.

Shariati's main criticism of Marxism was directed against the Marxist premise that gave a purely materialistic dimension to the struggle against exploitation and to class contradictions. Shariati believed this overemphasis on materialism was unnecessary, that the struggle against capitalism and the class system should have formulated its philosophy of history not by rejecting religion but by linking itself up with the struggles of the Prophets,[35] because 'without religion, it is not possible to have true socialism for creating a classless society'.[36]

Shariati and Mujahideen-e-Khalq: The Search for Models

During his stay in France, Shariati had reached the conclusion that an effective and meaningful struggle against the Pahlavi dictatorship had to be both ideological and military. It was therefore natural that he would develop close associations with the *Mujahideen-e-Khalq,* 'many of whom were Shariati's students at Hossienieh Irshad'.[37] When Hossienieh Irshad, which had become a fertile ideological centre for propagating revolutionary Islam, was closed down in 1973, an increasing number of Shariati's students found they had no alternative but to take up arms against the dictatorial regime.[38] Shariati had told his students that knowledge of 'self-consciousness', 'guidance', 'deliverance' and 'salvation' was not gained from books or taught in school or universities. 'It is taught in the field of struggle and through holy war *(jehad)*'.[39] The students who gained this knowledge would fight for freedom of mankind, for they were *'Mujahids* fighting for the sake of God'.[40]

Shariati remained a defender of *Mujahideen-e-Khalq* throughout his life, lending his ideological, spiritual and moral support and guidance to the organization 'during its days of persecution by SAVAK and persistent attacks by the reactionary Muslims lashing the *Mujahideen* with the whip of traditional Islam, and by the group of communist opportunists who having penetrated the organization were bent upon destroying it from within'.[41] In his article on the revolutionary movement of Imam Reza, Shariati argued that contrary to the claims of the apologists, guerrilla movements had come into existence in Iran after the death of Shia leaders like Imam Reza.[42] The *Mujahideen's* armed response, therefore, was justified, legitimate and correct.

Many of Shariati's students who were members of *Mujahideen-e-Khalq* were killed under torture or by the regime's firing squads or in shoot-outs with the Shah's Police. Those developments charged Shariati's writings with a power and animation born of a living experience on the battlefield of struggle. It was not possible to capture the revolutionary essence of Islam in the secluded corners of libraries or through endless and arid arguments over issues having little relevance to the immediate problems of an oppressed and impoverished people. Shariati compared the actions of the young and regenerated revolutionaries and those of the fossilized scholars crouched upon their escapist treatises, divorced from the social reality of their times, saying that 'half a dozen conscious, socially aware and conscientious high school students have far more worth than a large number of 'titled', 'turbaned', 'respectable' and 'ostentatious believers'. For the latter end up in meaninglessness and dogma, whereas the former kindle the sparks from which the flames of illumination, evolution, and revolution rage. Islam began with these flames and its reconstruction would also begin with them'.[43]

An essential part of this reconstruction required one to return to one's roots and culture and seek its pristine spirit[44] and ideal personality models. The Islamic tradition had many such 'models'. For example, Abraham was the model of man's revolt against enslavement of thought, intellect, and free inquiry. He was a symbol of man's rebellion against the enslavement of his beliefs and against physical, material, social and psychological bondage. Other 'models' which Shariati presented from a revolutionary angle included Prophet Mohammad and his companions, Hazrat Ali, and Abu Zar, the radical rebel who struggled against the emergence of aristocracy in the Islamic society to the end of his life. Also a model of immediate relevance to the Iran of the 70s suppressed by SAVAK was Imam Hosein, son of Ali and grandson of the Prophet. 1300 years ago, Hosein chose to defy the illegitimate authority of Yazid who had become the head of the Islamic State by setting a precedent for hereditary rule of the aristocracy hitherto foreign to Islam. Hosein and his small group of followers were killed to the last man in the battlefield of Karbala by Yazid's army in one of the most unequal military confrontations in history.

Shariati also hailed Muslims of the new age as 'personality models'. Among them thinkers like Afghani and Iqbal together with activists like Hasan and Mehbobeh — the young husband and wife *Mujahideen-e-Khalq* urban guerrillas who died fighting against SAVAK agents in the streets of Tehran in 1975. Shariati's search for 'models' for inspiring the contemporary Muslim youth was not limited to men only. He was equally concerned in drawing the Iranian women to the battle field of social and revolutionary struggle on the basis of the Quranic premise: 'Whoever performs right action, whether man or woman and has faith, is vitalised with good life'. It was crucial that Iranian women should reintegrate themselves with forgotten or suppressed models of womanhood in revolutionary Islam, which had been rejected through ignorance, prejudice, or outright feelings of inferiority by modern woman. Shariati worked for the assimilation of revolutionary models of Muslim woman by redefining for the contemporary Muslim woman the image of Fatima, the daughter of Prophet Mohammad, the socially aware wife of Hazrat Ali, the fourth Caliph, and the mother who reared revolutionaries like Hosein and Zainab, the brother and sister who so fearlessly fought against injustice and oppression. To dispel the dross which had shrouded the concept of woman in Islam over centuries of ignorance and misrepresentation, Shariati recalled the honours which Islam had bestowed upon woman. 'There is only one person buried at Kaaba, in the House of God, and that is a woman, a slave — Hajar — the second wife of Prophet Abraham and mother of Ismail.'[45]

Shariati presented Fatima as a firm and determined woman who spent her life in struggle resisting social pressures, poverty, and hardship. She continued to confront suffering and hardship even after she migrated to Medina with her father and began her married life with Ali. In his lectures to young boys and girls flocking to hear him at Hossienieh Irshad, Shariati told them that the contemporary Muslim woman was 'lost' because she either clung to the outmoded and anachronistic traditional model of womanhood, or to imported, synthetic and superficial models of the consumerist Western society. 'But with Fatima as our model we learn to fight injustice and oppression. We turn from ourselves to others. We become actively involved for eradicating the society's ills and changing a diseased social system'[46] based on capitalism. Fatima, therefore, was an ideal, a model, with whom modern Muslim females needed to identify themselves if they wanted to become authentic personalities and their 'true self'. But to become a Fatima was a challenge, because 'She is a holy trust, she should not have a single moment of peace in life for that might keep her from constant becoming. This is why Fatima must always be learning through involving herself on the scene of social struggle'.[47] To be the chosen one of God did not exempt one from hardship. If Muslim women wished to step on the path of true liberation, then they should be prepared to court great suffering and challenge as Fatima had done. To illustrate the place of affirmative suffering for seasoning the personality of the revolutionary, Shariati pointed out that 'there is no Prophet in the whole of Quran who is so punished and so criticized as Mohammad'.[48] This was so because 'none of the other Prophets were so beloved in the eyes of God and none of them so responsible to the people'[49] as Mohammad had been. The necessity for a revolutionary renunciation of material attractions was a first step on the path of social struggle and *Jehad fi Sabilallah* (sacred striving in the cause of God). Emphasizing the existential accountability of each individual in relation to the Creator, Shariati said that even the Prophet could not support Fatima when she stood in the Presence of the Creator, for His Judgment. 'The Prophet cannot protect Fatima from deviation. Fatima must become Fatima herself.'[50] 'No polluted and valueless man can pass the examination on the Day of Judgement unless he has learned in this world how to pass through to the hereafter by using the techniques of life, work, struggle, and service.'[51]

It was in response to this challenge for becoming a living expression of the idea of womanhood which Fatima as a revolutionary model presented that Fatima Amini, a school teacher from the conservative religious city of Mashhad broke the traditions of dogma and entered the field of social struggle as a *Mujahideen-e-Khalq* guerrilla. Her understanding and commitment to the ideology of revolutionary Islam developed gradually, over a period of several years through social and intellectual struggle. It was only after she had steeped herself in the revolutionary spirit of the Quran that she decided to become a member of the People's Mujahideen Organization. Joining the *Mujahideen* was a turning point in Fatima's life and in her struggle for finding an Islamic solution to the afflictions, exploitation, corruption, and oppression rampant in society. As early as 1962, when she was still a student at Mashhad's Teacher Training College, Fatima had founded the Islamic Women's Association to give direction to her search for developing the truth of Islam into a tangible, systematic ideological framework that could answer her questions and the question of the socially aware Muslims and meet the needs of the time.

Fatima Amini's life story was instructive. After graduating from Mashhad University in 1964, she decided to become a school teacher to give social awareness to the deprived children in her city. Having herself grown up in the low income areas of Mashhad, Fatima was more than familiar with the deprivations and poverty which the toiling masses had to daily experience as a result of the policies of the Pahlavi dictatorship, its comprador bourgeoie supporters, and imperialist masters. In 1970, she turned her partial association with the *Mujahideen-e-Khalq* into an enduring one by becoming a full member. A year later, she married a combatant member of the organization. As she once remarked, her marriage was a revolutionary bond that had been forged on the front of social and spiritual struggle.

Given her devotion and commitment, Fatima soon became an active and central figure in the organization. As part of her duties, she regularly visited families of political prisoners and survivors of *Mujahideen* killed by the regime, to look after their needs and extend moral support. Every fortnight, Fatima held a meeting for the female members of these families, where beside discussing their problems and coordinating their activities, she instructed them in revolutionary Islam by reciting verses from the Quran and interpreting them. In 1972, Fatima was instrumental in organizing the first major demonstration of *Mujahideen* supporters against the regime. Family members of martyred *Mujahideen* and of those in prison took part in this demonstration to protest against the execution of the five founding members of the organization.

Fatima Amini was arrested by SAVAK in March, 1974. For the next six months, she was subjected to gruesome tortures to extract organizational secrets from her. Part of her torture involved burning her body on electric steel 'trays' leading to her paralysis. But for a few fingers on her left hand and her tongue, Fatima was totally paralysed. SAVAK had tried to keep her alive by placing her in one of its hospitals with the hope of continuing its interrogation. In August, 1975, Fatima died without having revealed any secrets to SAVAK. Her story came to be widely known during the Islamic Revolution after political prisoners were released toward the end of October 1978.

Fatima Amini was the first female *Mujahid* to be killed under torture by SAVAK. At a time when her society had sunk into the swamps of cultural imperialism and runaway materialism, Fatima's life and resistance was an example that inspired other revolutionary women. She was soon followed by Fatima Sarwar Alladpush, a student of Ali Shariati at Hossienieh Irshad who graduated from Tehran University in 1975. Alladpush took up teaching in Tehran's slums for a while, but gave it up to devote all her energies to the precarious life of an urban guerrilla when she joined the *Mujahideen-e-Khalq*. In October 1976, Fatima Alladpush was gunned to death in a running battle with the Shah's police in Tehran streets. Other female *Mujahideen* who laid down their lives at a time when the Shah's formidable power had given his regime the semblance of invincibility included Sadiqa Rezai, 18, and Mehbobeh Motahedin, 24. In the booklet entitled 'The Story of Hasan and Mehbobeh',[52] Shariati summed up his agony at having to continue living in the face of the continual loss of his 'beloved pupils' to the despot's firing squads: 'To prove its truth and grandeur, Islam has gained two witnesses. And God has plucked two red roses from the desert of earthly existence, smelling their fragrance and caressing them. But their teacher is alone and suffers the agony of having been left alive after their martyrdom.'[53] In this work, Shariati hailed Mehbobeh as a contemporary Zainab and a befitting personality model for emulation by revolutionary Muslim women. He emphasised that personality was formed through social struggle, the evolutionary growth of the individual being an integrative, unifying process involving commitment to inner development (through the greater battle, *Jehad-e-Akbar*) and social action (the lesser battle, *Jehad-e-Asghar*); life being nothing but belief and *jehad*.

The theme of *jehad* and martyrdom was expounded further in Shariati's monumental book called *Shahadat* (Martyrdom). The work was based on four successive lectures delivered in 1973 in the context of religious meetings held during the sacred month of Muharram for commemorating Hosein's martyrdom on the battlefield of Karbala. The object behind these lectures delivered at Hossienieh Irshad was to inject the spirit of revolutionary uprising into the consciousness and experience of the young generation searching for a way to fight the 'invincible' Pahlavi regime. The contemporary spirit and immediacy that electrified these lectures making it Shariati's most moving and compelling work was 'directly inspired and generated by the martyrdom of Ahmad Rezai',[54] a leader of *Mujahideen-e-Khalq* and one of its intellectual founders. Ahmad Rezai was the first member of the *Mujahideen-e-Khalq* who died fighting the Pahlavi dictatorship. In a shoot-out against the Shah's Police in 1972, Ahmad Rezai had fought to the last bullet, then throwing away his gun he approached a group of SAVAK agents as if to surrender. But when he got near, he pulled the pin of the grenade he was holding in his hands, blowing himself to shreds and killing four security agents in the process.[55]

In *Shahadat,* Shariati presented Hosein's uprising against the despotic power of the time as an expression of man's historical struggle for breaking the barriers on the path towards liberation, salvation, and perfection, a theme Ahmad Rezai had also touched upon in the manual of revolutionary Islam he had published for his organization.[56] In recounting the battle at Karbala where Hosein and a handful of his revolutionary comrades faced a whole army of the establishment, the purpose was to grasp the meaning and message in this uprising, and use it as a manual and model for action in contemporary times. Hosein's stand aganist Yazid was a revolutionary response to the reactionary relationships that were beginning to dominate the Islamic society at the time. It was a fight against despotism, religious hypocrisy and exploitation that was being institutionalized in the name of religion by the ruling classes after the Islamic Caliphate had been converted into a monarchical form of dynastic rule. The spirit of Hosein's response over 1300 years ago, therefore, was inextricably linked to the unequal struggle which the tiny guerrilla organization of *Mujahideen* was now waging against the massive establishment of the dictatorial regime. As has been pointed out,[57] the greatness of Shariati's *Shahadat* does not only lie with its living and animated content, but also with the fact that he succeeded in publicly expressing these ideas at that particular stage in Iran's history. When he said during his lectures, 'today it is so difficult for me to speak', he did not mean that it was only because of the historical incident that had occurred in Karbala 1300 years ago[58] that he was feeling distressed. It was difficult for him to speak because so many of his students were getting killed in the 'contemporary Karbala' — the battlefield of struggle aganinst Pahlavi dictatorship, representing the contemporary Yazid. Given these cultural, moral, and spiritual aspects, it was not possible to evaluate armed struggle by a revolutionary vanguard in terms of the traditional criteria of victory and defeat. Failure and defeat were irrelevant in this type of battle. What was important was the spirit of the battle. As the *mujahideen-e-Khalq* saw it, Hossein set the example as to how to break the deadlock in social evolution when evil and reactionary forces were controlling the society. Under such conditions, anyone believing in the liberating spirit of truth had to put up a fight against falsehood, even if that meant sure death for oneself.[59] In the confrontation between a small group of revolutionaries and the despotic army of the dictators, only blood could distinguish the boundary between truth and falsehood.[60] Ali Asghar Baadizadegaan, a founder member of the *Mujahideen* had voiced similar ideas during his defence speech before he was sentenced to death in the Shah's military court, when he declared that the worth of an individual as an evolving being on the path of spiritual perfection was determined by the degree to which one was willing to giveaway and sacrifice in social struggle. One who had not given up anything in the cause of God and the people could not be regarded a revolutionary or a Muslim militant.'[61] Baadizadegaan said that it was from history that Hosein was receiving the response to his call urging people to rise up and fight against oppression. 'Whenever and wherever a liberated person has refused to submit to despotism and its attempts for distorting supreme values, and has preferred death to a dehumanized, purposeless existence under a monstrous regime and inhuman social system, it is a response to Hosein's call. Wherever there is struggle for liberation, Hosein is present on the battlefield.'[62] The *Mujahideen* placed the Hosein-Yazid contradiction in the framework of anti-imperialist struggle. 'In every age, a Yazid has been identified and a Hosein and his comrades have challenged him. Today, the Yazid of the world is imperialism, we who claim to be Muslims must bear in mind that Islam has a universal mission for people's liberation and their unity in a single community, the *Ummate'Wahadun*. To attain this objective, first and foremost it is necessary to efface imperialism, the greatest hindrance facing man's evolutionary progress towards perfection at this historical stage. This is how Islam, the harbinger of freedom and salvation for the oppressed and toiling masses of the world (the *mostazafin*) would spearhead the revolution for creating a new transformation in history to fulfil the Quranic promise that the *mostazafin* would inherit the earth.'[63] *Shahadat,* therefore, was to be the cornerstone of any revolutionary movement for breaking the deadlock and *status quo* imposed upon a society by a decadent regime. As Shariati saw it, *shahadat, taqia* (dissimulation) and *taqlid* (obedience) – among the basic concepts in Shia Islam – constituted the basic framework of any revolutionary guerrilla movement anywhere in the world. 'The best revolutionaries *(mujahideen)* in Latin America struggling for national liberation are conducting their struggle by observing three principles:

'(1) Subscribing to the conditions and requirements of guerrilla struggle;
'(2) unquestioned obedience in relation to instructions of leadership; and
'(3) preparendness for death.

'These three principles are the translation and explanation of no other principles than the three principles which the revolutionary Muslim *Mujahideen* observe: dissimulation, obedience, and martyrdom.'[64]

It was a great challenge for Shariati to go on living and carry on the struggle for propagating the message for which so many of his students and young revolutionaries were being tortured to death and getting killed by the regime. By putting himself and his role in historical perspective, Shariati compared his own situation to that of Hazrat Zainab, sister of Imam Hosein who returned from the battlefield of Karbala (after her brother and his comrades were all slain) to spread the message of her brother's mission among people. 'The messenger who has returned to the Capital of oppression (the allusion is to Tehran, seat of

Pahlavi dictatorship), has a most difficult task awaiting him—the responsibility to transmit the message of the silent martyrs to the people. He must become the voice of those whose tongues have been cut by the executioner's blade. If blood is without message, it remains dumb in history. If the blood of a martyr cannot convey its message to all generations, it means that the executioner has succeeded to imprison the martyr in the prison of a particular period in history. Zainab's mission (after her brother's martyrdom) is a message to all people — that life is nothing but belief in ideology and struggle for realizing it. Only those are worthy of life who can choose a worthy death.'[65]

Most of the slogans that characterized Iran's Revolution and gave it its authentic and distinct identity, such as, 'Every month Muharram, everyday Ashura, the whole earth a Karbala', and 'Every Revolution has two faces — blood and message,' had been circulated by Shariati. The most well known slogan 'Shaheed is the Heart of History,' came directly from the heart of Shariati's *Shahadat,* where comparing the martyr to the motor of history — its heart, Shariati said: 'Just as the heart injects life in the body by pumping blood through its dry veins, so the *shaheed* (martyr) is the heart that transmits his blood and gives life to the dried up and dying body of the society — a society where people have submitted to false values, coercion, and oppression so as to survive a little longer and are content with sheer physical survival'.[66] *Shahadat* was not an imposed death, but a goal, evolutionary and authentic. *Shahadat* was 'an invitation to all generations and for all times that if you can, then kill the oppressor, and if you can't, then die'.[67] Without making the supreme sacrifice, no movement in history was possible, nor any transcendence in dimensions of consciousness.

In his lecture, Shariati criticized the reformists, the moderates, the compromisers, and the reactionaries who invoked various justifications for their inaction and passivity against the 'invincible' apparatus of the dictatorship. By making allegorical references to the martyrdom of Ahmed Rezai in the context of his speech on Imam Hosein, Shariati said, 'The great teacher of martyrdom has risen to teach a lesson to those who believe that struggle against dictatorship should be waged only when victory is possible, and to those who have despaired or have compromised with the Establishment, or have become indifferent to their environment. Hosein teaches that *shahadat* is a *choice* through which the *mujahid,* by sacrificing himself on the altar of the temple of freedom and love, is irrevocably victorious. Hosein has come to teach the Children of Adam how to die. He declares that people who submit themselves to all forms of humiliations, injustice and oppression just to live a little longer are destined to die a 'black death'. Those who lack the courage to choose martyrdom, death will choose them.'[68] These ideas were echoed by Reza Rezai, another *Mujahideen-e-Khalq* martyr killed in 1973. According to Reza Rezai, the fate of a humbled people who accept to live in humiliation is a 'black death', whereas 'the warriors on the path of truth, justice, and unity live in blood and fire, affliction, pain and suffering so as to be the witnesses and harbingers of a great and certain victory.'[69] In the last letter Reza Rezai wrote to his mother before he was killed in a shoot-out with the Secret Police and which was, like other 'documents of revolution', among the most widely read materials, Reza Rezai reflected on the transpersonal and transcendental consciousness where *shahadat* was a point of intersection and inversion in continuous becoming. 'It is a thrilling moment when love for *shahadat* displaces the love for a mundane existence disgracefully lived under the heels of oppression, reaction, corruption, and decadence, without freedom and without evolutionary perfection. And today, all of us *Mujahideen-e-Khalq* are overflowing with this thrill! We must carve out with our blood the path of Truth, Justice, and Freedom's Victory.'[70] The greatest miracle of the revolutionary's martyrdom was that he gave an entire generation a new faith in itself, presenting it with a tangible and living model for emulation. Directly addressing his students in the heart of Tehran in what was to be one of his last lectures at Hossienieh Irshad Shariati said, 'My friends! We are passing through a bad period. All my hope and faith lies in you, our youth. After all, those who have "made it" in life, who enjoy position, power, money, and status have no other responsibility but to preserve what they have already achieved, or to get the better of it. But you who have been blessed with deprivation are capable of doing something to save that which is being lost and forgotten.'[71] It was therefore clear that what Shariati expected of the socially aware revolutionary Muslims was to get into the front line of resistance against 'Yazids' of the time, equipped with both the ideology and the gun to carry out a Hosein-like mission. However ideological struggle and propaganda — Shariati's mission — was as important, even more important than the 'red death' of the frontline revolutionary. For the cause and ideals motivating the martyr's struggle had to be propagated, so that the message of his blood was clearly comprehended by others, and the drops of his blood could raise the flood of revolution. According to Ayatollah Taleqani,[72] this was the function which *Mujahideen-e-Khalq* accomplished to bring about the Islamic Revolution. The *Mujahideen* pioneers were 'diamonds that sparkled in the dark night of dictatorship . . . they opened the way for *jehad*.'[73] It was 'the pure and innocent blood' of these 'devout and socially responsible believers' which raised the flood that swept away the Pahlavi dictatorship in 1979.[74]

Notes

1. A people's song from the Islamic revolution.
2. Ayatollah Taleqani's Speech at Tehran University, 16 May 1979.

3. *Taleqani der Faizieh* (Speech of Ayatollah Taleqani at Qom's Faizieh Theological School), p.10. Tehran, 1979.
4. *Doktor Shariati*, Shariati Foundation and Hamgam publishers, Tehran, 1979.
5. Shariati, A., *Chagon-e-Manden*, in *Payam-e-Khalq*, Number 15, 18 June 1979.
6. Gholam Abbas Tavassoli In, *On the Sociology of Islam: Lectures by Ali Shariati*, trans. Hamid Algar (Berkeley, Mizan Press, 1979) p.11-38.
7. Ibid.
8. Ibid. p.20-21.
9. Ibid.
10. Ibid., p.20-21.
11. Ibid.
12. Shariati, A., *Kavir*, Tehran, 1979. p.85-105.
13. Ibid.
14. Ibid.
15. *Doktor Shariati*, Shariati Foundation and Hamgam Publications, Tehran 1979.
16. Ibid., p.24.
17. Ibid.
18. Like all progressive Islamic forces, Iqbal was not spared the plague posed by the obscurantist *mulla* (clergyman). According to Iqbal, 'for the shortsighted, narrowminded *mulla* the concept of religion is to brand others as *kafirs*'. The *mulla's* religion served no function other than 'sowing corruption, perverseness and disruption in the name of God'. (In, *Life of Iqbal*, Volume 2, Ferozsons, Lahore, 1978, p.386). As Iqbal saw it, religion in its higher manifestation was 'neither dogma, nor priesthood, nor ritual'. (*Reconstruction of Religious Thought in Islam.* p.189).
19. *Doktor Shariati*, Shariati Foundation and Hamgam Publishers, Tehran, 1979.
20. Shariati, A., *Fatima is Fatima*. (English translation by Laleh Bakhtiar). Shariati Foundation and Hamdami publishers, Tehran, 1980.
21. Ibid., p.63.
22. Ibid., p.65.
23. Ibid.
24. Ibid.
25. Ibid.
26. Ibid., p.66-67.
27. Ibid., p.67.
28. Ibid., p.9.
29. Shariati, A., *Hajj*. Free Islamic Literatures Inc., Ohio, 1977.
30. Ibid.
31. Ibid.
32. *Doktor Shariati*. Shariati Foundation and Hamgam publishers, Tehran, 1979, p.107–8.
33. Shariati, A., *Touhid Va Shirk*.
34. 'The Spirit of Islamic Revolution. *Pakistan Times*, 9 June 1979.

35. *Doktor Shariati*, Shariati Foundation and Hamgam publishers. Tehran, 1979.
36. Ibid., p.106. According to Iqbal, while 'Bolshevism plus God is almost identical with Islam', pure materialism on its own cannot serve as a basis for human society, even in Russia. For as far as Iqbal knew, the Russians were 'really a religious people', and their negative state of mind about religion was not to continue for long. Since Islam, according to Iqbal, was 'a socialistic religion' and the Quranic teachings were opposed to the holding of land as private property, he would not be surprised 'if in the course of time either Islam would devour Russia or Russia Islam' As for imperialism, Iqbal believed it to be 'ungodly', because 'all States engaged in exploitation were Ungodly'. (*Life of Iqbal*, Volume 1, by Masud-ul-Hassan, Ferozsons, Lahore, 1978, pp.288-91).
37. *Doktor Shariati*, Shariati Foundation and Hamgam publishers Tehran, 1979, p.43.
38. *Payam-e-Khalq*, No.15, 18 June 1979.
39. Shariati, A., *Hajj*, Free Islamic Literaure Inc., Ohio, 1977, p. 62.
40. Ibid.
41. *Payam-e-Khalq*, 15 June 1979.
42. Ibid.
43. Shariati, A., *Zaminae-ye-Shenakht-e-Qoran*. (Context for Understanding the Qoran), p. 12.
44. Shariati, A., *We and Iqbal*, Irshad, Tehran, 1980.
45. Shariati, A., *Hajj*. Free Islamic literature Inc., Ohio, 1977.
46. Shariati, A., *Fatima is Fatima*. English Translation by Laleh Bakhtiar. Shariati Foundation and Hamdami Publications, Tehran 1980.
47. Ibid.
48. Ibid.
49. Ibid.
50. Ibid.
51. Ibid.
52. Shariati, A., *Qese-ye-Hasan-va-Mehbobeh*, 1976.
53. Ibid.
54. *Doktor Shariati*, Shariati Foundation and Hamgam Publishers, Tehran, 1979, p. 40.
55. *Anan kay Shahadat Ra Bargozedand*. (Those Who Chose Martyrdom). *Mujahideen-e-Khalq* Organization, 1975.
56. Rezai, A., *Rah-e-Hosein*. (The Way of Hosein) *Mujahideen-e-Khalq* Organization, 1971.
57. *Doktor Shariati*, Shariati Foundation and Hamgam Publishers, Tehran 1979.
58. Ibid., p. 44.
59. *Payvand-e-Pishtaz ba Khalq* (The Bond between the Vanguard and the Masses). Muslim Student's Association, Shiraz University, 1979.
60. Ibid.
61. *Anan Kay Shahadat Ra Bargozidand*. (Those Who Chose Marty-

rdom). *Mujahideen-e-Khalq*, 1975, p. 12.
62. Ibid.
63. *Ashura-Falsafa-e-Azadi*. (Ashura — the Philosophy of Freedom). Speech by Musa Khiabani at Tehran University Mosque 1979, p. 34 — 35.
64. Shariati, A., *Zamina-e-Shinakht-e-Qoran*, p. 35.
65. Shariati, A., *Shahadat*, p. 84.
66. Ibid.
67. Ibid.
68. Ibid., p.47.
69. *Sharh-e-Mokhtasar-e-Zindagi-e-Enqelabi va Namey-ha-va-Payam-ha-e-Mojahed-e-Shaheed Reza Rezai*. (A Brief Description of The Revolutionary Life, Letters, And Messages of Martyred Mujahid Reza Rezai) *Mujahideen-e-Khalq*. Second edition. October 1979.
70. Ibid.
71. Shariati, A., *Shahadat*, p. 73.
72. Ayatollah Taleqani's Public Statement on the Seventh Anniversary of The Execution of Founder Members of *Mujahideen-e-Khalq* Organization, Tehran, 25 May 1979.
73. Ibid.
74. Ibid.

8. Taleqani and the Revolution

'Taleqani had neither Left nor Right deviations.
He was on the straight path' — *Ayatollah Khomeini.*[1]

In 1975, SAVAK arrested Rahman Afrakhteh and Hasan Khamshi, two Marxists involved in the *coup* against *Mujahideen-e-Khalq's* Islamic leadership. Under interrogation, the two divulged many secrets of the organization including its connection with Ayatollah Taleqani. The most progressive of Iran's clergymen, Taleqani had been involved in the struggle against monarchy since the times of Reza Shah. During the Oil Crisis of the early 50s, he was among the few religious figures who continued their support of Mossadeq even after the political clerical leadership had abandoned him. After Mossadeq was overthrown in 1953, Taleqani resisted attempts by the royalist and conservative clergy to distort Mossadeq's role in Iranian history by forming the National Resistance Movement with Ustad Taqi Shariati, father of Ali Shariati, and Taher Ahmedzadeh a radical Islamic scholar.[2] His concern with developing a progressive Islamic ideology was channelised into the Liberation Movement which Mehdi Bazargaan and his foreign educated comrades had founded in 1962. The Liberation Movement presented an attempt by the religiously oriented Muslim intelligentsia to break the clerical monopoly over religion and develop a new approach to Islam that would synthesize the mild features of European Socialism with the progressive ideals of Islam.[3] It aimed at presenting Islam in a modern light that would be acceptable to the modern-educated middle class, the discontented intelligentsia and to the anti-Shah clergy, especially its junior ranks.[4] Besides helping the Liberation Movement to get started, Taleqani became the spiritual ideological guide for the younger members of the Liberation Movement who, in 1965, founded the *Mujahideen-e-Khalq* Organization.

The information revealed by Marxist members of the *Mujahideen* led to the immediate arrest of Taleqani. However, this was not the first time the Ayatollah was being taken to Pahlavi prisons. The greater part of his life had been interspersed with prison terms and exile. When Taleqani was arrested for the first time in 1935, he was placed in the same cell as a number of young communists who were later to form the Tudeh Party in 1941.[5] Taleqani had long discussions with his prison mates and tried to convince them about the validity of religious belief.[6] As a result of these discussions, Taleqani gained a first hand understanding of the goals and beliefs of communists, and in the years to come he developed a life long admiration for 'true communists' whom he had seen sacrificing their lives and getting mutilated under torture, 'for no personal gains of their own but for the sake of the ideal that at some future time, the toiling masses may live a better life.'[7] Over 30 years after his first imprisonment, Taleqani was in prison again where he once again became a witness to the transpersonal ideological commitment of young revolutionaries irrespective of their ideologies. As a part of psychological torture, Taleqani was taken to SAVAK's torture room where he was forced to watch the *Fedayeen* and *Mujahideen* revolutionaries brutally tortured. He was later placed in a cell located just next to the torture chamber so that he would hear the screams of prisoners being tortured. Another method SAVAK used for putting psychological pressure on Taleqani was to dump the battered, bloody, and often unconscious bodies of his students and other revolutionaries into his cell after they were tortured.[8]

Born in the Karaj district near Tehran in 1911, Taleqani's public career as an expounder of Islam as ideology began at the Hedayat Mosque in 1960. His discourses on the Quran and Islam at Hedayat Mosque marked the beginning of the progressive Islamic movement in Iran along well defined ideological and revolutionary lines. His weekly informal 'classes' at Hedayat Mosque were attended by students, intellectuals, bazaar merchants and teachers. These gatherings were the forerunners of the larger informal classes at Hosienieh Irshad where Dr. Ali Shariati began giving his lessons. Funds for the Hedayat Mosque were raised by a number of bazaar merchants, among them Haj Sadeq, a lifelong friend of Taleqani and father of Naser Sadeq, member of the Leadership Cadre (central committee) of the *Mujahideen-e-Khalq* Organization. 'We had never heard anyone speak about Islam with such freshness and clarity. On weekends, young men from neighbouring areas would travel 70 or 80 kilometres to attend Taleqani's lessons,' Haj Sadeq recalled after the Revolution. Although the number of people attending Taleqani's lessons at Hedayat Mosque remained limited these select gatherings furnished the base for an Islamic revolutionary vanguard which had a decisive influence on the course of the revolution. Among those who regularly attended Taleqani's lessons were Mohammad Hanif-nejad and Ahmed Rezai, the intellectual leaders of *Mujahideen-e-Khalq*. Later when Taleqani was in prison again, Mohammad Hanif-nejad was among his regular visitors and their exchanges on ideological issues continued. These meetings became more frequent after Taleqani was released from prison.[9]

Taleqani personally organized collection of funds among bazaar merchants for the *Mujahideen* as well as for families of political prisoners and revolutionaries executed by the Shah's regime.[10] He was also instrumental in winning the release of nine *Mujahideen* in 1974 who hijacked an aircraft belonging to Iran's national airline, to Baghdad. On reaching Baghdad, the *Mujahideen* hijackers were imprisoned and tortured by Iraqi security agents who suspected them of being SAVAK spies.[11] When Taleqani learned about the incident, he wrote Ayatollah Khomeini in Najaf a secret letter using invisible ink on the inside wrapper of a cigarette packet, requesting him to use his influence to get the *Mujahideen* hijackers released. However, it was through the help of a Palestinian leader that the hijackers were finally released.[12]

When the Liberation Movement was formed, Taleqani anticipated that the regime would employ all means at its disposal to discredit and destroy the movement and the image of its leaders among the people. 'Under conditions when to have personality and individual autonomy is a crime, the creation of a group by individuals with personality and character would become an unforgivable crime. Such a group would be branded with all the possible crimes, such as posing a threat to public security, opposition to the regime's reforms, or acting against the principles of religion and the wishes of the Prophet. Such a group, therefore, must be annihilated. Its members must be imprisoned and left to rot in prison cells for years without any human justification, under unimaginable torture and physical and spiritual suffering.'[13]

As Taleqani had predicted, before long the leaders of the Liberation Movement were arrested on charges of anti-State activities. When the younger members of the Liberation Movement went underground and formed the *Mujahideen-e-Khalq* Organization, the regime stepped up its propaganda campaign even more vigorously, claiming that since *Mujahideen* were opposing religion and Islam, shedding their blood was a religious duty.

While the principal target of Taleqani's lifelong struggle remained the despotic regime of the imperialist-backed Shah, much of his energies were taken up in resisting the destructive propaganda of obscurantist clergy against him and against other progressive Muslims like Dr. Shariati, Bazargan and the *Mujahideen-e-Khalq*. These clerics, whether they were royalists or formalists, had one common denominator, in that they labelled, according to Taleqani, 'every young and creative thinker an "infidel" '[14] and who believed that Muslim intellectuals 'wearing suits and neckties had no business mixing themselves with Islam'.[15] Many clergymen never forgave Taleqani for hiding Kasravi, a leading communist intellectual, in his house at a time when SAVAK was conducting a massive manhunt for him.

Leading the Islamic Revolution
After he was arrested in 1975 following the disclosure by the breakaway group of Marxist *Mujahideen*, Taleqani remained in prison until

October 1978. By then the demand to free political prisoners had become the Revolution's central issue, given its immediacy and tangibility, and a rallying focus for the Movement against the Pahlavi dictatorship. The regime found itself compelled to partly meet this demand and released Ayatollah Taleqani along with hundreds of political prisoners, including over a hundred members of the *Mujahideen* and *Fedayeen* in October 1978. Immediately after he was out of prison, Taleqani became the nucleus of the Revolution inside Iran. His popularity among the people and the trust most political groups and various classes of people had in him converted his house into the Revolution's headquarters. Taleqani thus became the voice and spokesman of the Revolution. He remained in direct contact with Khomeini in Paris apprising him of the day by day situation in the country. Taleqani's house, which had been converted into the 'office of Ayatollah Taleqani' became the centre for co-ordinating the Revolution. Most of the strikes and sit-ins in factories and offices were co-ordinated at this office. The most important strike organized by this office was that of the oil workers which gradually strangulated the regime. Thus, from November 1978 to January 1979, Iran was completely engulfed and paralysed by strikes. This period marked the space of time when the Revolution was dealing its most telling blows against the regime. In addition to strategically planning the Revolution, Taleqani's office also served as the centre for the monetary contribution people were making for the Revolution, as well as its distribution among the families of the wounded and the killed. The office had become the co-ordinating centre for information and for circulating the bulletins Khomeini issued from Paris. With the confrontation between the Army and people dragging on, Taleqani's house became the only refuge for soldiers and officers defecting from the Imperial army.

One of the most crucial decisions Taleqani made at his 'office' was the call for a public march on 10 December, the day marking *Tasu'a,* a day of special religious significance for Muslims, particularly Shia Muslims. On this day, mourning ceremonies for the martyrdom of Imam Hosein, grandson of Prophet Mohammad who was killed over 13 centuries ago by Yazid, the tyrant usurper of the Islamic State, attain a climax. Taleqani had given the call for a mass religious procession, defying the martial law General Azhari's military government had imposed. The regime had announced it would crush any violation of the martial law under any pretext without hesitation. In a bulletin he issued a day before the demonstration, Taleqani laid down the broad guidelines for politicizing this religious procession: 'All the banners and slogans during this period of mourning should be loaded with political content and protest against the existence of the Pahlavi regime in the country. The hands of the mourners used for hitting their heads and breasts should now become clenched fists of protest and resistance against the existing conditions. In the light of God's Will which endorses destruction and annihilation of the oppressor and victory of the deprived people fighting for their rights, the struggle of the Muslim people of Iran would continue until final victory is achieved. We should be aware that the Will of the deprived nations fighting for their rights is the Will of God, expressing itself through their hands, voice, and actions. Surely, Dawn is at hand.'[16]

Following this message, a number of conservative clergymen who feared massive massacre by the Shah's army, opposed the holding of demonstrations under Martial Law. Despite these objections, Taleqani, issued the call for the march.[17]

During the night before the demonstrations, the Military regime deployed tanks and armoured vehicles in different parts of Tehran for intimidating people and preventing them from participating in the march. The army-controlled radio and television kept on beaming sombre messages regarding the disastrous consequences if people took part in the religious procession. Soon the rumour began spreading that crack units of the Imperial Guards were preparing to attack Taleqani's house. Throughout the night, the telephone in Taleqani's house kept ringing as calls from various quarters, even from abroad, kept pouring in, urging him to cancel the procession in view of the feared scale of bloodshed.[18] Despite this atmosphere of tension, rumours, and uncertainty, Taleqani stood firmly by his decision.

On the morning of 10 December over one million people came on to the streets and marched along Tehran's main thoroughfare. The army which had threatened to crush the march had backed out in the final showdown. This meant the people had scored a decisive victory. The massive turnout in this demonstration, and in the still larger march that followed the next day, convinced the world of the popular breadth and intensity of the movement against the Shah. People from all classes had participated in this procession, which amounted to 'a vote of no confidence to the regime'.[19] It was after this massive show of force by the people against a regime they detested that America began thinking in earnest of salvaging its stakes in Iran even if it meant renouncing the Shah and the monarchy. The December demonstration became the first of the colossal demonstrations that made Iran's Islamic Revolution a unique revolution in history in terms of the mobilization of urban masses.

Taleqani and the Power Monopolists

In January 1979, when it became clear that Khomeini would be soon flying back to Tehran, a group of unknown or little known clergymen took the initiative in capitalising upon the occasion by forming the 'Centre for Welcoming the Imam (Khomeini)'. As a result, these clergymen effectively monopolized all arrangements relating to Khomeini's return and his subsequent installation in Tehran. Through the 'Welcome Centre', this group succeeded in making itself the counterpoint to 'Taleqani's office' and subsequently, the new power centre in the country. The Welcome Centre, began playing down Taleqani's role in the movement by ignoring him altogether. For example, Taleqani had suggested that since all classes and sections of the people were involved in the Revolution, representatives from all classes and sections of society, and not the clergy alone, should be allowed to participate in the special ceremonies for receiving Ayatollah Khomeini at the airport. The Welcome Centre, however, ignored this suggestion. Instead, it invited clergymen of its own choice to receive the Ayatollah at the airport. Moreover, while the Welcome Centre issued hundreds of special invitations to the clergymen it wanted, only four cards were sent to Taleqani's office,[20] that had so far been the nerve centre of the Revolution. A week after the Shah's regime had fallen, the men behind the Welcome Centre consolidated their gains and proceeded towards institutionalizing their authority by forming the Islamic Republic Party (IRP). After its formation was announced on 18 February 1979, many clergymen rushed to join IRP, for by associating itself with Khomeini it was evident that the IRP would become a major force in the country. Many of those flocking to join the Party had little, if any, revolutionary background. Others had been to prison briefly for opposing the Shah, but had regained their freedom and the Shah's favours by signing 'documents of repentence' for their anti-Shah activities. Only a few of its leaders were revolutionaries. Taleqani's remarks on these developments were placed in a historical context. Predicting that the Revolution would deviate from its progressive, anti-dictatorial, and anti-imperialist path he said: 'After every revolution, a group of opportunists stick themselves to the revolution. This causes the revolution to deviate from its path. However, this in itself is a factor in the evolution of the revolution, and revolution becomes a continuous affair.'[21]

Taleqani and the Communists

Throughout the Revolution, Taleqani remained the point of confluence for the various forces thrusting forward the Revolution—nationalists, communists, liberals and social democrats, progressive Muslims, clergymen and the masses. He was particularly concerned about dispelling the misgivings communists and their supporters might have had about the possibility that the clergy would once again use the pretext of 'Communist threat' for crushing the communists after the Revolution succeeded in overthrowing the Shah. At the same Ayatollah Taleqani made it clear to the masses in several public addresses that 'true communists' did not pose any threat to the revolutionary, dynamic, and anti-exploitive spirit of Islam — a conviction that was born of Taleqani's living experience and observation of those communist revolutionaries whom he had seen decapitated or killed under torture or by the firing squad for selflessly pursuing a motive that they themselves knew could never have led to any personal gain or advantage. In a speech he made at Hedayat Mosque on 18 January 1979, Taleqani said: 'I have witnessed the selfless sacrifice of these leftist youth, both inside and outside the prison. Their conscience, thought, and motive, their aspiration and quest, was the same (as that of the Muslims). (It was a quest) for freedom. Owing to internal and international reasons they are drawn to the Left. They have made sacrifices, lost their lives, and have given blood. We respect them because their conviction to fight for freedom and their (revolutionary action) has emanated from their true nature, from the depths of their conscience, and from the higher side of human nature. If they are prepared to lay down their lives, suffer pain, get killed under terrible and ghastly tortures so that the working classes may gain control of their factories in the distant future, it is because of their (intrinsic and higher) conscience. Their authentic inner nature and human conscience has propelled them to do this. They have not seen any clearly defined and precise religion to motivate them, and all this superstitious nonsense (about religion) has caused them to be dissatisfied with (formalist) religion and adopt a different path. They were dissatisfied because they wanted freedom and suffered its lack. I respect such selfless and strong people who have made so many sacrifices and have laid down their lives, who endured imprisonment for a quarter of a century. I respect them from the human angle, and not because they belong to a particular ideology. We do not, never, reject anybody (because of his ideology).'[22]

For Taleqani, the problem of Islam versus Communists, so compounded by imperialism, the obscurantists, and vested interests in Muslim societies for purely selfish reasons, needed a basic clarification. He dealt with this issue in the heart of Iran's religious centre, the city of Qom, at the Faizieh Theological School, one of the most famous religious schools in the world where Ayatollah Khomeini had taught Philosophy and Islamic law for many years.

Addressing thousands of students at the Theological School, Taleqani said, 'The problem of Communism is separate from the unscientific problem of materialism. In terms of its true and authentic linguistic meaning, Communism, that is, communal family life, has been founded by Islam. That's the way it was during the early days of the Islamic society founded by the Prophet. The life of the Prophet and his Companions, and the *Mohajerin* (those who migrated from Mecca to Medina) and the *Ansars* (residents of Medina) was like this. However, this does not include historical materialism and the primacy of matter. We must separate the two (i.e., communal way of living based on brotherhood and equality, from historical materialism).

'Communism is the child of political and religious dictatorship. In any country where there is despotism, exploitation, dictatorship, and deprivation among the masses, and where a distorted version of religion is supporting the despotism in power, communism would develop by itself. The issue of communism is different from the problem whether materialism is scientific or not.

'If we consider Islam so weak as to be incapable of confronting materialism, the history-based ideology of communism, it is because we have not understood Islam, or, indeed we (secretly) consider Islam to be inadequate. Islam is not inadequate. It is we who have not understood Islam and its direction towards equity and freedom.'[23] In an interview on 6 February 1979,[24] only five days before the Tehran Uprising put the final nail in the monarchy's coffin, a correspondent asked Taleqani whether there would be a place for communists in the Islamic Republic and whether he considered them to be Un-Islamic. Taleqani reiterated in his reply that the problem of ideology was different from the problem of struggle against imperialism and exploitation. 'From the point of view of struggle, we have ourselves witnessed that so many of them (communists) have been killed, have endured long prison terms, and without any doubt, had a share in this struggle. Our differences are ideological. We have no differences in our struggle.' Taleqani added that if the Iranian communists were not associated with foreign powers and were not opposed to 'our struggle against despotism, imperialism, and exploitation', they would have no contradiction with the Revolution. Noting that the communists considered themselves to be supporters of the impoverished masses and the deprived, Taleqani added, 'Our slogan is the same, that the oppressed and wronged against masses should be relieved and ameliorated. When we establish the Islamic Government on the basis of democracy and freedom, (communists) will be free also, both in expressing themselves and in organizing themselves.'[25]

That the Islamic Revolution was directed against despotism, imperialism, and exploitation remained the central theme of Taleqani's speeches. He saw no reason why all groups and forces who shared these objectives could not be included in the great task of restructuring and reconstructing the society. Unity of all anti-imperialist and anti exploitative forces remained the focal theme of his public speeches. He saw no reason why certain clergymen, in the name of Islam, or some communists, in the name of their ideology, exhibited the tendency for raising peripheral issues: 'What do we want? Is it anything other than severing the grip of imperialism and effacing exploitation? Are these not the problems with which Islam and the Quran deals? Or is it that we do not wish to acknowledge this fact. Either we are not aware of this (that Islam and the Quran are against imperialism and exploitation) or we do not want to become aware of this fact. Islam, the Islam that we know, the Islam which emanates from the Quran and the Sunnah of the Prophet, does not restrict freedom. Any group who desires to restrict people's freedom and their right to criticize, to express themselves, to discuss, and to argue, does not comprehend Islam. Any group which does not want that despotism, imperialism, and exploitation be uprooted has not understood Islam.'[26] Referring to the communists and other secular groups, Taleqani said, "What is it that these groups want? Is it anything other than equity, justice, and freedom? The secular groups also want equity and justice and effacement of exploitation and annihilation of imperialism. Who says that the Quran supports exploitation and imperialism?"

As Taleqani explained, the central economic and social concept that Islam lay stress upon was equity, which meant giving everyone the right that was his due and returning to him the fruits of his labour and thought. It meant the negation of exploitation of man by man 'which is the most evil phenomenon in human society since history began. It is the vilest and meanest of all phenomena that have emerged in history.'[27]

It was in this speech delivered to a crowd of over a million to commemorate the 25th anniversary of Mossadeq's national movement that Taleqani made some significant remarks about how Islam regarded those revolutionaries who were not religious and yet were selflessly fighting to bring equity and justice in human society. 'The problem of equity is of such great importance in religion and in Islam that the Quran places the murderers of even those persons who have nothing to do with religion, yet are fighting for the cause of equity, in the same category as the murderers of Prophets.'[28] Taleqani supported this contention by quoting from the Quran the relevant verse: 'Those who veil the verses of God, those who unjustly kill the Prophets, *and also unjustly kill those who have risen for equity,* promise them a painful agony.' (*Al-Imran:* 20). Elaborating this issue further, Taleqani said that those who were familiar with the interpretation of the Quran knew that in the above verse, the murder of those persons who have risen for establishing equity points to a group other than the Prophets. That is,

to a people who had not heard or comprehended the call of the Prophet. 'Such people are not to be accused, for, nevertheless they move on the path towards equity. They have risen for actualizing *qest* (equity). The Quran ranks their murderers with those who murder the Prophets. It has warned their murderers of a painful doom. This is the liberating truth of Islam since its first days.'[29]

A few weeks before his death, during a meeting with the first Cuban delegation to Iran, Taleqani spoke about the similarities and differences between the Islamic Revolution and other revolutions. 'We have common ideas with the Marxists in negating exploitation and imperialism, and for safeguarding freedom. What we do not accept is the primacy given to materialism (by the Marxists). We believe in the primacy of God. We believe in the Primacy of a Conscious and Creative Origin. We regard the Cuban Revolution a magnificent revolution. In fact, any revolution in any part of the world which is against injustice, despotism, and imperialism is, in our view, an Islamic revolution.'[30]

It was this liberating image of Islam that Taleqani and other progressive Muslims had projected which mobilized a whole nation to fight for its freedom in an Islamic framework, the ultimate framework for freedom. Taleqani had declared several times that 'under Islam we shall never tolerate despotism'.[31] This was a fundamental principle, 'an unalterable principle. An overall, irrevocable principle'.[32] On the basis of this principle, everyone had the right to be free and autonomous. No one had the right to take freedom away from man, for freedom was so sacred that 'man is prepared to give away all he has for it'.[33] The distinct feature of an Islamic government, according to Taleqani, was that no single individual or group could impose its will on the people or suppress them and control society... 'Nobody has been given this right. Even Prophets were not given this right. Similarly, no single individual or party has any right to impose its self-righteous control over others. Control and leadership are two different things. In the Islamic system of government, it is possible for a person to be in a position of leadership, but he has no right for controlling and dominating people'.[34] Surely then, it was this liberating and tolerant image of Islam that Taleqani had projected as the spokesman for the Revolution and its leadership which unified over 95% of the Iranian population under the banner of the Islamic Revolution. His death in September, 1979 removed one of the main hurdles in the way of religious monopolists to consolidate their dictatorship in the name of religion.

Notes

1. (Khomeini's address to the family of Ayatollah Taleqani, Qom), Kayhan, No.10807, 15 September 1979.
2. Afrasiabi, B. and Dehqan, S., *Taleqani and History*, Tehran, 1980.
3. Abrahimian, E., *The Guerrilla Movement in Iran.* MERIP. Vol.10, No.3, March-April, 1979, p.9.
4. Ibid.
5. Afrasiabi, B., and Dehqan, S., *Taleqani and History*.
6. Ibid., p.371-73.
7. Ibid.
8. Ibid.
9. Ibid.
10. Ibid., p.318.
11. Ibid.
12. Ibid., p.300-301.
13. Ibid., p.185.
14. Ibid., p.295.
15. Ibid.
16. Ibid., p.358-59.

17. Ibid.
18. Ibid.
19. Ibid., p.359.
20. Ibid.
21. Ibid., p.388.
22. Ibid., p.371–73.
23. *Taleqani der Faizieh.* (Taleqani at Faizieh). Tehran, 1979, p. 23-24.
24. Afrasiabi, B, and Dehqan, S., *Taleqani and History,* p.391.
25. Ibid., p.391-92.
26. Taleqani's Speech at Baharistan Square, Tehran, 21 July 1979.
27. Ibid.
28. Ibid.
29. Ibid.
30. Interview with Cuban delegation, 4 August 1979. Quoted in *Taleqani and History.*
31. Ibid., p.403.
32. Ibid.
33. Ibid.
34. Ibid.

9. The Islamic Revolution I

The Revolution began with the slogan 'Down with the Shah'. It needed no further elaboration. It simply called for the overthrow of a monarchical system that had sustained itself over the years through sheer tyranny. Torture, suppression and injustice had become synonymous with the Pahlavi regime. Religion came to this slogan's support and the Islamic Revolution was born.[1] Freedom, Independence and Justice were the objectives of this Revolution, and in so far as they were sought in an Islamic context, the Revolution was Islamic.[2]

The revolutionary process had been fermenting in Iran since America brought back the Shah to power in 1953, and was directly influenced by the international situation especially the political developments after Carter became President of the United States. When Carter stepped into the White House, the revolutionary process in Iran had already entered its final phase and was headed for an all out eruption.

It had taken a quarter of a century for the social, economic, political and intellectual forces to assume the constellation necessary for generating revolution. In the 25 years since the 1953 *coup,* a lot of economic development had taken place owing to the fact that Iran's oil revenues had sky rocketed from $ 34 million per year in 1953 to $ 20 billion in 1977.[3] Of the $ 54 billion in cummulative income during this period and despite the massive wastage of oil revenues for satiating the Shah's regal whims, nearly $ 30 billion were spent on economic and social projects for development. Particularly impressive was the expansion and growth in the educational and industrial fields as evidenced in the significant increases in the two modern classes — the salaried middle class and the urban proleteriat. During 1953—77, the modern middle class had increased from 324,000 to 630,000. In addition, there were nearly a million students in secondary schools, higher education, and foreign universities who intended to join the salaried middle class. The urban working class had also grown rapidly, from 30,000 in 1953 to 1.7 million in 1977.[4] However, the Pahlavi regime failed to win support from either the salaried middle class or the urban proletariat because of two reasons: 'First, the 1953 *coup* not only overthrew the popular leader Dr. Mossadeq, but also destroyed labour unions, professional associations, and all independent political parties, causing an unbridgeable gulf between the regime and the two modern classes. Second, the regime widened the gulf by implementing policies benefitting the upper classes rather than the middle and lower classes, who had no pressure group through which they could alter or peacefully oppose government decisions.'[5]

Moreover, the agrarian reforms of the 'White Revolution' had failed to liquidate large landholding. The glaring inequality in land ownership was compounded by the inequality in the cities, where the regime's strategy of developing the economy by helping private entrepreneurs had led to a dramatic increase in comprador capitalism. Thus, during the 70s the Iranian society represented 'one of the most inegalitarian societies of the world'[6] according to an unpublished report of the International Labour office. The top 20% of urban families accounted for as much as 55.5% of the total family expenditures, the bottom 20% for as little as 3.7% and the middle 40% for no more than 26%.[7] The socio-economic tensions, therefore, were aggravated 'not by modernization *per se,* but by the way the modernization was implemented and by the fact that the capitalist method of modernization invariably benefits the rich more than the rest of the society'.[8] By 1977, nearly two million rural migrants had clustered in the shanty towns around the Capital to provide the revolution with another active base.

While the Shah modernized society, he did little to broaden the support base for his monarchy by winning over the modern urban classes and by opening political channels for social forces and pressure groups.[9] Instead, he formed the Resurgence Party *(Hezb-e-Rastakhiz)* to 'transform his military monarchy into a fascist style totalitarian regime'.[10] The objectives of the Resurgence Party lay in tightening control over the intelligentsia and extending state power into the bazaars and religious establishment.[11]

While the Shah was burning his bridges to the salaried middle class and the intelligentsia, progressive Muslim intellectuals like Dr. Shariati, Taleqani and Bazargan were building a modern Islamic bridge to these groups. Given a revolutionary redefinition in progressive, anti-despotic, anti-imperialist and anti-exploitive terms, Islam was becoming a rallying focus both emotionally as well as intellectually among the middle class, the students, and intelligentsia — forces that had largely remained distant from Khomeini's formalist Islam during the June Uprising in 1963.

SAVAK and the Guerrilla Organizations
Perhaps more significant than all these factors in lending moral, psychological and human justification to the revolution was the distress and silent rage which the Shah had generated among people through SAVAK, his agency for repressive control. Students found in possession of ideological tracts, whether Islamic or Marxist, would be locked up in jail for as long as SAVAK wished. Such persons were brutally tortured,

Demonstrators carry portraits of Dr. Ali Shariati (left), the *Mujahideen-e-Khalq* emblem (centre), and Ayatolah Khomeini—the three Islamic forces in the Revolution (Tehran, 1978)

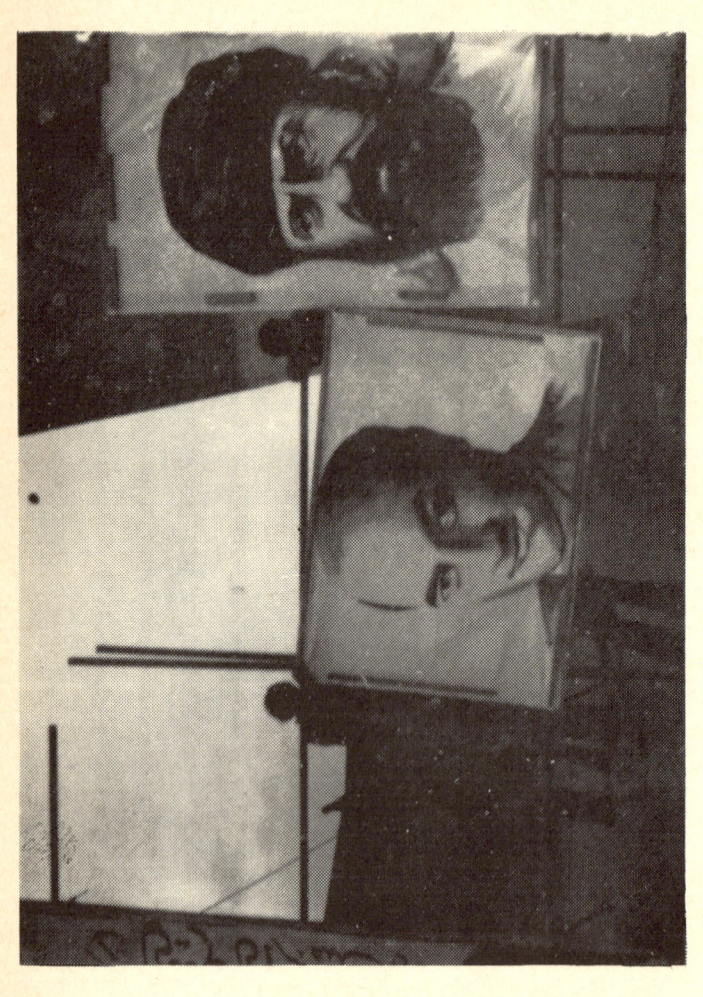

Huge posters of Syed Jamal-ud-Din Afghani and Dr. Ali Shariati on exhibition in Tehran during the Revolution.

Mehdi Bazargaan (centre), Professor of Physics at Tehran University and a leader of the Liberation Movement flanked by Ayatollah Taleqani (right) and Ali Asghar Baadizadegaan, Lecturer in Chemistry at Tehran University, a member of the Liberation Movement and a founder member of *Mujahideen-e-Khalq* organization (Tehran, 1965).

A group of *Mujahideen* after conquest of Tehran during the Constitutional Revolution.

Mirza Kuchak Khan with a group of *mujahideen* of the Jungle Revolution

Mirza Kuchak Khan (centre) as Leader of the Revolutionary Council of the Socialist Republic of Gilan photographed with other members of the Council and Soviet advisers.

Execution of *mujahideen* in the Jungle Revolution after arrest by Tehran Government.

Prime Minister Mossadeq at the military trial after the 1953 *coup*.

Ayatollah Khomeini in June 1963.

The Islamic Revolution. Below the *Allah* banner are pictures of founder members of *Mujahideen-e-Khalq* Organization executed by the Pahlavi regime in 1972. The three posters in the rear respectively show Mirza Kuchak Khan, Dr. Ali Shariati, and Reza Rezai, a *mujahideen* leader..

Dr. Ali Shariati — Architect of Islamic Revolution.

University wall in Tehran during the Revolution. Dr. Ali Shariati's picture Flanked by founder members of *Mujahideen-e-Khalq* organization. Photographs on top left show some of the *Mujahideen* members killed by the Pahlavi regime during 1972–77.

A giant Shariati poster in a mass demonstration against the Pahlavi regime. Below his picture is a passage from Shariati's book *Shahadat*. The banner behind Shariati shows members of *Mujahideen-e-Khalq* Ahmed, Mehdi, Sadiqa (concealed) and Reza – the three brothers and a sister from the Rezai family who were killed by SAVAK during *Mujahideen-e-Khalq*'s struggle against the Pahlavi dictatorship.

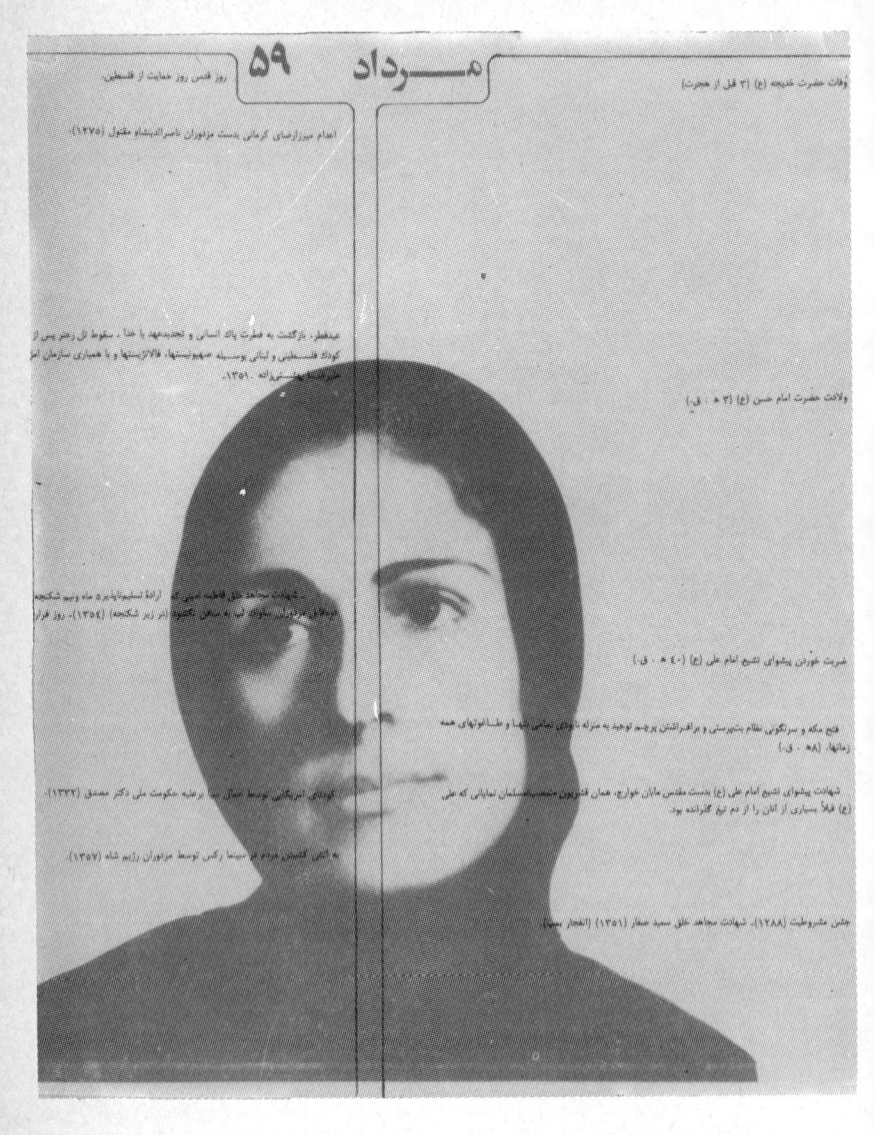

Fatima Amini, the first revolutionary Muslim woman killed under torture seen on the official calendar of *Muahideen-e-Khalq*.

A banner from the main movement against the Pahlavi dictatorship with pictures of Mehbobeh (first left) and her husband Hasan (third left) and other male and female *mujahideen* martyrs who became 'models' for the young Iranian revolutionaries.

Ayatollah Taleqani during confinement in Pahlavi regime's prisons.

Flanked by *Mujahideen-e-Khalq* guerrillas, Ayatollah Taleqani addressing a massive public rally a few weeks before the Pahlavi regime was otherthrown.

Ayatollah Taleqani (marked x) stands left out at Tehran airport as Ayatollah Beheshti and his Committee for Welcoming Imam Khomeini step forth to take over Komeini in a bid to take over the Revolution.

November 1978. Pahlavi regime's Imperial Guards attack Tehran University, nerve centre of the struggle against monarchical despotism.

Demonstrators against the Pahlavi dictatorship carry militant posters of *Mujahideen-e-Khalq* urging people for armed uprising. The model of the urban guerrilla erupted to life at a collective level in the general armed uprising on 10 February 1979.

Clad in blue jeans, progressive revolutionaries hold a roof top position against the Imperial Guards during the battle of Tehran.

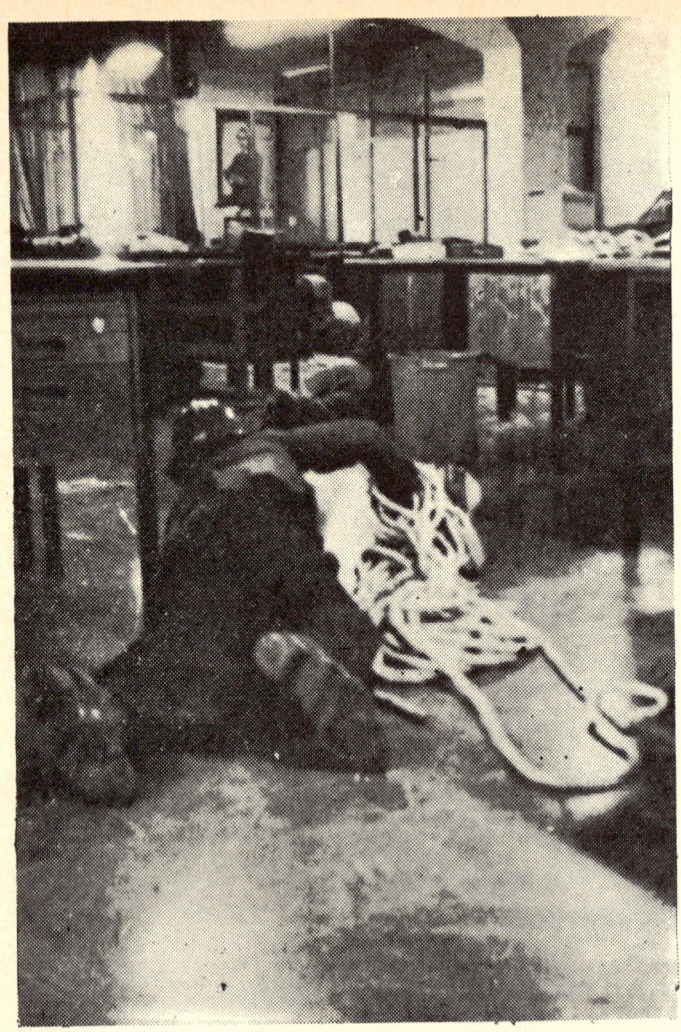

During the battle of Tehran, a *Fedayi* urban guerrilla who was manouvering for a better firing position for the control of *SAVAK* headquarters was shot by the Shah's forces. He fell from the fourth floor, crashing through the windows of the adjacent building housing the editorial offices of Ettela'at, one of the mass circulation dailies. Later the newspaper's staff placed red carnations on the spot where the young revolutionary passed away.

Masood Rajavi, member of *Mujahideen's* Central Committee addresses supporters at a Tehran rally in June 1980.

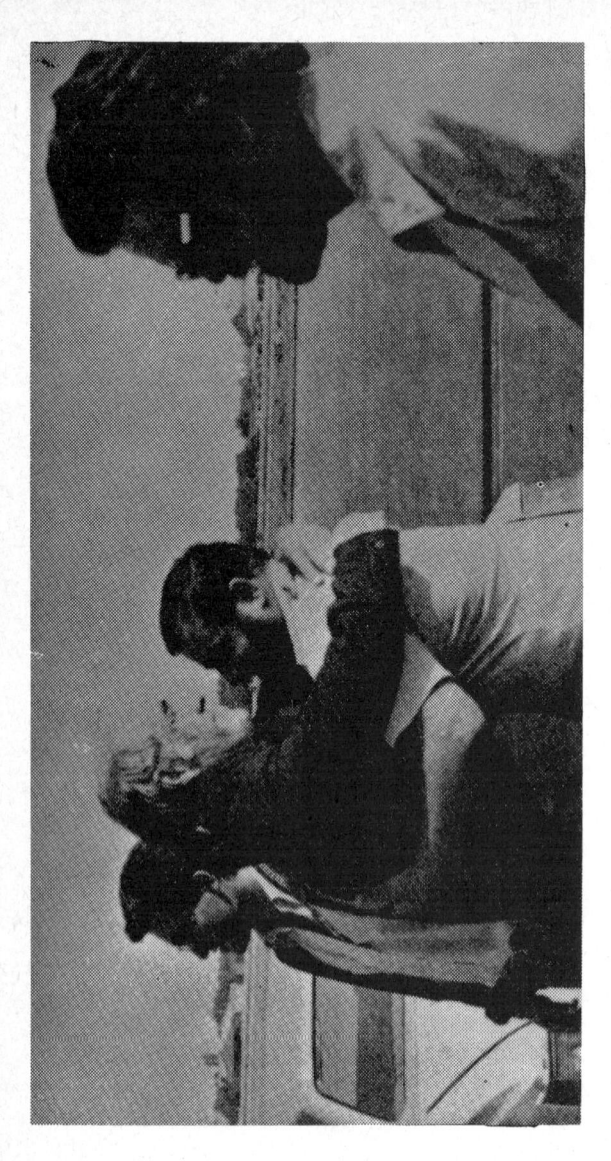

Mashallah Qasab, a former butcher and head of the Islamic Revolutionary Guards unit installed by Khomeini's regime at Tehran's U.S. embassy hugs Charles Naas, head of security office of the embassy, as he leaves for the U.S.

Wheelchair campaigner proves the popularity of PMOI candidate Mas'ud Rajavi.

A youngman who lost his leg to gunshot wounds during the struggle against the Pahlavi regime is seen campaigning for Masood Rajavi, a candidate for the Presidential elections held in 1980. Following Ayatollah Taleqani and some other progressive Muslims, *Mujahideen-e-Khalq* had also opposed a clause in the new Constitution legitimizing the absolute rule of Theolegians. Khomeini disqualified Rajavi from the Presidential elections for taking this stand.

A determined Sheikh Ezzedin Husseini, foremost religious leader of Kurdish Muslims, who supports Rajavi and *Mujahideen-e-Khalq*.

January 1979, Shah's soldiers shoot to kill a student *in front of* Tehran University.

Funeral procession of *Mujahideen* leader Shokrollah Moshkinfom, slain in Mashhad by 'Club-Wielders' during the 'Cultural Revolution' for closure of Universities in 1980.

Ayatollah Tehrani (centre) performing the funeral rites at the burial of a *Mujahideen-e-Khalq* leader at Mashhad's cemetry in 1980. On the Ayatollah's right stands Tahir Ahmedzadeh, one of the founders of The Progressive Islamic Movement in Iran. Ahmedzadeh, who was appointed Governor of Khurrasan Province by Khomeini after the fall of the Shah, resigned to show his protest against the street killings.

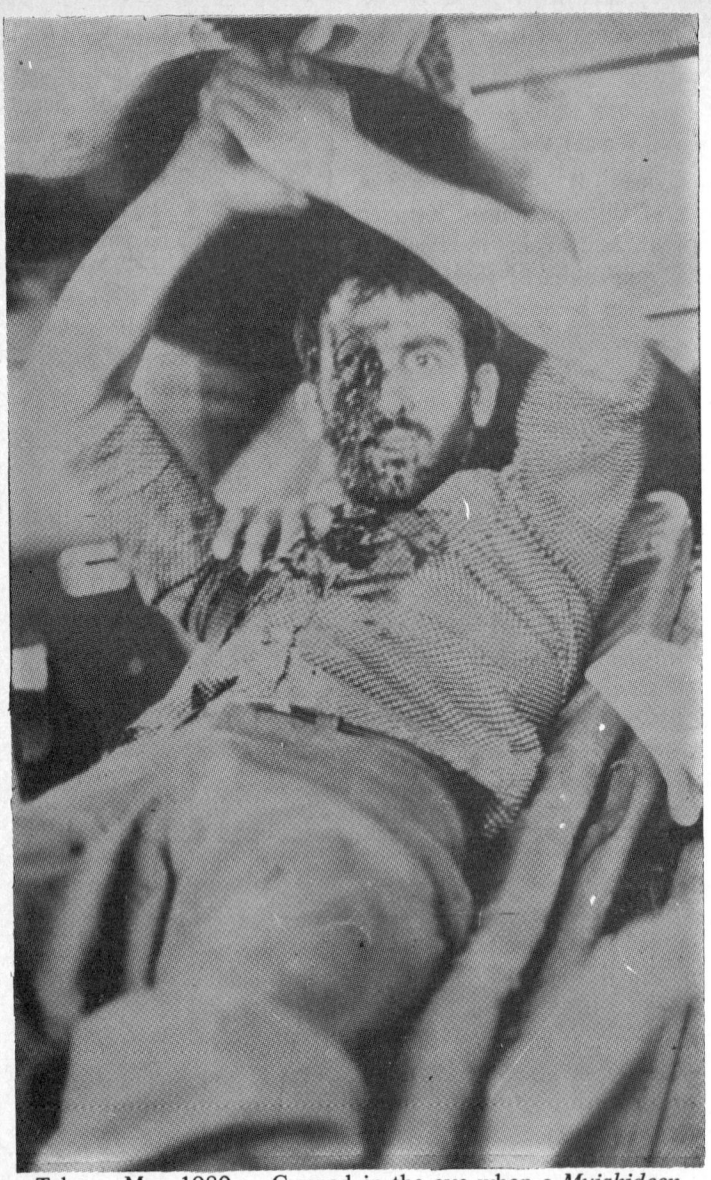

Tehran, May 1980 — Gunned in the eye when a *Mujahideen* rally in Tehran was held under the barrage of Khomeini's militia's bullets, this supporter of *Mujahideen* raises his arms as a symbol of unflinching resolve to the cause of freedom, as he is taken away on a stretcher to the ambulance.

A brooding Ayatollah Taleqani chooses to sit on the floor of the clergy dominated Assembly as a mark of protest against the abduction of the Revolution by the monopolist clergy.

A firing squad of the Islamic regime at work in Kurdistan. Those executed above included a wounded man who was brought for the execution on a stretcher. This execution which took place in August, 1979, was the forerunner of the large scale executions that have followed on a national scale after Banisadr was ousted from Presidency in June, 1981, with *Imam Jummas* of the Khomeini regime declearing in *Namaz-e-Jummas* that killing anti-Khomeini street demonstrators even if they were wounded, was *'halal'* (religiously sanctioned).

Mrs. Zahra Rezai, the mother who lost three sons and a daughter to the firing squads of the Pahlavi regime for membership in *Mujahideen-e-Khalq* during the early seventies, addresses a *Mujahideen* rally in Tabriz, a provincial capital. Several clerical leaders of Khomeini's regime have compared Mrs. Rezai to Hazrat Ayesha, wife of Prophet Mohammad, for opposing clerical regime.

Women supporters of *Mujahideen-e-Khalq* demonstrating against the Pahlavi dictatorship in January 1979.

The 19 year old Mehdi Rezai making his defence speech in Pahlavi regime's court of justice a few hours before he was executed.

Mehdi Rezai as last photographed by SAVAK during a break in the torture session that killed him. The above photograph became a revolutionary banner for the struggle of uncompromising progressive Muslims against dictatorship.

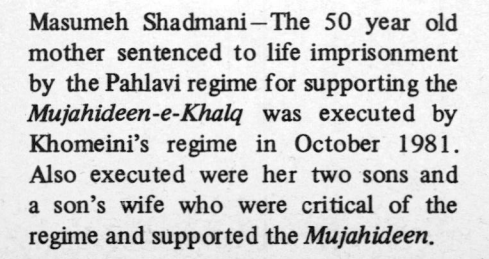

Masumeh Shadmani—The 50 year old mother sentenced to life imprisonment by the Pahlavi regime for supporting the *Mujahideen-e-Khalq* was executed by Khomeini's regime in October 1981. Also executed were her two sons and a son's wife who were critical of the regime and supported the *Mujahideen*.

Ayatollah Taleqani greets *Mujahideen-e-Khalq* leaders Musa Khiabani (R) and Masood Rajavi (centre) on being released from Shah's prison during the movement against the Pahlavi dictatorship.

April 1980. Khomeini's Revolutionary Guards gunning students *inside* Tehran University.

A unit of *Mujahideen-e-Khalq* guerrillas during the conquest of Tabriz on 11 February 1979. In the centre, raising a gun and a Shariati poster is Musa Khiabani, a top leader of *Mujahideen-e-Khalq*. Khiabani was killed by Khomeini's Islamic Guards in Tehran exactly two years after the above picture was taken.

sometimes leading to permanent physical impairment or death.

During the six years between 1971, when the *Fedayeen* and *Mujahideen* guerrilla organizations launched their operations and 1977, the year the Islamic Revolution began to unfold, SAVAK had killed, through bullets and torture, over 350 persons for their opposition to the regime. Almost 80% of those killed belonged to *Fedayeen-e-Khalq* and the *Mujahideen-e-Khalq*, and the rest to smaller Islamic and Marxist groups. Only two of the 355 killed by the regime were clergymen.[12] Countless others were imprisoned and tortured for suspected anti-state activities. It was in view of the torture meted out to members of guerrilla organizations often leading to their death, and their summary trials, often ending up in execution, that in 1975 Amnesty International credited the Shah's regime with 'the highest rate of death penalties in the world and a history of torture which is beyond belief'.[13]

In terms of class background, almost all the guerrillas came from the ranks of the young intelligentsia. They included nearly 150 students, and over a hundred engineers, teachers, office employees, professors, lawyers, architects and doctors. 14 housewives, all married to university graduates, and 22 factory workers were also among the 355 revolutionaries that SAVAK had killed.[14] The growth of the guerrilla movement in no way correlated with any decline in the economy. On the contrary, the movement developed at a time of middle class prosperity, rising salaries, employment opportunities for college graduates and a six fold expansion in university enrolment. In fact, almost all the dead guerrillas had been able to go to university either because they had won state scholarships or because their upwardly mobile middle class families could afford to pay the tuition fees. They took up arms as a result of social, moral, and political indignation, rather than as a result of economic deprivation.[15]

With the stepping up of guerrilla operations by *Mujahideen-e-Khalq* and the *Fedayeen-e-Khalq,* SAVAK's attempts at exterminating members and sympathizers of these organizations had become increasingly reckless. For example, SAVAK agents would pick up unsuspecting youngsters from university hostels, city streets, and the queues formed for entrance to cinema halls counting on the random possibility, that the victim might turn out to be a guerrilla sympathizer or contact. Before long, it was no longer necessary for a youth to look like a dissident or a guerrilla sympathizer in order to court the possibility of sudden arrest. In one of the better known incidents, a SAVAK agent shot and killed a man in a posh shoe store in front of the victim's wife and mother. The agent, who was accompanying the wife of a high ranking SAVAK official during her shopping, had become enraged by a remark the victim had made after the SAVAK agent had insulted his wife and falsely accused her of stealing his lady's handbag. Although the regime tried to cover up the incident, a journalist at *Ettela'at,* the daily with the largest circulation, decided to follow up the story. Since SAVAK could never allow such initiatives on the part of the press, it quietly killed the journalist. As for the lady's handbag, she found it where she had left it, in her car.

Carter and Human Rights

Given the configuration of internal tensions and contradictions prevailing in Iranian society, the coming of Carter to the White House affected the revolutionary process in a decisive manner.

By making the issue of 'Human Rights' the cover for the overall policy of imperialism, Carter helped, to his great dismay, to demolish the Pahlavi regime. The purpose of Carter's Human Rights policy was manifold. Primarily, it was to be used as propaganda against the Soviet Union and the Eastern bloc; and also for stemming the impending tide of popular uprising against American sponsored dictatorships by putting pressure on the dictatorial regimes to relent to liberalization. Iran being one of the most singificant bases of U.S. imperialism, this policy was first applied to the Shah's regime.[16] As the Human Rights issue became more pressing for the Pahlavi dictatorship, whose notorious nature was being exposed by political opponents of the Shah and international organizations and agencies, the Shah found himself compelled to acede to Carter's prescription for liberalization. It was in this context that as early as February 1978, after unrest in Tabriz led to attacks on cinema halls and burning of banks by demonstrators, the Shah declared that if disturbance by unruly mobs and damage to public property was the price the nation had to pay for freedom 'there was no alternative but to pay that price'. By August 1978, a month befor Tehran was touched by its first demonstration, Abdullah Riazi, Speaker of the Parliament, declared that 'the absolutely free elections' promised by the Shah for the next summer meant that any political group or individual could contest the elections because 'voting as well as candidacy will be free'.[17] But such overtures failed to attract even moderate forces like the National Front. 'People who have been involved in demolishing the very foundation of democracy in Iran and causing every kind of corruption for the last 25 years are not fit to form a transitional government or to hold free elections,' declared Karim Sanjabi, a National Front leader,[18] a day before Tehran was to witness its first major demonstration against the Pahlavi regime. Thus, given the repression, torture, and corruption which had sustained the regime for the past 25 years, to 'allow people any freedom was to allow them to fight against the regime'.[19] As a result, the moment the Shah began relaxing his iron grip on the society, it led to the eruption of long suppressed forces. Consequently the Shah lost control of the situation and failed in all his manoeuvres to tame the Revolution. Massacre of unarmed demonstrators, change in Government, even confession of past mistakes and a royal promise that things would be different in future, did not help the Shah in retaining his throne. The tyranny and cruelty with which the Pahlavi regime and the person of the Shah had come to be identified was of such magnitude that nothing less than a total annihilation of the regime was acceptable to the people.

It is therefore clear that besides the internal factors and contradictions, the contradictions in international policies and external events had a crucial role in intensifying the struggle of the Iranian people. America had failed to foresee the complications and setbacks which the slogan for human rights would generate against her own interests. Her insistence on moderating the Shah's repressive rule encouraged hundreds of middle class pro-West opposition elements to surface in Iran. Filing his report on the Iranian situation after his visit in April 1978, Helmut Richards, a long time student of Iranian politics, noted that the Shah, despite his 'liberalization', had taken to repressive measures against his moderate opponents. 'Now they are being beaten, their homes are being burnt, their demonstrations and meetings attacked, and their religious allies massacred on the streets.'[20] By September 1978, the alliance between the Westernized middle class liberals, Nationalists, Marxists, Maoists, progressive Muslim forces and the conservative religious elements 'had been sealed in blood'.[21] Revolutionary channeling of religious belief, blocking oil production, and the granting of religious sanction to strikes and to women's participation in anti-Shah demonstrations complemented the external influences and brought about the collapse of the Pahlavi dictatorship.[22]

Torture, Political Prisoners, and Revolution

Since the problem of suppression, imprisonment and torture of political prisoners had become a major issue and the opposition's most powerful weapon against the Shah's regime, the demand for freedom of political prisoners became a rallying point against the Shah. The two guerrilla organizations — *Mujahideen-e-Khalq* and *Fedayeen-e-Khalq* may not have succeeded, on their own, in directly mobilizing the masses in an armed uprising against the dictatorial regime. Nevertheless, they did succeed in exposing the brutal and ruthless nature of the Pahlavi dictatorship by refusing to submit to its torture and intimidation, and by manifesting a living image and a tangible model of what it meant to be a revolutionary. Above all, they presented the people with new 'personality models' — their 'heros' who had made the supreme sacrifice by offering their lives in the struggle against the imperialist backed dictatorship of the Shah. These models became the beacon for guiding people, particularly the young, into a higher dimension of human experience where commitment to a collective or transpersonal ideal assumed a new meaning. The heroic resistance which the revolutionary vanguard had displayed in the Pahlavi dungeons become a living experience shared by the people when the first hand accounts of torture in the Shah's prisons narrated by those who had endured them, had survived them, became available to the people. These narratives, along with the booklets, hand bills, and brochures detailing speeches that members of the guerrilla organizations had made in their defence during their trial by the Shah's military courts, became the most widely read material during the summer of 78 and after. These living testimonies gave an irrevocable forward thrust to the Revolution and to people's determination to oust the 'despotic regime of blood and torture' at any cost. One such document which almost every literate person involved with the Revolution had read was the letter of Reza Rezai, a fifth year medical student from Shiraz University and a leading member of *Mujahideen-e-Khalq,* which he had written and sent abroad after making his escape from SAVAK's custody in 1971. Reza was subsequently killed by SAVAK during a gunbattle in Tehran two years after his escape. Two of his brothers, Ahmad Rezai and Mehdi Rezai who were also among the pioneer members of *Mujahideen* had lost their lives in the struggle against the Pahlavi dictatorship. Excerpts from Reza Rezai's letter read:[23] 'Unfortunately, among those who were tortured the most savagely by SAVAK, none is able to describe them to you. Some of them have died under torture, others were shot to death.'

Through torture two goals are sought to be reached. First, to frighten those who fight the regime so that they will surrender their sacred fight. Second, to make a political prisoner talk about his organization, and thereby, reveal the names of active opponents. Since the birth of the urban guerrilla in Iran, the intensity of torture increased, especially with regard to those who belonged the different guerrilla groups.

'A guerrilla is under the most intensive torture during the twenty-four hours which follow his arrest. The most violent tortures are the whip made of electrical cables, then blows given by people who know karate and judo. Consequently, the prisoner falls into a coma. His feet swell because of the lashes from the whip, which prevent him from walking. Generally, either the hands, or the feet, or the nose is broken. None can bear these tortures, especially when the body is already ill. Then the agents of SAVAK come for the prisoner's confession. He has to sign his confession, asserting that he was not tortured and that he is well. The SAVAK is totally free to do what they want, but in order to abuse public opinion, they proceed with the construction of a legal file.

'Torture with electric and automatic electric prods is the most popular at present. The shocks leave no mark, but totally paralyze the body. Injecting drugs such as Cardiozol,or pulling fingernails out are also common as is the use of weights attached to the hands. The prisoner is also submitted to intense light of big projectors, to ultrasonic waves, and electrical shocks to the head which provoke madness, blindness, and deafness.

'To enlighten the public opinion, I describe tortures that I have witnessed. The agents of the SAVAK forced Ali Asgher Badizadegan, (co-founder of *Mujahideen-e-Khalq* organization), an engineer, to sit on a kind of electric chair and burnt him for four hours. He fell into a coma because of the intensity of the burns. The burns had reached the spinal column, and he was close to death. They stopped the torture and he was left alone for a week without any care. In the cell, the horrible smell of the burns spread in such a way that no one would come close to the cell. After three operations on the spine, he did not die but no longer can walk, and uses his hands to crawl about.

'The Engineer Abbas Meftahi (who belonged to *Fedayeen-e-Khalq* organization) suffered through 15 days of continuous torture, but never confessed. Mehdi Savalani, (also in the *Fedayeen-e-Khalq* group), can no longer walk, as his two legs were broken with a steel bar.

'I, myself, saw a prisoner go mad and several blind or deaf. Another was unable to urinate, since they had hung weights to his genitals. Another had the neck of a bottle forced through the anus.

'The regime takes no pity on the prisoners' families. They take members of the family as hostages, even old people and children, in order to capture whomever they want.

'Prisons are so dark and humid that even the guards refuse to work there. A cell is 4 feet by 7 feet and 6½ feet high, with a small window of 12x16 inches. There is no lamp inside the cell. The light comes from a lamp outside the cell or from the window. Sometimes the lamps are out and we cannot distinguish day from night. A cell is already small for one person. There were sometimes three of us living in one cell together. The cell is so humid that sugar melts and attracts ants.

'The guards are mere soldiers. They repeat every day that we are traitors and murderers, thieves and adulterer's sons and that they have to watch out for us since we would not hesitate to kill them. In spite of this 'propaganda', they are influenced by our behaviour and attitude. They wonder why the regime tortures us, when we are mostly engineers doctors and students. When we pray or when we read the Quran, they look at us with wonder, and one day one of them asked us: "Are you really Muslim?" A soldier said: "If ever I'm forced to kill you I'll kill my commandant first and then kill myself."

'The group of guards is changed from time to time, but the regime is far from being able to answer the questions they have. To tell the truth, the (prison cells) are really only war hospitals for the wounded, since everyone suffers from the wounds caused by torture.

'The daily programme of a prisoner can be summarized by enduring torture, sleeping, and eating. We cannot see the sun.

'I want to declare that the prisoners who have been arrested for the cause of their compatriots do not complain of their condition of life in prison and do not ask for the assistance of International Organizations in order to get better food, a more comfortable place, and daylight. They protest vehemently against the inhuman arrests of the regime and the extermination of the most talented children of Iran who are loyal patriots.

'Listen to the screams of those who resist in spite of the intense tortures of the SAVAK. Have your eyes wide open to see their bodies covered by the marks of torture. Let world opinion know about these things.'[24]

The world came to know about these things in 1975, when the *Sunday Times* of London published a report on torture in Iran after two years of investigation 'based on personal testimony from prisoners, interviews with prisoners' families and reports from impartial observers'. The evidence produced by this investigation confirmed much of what Reza Rezai had described about torture and the state of political prisoners in Iran. The Persian translation of the *Sunday Times* report as well as many other reports and speeches of the revolutionary vanguard began finding their way to the people during the Shah's experiment with liberalization.

The *Sunday Times* report stated that tortures most commonly applied to prisoners included 'felacca, the sustained flogging of the soles of the feet, extraction of finger and toenails, electric shock treatment to sexual organs, and the thrusting of a broken bottle into the anus of prisoners suspended by their wrists from a beam'.[25] Prisoners were also subjected to psychological torture. This included being forced to watch their children savagely mistreated. 'I found it so unbearable,' one man reported, 'that I wished I had a knife so that I could kill my son myself, rather than see him suffer like that.' Part of the psychological torture consisted of preparing the prisoners for their execution, leading them to the edge of a freshly dug grave or the prison compound where executions are carried out, blindfolding them, and then firing shots in the air. The prisoners would then be told that they had been 'reprieved' and taken back to their cells. The *Sunday Times* report also pointed out SAVAK's 'grim distinction of having invented an instrument of torture which victims call the Hot Table – an iron frame, rather like a bed frame, covered with wire mesh which is electrically heated like a toaster. Prisoners would be strapped to the table while it was heated until it became redhot'. Ahmadzadeh, one of the leaders of *Fedayeen-e-Khalq* managed to show scars on his back and chest – the result of being tortured on the Hot Table – to two French lawyers during his trial. The regime had allowed the French lawyers representing international organizations to attend the trial to demonstrate to its critics that political prisoners were not executed without trial. The lawyers also interviewed two political prisoners, Nasser Sadegh, and Ali Mihandoust, members of the central committee of *Mujahideen-e-Khalq*. Both political prisoners described the same torture methods being used on themselves and other prisoners, including Ahmadzadeh. Before he was executed, Nasser Sadegh repeated his statements about torture to another foreign observer.[26]

Ashraf Dehqani, a Marxist *Fedayeen-e-Khalq* leader wrote *Epic of the Resistance* in 1975 after escaping from the custody of SAVAK in a daring episode in which she was helped by Masume Shadmani, a 47 year old *Mujahideen-e-Khalq* housewife. In the above document, Ashraf wrote that her brother, Behrooz Dahqani, a member of *Fedayeen-e-Khalq* had been tortured to death in front of her, and also that her family was brought to prison and tortured and abused in front of her to make her confess. Ashraf then described how she was savagely raped by half a dozen guards during a torture session. She was whipped with cables day after day. 'I was like a mother delivering a baby. The pain is there and goes on. Nothing can be done but to wait for the birth of the child. And in that situation, the birth of the child was the arrival of death. I had to wait for that. Niktab (the chief torturer) ties me on my stomach on the bench. He rapes me to humiliate me and crush my spirits. I'm enraged to madness, but I try to look calm and indifferent, so that they be the ones who look humiliated and vile, not me. I want to make clear to them that their baseness does not reach me.

'Indeed, what difference does it have from whipping? Both were means of torture. Both had the same sordid goal: to force me to reveal my secrets. If I endured them, it was for the same reason: to advance the great and noble ideal and to keep the information that was not yet known, from the enemy. It was my contribution to the fight and the revolution. Besides, these infamies and these humiliations were for a short time and temporary. I endured them by imagining the cries of the working people, not only for an hour or a day, but at any instant of their oppressed life . . . Pain caused by the whip becomes more and more intense. I call Ipak, Reyhan, Robabe, Ghasem and others. They are oppressed and working men and women of the village where I was a school teacher. I feel their eyes fixed on me, as if physically I felt that they are wanting to assure my fidelity and my devotion to them. I read in their loving eyes their justified hope.'[27]

When the regime was forced to release hundreds of political prisoners in October 1978, the tales that surviving revolutionaries brought from the dark days of their tortured confinement flooded the press which, at that time, was enjoying its brief spell of full freedom. Thousands flocked to receive the prisoners being released every day. The released political prisoners formed their own association and intensified the revolutionary process further through their public speeches.

Families of revolutionaries began revealing their side of the story, how they were harassed, beaten, and tortured in front of a son or a daughter whom SAVAK had taken away. Many parents of executed revolutionaries complained they were never told the location of their children's graves or given the bodies of their daughters and sons for security reasons. Another security measure prohibited the martyr's family from holding memorial services for the deceased member of the family.

When defying this rule the mother of Mehdi Rezai, the 19 year old *Mujahideen* guerrilla killed under torture in 1972, held the traditional religious ceremony at her house after learning of her son's death, her entire family, including an infant grand-daughter were thrown into jail. Although the children were subsequently released, Mrs. Rezai remained locked up in jail, probably because of the special contempt SAVAK had for her — Mehdi was the fourth among her children who had got killed by SAVAK for resisting the Pahlavi regime. A fifth daughter, Simin Rezai was given a life sentence for writing an essay critical of the Shah's White Revolution as a high school student. Her school teacher had sent over Simin's essay to SAVAK. Both Mrs. Rezai and her daughter Simin were released in October 1978.[28]

Also among those released was Masume Shadmani Kabiri, a 47 year old supporter of the *Mujahideen*. Speaking to journalists after her release she said: 'I was arrested because of my sympathy and support for those families whose sons and daughters were the Shah's political prisoners. It was the month of Ramazan and I was fasting when I was arrested. I was taken for interrogation rightaway, where I was kept till sunset *(iftar)*. Then I was taken to the torture hall — I was stripped and beaten with an electric cable, then suspended from the ceiling. This went on for several days. They wanted me to tell them about the whereabouts of my son, Ali Reza, a member of the *Mujahideen-e-Khalq*. My silence angered them further. They decided to torture my other son, Hasan, who was in their custody and arrested two years ago, in front of me. When Hasan was brought to the hall, I did not recognize him. It was only after he had spoken and I heard his voice that I realised he was my son. He had been tortured beyond recognition. They took him to an adjoining room and beat him up severely. I could hear him scream, but there was nothing I could do but pray. I was determined not to give them any information, for I was committed to the *Mujahideen's* organization and ideology. I would have remained silent to my last breath and heart beat. Finally, I was taken to my cell, and after 11 months of torture, sentenced to death. The sentence was later commuted to life imprisonment. For the next two years there was no physical torture. Then one day I was taken again for interrogation, where I was told that my son, Ali Reza, had also been arrested. If I gave no information and refused to cooperate, both my sons, Ali Reza and Hasan, would be killed. Then both my sons were brought into the torture room and all of us were strapped to a steel bed. Our hands were squeezed in a vice, while we were being beaten. They did whatever they could to intensify the pain. None of us told them anything. I was then taken back to my cell'.[29] Like other torture victims, Masume Shadmani said that the tortures used most frequently involved pulling out the nails of the hands and feet, whipping with cables, heavy beatings, and suspension of the prisoner's body from the ceiling. Equipped with the most sophisticated tools of torture, SAVAK had acquired its techniques under the expert supervision of MOSAD the Israeli Intelligence agency and the CIA. Over the years, SAVAK had acquired such proficiency that it was exporting its expertise through the CIA to help security agents in Taiwan, Philippines, and Indonesia.[30]

In a visit to SAVAK headquarters in Tehran after the Islamic Revolution, Mohammad Heikal, the Egyptian journalist, reports seeing a film which was part of SAVAK's programme for training new agents. The film showed how to be more effective in burning the nipples of a girl with a lit cigarette. One could assume that the victim in the above film was either a *Mujahideen* or a *Fedayeen* revolutionary, for these were the only two organizations where Iranian women were as actively involved in the struggle against the Pahlavi dictatorship as the men.

A lot of documentary evidence substantiating the claims of political prisoners began pouring forth after the ban on the press was lifted by the tottering regime. One leading Tehran daily published the grisly photographs of naked, dead bodies of women, mutilated, tortured and killed by SAVAK during imprisonment. SAVAK used these photographs for intimidating political prisoners and forcing them to co-operate with the regime before submitting them to similar treatment. Other accounts told of a young mother whose infant son was tortured in front of her. The mother was forced to watch the flesh of her child getting clipped by a nail cutter. The infant later developed heart trouble.

Then there was the first hand account by a brother whose sister Fatima Amini, had been made to die a slow death under protracted torture. A 27 year old school teacher Fatima Amini was a member of *Mujahideen-e-Khalq* whose body was systematically burnt in front of her brother. The burning sessions were repeated over intervals to prevent a quick death. Due to repeated exposure to heat, most of her flesh was burnt out and Fatima became totally paralysed. Her state dragged on for another five months before she died, without telling SAVAK anything about the *Mujahideen-e-Khalq*. Her brother survived two years of solitary confinement and was able to narrate his sister's story after he was released in October 1978. 'It was hell, a thousand times over, but the thing that pulled us through was the feeling that I was suffering so that somebody else would live,'[31] a young girl said after her release from prison. To endure the agony of torture and suffering so that people should be free was the motive one came across most often among these revolutionaries. A journalist who visited the underground labyrinth of solitary confinement cells in a Tehran prison after the fall of Shapur Bakhtiar reported seeing a verse minutely etched with a prisoner's fingernails in the corner of a solitary confinement cell. The verse read: 'The agony of the whiplash is just a matter of days. If you are the people's confidante you'll live for ever.'

With communications cut from one another, the prisoners had to find the subtlest ways to convey their solidarity. Poems might be scrawled in the most unlikely places — classical lines from a Sufi poet or modern free verse from a revered contemporary, or a poem created by the prisoner himself, like the one above.

There is no denying the fact that disclosure of the agony which political prisoners were subjected to had a great effect on the nation's resolve to obliterate a system erected on the blood, bones, and tortured screams of the best of its youth. The Press and other media did a remarkable job in helping the masses catch up with the struggle of the revolutionary vanguard.

Although Iranian students abroad and exiled writers had published books and pamphlets revealing crimes of the regime against political prisoners, and even though the ideological tracts and defence speeches of the revolutionaries executed by the regime enjoyed a clandestine circulation inside the country, it was not until September 1978 that these books invaded Iran as 'White Cover books'. In the three months following the first anti-Shah demonstration in Tehran on 4 September 1978, until General Azhari's military government was clamped on Iran in November, nearly ten million copies of the forbidden books were sold.[32] One of the managers of Amir Kabir, the largest publication company in the country later disclosed that during the 12 months of Revolution, from March 1978 to March 1979, his company alone had published 580 books with a circulation of eight million[33] — a remarkable figure by any standard for a country of 36 million with 40% literacy. Marketed under a plain cover, these books presented a most remarkable phenomenon in the history of books and publication and played an indisputable role in consciousness-raising during the revolutionary process. Few people knew where the books came from because no information appeared on the cover except its title. Almost all of these books related to the works of Dr. Ali Shariati, the *Mujahideen-e-Khalq*, and progressive literature, generally. The distribution system of these books was unique in itself. When most book stores were closed under General Azhari's military government, the students organized distribution of the books in almost every part of Iran. When one group was arrested by the military forces, another would quickly replace it, thus reflecting the fact that the Revolution had become the determined struggle of an entire nation for freedom.

The Revolution for Freedom

The common denominator of all the forces that joined together and generated the Islamic Revolution was freedom—freedom for individual expression and thought, and freedom from despotism, exploitation, and imperialism. Expressing this objective of the Islamic Revolution on 18 January 1979, just three weeks before the movement climaxed in an armed uprising, Taleqani said, 'This Great Movement was born of the struggle for freedom and its success would mean freedom for all the people. This movement has not been brought about by any single individual, group, or ideology. It is not born of hero worship or efforts of political parties. Struggle against *shirk* (Polytheism) means struggle for human freedom'.[34] Urging the revolutionaries, whether Muslim or Communists, to remain united in the struggle against the Pahlavi dictatorship, Taleqani said, 'Our nation at this critical stage in its history and destiny is not after any ideology. It is fighting for freedom. It is concerned lest it is dealt another blow (by imperialism and reaction) and another despot comes into power. This is what I am worried about most. I request you to unify behind a single goal and a single slogan. Fight for people's freedom and struggle against imperialism and exploitation. If you are Muslims, for the sake of God and the Prophet, and if you don't believe in religion, then for the sake of human dignity and human reality, let us have one voice on the basis of what we have in common among us all — (to fight for) freedom. Freedom for a nation robbed of its wealth and capacities which must be restored back to it. This nation knows what to do with its future destiny. It is able to find its way. There is no need for any ideology, any party or any particular group to impose itself upon this Movement. Our call is freedom for the people. And that means effacement of despotism, imperialism, and exploitation and all that arises from these evils.'[35]

Taleqani declared that in the Islamic Iran that he envisioned, 'We shall not suppress freedom. It is not for me or anyone to say this, the Quran declares this, that there is no compulsion in religion. Everyone has the freedom to say and think whatever he wants. Those who are afraid to give freedom, those who do not want others to criticize their ideas or do anything against their interest, do so because of their own weakness and because they are afraid of their own ideological inadequacies. Although it is not possible to curb freedom in Islam, yet they have always clubbed us by calling us "Communists" and using the whip of "Communist Danger and Communist Plot" against us. They clubbed us with this stick in 1953. Do not allow this slogan and this problem to be exploited again (by your enemies).'[36]

The issue of 'freedom', therefore, was fundamental and dominated the Revolution. When a correspondent asked Khomeini during the revolution as to why the Iranian people had started the movement against the Shah's regime, Khomeini said it was because 'repression practiced by the Shah' had spread to an 'intolerable degree', and that people were denied 'freedom, independence, and well being'.[37] Khomeini voiced the sentiments and demands of the people and the progressive, democratic, and national forces when he declared: 'Our first concern is to bring down this autocratic regime.'[38] Khomeini made it clear that repression, censor, and suppression of thought and political activities would not be tolerated in the new society the Revolution aimed to establish after overthrowing the Pahlavi dictatorship. Even the Marxists would have full freedom to express themselves and there would be no restrictions on their legitimate organizational and political activities. 'In the society that we intend to establish, the Marxists would be free to express their opinion, for we are convinced that Islam has all the answers our people need. We have never denied them their freedom nor infringed upon it. Everyone is free to express his opinion.'[39] Khomeini reaffirmed his belief in this fundamental objective of the Revolution after his return to Iran by categorically discounting the possibility of suppressing people by 'the army and a new Savak-like police', in the name of reimposing law and order. 'Our people have been in prison for 35 years, no government is going to put them in prison again. They must be given a chance to express themselves as they wish, even if it means a certain degree of chaos.'[40]

Why Khomeini's Leadership?

No political organization was capable of assuming the leadership of the Islamic Revolution. This was not only due to the severe blows the regime had dealt the guerrilla organizations and other political bodies during the past years, but also due to the fact that the Movement was going ahead at such a rapid pace that political organizations had no option but to follow the massive spontaneity of the Movement. In this respect, only the clergymen, given their national organizational network in the form of mosques, their direct contact with people, and the uncompromising leadership of Ayatollah Khomeini calling for the overthrow of the monarchy appeared to present the only possible avenue for leading this movement.

Moreover, Khomeini was the only well known opponent of the Shah who had not been physically eliminated by the regime or confined to imprisonment. His past performance in confrontation with the Shah left no doubt in the people's minds that Khomeini would never compromise with the regime. Khomeini led the Revolution because, 'from the sociological perspective, he represented popular unity; and because people had to act with complete unity in order to succeed in overthrowing the regime'.[41]

During his exile, Khomeini had succeeded in projecting himself as a progressive and open minded revolutionary, thereby making his leadership irresistible even to those sections and groups who might have otherwise equated him with reactionary clergymen. For example, when Khomeini was asked by the French Radio and Television in September 1978 whether an Islamic government would mean that religious leaders were to run the country, Khomeini gave a categorical 'No' as reply. He said that an Islamic government did not mean that 'religious leaders should themselves run the affairs of government'. The clergymen were to only 'lead people in defining their Islamic demands'.[42] When asked whether he would personally assume a role in the new government,

Khomeini replied 'neither my age, nor my desire, nor my (religious) position permits such a thing'.[43] Khomeini left no doubt in people's minds that his role as well as that of the clergy in the Islamic government would not amount to actually running the affairs of State. Their role would be one of 'guidance and counselling', so that 'there were no deviations and people were not subjected to oppression'.[44] His views about women's rights were equally progressive. In the Islamic government that Khomeini envisioned, women were to be free in 'choosing their profession, activities, and destiny'.[45]

Primarily, however, it was by successfully blending politics and religion in an anti-imperialist and anti-dictatorial framework that Khomeini succeeded in making his leadership attractive and acceptable to various sections of society. By insisting that politics and Islam were inseparable, Khomeini had followed the path laid down by Syed Jamal-ud-Din Afghani a century ago. Expressing this point of view in a speech shortly after the Tehran Uprising in February 1979, Ayatollah Motahari, the Islamic ideologue closest to Khomeini and the then Chairman of the Revolutionary Council, the supreme body to take control of Iran, said: 'Khomeini not only believed that politics and religion were inseparable, he declared that indifference to politics and keeping one's self away from it was tantamount to keeping one's self away from religion. Khomeini's secret of success, therefore, lay in the fact that he carried forward the struggle in the mould of Islamic concepts as Syed Jamal had done. He fought oppression but presented the necessity of fighting oppression in terms of Islamic criteria. Similarly, he stressed the necessity for fighting injustice, imperialism, and exploitation by repeating the call that it was a disgrace for a Muslim to submit to oppression and be under the domination of an infidel ruler.'[46] Motahari believed that if Khomeini had attempted to bring the problem of class contradictions or the concepts of freedom and justice to people's awareness in the framework of ideologies of the East or the West, it would not have met with receptivity in the Iranian society. 'He presented the concepts of class contradictions, freedom, and justice using Islamic criteria and the rich background of Islamic culture. The society received these ideas in good faith.'[47] Thus, 'the people realized that freedom was not merely a political issue. More than anything else it was an Islamic issue. A Muslim ought to live in freedom and be a freedom fighter.[48] The Iranian Revolution, therefore, could be regarded as an Islamic Revolution, because even though Justice, Freedom, and Independence were the objectives of this Revolution, they were sought in terms of symbols and expressions that stemmed from an Islamic tradition. People had risen not only because of a revolutionary religious idiom, but also in terms of it.

Notes

1. Ahmedzadeh, T., Introduction to Chapter 3 In, *Taleqani and History*.
2. Ayatollah Motahari, *Pira-mon-e-Enqelab-e-Eslami*. Sadra Publications, Tehran 1979.
3. Abrahimian, E., *Structural Causes of the Iranian Revolution*. MERIP. Vol.10, No.4, May, 1980.
4. Ibid.
5. Ibid., p.22.
6. Ibid.
7. Ibid.
8. Ibid., p.23.
9. Ibid.
10. Ibid.
11. Ibid.
12. Abrahimian, E., *The Guerrilla Movement in Iran*. MERIP. Vol.10. No.3, March-April, 1979.
13. Ibid., p.4.
14. Ibid.
15. Ibid.
16. Afrasiabi, S. and Dehqan, D., *Taleqani and History*.
17. *Kayhan International*, 12 August 1978.
18. *Kayhan International*, 5 September 1978.
19. *Kayhan International*, 20 March 1979.
20. Helmut Richards in *Iran Erupts*. The Iran-America Documentation Group. Stanford, 1978. Nobari, A. (ed), p.113–14.
21. *Le Monde* editorial September 10-11, 1978. quoted in *Iran Erupts*, p.220.
22. Afrasiabi, B. and Dehqan, S., *Taleqani and History*.
23. Nobari, A., *Iran Erupts*. The Iran-America Documentation Group. Stanford, 1978, p.154–57.
24. *The Sunday Times*, 19 January 1975. Quoted In *Iran Erupts*.
25. Ibid.
26. Ibid.
27. Nobari, A., *Iran Erupts*. The Iran-America Documentation group. Stanford, 1978., pp.159–61.
28. After her release, Simin Rezai remained an active member of *Mujahideen-e-Khalq* and married Musa Khiabani, one of the surviving *Mujahideen* leaders. Both Khiabani and Ms Rezai, as well as the wife of *Mujahideen* leader Masood Rajavi were killed by Khomeini's Revolutionary Guards during a raid on their apartment on 9 February 1982.
29. 'The Way of Iranian Mujahideen.' *The Pakistan Times*, July 1970.
30. Heikal, M., *The Return of the Ayatollah*. Andre Dentsche, 1981.
31. *Kayhan International*, Tehran, 1979.
32. *Iranweek*, 31 August 1979.
33. Ibid.
34. Afrasiabi, B. and Dehqan, S., *Taleqani and History*, p.371.
35. Ibid., p.374–75.

36. Ibid.
37. Khomeini's interview with Lucien George in *Le Monde;* English text printed in *Manchester Guardian,* 21 May 1978. Quoted in *Iran Erupts,* p.11-14.
38. Ibid.
39. Ibid.
40. Heikal, M., *The Return of the Ayatollah.* Andre Deutsch, London, 1981, p.180–81.
41. Abol Hasan Banisadr's interview in the Paris daily, *Le Quotidien du peuple,* 19–22 September 1978. Quoted in *Iran Erupts,* p.128.
42. Quoted in *Khomeini Chay Goft, Khomeini Chay Kard* (What did Khomeini Say, What did Khomeini Do?). Peoples Fedayeen Organization, 1982.
43. Reported by Assocated Press, 7 November 1978, Quoted in 'What Did Khomeini Say, What Did Khomeini Do?'
44. Ibid.
45. Khomeini's interview in *Al-Mustaqbil.* 6 November 1978. Quoted in 'What Did Khomeini Say, What Did Khomeini Do?'.
46. Ayatollah Motahari, *Pera-mon-e-Enqilab-e-Islami.* Sadra publications, Tehran, 1979, p.51–53.
47. Ibid., p.51.
48. Ibid., p.53.

10. The Islamic Revolution II January 1978 - February 1979

From Qom to Tabriz

It was the Shah's regime itself which struck the first spark for setting the revolution in motion by planting a slanderous letter against Ayatollah Khomeini in the government controlled press on 7 January 1977. The letter called Khomeini 'a foreigner of Indian origin' who was making false pretences against a people and a country that had given him refuge. It also called Khomeini 'a sentimental poet' who used to occupy himself with romantic poetry during his years of obscurity in India. The appearance of this letter in *Ettela'at*, the nation's largest daily, shortly after Mostapha Khomeini, the Ayatollah's eldest son had died under mysterious circumstances, caused grievance to many people. In Qom, thousands took to the streets and demonstrated in front of the local office of *Ettela'at*. The regime's response was typical. It sent in its troops who opened fire on demonstrators, killing and wounding many. 40 days after the killings in Qom, memorial services for the dead were held in all the major cities. While these services had proceeded peacefully in many mosques, in Tabriz, capital of East Azerbaijan Province, police opened fire on a procession of mourners demonstrating in the streets. This enraged the demonstrators, who reacted by attacking the city's banks and cinema halls and set many of them on fire. The police responded with more gunfire. By the end of the day over a 100 demonstrators were killed and wounded. Following this incident, cracks began appearing in the country's monolithic Rastakhiz (Resurgence) Party. The first blow came from Ahmad Bani-Ahmad, member of Parliament for Tabriz who dropped a bombshell by introducing a motion against the government for police atrocities during the anti-Shah demonstrations. Even more distressing for the Shah than this open condemnation was that Bani-Ahmad had dared to announce his withdrawal from the Shah's Rastakhiz Party, which he stressed was unconstitutional—an act unthinkable in the SAVAK dominated Iran.[1]

After the Tabriz demonstrations, the religious protestors changed their tactics, using small groups to attack banks, cinemas, and local offices of the Rastakhiz Party. Both *Mujahideen-e-Khalq* and *Fedayeen-e-Khalq* organizations were active in many cities and security forces were unable to prevent the publication and circulation of their pamphlets. The Shah's inability to extinguish popular resistance to his autocratic rule despite possessing 'possibly the largest repression system *per capita* in the world',[2] and SAVAK's inability to decapitate the *Mujahideen* and *Fedayeen* despite the severe blows it had dealt these organizations since they began armed struggle in 1971, 'was testimony to the fortitude of the Iranian people'.[3]

From Rex Cinema to Black Friday

One of the main sparks that ignited the revolution and enflamed larger uprisings against the regime resulting in its eventual destruction, was the Rex Cinema inferno at Abadan. Six hundred people—men women and children—were burnt alive when the Rex Cinema hall was set on fire on 19 August 1978. People spared no time in crediting the Shah and SAVAK for this horrible crime. In vain the regime tried to put the blame on 'religious fanatics' and 'terrorists'. The funeral for the victims turned into a massive anti-regime demonstration, with thousands of people screaming that the grisly fire was the Shah's work.[4] Although cinema halls and banks, regarded by many militant elements as symbolizing corruption and capitalism, had become the target of militants since the Tabriz riots, such attacks by the religious opposition were usually carried out during hours when there was the least possibility of loss of innocent lives. Many people therefore believed that the Shah's regime had deliberately set the cinema hall on fire in a desperate attempt at discrediting the religious opposition as 'barbarous fanatics'. The regime's motive, the argument ran, was to direct the public rage and bitterness that would be elicited by this shocking tragedy at the 'religious fanatics'. Therefore, from the popular point of view, 'this horrible crime proved that there was no limit to the Shah's callousness, that for keeping his demonic dynasty in power, he was prepared to commit the most unimaginable crimes. Thus with the Rex cinema holocaust, people's resentment against the regime turned into boundless, even sacred, hate.'[5] In Abadan, angry demonstrations in front of the city's fire brigade and police office became a daily affair. To help calm the vengeful rage of the aggrieved people, Abadan's city council, in a dramatic switch, disqualified the police and ordered the boy scouts to take charge of enforcing law and order during the mass mourning at Abadan cemetry. The way the boys ran the show was disarming. Some barely ten years old, their faces streaked with tears or choking back sobs, comforted and held in check men and women who writhed about in the dust and poured earth on their heads in grief when the hundreds of charred and crumbled bodies, packed in polythene bags, were lowered into the mass grave. These young boys provided a foretaste of the heroism of the streets fighters which became commonplace later in the year. They took on the Shah's troops for months using nothing but their bare hands and rocks. When they did finally pick up guns instead of rocks, the Shah's dynasty fell before their onslaught like a house of cards.[6] The national rage generated by the Rex Cinema tragedy was so intense that within a week of the fire, Prime Minister Amouzegar was fired and replaced by Sharif Emami, the soft spoken ageing courtier with religious pretensions.[7] Calling his government the 'government of national reconciliation', the 71 year old Prime Minister declared he would 'make the country's laws according to Islam'[8] and put an end to prostitution and gambling'.

The new Prime Minister also declared that Iran would no longer be a single party State, and that Khomeini would be allowed to return to Iran. As in the past when threatened by a popular movement, the monarchy once again assumed an acquiescing posture to stem the movement from swelling further. But even the moderate Ayatollah Shariatmadari, one of the prominent Shia leaders equal in religious rank to Ayatollah Khomeini, seemed to have sensed that Emami's government was unlikely to last. 'The government will collapse in three months if it does not comply with the religious demands', Shariatmadari told the French news agency in an exclusive interview held at Qom,[9] shortly after Emami became Prime Minister.

On 4 September 1978, almost two weeks after the Rex Cinema incident, Tehran had its first major demonstration. Almost a hundred thousand people took part in a public march which started off from the affluent north end of the city, after the participants had said their prayers together to observe the end of the holy month of Ramazan. Thousands joined the procession as it marched towards the southern end of the city voicing the demand for freedom, independence, and Islamic government.

After the procession ended peacefully, the organizers of this march decided to hold the next protest demonstration on Thursday, 7 September. However, the government issued a statement on 6 September forbidding demonstrations and threatened to use force for dispensing 'unauthorized meetings on public highways'.[10] As a result of this threat those who had called for the demonstrations—the *Ulama* and religious leadership in Tehran, the National Front, and the *Bazaris* Association—called off the march.[11] Nevertheless the demonstration went ahead as originally planned and as compared to the march held three days before, almost twice as many people took part in it. It was during this procession that people freely shouted, for the first time since 1963, 'Down with the Shah'. That the eruption of this slogan was spontaneous and contrary to the clergymen's instructions is indicated by the fact that although many clergymen tried to stop people from saying it for fear of provoking the Shah's machine guns into action, the full—throated slogan lent the crowd an ecstatic electrification. Rising from the depths of the people, this long longed for utterance represented 'the crossing of a major hurdle in a country where for 25 centuries, and by sheer force, the Shah had been portrayed as the shadow of God.'[12]

The shout 'Death to the Shah', therefore, meant 'death to dictatorship' and it set into motion the crumbling of an idol and with it, the crumbling of a tyrannical dynasty.[13]

The Shah's regime well realised where this movement would lead if people were allowed to shed their fear. The regime, therefore, was determined to kill this courage. General Oveissi, Military Commander of Tehran, issued the final instructions to his soldiers following the demonstration on 7 September — if demonstrators appeared on the streets again, soldiers were to shoot to kill. By the end of the day Tehran was under Martial Law. But the young militants had already decided to meet the following morning, Friday 8 September at Jaleh square in the congested southern part of the city. Even though the *Ulama* had not planned another demonstration,[14] a crowd of about five thousand gathered at Jaleh square on the morning of 8 September. It was there that the unbelievable slaughter occurred.

Reporting the event in *Le Figaro* the next day, Yves-Guy-Berges, the French journalist who witnessed and survived the killing wrote: 'This is not a fight; this is a massacre. A firing squad at its work. The street one minute beforehand darkened with people, is strewn with bodies, shoes, trampelled banners, the wounded crawling towards each other, struggling to reach each other. I count 30 to 40 dismembered bodies. In their heart, no one believed that the army was going to shoot. Two students hail a motorcyclist for me and put me on the seat. "Leave! Leave! Tell what you have seen".'[15]

While people claimed that thousands had died in the Friday Massacre, General Oveissi, The Martial Law administrator responsible for the shooting conceded only 58 killed and 205 wounded. The Foreign Press put the figure around 500. General Oveissi blamed the shooting on 'a group of demonstrators supported and financed by foreign elements'.[16] According to General Oveissi, the military only acted in 'legitimate self-defense'—the demonstrators 'had attacked citizens and their property in different parts of Tehran killing several soldiers'. The officers responsible for maintaining martial law were thus 'forced to react and disperse the demonstrator to protect law and order'.[17]

With the beginning of the new academic year three weeks after the 'Friday Massacre', the Revolution entered its decisive phase. The geysers of revolutionary consciousness, Shariati, *Mujahideen-e-Khalq* and the revolution's vanguard had released in the minds of young students, began pouring forth from the universties to engulf the whole nation.

The University and the Revolution

When universities, colleges and high schools reopened late in September 1978, they became consciousness-raising centres in the revolutionary process. 'Teachers have taken their classes to the streets',[18] declared a bannerline in *Kayhan*, the nation's second largest newspaper. The last week of October saw the unfolding of 'Solidarity Week', an initiative which Tehran University, the largest and oldest university in the country, had taken for co-ordinating the struggle of the teachers, students and people, who had been separated by the SAVAK for a quarter of a century. The grounds, halls, and lecture theatres of educational institutions all over the country became centres for public meetings and for raising the political, social and religious awareness of the people and channeling it into an anti-imperialist direction. Slide shows and films depicting the atrocities of the Pahlavi regime against its opponents, and public addresses by political prisoners giving details of vicious tortures and appalling conditions in Pahlavi dungeons, gave the Revolution an irreversible thrust. Also, the emergence and exhibition of revolutionary art based on the resistance of vanguard revolutionaries of the two guerrilla organizations became a major event in the new revolutionary culture. The entire two floors of the College of Fine Arts at Tehran University was taken up for the exhibition of revolutionary art by *Mujahideen-e-Khalq* and *Fedayeen-e-Khalq* supporters. Splashed by the banners, giant portraits of martyred guerrilla leaders, and fragments of their defence speeches, the universities had become the guerrilla organizations.

On 4 November 1978, about a hundred thousand high school and university students had assembled in Tehran University campus to hear Taher Ahmadzadeh, the hard core revolutionary just released from the Pahlavi prison, and Dr. Habibullah Paimann, an Islamic ideologue, speak. However, before the speeches had gotten underway units of Imperial Guards broke into the campus, gunning to death scores of students and wounding four hundred. Following the soldiers rampage, thousands of students took to the streets, waving placards smeared with the fresh blood of students killed moments ago, screaming the slogan, 'Soldiers Killed 65 Students in the University'.

That same night, administrators of the national television network, sympathetic to the Revolution took advantage of Sharif Emami's professed 'liberal policy' for national reconciliation and screened the film of the massacre of students at the University, just after the news bulletin, the peak viewing hour. The scenes were so shocking that even those Iranians who might otherwise have been lukewarm to the Revolution and had never participated in anti-Shah demonstrations came face to face with the stark evidence of the ruthlessness of which the regime was being so widely accused. Reaction to the film was instantaneous. Tens of thousands of people poured out into the streets with voices full of rage, shouting slogans against the regime. In central Tehran, a cinema hall and a multi-storeyed bank were set ablaze and shops specializing in luxury goods attacked. Next morning Iran was under Martial Law. Sharif Emami had stepped down from the rostrum of 'liberalization', and after six hours of talks between Brezinski and the Shah, General Azhari, Chief of Staff of the Armed Forces, had been made Prime

Minister.[19] Tehran University came under military occupation on 6 November. Following the University Massacre, Khomeini, now in Paris, issued a statement in which he accused the Shah of 'turning our universities into a slaughter house for our youth'.[20]

Despite the Martial Law, the students and teachers were determined to continue their struggle which had now been given an immediate and tangible objective—regaining control of the University and evicting the army from the campus. These demands were expressed within the framework of the overall demand for the overthrow of the 'treacherous Pahlavi regime'. To press their demands, several hundred faculty members of Tehran University, joined by teachers from other educational institutions in the city, began a sit-in on 23 December 1978, at the Ministry of Education, a few blocks away from Tehran University.

The sit-in had actually begun three days earlier at Tehran University when a group of professors locked themselves up in the administrative building on the campus to protest against the military occupation of the University. Lasting for 25 days, the sit-in was splashed with blood when on 26 December, Professor Nejat-Ullahi, a young faculty member of a Tehran college, was shot and killed by the soldiers, laying siege to the Ministry of Education. The massive funeral procession for the slain professor became yet another catalyst for the continual mobilization of urban masses, a distinctive feature of the Islamic Revolution. A crowd of four hundred thousand, among them tens of thousands of students and teachers who had come to Tehran from all over the country, took part in the funeral march. The funeral march yielded its own martyrs when soldiers opened fire on the people.

Ayatollah Taleqani joined the teachers at the Ministry of Education on 13 January 1978, the day they had arranged to end their sit-in. He made a speech, lauded the role of the teachers in the movement, spoke about his 'son and brother,' Dr. Ali Shariati, and the progressive revolutionaries who had, during previous years, laid down their lives to fuel the present movement. A few hours later, the teachers led by Ayatollah Taleqani and accompanied by hundreds of thousands of people, marched towards Tehran University and 'liberated' it. Once again, Tehran University was the 'Central Fort of the Revolution', pumping consciousness, awareness and activism into the people.

There was nothing new about the University's tradition as the 'Fort of Freedom and Resistance', except the magnitude of its activism and the extent of its centrality in the present movement. Ever since the reinstallation of the Shah in power in 1953, it was primarily at Tehran University that the silence imposed by SAVAK had been intermittently broken. Shortly after the August 1953 *coup*, Richard Nixon arrived in Tehran as the special American envoy to dictate the new U.S. policies to the Shah. At that time the only expression of opposition to his visit came from Tehran University. Student supporters of Mossadeq and the Tudeh Party held a protest rally on the campus and declared, addressing the Shah: 'Even if you kill everyone everywhere, this Fort of resistance (the University) will continue its struggle until final victory is achieved.'[21] The regime retaliated quickly. Its paratroopers invaded the campus and using their guns, broke up the demonstration. Three students, supporters of the Tudeh Party, were killed and scores were injured. The day of the killing—7 December 1953—became a permanent page in the history of the resistance movement for the young, to be commemorated every year by future student generations. Shortly after the '7 December Massacre', 11 professors from Tehran University formally attacked the regime for submitting to an American-imposed 'agreement' that gave the newly formed oil Consortium, a creation of Western capitalism, full control of Iran's oil. The Shah ordered the immediate expulsion of these professors. When this order was turned down by the University's Chancellor, he was replaced by a man more convenient to the regime.[22] Then in 1961, the regime arrested 700 students who had formed a student's association for co-ordinating their struggle against the Shah's regime. This led to the first major protest against the regime and four thousand students and teachers held a sit-in at Tehran University.[23] A year later, when the Shah declared the launching of the 'White Revolution', the University lay bare the fact that these social reforms were designed by the Kennedy administration for popularising the monarchy, and in consequence, perpetuating imperialist control on Iran. Opposition to the Shah became more intense that year when Khomeini began criticizing the monarch, leading to the uprising in June 1963. The University was accorded punishment for its share in this movement. Once again, crack units of the Imperial Guards invaded the University, broke into the class rooms and laboratories, and mercilessly beat up boys and girls. 'The corridors of the Medical School and School of Science were drenched with students' blood,'[24] said a university professor after the rampage.

With Khomeini's exile in 1964 and the suppression of the opposition by SAVAK, the University became the crucible for the crystallization of a new and more enlightened breed of revolutionaries who inaugurated a new era in the history of resistance movements in Iran. Both the *Mujahideen-e-Khalq* and *Fedayeen-e-Khalq* were founded by socially committed revolutionary students and fresh graduates. The military operations carried out by these organizations and their underground newsletters and literature were a major factor in keeping alive the resistance movement and generating revolutionary awareness among people, particularly students. The defence speeches *Mujahideen-e-Khalq* revolutionaries delivered in the Shah's Military Court before they were killed under torture or by the firing squad were published and circulated by the organization and its supporters both inside and outside the country. These speeches as well as ideological tracts of *Mujahideen-e-Khalq* were distributed by the Muslim Student's Association, the network formed by the Iranian students studying in the West, as well as by the Liberation Movement and its affiliates. The 'Defence Speeches' shed light not only upon the ideological aspects of the organization, but also upon the bizzare conditions in the regime's prisons and the torture and humiliations the political opponents of the Shah had been subjected to.

By the mid 70s, Tehran had become the centre for underground resistance to the regime. The Shah was realizing too late that the centralizing of advanced education in Science, Tehnology, and Social Sciences at Tehran had suddenly brought his regime face to face with students—its most courageous and intelligent enemy. It was in this perspective that the Shah proceeded to dismember the Aryamehr Industrial University (re-named Sharif Industrial University, after Sharif Vaqafi, a senior student of the University and *Mujahideen* martyr). A highly sophisticated institution for scientific and technological education, this University had established itself as the leading centre of excellence in the country and the region under the generous allocations of funds made available by the regime. The huge educational complex was staffed by highly qualified Iranian professors with international standing, and its student enrolment, both at the undergraduate and the graduate levels, had swelled considerably over the years. The decision for dismembering the University and transferring it around five hundred kilometres to the south west of Tehran, on the outskirts of Isfahan, was finalised in 1977. The regime had been motivated to take this decision because the University had become a major centre for student resistance and a channel for students to join underground organizations opposed to the regime. Thus the University was producing not only brilliant engineers and scientists, but daring and imaginative urban guerrillas as well. In 1976, *Mujahideen* supporters had successfully carried out a strike at this University to observe the fourth anniversary of the execution of the founders of their organization.

As for the Government's plans to shift the University to Isfahan, the University faculty was united in its opposition to this plan. When the regime made it clear that the faculty had no choice but to submit to the government decision, the professors went on strike. The regime then began various attempts to persuade the faculty to acquiesce to its plans for shifting the University. It even offered to pay the professors, in terms of bonus and fringe benefits, twice the salary they were receiving in Tehran. This meant that an associate professor could expect a salary of up to $50,000 per annum were he to serve in Isfahan. The faculty turned down this offer and attacked the regime for its 'unethical and debased' attempts at bribing them. Following this rebuke, the government announced it would stop payment of salary to the professors as long as they remained on strike. This triggered a spontaneous reaction of support among the people. They immediately opened a special bank account for the striking faculty to meet their monetary needs. Within weeks of opening this account, millions of rials had been deposited, with large donations pouring forth from the bazaar merchants and the middle class. Thus, while the rural migrants in Tehran's shanty towns were motivated by economic considerations to take part in the Revolution, it was the economic security and relative affluence of professional classes that had given them strength to stand up against the regime and step into the streets for political reasons, and because of their disgust with a despotic and suppressive regime. The Pahlavi dynasty appeared to be losing every battle, even before the revolution had really taken off.

The massacre of students was not limited to the campuses alone. Infact, one of the most brutal massacres involving thousands of students took place on Friday, 8 September 1978, better known as 'Black Friday'. It will be recalled that despite the declaration of Martial Law, a few thousand people had gathered at Jaleh square on 8 September. A majority of these people were students, as confirmed by 'unimpeachable witnesses' and a French journalist's report of the incident which reads: 'Army troops were brought in to face over two thousand unarmed students. The soldiers fired point blank. Coldly and deliberately. An Italian journalist who was at the scene said that he felt like he was watching a firing squad. The students, who with rare courage had exposed their bare chests to the guns, were deeply convinced that the soldiers, their brothers, would never open fire on them. News of the Jaleh massacre spread like lightning throughout Tehran, touching off demonstrations against the regime and Martial Law.'[25]

Four months after this massacre, during the final days of Bakhtiar's premiership, Tehran University had become a beleagured people's fort, lined by sand bags stacked by students, and guarded round the clock by thousands of young males and females who had flooded the campus to protect it against possible invasion by the army. At the Revolution's high noon, the headquarters of the main guerrilla groups—the *Mujahideen* and the *Fedayeen* - were firmly entrenched in the University blocks. The campus became Republican Iran's first military training camp as the *Fedayeen* and *Mujahideen* began teaching eager Iranians the art of handling a machine gun.

From Martial Law to Bakhtiar

General Azhari's Military government was helpless in stemming the Revolution. Despite Martial Law, people were continuing their struggle and had invented new and relatively safer ways to do so. Hundreds of thousands of people began going to the roof tops at night to shout religious slogans, symbolizing defiance to the Pahlavi regime and the fight for freedom. Soldiers patrolling the streets reacted to these slogans by shooting indiscriminately at the night sky to frighten the callers. During these nights, demonstrators also took to the streets. In certain areas, officers and soldiers sympathetic to the people actually guarded a perimeter within which people could demonstrate safely.[26]

The helplessness of General Azhari's regime had become clear as early as 10 and 11 December, when millions had staged massive demonstrations in response to Ayatollah Taleqani's call to affirm the sanctity of their struggle against a tyrannical regime. These demonstrations had conclusively shown the broad base which the revolution enjoyed against the Shah's dictatorship. The Western press, radio, and television had declared these December demonstrations as a 'massive vote of no confidence' the Iranian people had given the Shah.[27]

Thus, when General Azhari became hospitalised with a heart attack late in December, the stage was already set for the next move by the West. Shapur Bakhtiar, once a second rank leader of the National Front, became Prime Minister on 6 January 1982. Ten days later the Shah and his wife left on what had been officially described as a 'holiday', but what the people knew for certain was permanent exile.

The spontaneous eruption of euphoria and jubilation with which people greeted the news of the Shah's exit from Iran simply proved how unbearable and hateful the detested regime of 'torture and repression' had become for the people. Streets in Tehran and other cities overflowed with joy as people danced and sang on the streets and strangers hugged, kissed and greeted each other. Tears of joy and relief streaked a thousand Iranian cheeks as men and women cheerfully shouted, 'Shah has fled, SAVAK is fatherless'. The collective intensity of joy overflowing Iran on 2 p.m., 16 January — after the radio announced the Shah's departure—was perhaps unprecedented in any nation's history. People genuinely believed that 'the regime of torture, execution, and repression' had forever come to an end.

However, Bakhtiar did not declare the end of the monarchy, though gradually, during his final days in office, he began hinting about the possibility of forming a Republic through a referendum. Meanwhile demonstrations against Bakhtiar, whom people regarded as 'America's last card' continued. In one confrontation near Tehran University on 28 January, Royalist marksmen who had positioned themselves on roof tops around the square adjoining Tehran University, opened fire on student demonstrators, killing and wounding over five hundred students. Tehran was plunged in chaos as students lined the streets, pleading with motorists to deliver medicines, bandages, and mattresses to assist doctors and nurses in the hospitals overflowing with the wounded. The spontaneous compliance of the motorists with these requests was another reflection of the incredible solidarity that characterized the revolution for freedom. The scale of this massacre can be judged by the fact that within the first hours of the shooting, a journalist contacting the hospitals in Tehran reported 30 dead and over 300 injured.[28] Meanwhile, Khomeini had declared he would be returning to Iran any day. To prevent Khomeini from making a possible landing at Tehran's Mehrabad airport, Bakhtiar deployed army tanks and armoured vehicles on the tarmac. However, these manoeuvres only succeeded in postponing the Ayatollah's return by a few days. On 1 February, Khomeini made his victorious entry to Iran. The 32 kilometre route from the airport to Beheshte Zahra, the cemetry where those killed during the Revolution were buried, was lined by millions from all sections of society. At this moment in the nation's history, the overwhelming majority of people, regardless of their social, political and economic background, regarded Khomeini as leader of a revolution that had ended the tyranny of the monarchy.

In view of the central role the students and the universities had played in the Revolution, Khomeini had planned to deliver his first speech in Iran in front of Tehran University, immediately after his arrival from Paris. But the cramming crush of the millions who had turned out to welcome him jamming all the streets around the University, made it impossible for him to do so. A few hours later, it was at Beheshte Zahra that Khomeini delivered his first speech and where he had to be taken in a helicopter that Shapur Bakhtiar had sent.

The Tehran Uprising

On 5 February, four days after his arrival, Khomeini appointed Mehdi Bazargan Prime Minister of the provisional government. Bakhtiar called this move a 'joke,' saying that he would take no action as long as it remained a joke. With a crumbling army and an indecisive America behind him, Bakhtiar still believed himself to be the legal Prime Minister of the country.

America's primary concern at this stage was to avert the possibility of civil war, for that would have radicalized the masses further and strengthened the guerrilla organizations. The army therefore, had to be kept intact at any cost, even if that meant a tactical withdrawal and accommodation with Khomeini. It was in this context that General Huyser, Carter's special envoy who arrived in Tehran on 3 January 1979, and General Qarabaghi, Chief of the Iranian Military Forces and a trusted lieutenant of American interest, had begun secret negotiations with Khomeini's principal aides — Mehdi Bazargan and Ayatollah Beheshti, who later became Secretary General of the newly founded Islamic Republic party. While Bazargan and the clerical leaders on behalf of Khomeini were secretly negotiating with the U.S., the SAVAK Chiefs and the Chief of Staff, for an orderly transfer of power, the guerrilla organizations, prompted by the sudden revolt of young Air Force cadets and technicians at an Air Force base in Tehran, mounted a major assault on the remnants of the army.[29] This sudden development disrupted the negotiations and brought the Islamic Revolution to its climax — a general armed uprising and the quick victory of people's forces. There is little ambiguity about the events that led to the Tehran Uprising on the night of 9 February 1979. On that particular night, the Army controlled television screened the film of Khomeini's arrival as a prelude to its accommodation with the nation's new leader. Among those who were watching this film in the hall of the Air Force base at Farahabad, in the southern part of Tehran, were the Air Force cadets and technicians, called *Homafars*. These young cadets raised slogans in support of the Revolution and Ayatollah Khomeini as they watched the film. Members of the Imperial Guards who were also present in the hall resented this and fighting broke out between the *Homafars* and the Imperial soldiers. The *Homafars* entrenched themselves in their block after driving out the soldiers. The soldiers regrouped and laid a seige of the *Homafars* block.

As news of the fighting spread, people rushed to Farahabad to help the *Homafars*. Before midnight, thousands had gathered in the streets around the air base. A clergyman present at the scene pleaded with the people to disperse to avoid bloodshed.[30] But the *Homafars*, using megaphones from their block, urged the people to stand by them. Meanwhile, the two guerrilla organizations having learnt about the Farahabad fighting mobilized their members, distributed guns among their sympathizers and rushed in full force to help the beseiged cadets and technicians.[31] They dug trenches, raised sand bags, and took positions on roof tops of houses around the cadets' block. The battle for liberation had begun. Before additional units of Imperial Guards from the northern end of the city could reach Farahabad, the *Homafars* had discovered the secret armory located in their block and got hold of long longed for guns and grenades. They also distributed a large number of arms among the people. During the street fighting between the people and guerrillas on one hand, and the Imperial soldiers on the other, one could see children, some of them barely ten years old, passing Molotov bombs by the hundreds, made with Pepsi Cola bottles, to the combatants.[32] The Imperial Guards lost several tanks to these Pepsi Cola bombs.

Bakhtiar and the Generals knowing that the situation was now beyond their control, declared Martial Law effective from 4 p.m. on 10 February. Khomeini declared the Martial Law to be illegal and urged people to stay on the streets. He condemned the attack by Imperial Guards on Farahabad and warned the army that if soldiers did not return to their barracks, he would issue the religious decree *(fatwa)* giving people permission to take up arms against the regime.[33] But people had already taken up arms without waiting for Khomeini's decision and religious permission. By the morning of 11 February, Tehran was an embattled city. People had erected barricades on the streets and on roof tops in all parts of the city. By 11 a.m., the guerrillas had successfully beaten off the Imperial Guards and spent the next two days, from 11 February to 13 February in neutralizing SAVAK strongholds, occupying police stations, opening up the prisons, the armories, and the five major military bases in Tehran. Similar events took place in the provincial cities.[34] The struggle and resistance of *Mujahideen* and *Fedayeen* revolutionaries that had become ingrained in the minds of the people during the revolutionary process as a model and ideal of revolutionary action, spurred them to life during the national armed uprising. Besides the crucial influence the revolutionary vanguard had on the young by giving them personality models who had risen from amongst themselves, the *Mujahideen* and *Fedayeen* guerrillas played a significant role in the Tehran Uprising. Young Air Force cadets who began the armed uprising on 10 February, confirmed during an on the spot interview that they were greatly helped by the *Mujahideen-e-Khalq* and *Fedayeen-e-Khalq* guerrillas and the revolutionary people[35] when fighting broke out with the Imperial Guards. As reported by a national newspaper, in Tehran alone, 654 persons lost their lives and 2804 suffered serious injuries during the 'final three days that shook the foundations of 2500 years of the Monarchy.'[36] *Kayhan*, one of the largest newspapers in Iran, wrote that in 'these final days, the decisive role had been played by the *Mujahideen*, the *Fedayeen*, the *Fedayi Munsha-ab* (a pro-Tudeh off-shoot of *Fedayeen-e-Khalq* and the Tudeh Party).'[37] *Le Monde* reported that mere guerrillas had successfully snuffed out the once formidable army.[38] Soon after forming his government, Bazargan told interviewers from French Television that 'the Revolution would not forget the role played by the guerrillas and the Tudeh Party.'[39] Before sunset on 11 February, the radio and television announced the fall of Tehran. The first person to appear on television to congratulate the nation on its victory was Khalil Rezai, father of Ahmad, Mehdi, Reza, and Sadiqeh— the four members of *Mujahideen-e-Khalq* organization killed by SAVAK during the years of struggle of the resistance movement. During the Revolution, Khalil Rezai and his wife had addressed numerous meetings, both in Iran and abroad, recounting the crimes of the Shah's SAVAK and the torture and killing of political dissidents. The tape recording of Mr. Khalil Rezai's narrative about the struggle and execution of his children was one of the cassettes most Iranians had acquired during the Revolution. The suffering of the Rezai family for the cause of the Revolution had thus become a shared experience for the nation, and a living testimony to the illegitimacy of a regime that was erected on repression, torture, and execution. The appearance of Khalil Rezai on television during the first moments of the birth of the new Iran, immediately followed by a speech by Ayatollah Taleqani, was a solid confirmation of the fact that the progressive and democratic vanguard of Iran's Islamic Revoluiion had played a decisive role in overthrowiing the Pahlavi dictatorship. As in the Sandinist Revolution in Nicaragua, the guerrilla activity in Iran during 1971–77 had served as a 'prop for the masses, who crushed the enemy by means of insurrection.'[40] Perhaps the Shah had been right after all when he told journalists in Egypt, where he was mourning the demise of his monarchy, that 'the greatest mistake of my career' was to set *Mujahideen* and *Fedayeen* 'terrorists' free.[41]

During the brittle hours of victory, given the absence of a unified command structure for co-ordinating the armed activities of various groups, the National Radio and Television became the co-ordinating centre for the people's Revolution. It urged people to stay constantly tuned to the radio and sent urgent pleas to *Mujahideen* and *Fedayeen* guerrillas to rush to different trouble spots, including the Radio and Television station, which had come under attack by royalists and SAVAK agents. For sometime after the Tehran Uprising, *Mujahideen* and *Fedayeen* continued guarding strategic buildings in the Capital and elsewhere. The slogan 'Hail the *Mujahid!* Hail the *Fedayi*,' so often raised during the Revolution, could still mix freely with 'Hail Khomeini' slogans. As in the revolution in Nicaragua, it was the popular demand for 'arms, leadership, and organization' that had provided the incredible impetus for unity among conflicting revolutionary tendencies, namely traditional Islamic, progressive Islamic, communist, nationalist, as well as liberal, under Khomeini's overall leadership. The Revolution began to fall apart when the fusion generated by these tendencies began to be eroded by the power drive of a clerical faction callng itself the Islamic Republic Party. Dominated by formalist clergymen and founded only after the collective power of the above forces had overthrown the Pahlavi regime, the Islamic Republic Party (IRP) made the blind obedience of its policies and religious edicts the sole criteria for distinguishing between the 'Islamic' and the 'Un-Islamic,' revolution and counter—revolution.

Notes

1. *Kayhan International*, 20 March 1979.
2. Helmut Richards in *Iran Erupts*, p. 113.
3. Ibid.
4. *Kayhan International*, 20 March 1979.
5. *Mojahed*. Number 5, 19 August 1979.
6. *Kayhan International*, 20 March 1979.
7. After the Shah was overthrown, the reluctance of the new Islamic regime to follow up public enquiry into the Rex Cinema tragedy began giving rise to rumours and suspicions that a diseased mentality, using a religious pretext, might have been behind the inferno. The 170 families who had lost their loved ones in the Rex Cinema formed an informal association to press the Islamic government to carry out a public investigation of the tragedy. Faced with the reluctance and delays by the Islamic regime in doing so, these families staged a sit-in in Abadan. In August 1979, one year after the Rex Cinema incident, Mr. Sazesh, spokesman of the bereaved families told reporters that 'all available evidence shows that officials of the Shah's regime or SAVAK were not involved

in the incident. Otherwise the present authorities would not be so reluctant to investigate the case.' ('Search for the Truth', *Iranweek*, 24 August 1979, p. 19). Mr. Sazesh also pointed out that although the central figure involved in the incident —a young man named Hosein Takbalizadeh — had been arrested, he had been allowed to escape from prison several times. 'But people arrested him and handed him over to the officials telling them that if they could not keep him in jail, people would take the responsibility themselves.' (Ibid)

Actually, Hosein Takbalizadeh, a deeply religious person who hated movies, had set fire to the Cinema to further the cause of religion and revolution. It took the Islamic regime another year before it decided to go ahead with his public trial. During one of the trial sessions reported in the press, Abdulla-lur-qaba, an accused in the case and Takbalizadeh's confidante, was questioned by the Court as to why he did not report Takbalizadeh's crime to the Police since he knew about it. 'For the sake of Revolution,' Abdulla-lur-qaba replied. (*Kayhan*, No. 11087, 6 September 1980).

Takbalizadeh as well as nine others, mostly SAVAK agents, were given the death sentence on 6 September 1980, by Hujat-ul-Islam Moussavi Tabrizi, President of the Islamic Court. In his final remarks concluding the 18 sessions the trial had lasted, Hujat-ul-Islam Tabrizi transferred the burden of the crime from the 'religious' Takbalizadeh to SAVAK with the remarks, 'In this trial, the possibility can be conceded that SAVAK took advantage of Takbalizadeh's simplicity', and made him a tool of its own designs. Moussavi Tabrizi, who today is the Chief Prosecutor of Islamic Courts then made a surprising attack on 'Marxists — Leninists', who were in no way connected to the Abadan tragedy. His remarks insinuated that only Marxists were capable of committing such a crime because it was impossible for a Muslim to do so. 'How can one imagine that a Muslim should burn alive 400 people so that the Revolution attains victory? It is the Marxist—Leninists who say that ends justify the means, but Islam does not believe in this.' (*Kayhan*, No. 11087, September 1980).

8. *The Revolution which Islam brought.* Ministry of National Guidance, Tehran, 1980.
9. *Kayhan International*, 5 September 1978.
10. Nobari, A., *Iran Erupts*, p. 194.
11. Ibid.
12. Ibid.
13. Ibid.
14. Ibid., p. 195.
15. Yves-Guy-Berges, *Le Figaro*, 9—10 September 1978. Quoted in *Iran Erupts*, p. 200.
16. *Le Monde*, 11 September 1978. Quoted in *Iran Erupts*, p. 202.
17. Ibid.
18. *Kayhan*, No. 10593, 23 October 1978.

19. *Kayhan*, No. 10776, 7 August 1979.
20. Nobari, A., *Iran Erupts*, p. 225.
21. Maleki, H., *Daneshgah-e-Tehran va Jae-e-pa-e-Emperialism*. (Tehran University and Footprints of Imperialism). Tehran, 1980, p. 10.
22. Ibid.
23. Ibid.
24. Ibid.
25. *Le Monde*, 11 September 1978. Quoted in *Iran Erupts*, p. 202–3.
26. *Kayhan International*. 20 March 1979.
27. Ibid.
28. *Tehran Journal*, 29 January 1979.
29. Abrahimian, E., *The Guerrilla Movement in Iran*. MERIP. Vol. 10, No. 3, March-April 1980.
30. Afrasiabi, S. and Dehqan, B., *Taleqani and History*.
31. Ibid.
32. Afrasiabi, S. and Dehqan, B., *Taleqani and History*.
33. Khomeini's bulletin on 10 February 1979.
34. Abrahimian, E. The Guerrilla Movement in Iran. *MERIP*, vol. 10.
35. *Kayhan*, 12 February 1979.
36. Quoted in *The Guerrilla Movement In Iran*. MERIP. Vol. 10, No. 3, March-April 1980.
37. Ibid.
38. Ibid.
39. Ibid.
40. 'Can Sandinism Survive Reagan?' *The South*, May 1982, p. 65. Remark attributed to Sandinist leader Humberto Ortega.
41. *Mojahed*, June 1980.

11. The Runaway Revolution

We will murder any member (of Parliament) opposed to Imam Khomeini's Line of Thought.[1]

— Hujat-ul-Islam Hadi Ghaffari

In November 1981, Dr. Ali Shariati's house in Tehran was the venue of a meeting by Progressive Muslims for discussing the state of Iran's Revolution. 'Revolutions have always ended up in reaction when the illegitimate sons of the revolutionary movement have taken control of the revolution',[2] declared Ayatollah Ustad Ali Tehrani, the prominent religious leader from Mashhad and lifelong admirer of Ali Shariati, in his speech at the meeting. According to Ayatollah Tehrani, the main reason that most popular movements have ended up so miserably, particularly in the East, is hero worship and emergence of a personality cult. This tendency for idol worship has always led to a situation where the leader of a movement, surrounded by opportunists, begins to be idolized in a personal sense. Tehrani made these remarks at a time when the Islamic Revolution was being usurped by the Islamic Republic Party (IRP). Dominated by the clergy, the IRP was created shortly after the monarchy was overthrown and had campaigned for projecting itself as the only Islamic group loyal to Khomeini and the Revolution. But were Khomeini to be monopolized by a single Party, it would have cancelled his non-partisan image as a unifying force for the whole nation, a function which he had so successfully carried through during the mass movement against the Pahlavi dictatorship. The inevitable consequence of Khomeini's monopolization by a single Party, and his identification with it would have meant that the Party could invoke Khomeini's religious authority and leadership for creating its own dictatorship in the name of Islam.

Sensing this danger, Ali Asghar Haj Syed Javadi, a progressive Islamic intellectual whom Dr. Shariati had once lauded as a model of 'human dignity and freedom's resistance', for his struggle against the Pahlavi dictatorship, pointed out in an article that Khomeini's leadership had been the 'bond of unity' and the 'axis for political balance' in the country. 'This should create a strong and unified political leadership by all forces faithful to the Revolution and opposed to reaction, despotism, and imperialism'.[3] Javadi stressed in his article that Khomeini's leadership should not become propaganda material through monopolization and commercialization by any particular Party. Statements such as this were indicative of the direction towards which the IRP was leading the country by claiming for itself the absolute right to lead the Revolution, and invoking religious justification for suppressing and violating the legal rights of other political groups, which the IRP sponsored constitution had itself promised. In less than a month after the IRP was formed by Ayatollahs Behsheti, Rafsanjani, and Khamanei, the situation created by its power drive had begun to reflect itself in concrete terms in society. For example, although complete freedom of the press had been one of the principal demands of the Revolution, the press was being subjected to an 'unprecedented campaign of intimidation'.[4] Physical attacks by club-wielding gangsters invoking Khomeini's divine leadership against newspapers were being organized to force the press 'to express one and only one line of thought and opinion',[5] as the case had been under the Pahlavi monarchy. Commenting on the state of the Revolution barely five weeks after the Pahlavi dictatorship was overthrown, the *Tehran Journal* made the observation that during the Revolution, the monarchy had come to be called *Taghoot,* meaning a government based upon the worship of idols. But it was becoming clear now that even though the imperial idol had fallen, the idol worshippers were still around, sparing no time in substituting a religious idol for a royal one. As a result, people had already begun to question whether the new regime was 'walking in the way of God' as it claimed or whether it was bound to 'incur the wrath of God for taking the path that was ungodly'.[6]

A rather crude exhibition of this 'walk on the ungodly path' was publicly demonstrated on 13 April 1979, when a group of Islamic Revolutionary Guards abducted the sons and daughter-in-law of Ayatollah Taleqani from a central Tehran street in broad day—light, brandishing automatic weapons and using rifle butts on the Ayatollah's sons. The abduction of Taleqani's sons, who were returning from a meeting they had held with the Palestinian representatives in Tehran on their father's instructions, simply confirmed the fact that freedom, which had been the primary objective of the Revolution, was becoming the target and victim of a group who wanted total control of the Revolution. For Taleqani represented a distinct line of thought in the Revolution's leadership, where Islam was dynamic, assimilative and creative, and where freedom was a basic principle. Moreover, Taleqani did not endorse the IRP view that since the monarchy had been overthrown, the revolutionary vanguard groups and other secular forces that had fought against Pahlavi dictatorship be suppressed, and all power monopolized by a particular religious group with a restrictive outlook. The abduction of Taleqani's family members triggered massive demonstrations in his support. These demonstrations did not merely reflect public protest against an individual incident. Rather, they expressed the rage stemming from the general feeling that the Revolution was being abducted in the name of Islam by 'power monoplists' — the term Taleqani began using for IRP leaders who were determined to entrench their position by instituting a dictatorship in the name of religion. After three days of pro-Taleqani demonstrations had rocked the country, Taleqani, broke his silence and issued a statement emphasizing the point that the disgust he had felt at the abduction of his children and his departure from Tehran in protest 'was in no way personal'. It was simply born of the concern for 'safeguarding the freedom and independence' of the people and preventing a regression 'into the lap of dictatorship and despotism'.[7]

Mujahideen-e-Khalq also condemned the incident and warned people about the new fascistic tendency seeking to impose itself through a group 'who arrogate to themselves the right to do as they please in the name of Islam and deprive others of civil liberties through violence.'[8]

The mood being generated by the 'power monopolists' was poignantly reflected in 'The Sound of Fascism's Footsteps', an article Ali Asghar Haj Syed Javadi wrote immediately after the abduction incident. Part of this article, among the last to appear in the national press before Javadi was banned from writing and most newspapers were closed down, reads: 'For years we had protested against the Shah's SAVAK for abducting people in broad day-light and subjecting them to beatings and torture during interrogation in isolated quarters. And now, in the name of Islam and the Islamic Republic, SAVAK and its apparatus of suppression, repression, violence, and intimidation is being reintroduced on a far more extensive scale. If a blind, crude, and violent fascism is rising to replace Pahlavi fascism, of what use would it be if it calls itself by a different name and hides itself under an "Islamic" cover?'[9] The article recalled that the former Shah had violated people's rights on the pretext that he was fighting 'communists' and 'terrorists'. Now it seemed that those who had decided overnight to become revolutionaries and jumped on the bandwagon the revolutionary vanguard got started, were shamelessly following in the Shah's footsteps to strengthen their power. 'A blind, raw, cruel, and fascistic show of force is developing in order to intimidate people and to send them to the valleys of silence. Threats, violent attacks, beatings and insults are being used to stifle the voices of protest, so that the late-comer revolutionaries may get hold of the Revolution's reins.'[10] The concluding note of this article was prophetic in that it predicted that the liberating Islamic Revolution which progressive revolutionaries like Taleqani, Shariati, *Mujahideen-e-Khalq* and others had been struggling for and propagating, would deviate from its path after confrontation with regressive elements. As a result, the Revolution would 'eventually fall into the lap of internal reaction and international reaction'.[11] Faced with this disaster, it was vital for every person to act according to one's responsibility and to put up a fight 'even if this leads to one's annihilation or death. For life is nothing but belief and *jehad*',[12] Javadi concluded, quoting Imam Hossein, the religious model of resistance against religious reaction.

The violence being unleashed by the 'power monopolists' was getting so widespread that the revolutionary groups, who were its primary targets, had to print booklets for keeping a record of the attacks they were being subjected to. Barely three weeks after the Tehran Uprising, *Mujahideen* headquarters in three provincial cities[13] were simultaneously attacked by club-wielding and gun-slinging groups. In Torbat-e-Heydariyeh, a town in Khorassan Province, the building of the Muslim Youth Association supporting the *Mujahideen* was attacked and ransacked by a group of people brandishing picks, shovels, knives, and clubs. The mob had been raised by a preacher in one of the town's mosques, who ruled that 'shedding of *Mujahideen* blood was lawful'.[14] Since the new regime had come to power, the mosques were being increasingly used as the platform for campaigning against *Mujahideen*, with Sheikh Khaz'ali assuming the role of a roving propagandist, preaching in towns and villages that *Mujahideen* were hypocrites, apostates and 'worse than Marxists'. The Sheikh gained recognition by his now famous statement that if the need arose, the clergy would rather compromise with the Shah than with Rajavi, the *Mujahideen* leader.[15] News items from a single issue of *Ettela'at*, the largest daily, are indicative of the scale and nature of the IRP—orchestrated violence against its potential political foe. In its issue dated 23 February 1980, barely a year after the Pahlavi dictatorship was overthrown, the paper reports that several bookshops in the city of Mianeh were attacked and set on fire by 'a group of people',[16] while in Qa'emshahr 'a group of people' attacked a meeting of *Mujahideen* supporters, killing one person and wounding three hundred. The paper also reports that in Shiraz, the southern provincial capital, five hundred persons were injured when 'a group of people' attacked the *Mujahideen's* main office but faced resistance by *Mujahideen* supporters. In Tehran, the same paper reports, 'countless' people were injured when a *Mujahideen's* meeting at Tehran University was attacked. Only a few weeks earlier *Ettela'at*[17] had reported that a group of people shouting, 'The only permissible party is God's party, Khomeini, God's spirit, is the only leader', had attacked a meeting of *Mujahideen* supporters in Tehran University armed with daggers and ironbars.

Between 20 March and 20 April 1980, more than 80 incidents were reported in over 40 cities where *Mujahideen* supporters had been attacked, beaten, gunned down, harrassed, arrested, and stabbed. In some cases, Molotov bombs were thrown into homes of *Mujahideen* sympathisers. At least in two instances, high school students selling the *Mojahed* newspaper were stabbed to death.[18] The attack on the *Mujahideen's* office at Mashhad resulted in the killing of one member of the organization and wounding of four hundred supporters. Attacks on bookshops were not confined only to those selling communist literature. The entire book-bazaar in Tabriz, capital of Azerbaijan Province was attacked and ransacked. Libraries and bookshops selling revolutionary Islamic literature by Shariati and *Mujahideen-e-Khalq* were also attacked and set on fire.[19] In the attack on the heart of Iran's book-bazaar, just next to Tehran University, three employees of a bookshop sustained severe injuries,[20] when the bookshops were invaded by men armed with clubs and axes.

Even declaration and demonstration of support by non-IRP groups for Khomeini's anti-imperialist measures were not tolerated—when the *Fedayeen-e-Khalq* staged a street procession to express solidarity with 'Muslim student followers of Imam Khomeini' who occupied the American embassy in Tehran, they were attacked by a group of IRP supporters led by Hujat-ul-Islam Hadi Ghaffari, leader of a power pocket within IRP. The violent attackers disrupted the *Fedayeen* procession shouting, 'We shall turn Iran into *Fedayeen's* graveyard'. The *Fedayeen* resisted with the slogan 'We shall turn Iran into America's graveyard'.[21] A few weeks later, an authorised meeting of the *Fedayeen-e-Khalq* supporters, permission for which had been legally granted by the regime, was attacked by 'a group of people' with Molotov bombs and guns. Two persons were killed and 25 were injured[22] after the 'Hezbollahis' had disrupted the meeting.

Steps for Erasing Personality Models
From their standpoint, the formalist clergymen believed their campaign against revolutionary groups, in particular the *Mujahideen*, was justified. All signs testified that the *Mujahideen* were growing as an avalanche of revolutionary Islamic consciousness. Over four million copies of the *Mujahideen's* ideological and revolutionary literature had got into circulation since September 1978. Their newspaper, the *Mujahid*, had hit a circulation touching the half million mark. In addition, *Mujahideen* began publishing their journal in English and translated some of their ideological material into the Arabic and English languages. When the new academic session began in September 1979, courses arranged by *Mujahideen* student supporters on 'Dynamism of the Quran' drew a large enrolment all over the country. At Tehran's Sharif University of Engineering and Technology alone, ten thousand students had registered for this course, in what was a too obvious reminder of Dr. Shariati's lectures at Hossienieh Irshad. As its name indicated, the lectures on 'Dynamism of the Quran' dealt with a dynamic redefinition of Islam within the framework of the present age. The course on Islamic ideology was essentially structured along the same instructional lines as the education which *Mujahideen-e-Khalq* members used to secretly receive

in clandestine study cells during the repressive years of the Pahlavi dictatorship. After the Pahlavi regime was overthrown, this wave of revolutionary Islamic consciousness had become so popular and generalized that it dominated the educational centres and other institutions. Another indication of its popularity could be seen in the new names the universities, colleges, schools, streets, hospitals and libraries had adopted. While Tabriz University, the second largest in the country, had been named Hanif-nejad University, after one of the co-founders of the *Mujahideen-e-Khalq* organization who hailed from Tabriz and was executed by the Shah in 1972, Iran's leading University of Engineering and Technology was given the name of Sharif Vaqafi, another *Mujahideen* martyr of the Pahlavi era. Iran's only university for women at Tehran was named Motahedin University, after Mehbobeh Motahedin, the *Mujahideen-e-Khalq* urban guerrilla who was killed in a gun battle with the Shah's security police and whom Shariati had eulogised as a contemporary personality model for Muslim women. Literally, hundreds of colleges, hospitals, institutes, libraries, streets and city centres were named after Dr. Shariati and *Mujahideen-e-Khalq* martyrs. The country's only heart hospital, one of the best in the region, was named Mehdi Rezai Heart Hospital, after the 19 year old *Mujahid-e-Khalq* guerrilla who was tortured to death in 1972 and whose defence speech in the Shah's military court has registered for posterity his defiance and contempt for the Pahlavi regime. Moreover, the revolutionary songs and music dominating revolutionary Iran was entirely derived from *Mujahideen* and *Fedayeen* sources. These revolutionary songs and poetry of resistance, born of the living experience of revolutionaries on the battlefield of struggle, had been in secret circulation in previous years.

While it was possible for the religious monopolists to ban *Mujahideen* music on radio and television and erase the names of *Mujahideen* martyrs from sign boards on schools and streets, there was little they could do to erase the 'personality models'—blueprints for a revolutionary personality—which the *Mujahideen* vanguard had etched through their revolutionary life, struggle, and death, in the minds of the young. Nevertheless, the IRP clerics, by employing various tactics, attempted to render these personality models redundant by attacking the *Mujahideen's* ideology and creating ambiguities about their loyalty to Islam. An example of this is provided in the public trials which were held for SAVAK agents whose role as torturers and executioners of revolutionaries under the Pahlavi regime was undisputed. Initially, these trials were shown live on television in view of the popular demand for their exhibition. As a result, the trials had become propaganda channels for *Mujahideen* and *Fedayeen*, for almost all the persons who had been killed under torture or executed during 1971–77 belonged to these groups. However, later the ruling regime attempted to use these trials to its own advantage by converting them into a platform for propaganda against the *Mujahideen* and *Fedayeen*. For example, a notorious SAVAK agent by the name of Tehrani, who was responsible for carrying out some of the most brutal tortures against revolutionaries, defended himself in the Islamic Court by pleading that he had interrogated or sometimes beaten 'only communists and Islamic Marxists', and that he had never tortured any clergymen whom he revered and held in high esteem. Tehrani's statement struck a sympathetic chord in extremist clerical quarters, some of whom even began campaigning that the SAVAK agent be 'forgiven' and his services be used against the enemies of Islam. Also present at Tehrani's trial were some *Mujahideen* who had served prison terms during the Shah's Iran and were tortured by Tehrani. But they were prevented from giving statements in support of the accusations against their former torturer in the Islamic Court of justice. A case in point being that of Masumeh Shadmani Kabiri, a 50 year old house-wife who was given a life sentence by the Pahlavi regime for resisting the monarchy. In her open letter to the Revolutionary Council, the former victim of SAVAK's tortures complained of the 'insulting treatment' accorded to her during the trial of her former tormentor which she had attended as a witness for the prosecution. Mrs. Kabiri stated that when Tehrani, the SAVAK agent, had made 'completely false and fictitious remarks' about some of the martyrs in the court room, the officials of the Islamic Court did not permit her to speak and clarify the accusations. When Masumeh insisted on speaking as a 'witness', the official called her a 'trouble maker' and ordered her out of the hall. Masumeh, who had herself been tortured and seen others tortured during her imprisonment, told the Islamic judge that the Shah 'also called us trouble makers'. She recounted that until a few months ago, she was a prisoner 'in these very rooms and cells of the Qasr prison', where the trial was now being held. 'I have not yet forgotten the heart—rending screams of women under torture, whose bodies had been burnt. Do I have to hear from you what I have been hearing from the Shah's regime?' However, the Islamic judge could not turn Masumeh out of the court because those present at the trial took her side and refused to support the Islamic official's 'Un-Islamic and immoral attempt' at converting the SAVAK agent's trial 'into the trial of a *Mujahid-e-Khalq* supporter'. In her open letter, Masumeh asked whether the Islamic Court's refusal in allowing a witness to speak against the slanders of her tormentor was not indicative of a 'sinister plot for discrediting the pure and selfless sons and daughters of the people and God. Should those who were tortured, murdered, imprisoned, and subjected to insults and humiliation during the dark oppressive reign of the Shah be made the sacrificial victims of sinister and inhuman plots, so that the way for compromise and capitulation is opened?'[23]

Also illustrative of the compromising stance of the Islamic 'power monopolists' with SAVAK agents is another open letter[24] which the mother of three *Fedayeen-e-Khalq* members wrote to the Prosecutor General of the Islamic Court. The letter also appeared in the national

Press. Mrs. Sanjari, the mother of three *fedayis*, stated that two of her sons were killed by SAVAK in 1975 and 1976 respectively, while a third son had been tortured to the extent that he had lost his sanity and had to be institutionalized. Her own husband had died of a heart attack when SAVAK agents suddenly burst into their home during the night to arrest one of her sons. Mrs. Sanjari complained in her letter that although she had been present in the Islamic Court where a SAVAK agent responsible for the death of one of her sons was put on trial, she was not allowed to speak as a prosecution witness. And although the SAVAK agent had confessed he had had a hand in the death of Mrs. Sanjari's son, he was given only a two year prison term. Mrs. Sanjari expressed surprise that while only a few days ago an Islamic Court had sentenced five members of a revolutionary group to death in a single day, and had consigned them to the firing squad immediately without even explaining to the people the charges levelled against them, the same Islamic Court had given a two year sentence to a SAVAK murderer who had confessed his crimes. 'Is there not a definite purpose behind sparing people like my son's murderers from getting the punishment they deserve?' Mrs. Sanjari asked. She added that concessions of this type and the light sentences that were being handed to SAVAK agents pointed to the fact that the Islamic regime planned to reorganize SAVAK and employ its qualified agents and specialists, who had brought universal shame and hate against the Shah's regime, for its own purposes.

There seemed to be considerable substance in the allegation about SAVAK agents being retained for use by the Islamic regime for its own security. A glance at the issues of *Ettela'at* during June-July 1979, reveals that during the period of a single month, hundreds of 'SAVAKIS' were released from prison. It was also reported that the former head of SAVAK in the city of Arak 'who had repented for his past deeds in the presence of Hujat-ul-Islam-al-Eshaq', was helping the Islamic regime in apprehending 'counter revolutionaries',[25] the term the Islamic regime now used for its political opponents. Before long, the revolutionary groups began complaining that while the prisons were becoming empty of SAVAK agents, they were getting filled with revolutionaries and their sympathisers. Commenting on this state of affairs, Hujat-ul-Islam Karubi, an aide to Khomeini, conceded that criminals of the previous regime were being allowed to move about freely in the country.[26]

The problem with the ruling clergymen's regime was that although they had abducted a revolution, they had no revolutionary models of their own or a revolutionary background upon which to project themselves. Khomeini's image as the overall leader of Revolution could give them the religious legitimacy they longed for, but it was not enough. For this religious legitimacy was something quite different from the tangible grip which personality models like Mehdi Rezai, Fatima Amini and other martyred revolutionaries exercised on the young.

The impact which the *Mujahideen-e-Khalq* pioneers had had on the Revolution through their posthumous, yet constant presence, in the minds of the young as the ideal embodiment of selfless revolutionaries, was pointed out by Ayatollah Tehrani. In an interview the prominent Ayatollah from Mashhad had given to a group of students and which was printed and circulated by the students themselves after the clergy controlled press censored the interview, Ayatollah Tehrani said that during the struggle against the Shah, there were two categories of clergymen who participated in the demonstrations against the Pahlavi regime. The first category, consisting of only a few clergymen, comprised of those who 'daily used to go with the young, with the university fellows and students to face the tanks and guns'. The second category of clergymen were those who used to take part in demonstrations only after they had sought permission in advance from military authorities. It was only after this permission for taking out a procession had been granted that these clerics (who were now in power) joined the folds of the street demonstrations against the Shah. 'But the real demonstrations,' emphasized Tehrani, 'were those which were held under the barrage of machine guns, tear gas shells, and rumbling tanks. These young students would take care of us and attend to us when we could see no longer, blinded by the tear gas and the smoke. These same young men, these young university students who are now among the *Mujahideen*, who joined the *Mujahideen*, are the ones who followed the example of *Mujahideen* martyrs and were at the fore-front of the struggle. When the soldiers started shooting, everyone would run away and disperse. No clergyman would be in sight. It was these young fellows who surrounded the tanks, set them on fire and disarmed the soldiers. Look at their defence speeches, the tortures suffered by Saeed Mohsen, Hanif-nejad (co-founders of *Mujahideen*) and others, which gave so much morale to our people.[27]

To counter the appeal of *Mujahideen-e-Khalq* 'personality models', another manoeuvre the IRP and its formalist clerics attempted was to invoke the posthumous support of a few young revolutionaries who were not regular members of the *Mujahideen* and were executed by the Pahlavi regime for their armed struggle against the Shah's dictatorship. An example of this attempt can be seen in an interview published in IRP's newspaper *Jumhuri-ye-Islami*[28] by Ayatollah Rabbani, a top ranking IRP Ayatollah and Khomeini's personal representative in Shiraz.[29] In this interview, Rabbani claimed that members of the Abu Zar Group, a small Islamic guerrilla organization formed in the city of Nahavand, four of whose members were executed during the Pahlavi era, 'were in no way linked with *Mujahideen-e-Khalq*'. Furthermore, he claimed that members of the Abu Zar Group, who were the 'purest of all groups', had contacted him several times 'and asked for my guidance'. However, the IRP failed in its attempt at using the Abu Zar martyrs as parallel models against *Mujahideen* revolutionaries like

Mehdi Rezai, because of the disclosures made by survivors of the Abu Zar Group. In an open letter written in response to Ayatollah Rabbani's interview, Alireza Karmali and Hujatullah Avarzamani, the two survivors of the Abu Zar Group stated that their Group had been inspired in its 'sacred armed struggle' against the Pahlavi dictatorship by the *Mujahideen-e-Khalq*.

'The Defence Speech of Mehdi Rezai, the Red Rose of the Revolution, had ignited a fire in our breasts, impelling us to seek the *Mujahideen*. Even when we contacted Mr. Rabbani we requested him to help us get in touch with the *Mujahideen*.' The survivors of the Abu Zar Group[30] then asked people to read the 'Defence Speeches' their martyred brothers in the Group had delivered in the Shah's Military Court, in order to find out for themselves whether the martyrs of the Abu Zar Group were associated with the *Mujahideen-e-Khalq* or not.

It was within such a context that the student supporters of the IRP clerics decided to take over the American embassy in Tehran.

The Hostage Crisis

Two main reasons prompted the clergy sponsored students to occupy the American Embassy in Tehran on 4 November 1979. One of these reasons was to strengthen the IRP in its power struggle against the liberals in the government headed by Bazargaan. The other was to win popular credit for student supporters of IRP by portraying them as a revolutionary force. After all, student supporters of the IRP were clearly in a minority compared to the huge following the *Mujahideen* and *Fedayeen* commanded among students and the young. After the takeover of the U.S. embassy, student supporters of IRP could also compete with the two revolutionary groups by taking credit for their 'revolutionary' and 'anti-imperialist' action. However, it needs to be recalled that it was the *Fedayeen-e-Khalq* guerrillas who first occupied the American Embassy in Tehran on 14 February 1979, only three days after the Pahlavi regime was overthrown. At that time the *Fedayeen's* action was condemned by the clergy and the Revolutionary Council. Even Tass, the official Russian news agency, condemned the action of a Marxist-Leninist group, which, unlike the Tudeh Party, had developed and acted independently of Russian influence. The Russian news agency branded *Fedayeen* as 'Western spies'.[31] The *Fedayeen* were subsequently forced to leave the U.S. embassy, and a special unit of Islamic Revolutionary Guards, headed by Mashallah Qasab, was installed by the regime in the embassy for protecting the American diplomats. In May 1979, the Revolutionary Guards of the American Embassy abducted Reza Sada'ati, a leading *Mujahideen-e-Khalq* member from his apartment. The handbills circulated by these Revolutionary Guards and their supporters accused Sada'ati of spying for Russia and undermining Iran—U.S. relations. Officially, the Islamic regime disowned having anything to do with the Revolutionary Guard's unit at the American Embassy or with Sada'ati's detention. Nevertheless, the Islamic Court took charge of Sada'ati when he was handed over to it by the American Embassy Revolutionary Guards. Although Ayatollah Taleqani had dismissed the espionage charges against Sada'ati saying that his arrest had 'nothing to do with spying',[32] implying that it had more to do with the power struggle within the Revolution, Sada'ati was detained for a whole year before he was given a trial in August 1980, and sentenced to ten years imprisonment.

After the American Embassy was taken over by 'Student Followers of Imam Khomeini', they began using the secret documents at the Embassy primarily as a tool for discrediting the Western educated liberals in Bazargaan's government as 'American agents'. Any document indicating that a non-cleric had contacted an American official was used as evidence for accusing the person in question of being an 'American agent'. The students never revealed the documents dealing with negotiations clergy leaders like Ayatollah Beheshti and Ayatollah Rafsanjani had held with the Americans and the Shah's generals for sorting out the conditions for a smooth transfer of power to the clerical leadership[33] during the mass movement against the Pahlavi regime. Also, those documents which referred to the *Mujahideen* as radical anti-imperialists were not made public nor was the fact that Mashallah Qasab, abductor of a *Mujahideen-e-Khalq* leader, had been appointed to the U.S. embassy by Mehdi Hadavi,[34] Chief Prosecutor of the Islamic Court. While Khomeini's regime had denied it had anything to do with Mashallah Qasab, documents found at the American Embassy described Mashallah Qasab, the zealous supporter of American interests in Iran, as some one 'who has two warrants authorizing his presence at the Embassy, one from the Revolutionary Prosecutor General, Mehdi Hadavi, another from Revolutionary Guards Headquarters'.[35] The secret document conveying 'a summary of significant information developed on Mashallah (Qasab) Kashani',[36] also confirmed that the American agent was 'in direct contact with Hadavi'.[37] Although these documents confirmed the role of the American Embassy and its Revolutionary Guards authorized by Khomeini's Islamic regime in creating the Sada'ati scenario, the latter's confinement in prison continued on the basis of charges of spying for Russia. In August 1981, after the spate of executions of anti-regime demonstrators was well under way, Sada'ati was removed from his cell in Evin prison. Despite the ten year prison term he had been handed by the Islamic Court, Sada'ati was executed by the firing squad in the prison courtyard,[38] for belonging to an organization which the clerics were now describing as composed of 'American agents'.

The declared objective of the occupation of the Embassy by student followers of Imam Khomeini was to force America to hand over the Shah to Iran. This demand had been raised for lending justification to the Embassy take-over because the Shah continued to be a detested figure. By giving refuge to him on the pretext of medical treatment on its soil, America had further inflamed the anti-American feeling prevailing in the country at the time. The students therefore simply demanded that in order to get the hostages released, all that America was required to do was 'to hand over the treacherous Shah to Iran', and 'the question of negotiations with the U.S.' on this issue did not arise.[39] Also, the students warned the Islamic government that any attempt to draw their 'authentic' and anti-imperialist action to the negotiating table would amount to a 'betrayal' of their 'glorious and Divine movement'.[40] However, with the death of the Shah and the concentration of power with the IRP after Prime Minister Bazargaan's resignation, the clergy sponsored students tabled four conditions for releasing the hostages:

a. Returning to Iran $24 billion of the Shah's wealth the Islamic regime believed he had amassed in America.
b. Formal apology by President Carter to the Iranian people for the mistakes and crimes America had perpetrated against the Iranian people in the past.
c. An assurance by the American government that American companies and organizations which had been contracted for various development projects in Iran would not take legal action against Iran and demand compensation for annullment of their contracts.
d. A 'promise' by the United States government that it would not interfere in the internal affairs of Iran.

The Islamic regime confirmed that these conditions were 'final'. There could be no negotiations on them, and if America failed to comply with all these conditions, the hostages would be put on trial on charges of espionage. America refused to acquiesce with these demands.

Having achieved part of its objectives on the domestic political scene, and confronted with America's adamant refusal to submit to its demands, the IRP decided that there was nothing it could achieve by prolonging the crisis. The result was that within a year of taking American diplomats hostage, those clerical leaders who had argued that putting the hostages on trial would be 'the supreme index of their anti-imperialist struggle', began soliciting the freedom of the hostages. They now reasoned that the struggle against imperialism could not be gauged by merely keeping 52 hostages. Because, regardless of whether the hostages were freed or not, America would not renounce its designs against Iran. Moreover, after Carter's defeat in the Presidential elections in 1980, IRP leaders were keen to settle the issue with the 'moderate' Carter (while he was still in the White House) rather than face Reagan. For the later had declared that he would re-negotiate the whole hostage issue Carter was trying to resolve on what Reagan believed to be non-punitive terms. Also, the statement[41] by General Graham, a prospective military adviser to Reagan, pointing out the possibility of laying mines around the 'oil ports of Iran' as a step for winning the hostage's freedom, had sent the clergymen scurrying for a settlement with Carter at all costs. In this connection, it is worth noting that Behzad Nabavi, the IRP-sponsored spokesman for the Islamic government, was desperately driving home the point that Carter would not be able to officiate as President after 16 January 1981. He pointed to the necessity for accepting Carter's conditions for releasing hostages, pleading that 'if we do not reach any result (in our negotiations with Carter) by then (16 January), it cannot be said what form our negotiations would take with the new (U.S.) government. We have therefore decided to reach an acceptable agreement (with America) and bring the hostage problem to an end.'[42]

Clearly then, it was America who dictated the final terms on the hostages issue and not Iran. The American terms were not any different from those it had already offered during the initial weeks of the hostage crisis: America refused to offer an 'apology', a condition which Khomeini had so vehemently stressed, and she also refused to return the Shah to Iran while he was alive. After the Shah's death, the wealth he was alleged to have amassed in American banks was to be viewed as an issue to be settled in American courts through formal legal procedures, a proposition American had originally offered a year earlier. America concluded the hostage crisis by accepting only two of the conditions Iran had originally proposed—an assurance to Iran that she would not interfere in Iran's internal affairs, and agreeing to defreeze the $13.9 billion of Iranian assets she had frozen after the students took over the Embassy. Even these two conditions were met not as Iran wanted, but as America had deemed desirable. For example, in meeting the first condition, America made it categorically clear that 'U.S. policy is not based on interference, and America does not interfere in Iran's internal affairs'.[43] The above statement showed that America had not only refused to offer an apology for past interference in Iran's internal affairs, indeed it even denied any interference, whether in the past or the present by declaring that 'such a course of action did not constitute American policy'.[44] As for the second condition, Iran did not get its $13.9 billion that America had blocked. The agreement signed between Iran's Islamic regime and America provided for a release of these assets in three stages. In the first stage, Iran was to receive $1.7 billion. As for the remaining amount, it was to be decided in accordance with Iran's problems vis-a-vis the claims of the 250 American companies demanding compensation for cancelled contracts, and Iran's balance of payment on outstanding loans. While making these aspects of the negotiations public, *Enqelabe Islami* editorially extended a blistering greeting to the IRP clergymen for settling for a mere

$1.7 billion instead of their 'final and irrevocable' claim for $24 billion. The editorial summed up the 14 month long episode of the American hostages, stating that the IRP students had taken this step to force America to accept the following conditions:

    a. Returning the Shah to Iran and the Shah's wealth amounting to $24 billion.
    b. A formal apology by Carter for the crimes committed by America in Iran.
    c. An assurance to Iran that in future, America shall not interfere in Iran's internal affairs.
    d. Affirming that American companies shall not file legal suits against Iran demanding financial compensation for cancelled contracts after the Revolution.

Literally, none of these conditions were met by America in any real and meaningful sense. However, America did release a part of Iran's blocked assets that it had frozen and also agreed to lift the economic blockade of Iran. But America had taken these two steps only after the hostages were taken, in order to force Iran to release the hostages. And once the Islamic regime had agreed to release them, there was no longer any reason for America to persist with its initial sanctions against Iran.

Notes

1. *Ettela'at.* No.16095, 11 March 1980.
2. *Kodamin Rah-e-Sayyum?* (Which Third Way?). Published by supporters of the banned 'Institute For Propagation of Shariati's Thought'. Tehran, November 1981.
3. *Kayhan.* No.10776, 7 August 1979.
4. *Tehran Journal.* No.16095, 20 March 1979.
5. Ibid.
6. Ibid.
7. Taleqani's Statement on 17 April 1979. Quoted in *Mojahed,* May 1980.
8. Ibid.
9. Javadi, A., 'The Sound of Fascism's Footsteps.' *Ayndegaan,* No. 3335, 17 April 1979.
10. Ibid.
11. Ibid.
12. Ibid.
13. *Ettela'at.* No.15799. 4 March 1979.
14. *Mojahed.* June 1980 (editorial).
15. Ibid.
16. 'Group of people' was the term the press indirectly used for

IRP — sponsored groups of club-wielders who attacked political opponents of IRP, chanting the slogan *'Hezb Fa qet Hezb'ollah, Rahbar fa qet Rub'ollah'*, meaning 'The only permissible Party is Allah's Party, (Khomeini) God's spirit, is the only leader'. These gangs came to be known as the 'Hezbollahis', since they claimed that only they represented God's Party.

17. *Ettela'at.* 31 January 1980.
18. *Mojahed.* May 1980.
19. *Ettela'at.* 8 May 1979, 9 December 1979.
20. Ibid. 22 April 1979.
21. *Ettela'at.* 26 November 1979.
22. Ibid. 16 February 1980.
23. Masumeh Shadmani Kabiri was 40 when she first got acquainted with the *Mujahideen* in 1971. Two of her sons were *Mujahideen* members sentenced to life imprisonment by the Shah's regime. During the early 70s, Masumeh was among the few women who actively participated in the protest movements made by families of imprisoned *Mujahideen*. Following her release from the Shah's prison during the Islamic Revolution, Masumeh was subjected to continuous harrassment by the new Islamic regime. Even the house she lived in was confiscated. In October 1981, Masumeh was arrested by Khomeini's Revolutionary Guards and sent to Evin prison. According to the *Mujahideen*, she was 'tortured in the most violent and inhuman conditions by mercenary beasts' before she was formally handed the death sentence and executed by a firing squad. Her two sons and a son's wife had been executed two months earlier.
24. Open Letter of mother of Martyred *Fedayeen-e-Khalq* Khashayar and Keyumars Sanjari. In, *Ayandegaan*, No.3418, 6 August 1979.
25. *Ettela'at.* 7 April 1979.
26. *Ettela'at.* 5 November 1979.
27. Ustad Ali Tehrani's interview, 26 June 1980.
28. *Jamhuri-ye-Islami.* 6 July 1980. Quoted in the open letter of survivors of Abu Zar Group.
29. Ayatollah Rabbani, whom Khomeini had appointed as a member of the powerful Guardian Council died in a car accident in February 1982.
30. Alireza Karam Ali and Hujetullah Avarzami, the two surviving members of the Abu Zar Group, were sentenced to life imprisonment by the Pahlavi regime. They were among the last batch of political prisoners released by the Shah before the general uprising in February 1979, toppled his regime. Hujetullah Avarzami was executed by Khomeini's regime in September 1982, while Karam Ali is reported missing.
31. *Kayhan*, No.11499, 2 February 1982.
32. *Ettela'at*, 1 July 1979.
33. During Ayatollah Ustad Tehrani's three day stay with student followers of Imam Khomeini at the American embassy, the students showed him documents revealing that some of the most vocal 'anti-imperialists' among the clerics had American contacts.

Ayatollah Tehrani is known to have filed a report on these 'pro-American anti-imperialists' and handed it over to the Grand Ayatollah Khomeini.
34. *Mojahed*. No.106, 20 January 1980.
35. Document at the American Embassy entitled 'Secret, Tehran, 08947', No.0091245 dated August 1979. Published in *Mojahed*, No.106, 20 January 1980.
36. Ibid.
37. Ibid.
38. Also executed under detention was Saeed Soltanpur, a leading poet and intellectual who, as a member of the *Fedayeen-e-Khalq*, had struggled against the Pahlavi regime for the past seven years and had spent four years in the Shah's jails. Arrested on his wedding day in April 1981, on charges of smuggling currency, Soltanpur was in prison when the demonstrations against Khomeini broke out in June 1981. He was, however, executed on charges of participating in the demonstration against the Islamic Republic in August 1981.
39. Student Followers of Imam Khomeini. Bulletin No.19. Quoted in *Mojahed*, No.105, 13 January 1981.
40. Ibid., Bulletin No.32.
41. *Kayhan*, 31 December 1980.
42. Kayhan, 12 January 1981. Quoted in *Mojahed*, 20 January 1981.
43. 'Which Victory?' (editorial) *Enqelabe Islami*, No.956, 23 January 1981.
44. Ibid.

12. Elections in the Islamic Republic

> *People were made to vote for IRP candidates through the use of deception, intimidation .... mass imprisonment and murder.... I am grieved to declare that at no period (in history) acts such as these have been witnessed. People did not expect the Islamic government to act in this manner.*
>
> *– Ayatollah Pasandeedeh, elder brother of Ayatollah Khomeini.*[1]

The Presidential Elections

Abol Hassan Banisadr, the French educated economist and a close associate of Ayatollah Khomeini, pocketed 75% of the 14 million votes cast in the country's first Presidential elections held in January 1980. His promises during the election campaign included the nationalization of banks, insurance, foreign trade and heavy industry. A year later, he also promised to 'resist efforts being made to create an atmosphere of terror, suppression, and censor' for decimating the people's fundamental rights and their 'courage to criticize'.[2]

The turn out in the January elections showed that nearly 7 million voters had stayed away from the polls. Only ten months earlier, in April 1979, over 20.4 million votes were cast in the referendum for the Islamic Republic, of which 98% supported the new republic. The lower turn out in the Presidential elections showed that things had changed considerably since the days of the referendum, and that people's enthusiasm, hope, and trust in the Islamic Republic was being frustrated as a result of the uneven policies of the formalist clerics in the IRP. Hasan Habibi, the candidate IRP had supported in the elections against Banisadr, got only half a million votes compared to Banisadr's 11 million.

That the IRP clerics had sensed that there was little chance of them winning the Presidential elections was reflected in the pressure which different religious quarters, with an outlook similar to the IRP's, were variously applying to dispense with the need of holding elections altogether. Their argument was that a group of clergymen nominated by Khomeini should get together and select a suitable candidate from among themselves for the President's office. An open letter addressed to Ayatollah Khomeini and published in the ultra-right wing *Sobeh Azadegaan* indicating this line of thought partly reads: 'We beseech the Imam, the Great Leader, the Grace of God on earth, to order competent individuals such as the learned *Ulama* and teachers of theological schools, and those who have been elected to the Assembly of Experts (for drafting the Islamic Constitution); or anyone whom (you) consider suitable, or unsuitable, to get together, and in the shortest possible time, consensually nominate one person as the candidate for the President's office, so that by avoiding Un-Islamic propaganda, the best possible person may be selected for this crucial office'.[3]

As for the *Mujahideen-e-Khalq*, Khomeini disqualified Masood Rajavi, their candidate, after large numbers of the nation's youth embarked upon a vigorous election campaign for Rajavi and the Kurdish political and religious leaders declared that the six million Sunni Kurds would be voting for Rajavi. The official reason given for Rajavi's disqualification was that the *Mujahideen* had objected to a number of articles in the draft Constitution of the Islamic Republic, among them articles 107—10, which vested absolute powers with a council of Ayatollahs or a leading Islamic jurist. These articles according to the *Mujahideen*, posed an inbuilt contradiction in the Constitution. On the one hand, the constitution recognised the sovereignty of the people through direct and free elections for the Parliament and the Presidency. On the other hand, it gave the Islamic jurists final authority over and above the Parliament and the President, the right to over rule any bills passed by the Parliament which the top Ayatollahs decreed as being Un-Islamic, and the power to dismiss the President. Commenting on this contradiction between simultaneously accepting the people's sovereignty on one hand and rejecting it on the other, an editorial in *Enqelabe Islami* said that if people's votes were to be made the basis for forming the government of the Islamic Republic, it would lead to one form (democratic) of regime. But if the principle of universal suffrage were not upheld as the basic principle in the Constitution, and final sovereignty was given to some institution such as the Council of Ayatollahs, the country would end up in a dictatorship 'no better than that under the Pahlavi dictatorship'.[4] This fundamental contradiction in the constitution 'could lead to resentment and reaction against it and bring to power a secular government',[5] the editorial concluded. The constitutional contradiction was summed up by Ayatollah Taleqani, who was among those voting against article 110. In one of the last statements he made before his death in September 1979, Taleqani said he was 'afraid' that as things were going, 'the standard and level of the (Islamic) Constitution would be much inferior to the one we had 70 years ago.'[6] It was for these reasons' that *Mujahideen-e-Khalq* had publicly declared that they would not vote for the new constitution unless what they believed to be 'undemocratic, sectarian, anti-people and class based principles' were removed from the Constitution. Following Rajavi's disqualification, the Kurds boycotted the Presidential elections and persisted with their boycott in the Parliamentary elections that followed shortly, with the result that the Kurdish Sunnis, accounting for almost 15% of Iran's population, have no representative in the Islamic Parliament. The Tehran Government had dissolved even the local councils which, following Ayatollah Taleqani's trouble shooting trip to Kurdistan, were established in some towns in Kurdistan. After Taleqani's death, these popular councils were dissolved on the pretext that 'communists' had infiltrated them. That Kurdish people were denied representation in areas with Kurdish population is evidenced in the open letter Abdur Rahman Qassemlu, Chief of the Socialist Kurdish Democratic Party, the largest political organization in Kurdistan, wrote to Khomeini in August 1979. In his letter, Qassemlu stated that the Kurds had been frontline revolutionaries in the struggle against the Pahlavi dictatorship and had accepted Khomeini's leadership in the anti-imperialist Islamic Revolution. But after the monarchy had been overthrown, Qassemlu said, problems were on the increase because of the sectarian and prejudiced position of religious authorities in Tehran. 'You told us during our meeting that in the Islamic Republic there would be no discriminations (against minorities). Then why a single Kurd has not been allowed to become member of the Revolutionary Islamic Council in the cities of Urumieh, Salmas, and other towns where hundreds of thousands of Kurds live?'[7]

After Banisadr became President, there were two distinct groups in the Islamic regime contesting for power. On the one side was Banisadr and a government incorporating a 'liberal' approach and on the other were the 'reactionaries' designing to promote their monopolistic aspirations through the IRP. The main thorn in the side of the IRP was the existence of progressive revolutionaries, who were opposed both to the 'liberals' as well as the monopolistic reactionaries. Hence the IRP's main concern was to consolidate its power, even if that meant diverting the Revolution from its principal anti-imperialist course into divergent areas such as military action in Kurdistan, attack on the universities, suppression of religious minorities and women's rights, and suppression of other anti-imperialist forces in the country.

The IRP controlled the radio and television, the Revolutionary Guards, the Islamic courts and the Parliament. In religious terms, this latter group believed in blind obedience to authority and invoked the legitimacy of religious decrees *(fatwa)* for silencing and suppressing criticism and alternate viewpoints in the name of Islam and struggle against imperialism. As for the liberal bourgeoisie, while this group also declared itself anti-imperialist, believing in the overall system of an anti-imperialist government, it differed from the IRP in its emphasis on a free press, a censor-free radio and television accessible for open debate on political issues to other groups, and recognition of individual and social liberties in the practical sense. According to this viewpoint, there was no need to sacrifice freedom in the struggle against imperialism because the aim of anti-imperialist struggle was the liberation of people from domination and from all forms of exploitation, including exploitation in the name of religion. Moreover, the violation of basic rights and civil liberties by the very people who had drafted the Constitution, was already becoming commonplace, making the struggle for the defence of freedom as basic an issue as it had been during the struggle agaiinst the Pahlavi dictatorship.

Initially, the revolutionary groups were not associated with either of the above groups and were critical of them for being 'reactionary' and 'liberal'. However, with the polarization of forces the revolutionary groups could not retain their independent 'neither reactionary, nor liberal' position. Wedged between the liberals and reactionaries, the *Mujahideen* reasoned that if the course of development of the Iranian society was not to be a revolutionary one, in the very least it should follow the course preferred by the liberals. For social, political, and historical necessities had shown that, as compared to reactionaries, the liberals had a greater capacity for organizing a viable system of government. Moreover, in the context of long term strategy, the *Mujahideen* reasoned that the liberals would not last for long. While it was possible for the liberals to end up in the trap of the comprador bourgeoisie, the *Mujahideen* did not see in it as lethal a danger as fascistic reaction, because the stage of the comprador bourgeoisie in Iran had reached its peak during the Pahlavi years of the 70's, and the social contradictions had 'risen to a higher stage where labour and anti-capital elements had come out clear'.[8] Furthermore, the *Mujahideen* thought it was necessary to fight against the reaction and religious fascism of the IRP because the IRP was imposing reaction and fascism in the name of Islam and as a means for foisting itself on the people.[9] IRP's attacks against *Mujahideen*, branding them as 'infidels' and 'heretics' were viewed by the *Mujahideen* in the historical perspective of the war of religion against religion. The *Mujahideen* pointed out that just as Hazrat Ali and Imam Hosein in their time had been dubbed as 'infidel' and 'heretic' by their political contenders and power monopolists, so were the *Mujahideen* being made the target in the war of epithets in order to create a false contradiction between the 'faithful' and the 'infidel'.[10] Moreover, the *Mujahideen* were suspicious of the IRP leadership's claim about waging an anti-imperialist struggle because, 'these gentleman sat down at the negotiating table with General Huyser, Shapur Bakhtiar, and General Qarabaghi (last Chief of Staff of the Shah's army) to work out details for the transfer of power from Shapur Bakhtiar to Mehdi Bazargaan, Khomeini's Prime Minister designate for an Islamic Republic.'[11]

The Parliamentary Elections
The IRP scored a major victory and succeeded in making up for its defeat in the Presidential elections by winning a majority of seats in the

Islamic Parliament. The Parliamentary elections, held two months after the Presidential elections, gave rise to widespread allegations that through 'coercion, deceit and intimidation', the IRP had rigged the elections. Since Banisadr, as the country's newly elected President, still enjoyed some powers and was regarded as a favourable alternative to the power drive of the religious monopolists by many Ayatollahs, his office became the recipient of protests filed by various sources against the rigging of elections. For example Ayatollah Syed Morteza Pasandeedeh, elder brother of Ayatollah Khomeini, accused the IRP of rigging the elections in his cable to the President. 'The elections have been rigged',[12] declared the elder Ayatollah. People had been made to cast their votes for IRP candidates through the use of 'deceit and intimidation'.[13] Ayatollah Pasandeedeh also said that on the day the elections were held, the judge of the Islamic Court in Khomein, Khomeini's hometown, disrupted the elections through coercion, mass imprisonment, and murder.[14] The cable concluded with the observation: 'I am grieved to declare that at no stage (in history) acts such as these have been perpetrated. People did not expect the Islamic government to act in this way.'[15]

Not only was the legitimacy of the elections that flooded the Parliament with IRP sponsored clergymen being questioned, but also the integrity of some of those who had got elected. To quote one instance, Ayatollah Tehrani, the prominent religious leader declared that many of those who were elected to the Islamic Parliament in Mashhad, capital of Khorassan Province, were 'like the gangsters of the Shah's clubwielding gangs'.[16] Tehrani recalled that these elected members belonged to that category of clergymen who had openly opposed and insulted Muslim revolutionaries fighting the Shah's regime and had accused Khomeini of being 'the harbinger of the Marxist system in Iran', and who had preached that no struggle should be waged against the Shah's regime.[17] Ayatollah Tehrani therefore called for re-elections, saying that the elections held in his hometown were 'spurious' and had been marked by rampant rigging. He compared the composition of the Islamic Parliament to the Parliaments during the reign of the two Pahlavi monarchs. 'During Reza Khan's reign, (after 1925) the Parliament was made up of people who had been "bought" and "bribed" to favour Reza Khan. During the reign of his son, Mohammad Reza Shah (after Mossadeq was ousted in 1953), it was force and coercion that created the Parliament. But in the present phase, hypocrisy and deceit are the distinctive features of the Parliament.'[18]

Notes

1. Ayatollah Syed Morteza Pasandeedeh's cable to the President.

Enqelabe Islami, No.218, 19 March 1980, p.16.
2. *Enqelabe Islami,* January 1981.
3. 'Open Letter to the Imam of the People', in, *Sobeh Azadegaan,* No.27, January 1980.
4. *Enqelabe Islami,* No. 53, 23 August 1979.
5. Ibid.
6. Ibid., No. 67, 11 September 1979.
7. 'Open Letter of Kurdish Democratic Party to Ayatollah Khomeini', *Kayhan,* No. 10776, 7 August 1979.
8. *Mojahed.,* May 1980, p. 11.
9. Ibid.
10. Ibid.
11. Ibid.
12. *Enqelabe Islami.* No.218, 19 March 1980. Ayatollah Syed Morteza Pasandeedeh's Cable to the President's Office.
13. Ibid.
14. Ibid.
15. Ibid.
16. Ibid.
17. Ayatollah Tehrani, *Ari En Chay nin Shud, ba radar* (Yes Brother, That's the Way it Ended). Printed at Mashhad University Press. June 1980, p. 17. Henceforth to be called 'Yes Brother, That's the Way it Ended'.
18. Ibid., p. 19.

13. The University and the Islamic Republic

'Those who saved our nation are the people, these beloved universities, these beloved theological students.'[1]
—Ayatollah Khomeini

'All the troubles afflicting mankind have their roots in universities.'[2]
—Ayatollah Khomeini

That the universities were the centre of gravity of the Islamic Revolution remains an indisputable fact. Indeed, the Revolution had been germinated, sprung, and was sustained mainly by the universities.[3] This fact was unhesitatingly admitted by Ayatollah Khomeini during the course of his public addresses in the in the initial period following the overthrow of the Pahlavi dictatorship. In his message, to students and teachers, marking the beginning of the first academic session in the Islamic Republic in September 1979, Khomeini was full of praise and endearments for the students and teachers. Iranian teachers and students had 'faced deprivation, torture, and hardship during the long years of oppression'[4] by the Pahlavi regime. They were subjected to all forms of pressure, distress and intimidation because they had dared 'to stand up against dictatorship, despotism, and one upmanship with fearless courage. They had refused to submit to forces of evil.'[5] Six weeks later, on 4 November 1979, Ayatollah Khomeini issued another statement on the first anniversary of the student's massacre at Tehran University by the Shah's Imperial Guards. The Ayatollah recalled that last year on this day 'the abominable regime (of the Shah) attacked the universities and slaughtered our beloved students en mass.'[6] The Ayatollah said that since the Shah's regime was 'opposed to all expressions and symbols of civilization and progress in the country',[7] and universities and other educational institutions were symbols of civilization and progress, that was the reason why the Shah's soldiers would 'one day attack Fazieh School and other Theological Schools in the country, and another day they would attack Tehran University and universities all over the country.'[8] In this statement, Khomeini termed the universities as 'Centres of knowledge and the learned.' However, after the formalist clergymen teamed up in the IRP and began tightening their grip on the State apparatus, the universities continued their mission as consciousness — raising centres and dessimated information about the new fascism. Since IRP lacked support among students but had absolute access to Ayatollah Khomeini, it used him for attacking the universities and generating mistrust and resentment against educational institutions. As a result, Khomeini began calling the universities 'Centres of corruption' and 'licentious reveleries'.[9] The crescendo of Khomeini's incredible attacks against universities reached the unsurpassable point when he declared that all the troubles afflicting mankind had stemmed from universities. He said: 'If we extensively survey all the universities in the world, we will see that all the troubles that have afflicted mankind have their roots in the university.'[10] Khomeini even absolved the Shah for his 'crimes' against the nation and put the blame on the university educated Iranians for all the misfortunes in the country's history. His logic was simple: 'For 50 years, this country has had universities. The university professors and the universities drove our country into the lap of super powers.'[11] But the Grand Ayatollah Khomeini seemed to have overlooked the fact that the Pahlavi regime had remained in power for 50 years because it had enjoyed the blessings of the Grand Ayatollahs and religious leaders of the Shia world at a time when Khomeini was an ordinary Ayatollah. Moreover, the Grand Ayatollah Brujardi, who remained the supreme religious leader of the Shia world, by virtue of the consensual approval of the Grand Ayatollahs of the time, until his death in 1962, and his successor, the Grand Ayatollah Hakim who died in 1964, could have stripped the Shah of power or challenged his authority were they to decide that such a move was necessary for safeguarding Islam and the nation's interests.

The 'Cultural Revolution'

The anti-university atmosphere having thus been manufactured, the IRP mobilized its forces on 20 April 1980, and moved in to neutralize the challenge posed by the universities and centres for higher learning, using the pretext that universities had to be 'Islamized' through a 'Cultural Revolution'. By using violence for physically taking over universities, IRP hoped to achieve two objectives. Firstly, it hoped to 'purge' the educational sphere of supporters of *Mujahideen* and *Fedayeen* who constituted the majority, both among students and the faculty. Secondly, by resorting to its para—military forces and gangs of 'club-wielders', IRP aimed at creating a law and order situation in the country, then blaming 'an incompetent Banisadr' for the chaos and bloodshed, and demanding his ouster form the President's office. What happened during the week — long, nationwide disturbances when student supporters of the IRP, aided by Revolutionary Guards and backed by a violent mob attacked the universities, was unprecedented. The distressing letter of a female student from Mashhad University to Banisadr's office portrays the nature and scale of the events. Describing the carnage, she wrote that armed gangs of 'club-wielders' descended on the University. The letter, published in *Enqelabe Islami*,[12] partly reads: 'The University had become the venue for a book burning 'festival'. The Campus was strewn with torn pages of books. The *Hezbollahis* had invaded and conquered the University. They beat up the students, tore off the scarves that veiled the heads of Muslim girls, insulted and abused them, and did to them what I am ashamed to narrate. They unleashed a havoc that God alone is a witness of. They hit and split the head of a girl student, and as blood poured over her face they shouted "Kill her! her blood is *halal*" (religiously lawful). By God! they surpassed the atrocities of the Shah's gangs of "club-wielders". The dimensions of this tragedy are so vast, they are beyond my capacity to narrate.'

Also reaching Banisadr's office was a cable from Taher Ahmadzadeh, the progressive Islamic revolutionary who had spent long years in the Shah's prisons, and after the CIA *coup* against Mossadeq in 1953, had founded the National Resistance Movement with Ayatollah Taleqani. After the Pahlavi regime was overthrown Ahmadzadeh was appointed Governor of Khorassan Province, the streets of whose capital, Mashhad, were the scene of some of the ugliest clashes between the *Hezbollahis* and progressive Muslims. Ahmadzedeh, who resigned from his post because of differences with formalist clergymen, informed Banisadr that 'marauding hooligans of the Islamic Republic Party were on the loose in the city on a book burning spree'. The books that were becoming the fuel for the bonfires of religious monopolists were the progressive Islamic literature of Ali Shariati and *Mujahideen-e-Khalq*, as well as the ideological literature of *Fedayeen-e-Khalq*. A few months later, a *fatwa* of a small town *mulla*, giving religious sanction to the burning of books authored by Ayatollah Taleqani, stirred further controversy.

After the *Hezbollahis* gangs of club-wielders had occupied Mashhad University, they attacked the central office of the *Mujahideen-e-Khalq*, which still functioned as a legally recognized political organization. Thousands of *Mujahideen* supporters surrounded the office and defended it against the attackers. After four hours of pitched battle, four hundred supporters of the *Mujahideen* were wounded and a leading member of the organization by the name of Shokrullah Moshkinfam was killed. Arrested by SAVAK in 1974 for circulating Khomeini's bulletins and ideological tracts of *Mujahideen-e-Khalq*, the Pahlavi regime had sentenced Shokrullah to life imprisonment. He was among the last batch of hard core political prisoners composed of *Fedayeen* and *Mujahideen* who were released in January 1979, a month before the Tehran Uprising. The 100,000 strong funeral procession of Shokrullah was led by progressive religious scholars Ayatollah Tehrani, and Taher Ahmedzadeh. The slain *mujahid* was hailed as a martyr who had laid down his life in the struggle against religious reaction.

Statement by the father and son of Dr. Ali Shariati

In a statement that Ustad Taqi Shariati, father of Dr. Ali Shariati issued on the 'martyrdom of one of the sons of true Islam and Alavi Shiism,'[13] the elder Shariati expressed his profound grief and pain because 'such unfortunate' attacks were taking place in a system that called itself an Islamic Republic — 'A system from which we expected peace, harmony, equality, and brotherhood.' Following the tradition of Islamic revolutionaries, Ustad Shariati greeted the parents and wife of Shokrullah Moshkinfam because 'their religious family has presented a martyr to Islam and society.'[14]

Dr. Ali Shariati's 22 year old son Ehsan, working at the Centre for Propagation of Shariati's Thought at Tehran, was more vocal. In his statement, Ehsan Shariati termed the attack on the *Mujahideen's* office, the wounding of hundreds of their supporters and the death of Shokrullah, as a 'criterion and a sign of God' for distinguishing between Truth and Falsehood. 'What is most vitalizing is the fact that in the ever continuing battle of religion against religion, it is the true Islam of Alavi Shiism which has become the vanguard to stand up against reaction and ignorance. It has dug the ditch of differentiation (between Truth and Falsehood).' Quoting his father, Ehsan Shariati said, 'according to our Teacher, when blind force and coercion dons the garb of *taqva* (piety) it gives birth to the greatest tragedy. In unison with all the *Mujahideen* and freedom loving men and women who have defended the fort of consciousness, freedom, and creativity, I condemn this crime against humanity.'[15]

Conditions were much worse in Tehran University. 50 student supporters of *Fedayeen-e-Khalq* were killed when Revolutionary Guards stormed the campus making free use of heavy automatic weapons. Bodies of students killed by Revolutionary Guards were hoisted by students on their hands and taken to the streets. Shouting 'The Shah's Massacre of Students is Repeated', the students took their dead and wounded to the hospitals. The scenes created on Tehran streets were a replay of the student's struggle against the Pahlavi dictatorship a year ago. Said one *Fedayeen* student supporter with a Revolutionary Guard's bullet lodged in his body, 'the bullets that should be used against America are being bored into our anti-imperialist chests.'[16] Similar disturbances engulfed Rasht, capital of Gilan, the province in North Iran, when a machine-gun wielding *Hujat-ul-Islam* leading bands of *Hezbollahis* attacked Gilan University. 13 students were gunned to death and over a thousand injured when fighting spilled over into the city and engulfed the whole region. In Ahwaz, provincial capital of the oil rich Khuzestan Province, nearly a thousand students were arrested. Some of them were later killed when Revolutionary Guards opened fire on them in a prison hall, claiming that the prisoners had tried to escape.

In Zahedan, another provincial capital, Revolutionary Guards attacked the Baluchistan University, opened fire at the students' hostels, threw out the Marxists and Progressive Muslims from student dormitories, and 'turned the University into an army camp'. A statement issued by the University condemned the incident and posed the simple question as to why the Revolutionary Guards were so insistently imposing 'a particular brand of thought as being the true Islam'.[17] Also expressing disgust at the IRP's 'cultural revolution farce' was the cable that 152 faculty member of Shiraz University sent to Banisadr's office. The Shiraz professors condemned the drawing of barbed wire around the University and colleges by IRP students, the attack by clubwielders, and the indiscriminate hooligan assaulting, murder, and injury of university and high school students, and the destruction of colleges and classrooms.[18]

According to official figures published by hospitals in Tehran and the three provincial capitals of Ahwaz, Rasht, and Zahedan, over three thousand persons had been wounded and over 37 killed during the first three days of the 'Cultural Revolution'.[19] Clearly then, the assault on universities and the killing and wounding of students during the weeklong 'cultural revolution' was unprecedented in history.

Comments on the 'Cultural Revolution'

Condemning the Cultural Revolution as a 'plot' which the IRP had hatched 'for pitting the people against the President', *Enqelabe Islami* noted that there was nothing 'Islamic' about the violence which the IRP had used for violating the universities. 'The aim of the cultural revolution was to pit the students and people against Banisadr, and fanning this confrontation to the extent where violent clashes and deaths would occur,'[20] commented the newspaper's editorial. It reasoned that these casualties would have given the IRP the self-righteous pretext that 'they had given martyrs for the cultural revolution and in the struggle against Banisadr.' With this as a weapon for mobilizing its supporters, the editorial continued, IRP hoped to hound Banisadr out of office. Concluding its verdict on the 'cultural revolution,' Banisadr's newspaper commented: 'We cannot present to the world the ethics, morals, and actions we have witnessed during the last few days as our "cultural revolution". Those who have inaugurated the cultural revolution with sticks, clubs, and guns are not part of this nation.'[21]

Commenting on the 'cultural revolution', Ayatollah Tehrani remarked that historians would term those who had masterminded the 'cultural revolution' as more vicious than Shimr, the man who killed Hosein, grandson of the Prophet, and who is regarded in the Iranian tradition as the vilest of the vile for his crime. The progressive clergyman reasoned that the IRP people behind the cultural revolution were more wicked than Hosein's murderer because even Shimr had given the grandson of the Prophet a night in which to accept Yazid's terms. Shimr attacked only after the period for the ultimatum had lapsed. But the IRP which had first given a three day ultimatum to the *Mujahideen* and *Fedayeen* student supporters for vacating their offices on the universities, turned back on its own word. Even before the first day of the IRP ultimatum had passed, 'they launched their attack and violated the sanctity of these revered centres which were the standard bearers of the Revolution, and subjected them to the most obscene and shameless insults.'[22]

Interestingly enough, only four months before the IRP thought of its 'cultural revolution,' the Party had condemned in advance any prospective 'plots' for closing down the universities, and declared that only 'imperialism and its mercenary agents' could think of closing down the universities. Parts of the statement read out at an IRP student rally on 4 November 1979, commemorating the first anniversary of the massacre of Tehran University students by Imperial Guards, read: 'Imperialism and its mercenary agents are lying in ambush, waiting for a suitable moment to create chaos in our society by bringing about the closure of our cultural, educational and productive centres.'[23] However, in another resolution read at an IRP student rally the day universities were attacked and occupied by the IRP, Revolutionary Guards and violent mobs, IRP students called the universities 'the most genuine bases for American imperialism'. Having themselves now accomplished what only four months ago they feared 'imperialism and its mercenary agents' would attempt, IRP students now declared: 'So long as this base (university) is not annihilated, we cannot be sure about the eradication of U.S. imperialism in Iran. We must therefore try our utmost to destroy this American base (the universities) inside Iran.' Following Ayatollah Khomeini, who had declared that all the sufferings of humanity could be attributed to the universities, IRP students declared that everything that was wrong with Iranian society was 'only and only because of these universities.'[24] It was therefore vital, argued student followers of Ayatollah Khomeini in their statement, to bring about a revolution in the system of universities. Only then would the 'unhealthy' society become 'automatically pure and healthy'.[25] Thus, according to this logic and outlook, all the problems of the world could be 'automatically' solved by closing down all the universities in the world.

Notes

1. Ayatollah Khomeini's speech, Sunday, 26 August 1979, (4 Sha-

rivar, 1358). Quoted in, 'What Did Khomeini say, What Did Khomeini Do?' Published by *Fedayeen-e-Khalq* Student Supporters, 1982.
2. *Enqelabe Islami*, 20 December 1980, (29 Azar, 1359).
3. Ayatollah Tehrani, *Yes, Brother, That's the Way it Ended*, p. 19.
4. Ayatollah Khomeini's Message on 23 September 1979. Quoted in 'What Did Khomeini Say, What Did Khomeini Do?'
5. Ibid.
6. Ibid.
7. Ibid.
8. Ibid.
9. *Enqelabe Islami*. 2 July 1980.
10. Ibid., 20 December 1980.
11. 'What Did Khomeini Day, What Did Khomeini Do?', p. 13.
12. *Enqelabe Islami*, 22 April 1980.
13. Statement of Ustad Taqi Shariati on the martyrdom of *mujahid* brother Shokrullah Moshkinfam. *Mojahed*, 26 April 1980.
14. Ibid.
15. Ibid. The 'ditch of differentiation' alludes to the 'battle of the ditch' *(Khandaq)*, in which the Prophet of Islam dug a ditch around Medina to ward off the reactionary hordes from Mecca who had come to 'finish off' the Prophet's movement.
16. *Nabard-e-Danesh Amuz* (Struggle of High School Students). Special Issue, No. 18. 26 April 1980.
17. Statement of the Administrative Committee of University of Sistan and Baluchistan, In *Enqelabe Islami*, May 1980.
18. *Mojahed*, No. 64, May 1980.
19. *Nabard-e-Danesh Amuz* (Struggle of the High School Students). Special Issue. No. 18, 26 April 1980.
20. 'To tay eh (The Plot), editorial, *Enqelabe Islami*, April 1980.
21. Ibid.
22. Ayatollah Tehrani, *Yes, Brother, That's the Way it Ended*, p. 19.
23. Resolution of Islamic Students Association (Pro—IRP) on 4 November 1979. Quoted in *Mojahed*, 26 April 1980.
24. Resolution read at the IRP student rally in Tehran, 21 April 1980. Quoted in *Mojahed*, 26 April 1980.
25. Ibid.

14. Women and Religious Minorities in the Islamic Republic

On 31 March 1979, on the eve of the referendum for the Islamic Republic, Ayatollah Khomeini issued an appeal to Iranian women, urging them to vote for an Islamic Republic because Islam had given 'greater consideration to women's rights than men's rights'.[1] In this statement, Khomeini declared that in Islam, women had the right to vote and enjoyed rights which were more comprehensive than those of women in the West. 'Our women have the right to vote and the right to get elected. They have the right on all affairs relating to them. They have the right to freely choose many professions'.[2] Komeini promised men and women that 'in the Islamic government, each and everyone will be free, and all people will attain their rights'.[3] Regarding the problem of religious minorities, Khomeini had made it clear in the numerous interviews that he gave before coming to power that 'the religious minorities are Iranian and deserve the same respect as do Iranian Muslim'.[4] Khomeini also declared that 'Islam had granted more freedom to religious minorities than any religion or faith.' The religious minorities 'must enjoy the same intrinsic liberties that God has bestowed equally on all men, and we will safeguard them to the foremost', Khomeini affirmed in an interview with *Diw Weh Chronte*, the Dutch paper.[5] 'Not only are religious minorities free, but the government is responsible for the protection of their rights. All Iranians are entitled to civil rights regardless of whether they are Muslims, Christian or, Jewish.'[6] However as the Islamic and secular opposition to the Khomeini regime claims, since the institution of the Islamic Republic, restrictions, limitations and discriminatory measures against women and religious minorities have increased. This discrimination is reflected in the 'Retribution Bill' recently passed by the Islamic Parliament. The bill fixes the *dieh* or blood money for a murdered woman as half that for a murdered man.[7] Also according to the Islamic legislation, women witnesses in cases involving murder do not carry any legal weight.[8] Even if more than one woman were to give witness in a murder case, their account would still be unacceptable. As for women's participation in the legal profession, since women's right to form judgement is not recognized, it is not possible for them to become lawyers or judges. In short, the Retribution Bill indicates forthright and by implication that the 'value' of women is half that of men. Moreover, as a result of the introduction of divorce laws based on traditional Islamic interpretation, many women have been rendered helpless in cases where their husbands unilaterally declare they have divorced their wives. Legal sanction to polygamy and 'temporary marriage' *(muta)* has only eased the way for misuse of this legislation and for converting women into sexual objects by the affluent.[9] The 'Retribution Bill', as critics claim, does not recognize Muslims, Jews, and Christians as equals. If a non-Muslim is murdered by a Muslim, the murderer is not subject to retribution or sentencing provided he pays a certain amount of money as *dieh* or 'blood money'.[10] To further restrict the human, social, and political rights of religious minorities, other legislation is underway. One such bill, currently under consideration in the Parliament, states that religious minorities cannot live in an apartment on the first or second floors if a Muslim is living on a floor lower than that of the non-Muslim.[11] Another proposed clause prohibits the dissection of the corpse of a Muslim but permits the dissection of the corpse of a non-Muslim. As for taxes, the Islamic regime is preparing a bill which would require religious minorities to pay all the normal taxes in addition to an amount as *Jaziah* tax, an amount of money religious minorities must pay the Islamic Republic because they are non-Muslims.[12]

The problem religious minorities are facing in the educational sphere is reflected in a 20 point official circular issued by the Ministry of Education on 11 November 1981,[13] (20th Aban, 1360, of the Iranian calender). The handout calls for closure of all special schools run by national and religious minorities, removal of all non-Muslim school principals and their replacement by *Hezbollahi* teachers loyal to the IRP. As reported by opposition sources, non-Shia school teachers have been fired from their jobs on grounds that no follower of other creeds is capable of carrying on the mission of Islamic education.[14] The 20 point circular also calls for the cancellation of all school activities other than the lessons given during class hours. As a result, extra-curricular activities in the areas of sports, culture and art, hitherto organized by student societies, have been banned. The circular flatly contradicts the Islamic constitution drafted by the IRP dominated clerics by prohibiting the teaching of minority languages side by side with Persian as the national language.[15] The imposition of these reforms for Islamizing education generated intense resentment and protest on the part of minorities, to the extent that the Islamic regime had to withdraw some of the items from its 20 point list. However, despite the opposition of progressive and national groups to the discriminatory clause in the Islamic consititution according to which only a Shia belonging to the majority *Asna Ashri* sect can become the country's President, the Islamic regime has not altered this condition imposed on Presidential elections.

Notes

1. Quoted in 'What Did Khomeini Say, What Did Khomeini Do?' p. 7–8.
2. Ibid.
3. Ibid.
4. Interview in *Al Ghoami Al-Arabi*. Quoted in *Kar*, Vol. 1, No. 9, October 1981.
5. Quoted in 'What Did Khomeini Say, What Did Khomeini Do?'
6. Ibid.
7. *La-ye-hay-e-Qesas* (Retribution Bill) Tehran, 1981. Articles 5 and 46.
8. Ibid., Article 33 A.
9. 'What Did Khomeini Say, What Did Khomeini Do?' p.7–8.
10. Ibid., p.7.
11. Ibid.
12. Ibid.
13. *Kar*, No. 145, 26 January 1982.
14. *Kar*, (English edition) Vol. 1, No. 9, October 1981.
15. *Kar*, No. 145, 26 January 1982.

15. Progressive Muslims and the Islamic Republic

In June 1980, Ustad Ali Tehrani, the clerical leader from Mashhad, published a widely circulated epistle called 'Yes, Brother, That's the Way it Ended'.[1] The book was written in a literary style in response to one of Dr. Ali Shariati's well known works, and reflected the general disenchantment most progressive Muslims felt with the way the clerical leaders were derailing the Revolution. Summing up the views of the Islamic opposition to the clergymen in power, Ustad Tehrani stated that the Revolution had originally sprung from the inner depths of people's yearning for freedom and independence. Its objectives were to efface despotism, imperialism, and exploitation from the country. However, when the Revolution had reached a climax and victory was in sight, it was joined by those who had glorified the Shah and hailed him as the defender of the Shia faith. This was how opportunists and conspirators penetrated the clerical leadership of the movement. According to Ustad Tehrani, at one stage during the Revolution, some of these opportunist elements had negotiated with the Shah's military commanders for permission to stage demonstrations against the Shah's regime. These opportunist clergymen had participated only in 'arranged' demonstrations where they were sure beforehand that the soldiers would not be ordered to shoot. Ayatollah Tehrani then directed his criticism against the Revolutionary Council formed immediately after the monarchy was overthrown. The trouble with this council, according to Tehrani, was that it did not consist of people whose outlook and experience were born of active involvement on the battlefield of revolutionary struggle. The council consisted merely of those who had been close to Khomeini as advisers, sycophants, or fellow clergymen. As for the Provisional Government headed by Bazargaan, its leader had frankly admitted that he did not believe in revolutionary measures. His was a step by step reformist policy. The true revolutionaries, according to Ayatollah Tehrani, those who had struggled when silence, passivity, indifference, and compromise had depotentiated the resistance movement, had been turned out from the ranks of the Revolution. While the Revolution's vanguard were being projected as counter—revolutionaries and outcasts, the opportunists and religious monopolists seized the reins of revolution with their Islamic Republic Party. 'Through "coercion", "gold" and "deception" (*zoor, zar, va tazveer,* Shariati's terms for despotism, exploitation by capital, and religious hypocrisy) they secured the services of various forces and sections of people and chained them in a new form of bondage, through blind obedience.'[2] This is how the people, according to Ustad Tehrani, were made the tools of the Party's objectives. The Party began 'sowing seeds of discord and suspicion' to steer away the Revolution from its progressive, anti-imperialist, and anti-exploitive path. 'They printed articles against the Teacher of Revolution and his writings. One of their propaganda bulletins headlined "The Confrontation of Leader of the People (Khomeini) Against the Imperialist Culture of Dr. Shariati", reflected their approach. Shariati, who had spent an entire life struggling against cultural imperialism and reaction, who endured imprisonment, torture and laid down his life in the struggle against imperialist culture and reaction, was now being portrayed as the agent of imperialist culture.'[3] Ustad Tehrani's epistle graphically expressed the sharp increase in 'the savage attacks on the headquarters and offices of different political groups',[4] after Taleqani's death in September 1979. 'Club-wielding hoodlums' who had supported the Shah's regime, aided by those who had been duped in the name of religion by devious religious propaganda of power monopolists 'created havoc' and spilled blood in their confrontation against 'those opposed to blind religious obedience'. The Ustad also revealed that in a meeting with Ayatollah Khomeini, he drew Khomeini's attention to well known facts in the country's recent history. He reminded Khomeini that 70 years ago, during the Constitutional Revolution, much innocent blood of people opposed to the dictatorship of Nasir-ud-Din Shah, the then monarch, was spilled 'in the name of struggle against *Bahai* apostates.'[5] Khomeini's attention was specifically drawn to the fact that after the CIA sponsored *coup* against Mossadeq in 1953, 'innocent people had been liquidated in the name of struggle against Communism'. As a result, 'revolutionary individuals and true Muslims opposed to the Pahlavi monarchy were murdered.' 'And today,' Tehrani declared in his booklet, 'the same crime is being repeated by branding those who are being executed and killed as "counter revolutionaries" opposed to Khomeini's anti-imperialist line.'[6]

Similar views were expressed by Ayatollah Lahuti, the first chief of the Islamic Revolutionary Guards who later resigned because of differences with the 'power monopolists'. Speaking on the third death anniversary of Dr. Ali Shariati in Mashhad in June 1980, Ayatollah Lahuti declared that just as 'the opportunists, the ignorant, the reactionaries and the wealthy' had existed over 13 centuries ago to undermine the Islamic State during the early days of its inception, similar forces, in collusion with the false men of religion, were undermining the Islamic Revolution today.[7] In a bitter attack on the 'opportunist power monopolists' who claimed to be the only followers of Imam Khomeini,

Lahuti said that even if the family of the Shah were brought back to Iran, they would also declare their loyalty and devotion to Khomeini, because 'supporting Khomeini brings bread and position.'[8] The power monopolists, according to Ayatollah Lahuti, were not really interested in Imam Khomeini. 'From their point of view, Ayatollah Khomeini or Ayatollah Montazeri do not matter. Only they themselves really matter.'[9] There were good reasons for Ayatollah Lahuti's bitterness against the IRP. Tape recordings of Hasan Ayat, a prominent IRP strategist secretly recorded during a Party session, had revealed that the IRP was planning to overthrow Banisadr and gain total control of power. Moreover, to consolidate the IRP's position, Hasan Ayat had suggested that, 'We should inflate Montazeri (as Ayatollah Khomeini's successor) so that when Khomeini dies, our position remains all right.'[10]

A Meeting At Shariati's House
Six months after Ayatollah Tehrani's booklet appeared, his views were complemented at an informal meeting of progressive Muslims held at the house of Dr. Ali Shariati in Tehran. Besides Ayatollah Tehrani who spoke at this meeting, other speakers included Khomeini's son, Hujat-ul-Islam Ahmad Khomeini, Ayatollah Lahuti, Puran Shariati, wife of Dr. Ali Shariati, and Mrs. Zahra Rezai, the mother of four *Mujahideen-e-Khalq* pioneer members killed by the Shah's regime during the early 70s. Also present at the meeting was Mrs. Motahedeen, mother of Mehbobeh Motahedeen, the young revolutionary who, along with her husband Hasan, was killed in a gun battle against SAVAK agents in a Tehran street in 1974. Her revolutionary life and death had inspired Dr. Ali Shariati to write *The Story of Hasan and Mehbobeh,* a small book in which the Teacher of the Revolution praised the two revolutionaries as personality models for the new generation of Muslims.

In his speech, Ahmed Khomeini pointed out that two different and conflicting currents of thought and outlook were prevailing in the country at the time. These outlooks, according to Ahmad Khomeini, had nothing to do with individual personalities but represented 'a particular mode of approach to Islam and the Revolution.' Although Ahmed Khomeini did not specifically identify the first approach, he was unequivocal about the need to resist the second line of approach, 'a front created by the union of left opportunists (meaning Tudeh Party) and the extreme rightists (the IRP clergymen).'[11] The logic of the religious monopolists was that 'whoever is not with us, is not a Muslim and is against us.'[12] Ahmad Khomeini said that people were being arrested and beaten up, but what was more disturbing about the beatings and the torture was its justification under cover of Islamic punishment. There appeared to be good reasons for the widespread allegations that the religious monopolists were using torture and terror as State policy by 'Islamizing' it. Ali Mohammad Jahromi, a clerical member of the committee for the investigation of torture appointed by

Khomeini, felt no compunction in publicly declaring his contempt for those protesting against the use of torture. He said: 'Those who are spreading the rumours about torture are Westernized elements. They do not understand the meaning of Islamic punishment.'[13] Ahmed Khomeini's condemnation of right extremism and left opportunism did not amount to an automatic endorsement of *Mujahideen-e-Khalq*, the major opposition organization in the country. 'We should create a third line, a third front, one that could function independently of these two currents.'[14] He also pointedly declared that the major threat to the Revolution stemmed from religious reaction. 'The danger threatening the Revolution is the persistence of that line of thought and attitude which opposed Dr. Shariati.'[15] Ahmed Khomeini believed that attacks against Shariati and opposition to the teachings of 'the true Teacher of the Revolution' would destroy the Revolution. Because it was Shariati 'who presented the real Islam in such a way that if imperialism wanted to penetrate the ranks of true Muslims in Iran for using them against the Revolution, it must do so by first destroying Shariati.'[16]

The psychotic double-bind afflicting the religious monopolist's world-view is clearly reflected in their approach to Dr. Shariati. While officially, Shariati's portraits and posters are allowed in government offices, and all the colleges, institutes, streets and hospitals named after him still retain his name, an overt and covert campaign against Ali Shariati is operating at all levels—ranging from President Khamanei's speech in April 1982, urging people to read the works of Ayatollah Motahari the favoured ideologist of the IRP for 'right guidance', to the use of violence against sources of support for Shariati. For example, in December 1980, the Centre for Propagation of Islamic Truth founded in 1941 by Ustad Taqi Shariati, Ali Shariati's father, was attacked by armed gangs of *Hezbollahis*, an incident unprecedented in the 40 year history of the Islamic Centre. Following this incident, Ustad Ali Tehrani, the Ayatollah identified with Ali Shariati's Islamic approach, was prevented from addressing a public meeting in Isfahan where he was attacked by a 'group of people treacherously deceived in the name of safeguarding Islam.'[17] According to one non-IRP Ayatollah, these incidents showed that the ruling clerics were dragging off the Revolution from its course by 'doing things which are a disgrace to Islam.'[18] Before the end of 1980, the weekly magazines published by the Centre for Propagation of Shariati's thought were banned, as were the libraries, reading rooms and provincial offices of Shariati Centres established by Dr. Shariati's supporters after the Revolution. To neutralize Shariati's image as the architect of the Islamic Revolution, the clerical regime began projecting its protege, Ayatollah Motahari, a well read clergyman and lifelong employee in the Pahlavi regime's Ministry of Education, as the ideologue of the Islamic Revolution. Despite his academic association with the Shah's regime and the contribution of dozens of articles to the glossy magazine *Zan-e-Ruz*, (Women Today), the Pahlavi regime's equivalent of *Cosmopolitan* during the heyday of consumerist Iranian society in the 70s, Motahari was given a revolutionary aura when Khomeini appointed him as Chairman of the Revolutionary Council that took control of the country after the collapse of the Pahlavi regime. While the clerical leadership focussed on building up Motahari, a former student of Khomeini and his devout disciple, as the ideologue of the Revolution, many of Motahari's colleagues and Islamic academicians who had also served under the Pahlavi regime, but were reluctant to endorse the clerical leadership, were taken to task for 'collaborating with the Shah's regime'. For example, Dr. Hosein Nasr, a well known Islamic scholar and Motahari's colleague in the Pahlavi regime's Ministry of Education, had to flee the country under threats of possible execution for supporting the Shah's regime. Thus, while the clerical leadership formally acknowledged Shariati as a revolutionary Islamic ideologist, it suppressed the followers of his Islamic approach and even made it impossible for them to hold commemoration meetings on Shariati's third death anniversary. To quote one instance, Dr. Kazem Sami, leader of the Progressive Revolutionary Movement of Iranian Muslims *(Jama)* found the doors of a central mosque in Qom, where he was scheduled to address a commemorating meeting for Shariati, locked in order to keep him out. It was in the context of these developments that one Ayatollah declared, 'The blood-stained pages of Islamic history are tainted with similar violations of rights, veiling of the truth, and perpetration of injustice.'[19] However, despite playing down Shariati's role in the Revolution, IRP used Shariati whenever it suited the clerical regime and projected Shariati in a light to justify the clerical leadership. One method was 'to clip the tape recordings of Shariati's speeches and rearrange them to serve their own purpose,'[20] complained Mrs. Shariati. As one of the speakers at the meeting held at Dr. Shariati's house in Tehran in November 1980, Mrs. Shariati pointed out that while the books written by her husband were being 'removed from libraries, schools and mosques, handbills accusing Shariati as the "chief propagator of cultural imperialism" and "moral decadence" were being circulated in the country by the IRP.' They put such slogans on IRP posters, Mrs. Shariati said. Following the appearance of these posters, Mrs. Shariati said that she rang up the office of the IRP and requested Ayatollah Beheshti, the Party Secretary General, to stop the circulation of anti-Shariati posters. Ayatollah Behesti's response to Mrs. Shariati's request was typical of the cloak and dagger policy of the IRP— while Ayatollah Beheshti agreed with Mrs. Shariati that what was happening was a 'plot' to bring about a confrontation between supporters and opponents of Dr. Shariati, he did nothing to stop the posters' circulation, nor did be issue a denial on the party's behalf disowning the anti-Shariati campaign. Instead, the Party newspaper ridiculed Mrs. Shariati by insinuating that she was aspiring to become the new 'Empress' of the country. 'There is no need for me to say that they are decimating us,' declared Mrs. Shariati.[21] She then disclosed that although she had been teaching in schools for years, she was now banned from entering her school to teach. 'They have turned me out,' Mrs. Shariati said, leaving no doubts about the fact that she had been 'purged' alongwith thousands of school teachers and students during the IRP's cultural revolution. After all, one of the main objectives of this cultural revolution was to pave the way for recruiting only those persons as teachers who were loyal to the Party line. 'There are countless teachers like me whose voices of protest have been stifled with blood. Mothers of martyrs and revolutionaries come to me to complain that they are being harassed, beaten, imprisoned, and tortured. Today it is a crime to know Shariati,'[22] declared the wife of the Teacher of the Islamic Revolution. Even Shariati's daughter had been refused employment as a school teacher in the Islamic Republic, 'because they were afraid she will start preaching the progressive Islamic line of thought,' said Mrs. Shariati. She however added that her daughter was offered a teaching position only on condition that 'she does not reveal her identity as Dr. Shariati's daughter.'[23] Mrs. Shariati complained that the Grand Ayatollah Khomeini, had not 'even once' uttered a word of support for progressive Muslims.

It was Mrs. Zahra Rezai who spoke next. Until the beginning of 1980, Mrs. Rezai was being described as 'the noblest of mothers',[24] whose strength and inspiration had reared young revolutionaries possessing the highest moral and spiritual virtues. Revolutionary Iranians believed that with Mrs. Rezai as a model, motherhood in Iran had become, like the indomitable figure of Brecht's 'Mother Courage', 'inseparably linked with Revolution'.[25] Such glowing tributes to Mrs. Rezai came naturally, in view of the fact that her children were among those who led the struggle for the Islamic Revolution. That Mrs. Rezai's children and their comrades in the *Mujahideen* organization had 'provided a procession of models to a weary, corrupt and spiritless world',[26] was being officially acknowledged. Ahmad Rezai, her eldest son, among the intellectual founders of the *Mujahideen*, matched his intellectual genius with disciplined action. He trained cadres of dedicated young revolutionaries, morally and spiritually equipped to stand against the brutality of SAVAK which the Pahlavi regime used as a tactical and psychological device of suppression. Ahmad also wrote one of the most moving philosophical books of the struggle, *The Way of Hosein*, a poetically rich description of how the Islamic revolutionary carries on his battle in the image of Hosein — the fearless grandson of Prophet Mohammad. Reza Rezai, her second son, was a warm, extroverted person who forged strong links between family, friends, and comrades in the struggle. The letters Reza wrote to his mother at various stages of the struggle and which were later published by the *Mujahideen*, are regarded as 'a powerful documentation of how the greatest of human achievements are based on the foundation of the deepest human understanding.'[27] While both Ahmad and Reza were killed in direct confrontation with SAVAK agents in street battles, it was for Mehdi, their younger brother, to be martyred in the hardest way allotted to mankind — the way of inquisition, crucifixion and burning at the stake — the way of slow, unremitting torture that has been the lot of many prophets and saints. Mehdi died at the age of 19 under SAVAK's torture. Mrs. Rezai's fourth child, the 18 year old daughter Sadiqeh, was killed when she was forced to swallow a cyanide capsule at the end of an unequal confrontation against SAVAK agents. The surviving members of the family had their trials as well, for the struggle seeped into the lives of all of them. On one occasion, while looking for Sadiqeh, SAVAK agents packed up the entire family, including two infants, and kept them all in prison.[28] Even Mrs. Rezai and her husband were tortured physically and psychologically to force out a confession.

When she spoke in the meeting at Dr. Shariati's house, Mrs. Zahra Rezai described how the female relatives of the Islamic regime's political prisoners were being treated by Revolutionary Guards. She said that on one occasion, the Guards had arrested 70 women — mothers, and sisters who had gathered outside the prison to inquire about the conditions of their imprisoned children or brothers and sisters. These women were beaten and taken into the prison where they were tortured. One mother was slapped so ruthlessly that her ear drum ruptured. Another had her arm broken. A third woman was kicked so hard in her stomach that she had to be taken to hospital in a state of coma.[29] As for Mrs. Rezai herself, she stated that Molotov bombs had been thrown into her house on three occasions. She said that when Revolutionary Guards arrived at her home following the bombings to make inquiries, they accused her of having planted the bombs herself in order 'to become famous'. However, the third time a bomb was thrown into the courtyard of her house, the man responsible for it was arrested by the people and taken to the local police station. But the police were unable to file a case against the culprit, Mrs. Rezai said, because they were ordered to honourably release him.[30]

Progressive Muslims were not the only source of criticism against the clergymen in power. Conservative and moderate clerical leaders had also begun voicing their disgust with the state of affairs resulting from the power drive of religious monopolists. One of the rare criticisms which found its way into the national press in March 1980, was an interview that the Grand Ayatollah Qomi had given to journalists following a meeting he had had with the Grand Ayatollah Khomeini. In his candid interview, Ayatollah Qomi bitterly attacked the clergymen's Party ruling Iran. He said the IRP was 'striking Islam at its roots'[31] with its misdeeds, and that it was destroying Islam in the name of Islam.[32] Qomi complained that all the Islamic laws were being implemented in a manner that was Un-Islamic. Many of the trials being held were Un-Islamic as were the illegal imprisonments and killing of people. 'Those who had taken the affairs of the country in their hands under the pretext of a Crusade for Reconstructing Society have gone beyond the limits in tyranny',[33] and in committing gross violations against people's rights. The Ayatollah called the terror, tyranny and injustice being perpetrated in the name of Islam by the Party as 'indescribable'. He said that on the basis of first hand reports reaching him and which he had personally verified, it was clear that innocent people were being beaten, imprisoned and tortured.[34] By monopolizing the mosques, IRP had disarmed the clergymen who did not support it. 'I told Ayatollah Khomeini that the IRP was corrupt and rotten, and it was for him not to permit these filthy laws to come into force nor to allow a bunch of corrupt, irrelevant, and unqualified "experts" (IRP members of the Assembly of Experts that drafted the Islamic Constitution) to go ahead and constitute authority.'[35] The angry Ayatollah, who enjoys a religious rank equal to Khomeini's, declared that he did not believe in the legitimacy of the Constitution drafted by the Assembly of Experts because 'they took people's votes through hypocrisy and deception.'[36] The Grand Ayatollah then revealed that in a public statement he had issued before the Constitution was put to vote, he had declared that the Constitution was 'no good' and had to be amended because 'at least six of the articles were Un-Islamic'. But when the statement was read on the radio and television, it had been changed to convey the impression that Qomi fully supported the Constitution, and was urging people to go ahead and vote for it.[37] As Qomi saw it, the only way in which the affairs of the country could be sorted out in a proper manner and with religious legitimacy, was by delegating all authority to a Leadership Council composed of the Shia world's ten Grand Ayatollahs. 'When all the Grand Ayatollahs who command authority among people can consult with one another, then an order or a decree issued by the Council would be binding upon all people.'[38] Because leadership by the Grand Ayatollahs was a 'God given right' and not something 'which could be given or taken away' by ordinary people or put to question, or where the Leader could be punished.[39] Ayatollah Qomi's interview was among the last unmerciful criticisms of the clerics in power to appear in the national press. After this, criticisms by the Ayatollahs opposed to the IRP were phased out from the clergy controlled press. However, such criticisms continued to make their appearance in the form of booklets and 'Open letters to Ayatollah Khomeini'. In this respect, the criticisms which found a resonant audience were those made by Ayatollah Zanjani, the aged Ayatollah who continued to support former Prime Minister Mossadeq after the clergy had abandoned him, and Ayatollah Ustad Ali Tehrani.

The Fall of President Banisadr

By the autumn of 1980, the theme dominating the editorials in Banisadr's newspaper *Enqelabe Islami* and the *Mojahed*, now gone underground, conveyed the impression that the major threat to the Revolution resided within the Islamic forces. An editorial[40] in *Enqelabe Islami* noted that confrontation between various Islamic groups had brought the country to the verge of explosion. 'This is the greatest danger of all facing the Revolution. Today, the different Islamic groups and dispositions that struggled for the Revolution are not standing side by side, but against each other.' Another editorial noted that the Muslim intelligentsia was parting ways with dogmatic and formalist clergymen, and that the 'gulf separating the Islamic forces was becoming wider day by day'.[41] The editorial said that the 'great achievement' of Imam Khomeini, which was to bring together the intelligentsia and the clergy, was crumbling. This confrontation took an ominous turn with the uncovering of a plot alleged to have been made by extremist religious elements for killing Banisadr and announcing three days of national mourning.[42] Sensing that the tentacles of the power drive of religious monopolists were reaching for his own throat, Banisadr urged the people 'to stand up and resist'. 'If you do not resist today, tomorrow will be too late and a new dictatorship will impose itself upon you. You will be enslaved again by a regime against which you had revolted.'[43]

What brought the confrontation between Banisadr and the formalist clergy to a head on collision was the attack on Banisadr's political meeting at Tehran University in February 1981. Gangs of 'club-wielders' attempted to disrupt this meeting using their familiar methods. Banisadr's supporters captured over 40 of the attackers and found them carrying membership cards of IRP and its para-military affiliates. Banisadr spared no time in reading out the name and political affiliation of each 'club-wielder' on the microphone. This was the first time that IRP was being publicly named for sponsoring the notorious gangs of 'club-wielders'. IRP people denied the charges and called the disruption of Banisadr's meeting a 'plot' and a scenario Banisadr had himself screened by employing his own club-wielders to disrupt his meeting in order to malign the image of IRP. The Party mobilized the Parliament and Judiciary, the press and the radio and television under its control, and launched legal proceedings against Banisadr. As a result, it was Banisadr who was held responsible for the February disturbances at Tehran University. With its total hold on the media, and the unflinching support of the hard-core nucleus of a section of the religious populace devotionally loyal to Imam Khomeini, IRP stepped into the final phase of its campaign for removing the President from office. The campaign against Banisadr now claimed that he had 'betrayed Islam', and called for his execution. As for Banisadr, he declared in a speech to Air Force officers at Shiraz that he would resist the substitution of one dictatorship, meaning the Pahlavi regime, by another, meaning the IRP.[44] Banisadr made this statement on 28 May 1981, despite a warning issued by Ayatollah Khomeini a day earlier not to say anything against the clergy. Also, Khomeini had said that those who deviated from his guidelines would be declared *mufsid-e-fil-arz* (corrupt criminals of the earth), a charge punishable by death. Earlier, Khomeini had appointed a Commission composed of clergymen for investigating the allegations against Banisadr. The Commission duly declared that Banisadr was responsible for violating the Constitution, and that his speech on 28 May was unlawful. Following this, Khomeini publicly declared his support for Banisadr's dismissal from the Presidency by asking the President to 'repent' for his deviations so that he could be 'forgiven' by Islam. This gave Banisadr's dismissal the final religious sanction. Consequently, any demonstrations that were to be held in support of Banisadr would have been viewed as demonstrations against Islam. Also, any measures adopted for breaking up such demonstrations would have been Islamic and for the defence of Islam. It was for these reasons that the Islamic judges called the demonstration staged by 500,000 people in support of Banisadr on 20 June 1981, as an uprising against Islam. There could be no middle way for demonstrators arrested against such charges. Either they were to be executed, or if they repented, they were to be pardoned, one Islamic judge is reported to have said. 15 girls, the first group of demonstrators arrested on 20 June to be executed, were the 'unrepentent' ones. When the girls were brought before Ayatollah Gillani, the Islamic judge, and asked their names, each had in turn replied *'Mujahid'*. When the judge asked the name of the girls' parents, each had replied 'People of Iran'. The Islamic judge solved the problem of having the girls identity for his legal file by having them photographed. Then he consigned them all to the firing squad. The girls had raised their clenched fists and shouted 'Long live Freedom, Death to Khomeini' before their voices were silenced by the bullets of the Revolutionary Guards. The spate of mass executions unleashed by the Islamic Courts and the Revolutionary Guards following the 20 June demonstrations reached such an extent that according to conservative estimates, by the end of 1981, over four thousand persons, mostly supporters of *Mujahideen-e-Khalq,* had been executed. And as claimed by opposition sources in May 1982, the number of those exceeds 15,000. Although it is known that most of the executed were students and teachers, the first confirmation of this fact from the side of the clerical regime came only recently. During a meeting Mrs. Rajai, wife of the slain Iranian President, had with Pakistani women in her recent visit to Karachi, she was asked as to who were the women who had been executed in Iran. Mrs. Rajai replied that 'the women executed were mainly teachers.'[45] Mrs. Rajai thus confirmed that thousands of young Iranian women had aspired to become a 'Fatima' in the tradition of Fatima Amini—the young school teacher whose trail—blazing martyrdom under SAVAK's torture in 1975 became a beacon of inspiration for thousands of women, making them active participants in the field of social struggle, and drawing them into the folds of the *Mujahideen-*

e-Khalq. Documents retrieved from SAVAK archives confirm Fatima Amini as a revolutionary who was the epitome of faith and ideological commitment. These documents, which have since been published, reveal that the 15 girls, whose execution inaugurated the mass execution of political opponents of Khomeini's regime, had answered the questions of the Islamic judge exactly in the same manner as Fatima, the first female member of the *Mujahideen* executed by the Shah's regime, had answered in 1975. When the Pahlavi judge had asked Fatima her name, she had simply said *'Mujahid.'* And in response to his query about her parents, she had replied, 'I am the child of the people.' Like Fatima Amini, who used to recite verses from the Quran to boost her morale and spirits under SAVAK's lethal tortures, the *Mujahideen* girls faced the barrels of Islamic Guard's guns shouting the slogan 'Allah-o-Akbar' — God is Greatest, thereby refusing to submit or accept Khomeini as the Divine Authority. It may be recalled that the *Mujahideen-e-Khalq* began their urban guerrilla war only after the Islamic Guards of Khomeini's regime had killed 30 unarmed demonstrators on 20 June and had begun the mass execution of arrested demonstrators on the following morning. The *Mujahideen* invoked these hurried executions for justifying their all out offensive against the Khomeini regime. However, their military operations, which had taken off splendidly initially, strengthened the clergy's self-justifying claim that it was fighting a 'holy war' against 'hypocrites,' meaning *Mujahideen,* and that the killing of those who were demonstrating against the 'Islamic Republic' was the religious duty of all believers. However, as Mehdi Bazargaan, Khomeini's first Prime Minister, complained in the Islamic Parliament, many of those killed were neither members of the *Mujahideen,* nor necessarily subscribing to their ideology, but had simply joined the demonstrations to protest against dictatorship. The indiscriminate executions of young boys and girls led Bazargaan to declare that 'blind revenge' was depriving the nation of its 'most precious and dearest asset' — the young generation. However, even Bazargaan, representing 'loyal opposition' to Imam Khomeini, could not continue his speech because the wires of his microphone were disconnected by Parliament deputies. In other words, in Iran, the word 'terrorist' has come to mean a general term for political dissidents—teachers, lawyers, students and journalists who subscribe to a particular ideology or outlook. A member of the Islamic Parliament has justified the mass executions of political opponents by arguing that 'just as the excesses of the French Revolution were excused 20 years later, so the excesses of the Islamic Revolution would be forgotten and accepted.'[46] Iran's clerical rulers have been blessed with the war against Iraq that has unified the fiercely nationalist Iranians and their strongly religious counterparts against a common enemy. With all the support of its firing squads and its claims to religious monopoly, the clerical regime has been unsuccessful so far in totally liquidating opposition to its rule.

One year after the clergymen began their crack-down against *Mujahideen-e-Khalq*, the latter are still reported to be engaging the Islamic Guards in military operations in Tehran and other provincial cities, despite the heavy losses they have suffered.

Islam vs Islam: Letter from the Sons of an Islamic Judge to their Father

Ayatollah Mohammadi Gillani, the Islamic judge who sent the 15 girls, the youngest of whom was only 13 and the eldest 17, to be killed by the firing squad, appeared on the national television in an interview following the executions, to give justification for his religious judgement. One reason Judge Gillani cited for 'Islamizing' the execution of *Mujahideen* women was by drawing a comparison between the *Mujahideen* women and Hazrat Ayesha, wife of the Prophet Mohammad, traditionally regarded with disfavour by Shia Muslims. By comparing *Mujahideen* women to Hazrat Ayesha, Ayatollah Gillani termed them to be 'fit for extermination'.[47] The Islamic judge had also stressed in his television appearance that anyone wounded in anti-Khomeini demonstrations was to be killed on the spot. This verdict of the Ayatollah was echoed nationwide during the Friday prayer congregations by the religious leaders and also through the rhetorical speeches of Ayatollahs broadcast on the State radio, urging 'believers' to kill the wounded instead of taking them to hospitals.[48]

Following the appearance of Judge Gillani on television, two of his sons, Kazem and Mohammad, wrote him an open letter. The sons of the Ayatollah, who support the *Mujahideen*, compared their father to the Islamic Judge of Yazid who gave the ruling that killing Imam Hosein, Prophet Mohammad's grandson, was lawful because Imam Hosein had become an 'apostate'. Since Mohammadi Gillani had given similar reasons for sentencing the regime's opponents to death, his sons equated him with Yazid's Islamic judge. Such misuse of Islam, according to the *Mujahideen*, was being carried out by a brand of religious monopolists whose ideological ancestors had labelled Hazrat Ali, the Islamic Caliph, as 'infidel' and 'hypocrite', and called Imam Hosein an 'alien', and who even demanded that Ali must 'repent' for pursuing an Un-Islamic way. The power monopolists of the past used the very slogan which the Prophet had uttered in the battle of Badr, for attacking Imam Hosein's encampment at Karbala. The conflict between the two camps, the hypocritical and monopolistic version of Islam on the one hand and true Islam on the other, was to continue in the never ending battle of religion against religion until all forms of exploitation and oppression were effaced. Parts of the letter the sons of Ayatollah Gillani wrote to him read: 'You took no pity on our innocent 13 year old sister whose execution you ordered. You justified the massacre by invoking religion. By doing so, you have committed the unpardonable crime of attributing your own crime to God. No one is more vicious and vile than the person who belies God. (The Holy Quran *A'raf:* 37).

'It was a repulsive experience and a stigma for us to see your interview on television. Until recently, you believed in *Mujahideen's* honesty, selflessness and purity. It was you who used to say that the *Mujahideen* were the most honest and upright among the young, and that Masood Rajavi was fit for becoming the country's President. You even expressed your opposition when violence began to be increasingly used for crushing the *Mujahideen* by reactionary agents. What happened that now your hands are splashed with our blood? You have even surpassed your murderous act by declaring on your propagandist television that the wounded and the injured street demonstrators must be killed.

'It was your Revolutionary Guards who opened fire and massacred people demonstrating against the imposition of despotism and dictatorship under cover of Islam. Those arrested during these demonstrations, as well as the injured, were taken to a Court where they were provided with neither a lawyer nor the opportunity to defend themselves. By your order they were consigned to the firing squads. You do not allow political groups to publish and distribute newspapers and bulletins, or hold meetings. You have blocked all channels of expression. Then tell us, how do you expect people to express their protest? Your repressive measures clearly reveal your fear of the people. Your regime must daily line up scores of *Mujahideen* and other revolutionaries in front of its firing squads for its survival. Yet, despite all your barbarity, you have witnessed that our 13 year old sister and all those young girls whom you killed remained firm and unafraid of your despotism, and greeted death for the sake of Freedom. The last shout of our sisters is the angry voice of a people who are no longer prepared to live under dictatorship, torture, and despotism imposed in the name of religion. They shall not allow that people's freedom be crushed under the boots of those reactionaries who are using Islam as a cover, who are distorting the pure face of Islam with their horrible crimes.' One could say that the religious outlook which gave religious justification to the killing of unarmed and wounded street demonstrators was similar to the diseased religious self—righteousness which burnt down a cinema hall packed with innocent victims, for the sake of religion and revolution, in Abadan in August 1978.

The confrontation between Ayatollah Gillani's Islam and the Islam of his sons poignantly expresses the evolutionary movement and expansion in consciousness born of conflict and symbolized by the idol breaking tradition of Prophet Abraham. Symbolically, Abraham's act represents an archetypal stage in the intellectual and spiritual development of man towards Perfection. As Shariati has pointed out, Abraham was brought up in the house of Azar, the idol worshipper hooked to the blind dogma of his times. But when Abraham grew up and was blessed with consciousness, he broke the bondage 'the idols' of dogma and blind obedience had imposed on his society, thereby accelerating the social and spiritual evolution of his people and society. Therefore what the young generation in Iran had undertaken in the fight against religious dogma and obscurantism was a collective expression of the archetypal mission of Abraham. In the words of a *Mujahideen* woman recently martyred, the young Iranian generation 'has made an epic out of every single life and has itself become an epic. Where in history can one find a people whose 13 year old children kiss the gallows before being hanged, and stand firm on their ideology and opinion? Perhaps it is far too early for our generation and ourselves to appreciate the magnificence and depth of such heroism.' The above message addressed to Iranian women, was issued by Ashraf Rabii, a woman leader of the *Mujahideen* organization and wife of Masood Rajavi, in September 1981. Before she was herself killed by the Revolutionary Guards in February 1982, she declared that 'the *mujahid* woman had no second thoughts about standing firm for the sake of freedom and human dignity.'

Another expression of the confrontation between dynamic Islamic spirit and the deadlock posed by dogma is reflected in the statement of Hosein Khomeini, grandson of the Grand Ayatollah Khomeini, describing the religious dictatorship in Iran as 'worse than the Shah's'. The young Khomeini observed that under the religious monopoly of the new dictators, Iran was 'governed by fascists more dangerous than the founders of fascism', and that 'the revolutionary courts were treating our people with more brutality than the Mongols did'.[49] Clearly, then, it was evident from Hosein Khomeini's statement that the Islamic Republic as it existed was unacceptable to all those opposed to fascism and oppression. It also meant that the religious dictatorship, by surpassing the Shah's regime in persecution, torture, and execution of its political opponents dwarfed the despotism and oppression of the Pahlavi dictatorship into insignificance. One could even say that if the Iranian religious dictatorship had the technology and industrial base of a highly developed country at its disposal, enabling it to create a military machine, it would have embarked upon a course of expansionist action that would have made a caricature of Hitler's misdeeds. As for the Islamic Republic the younger Khomeini had in mind, it was no different from that envisioned by progressive Muslim revolutionaries. Based on freedom, independence, and democracy, such a Republic could be established, according to Hosein Khomeini, on the basis of 'a common ground' that would unite the different forces and viewpoints by their adherence to an all encompassing universal principle. 'When the Muslim, the Marxist, the Jew, the Christian, the Zoroastrian and other minorities are allowed to get together in one Parliament, this would mean that they would be faithful to the basic democratic foundation of the system and would readily accept leadership of its President and Judiciary. This is how it is possible to achieve a basis, the common ground necessary for creating a common faith and universal acceptance of the system,'[51] Hosein Khomeini said. 'If we do not accept realities and deny their existence by resorting to coercion and deception, consequently people would not accept the system and will have no mutually shared framework and no common basis for endorsing the Islamic Republic. In that case, their primary demand would be the overthrow of the Islamic Republic'.[52] In the three years since Hosein Khomeini made the above statement, the refusal of 'power monopolists' to respect and uphold the basic principles of human dignity and freedom has further strengthened the determination of progressive Muslims to rid Islam from the pernicious grip of self — righteous monopolism of any particular class. It is in this sense that the Islamic Revolution is a continuing revolution. Just as the origins of the Scientific Revolution can be traced to the battle between dogma and progress, symbolized by the trial of Galileo who threatened the obsolete world-view of the Church, so the ongoing struggle in Iran between dogmatic and dynamic approaches to Islam symbolized the beginning of a new era for Muslims. Iran's Islamic Revolution today is a 'War of Liberation' which progressive Muslims are fighting for rescuing Islam from the shackles of an obsolete dogma,[53] the base for reaction and imperialism, and for steering society towards freedom, independence, human dignity and perfection. Ayatollah Jalal Ganjae, a former student of Ayatollah Khomeini and Professor of Islamic theology who recently escaped to Paris to join the *Mujahideen-e-Khalq* has described the current conflict in Iran as "a battle between two Islams: the Islam of freedom and human dignity *vs* the Islam of torture and tyranny, the Islam of progress *vs* the Islam of backwardness, the Islam of social justice *vs* the Islam of a privileged, ruling priestly class."[54]

Notes

1. Ayatollah Tehrani, 'Yes Brother, That's the Way it Ended'.
2. Ibid., p.11-12.
3. Ibid.
4. Ibid.
5. Ibid., p.21.
6. Ibid.
7. *Kayhan,* No.11027. 23 June 1980.
8. Ibid.
9. Ibid.
10. Ibid.
11. *Kodamin Rah-e-Sayyum?* (Which Third Way?), p.22-25.
12. This logic applies not only to the Islamic regime's domestic opponents but to international Muslim organizations as well. For example, Iran's ruling clergymen accuse *Ikhwan-ul-Muslimeen* of

having 'Zionist Connections' against Syria because 'traitorous elements' have penetrated the *Ikhwan's* organization. (Arabia No.8, April 1982, p.31).
13. *Enqelabe Islami,* No.453, 21 January 1980.
14. *Which Third Way?* p.22-25.
15. Ibid.
16. Ibid.
17. *Enqelabe Islami,* No.426, 16 December 1980.
18. Ayatollah Mossavi Gharavi's cable to Banisadr, *Enqelabe Islami,* No.426, 16 December 1980.
19. *Enqelabe Islami,* No. 426, 16 December 1980.
20. *Which Third Way?*
21. Ibid.
22. Ibid., p.28-30.
23. Ibid.
24. 'Mrs. Rezai Provides a Model For Today's World.' *News And Views,* Vol. 1, No.109, 15 December 1979. Department of Information and Publication, Ministry of Foreign Affairs, Islamic Republic of Iran.
25. Ibid.
26. Ibid.
27. Ibid.
28. Ibid.
29. *Which Third Way?,* p. 33-34.
30. Ibid.
31. Interview of Ayatollah Qomi in *The Bamdad,* 9 March 1980.
32. Ibid.
33. Ibid.
34. Since the rise to power of the clerical regime, the use of torture against political dissidents has sharply increased. The present rulers in Iran no longer consider Felacca and whipping as forms of torture but as religiously sanctioned 'corrective punishment'. The use of 'mock firing squads' by Islamic Revolutionary Guards was reported to be widely in use only a few months after the Pahlavi regime was overthrown. In its news bulletin in January 1982, Amnesty International has noted the use of torture by Iran's Islamic regime that includes burning the victim's body. The recent allegation by *Mujahideen-e-Khalq* (*Mojahed,* No.15, Nov. 1981) that Revolutionary Guards burnt alive seven of their supporters seems to be supported by a news item published in *Jumhuri-yeh-Islami,* newspaper of the ruling Islamic Republic Party (*Jumhuri-yeh-Islami,* No.698, 9 Aban, 1360) 31 Oct. 1981. The paper reports the burning to death of seven 'hypocrites', (the term IRP employs for *Mujahideen*) when the car in which they were trying to escape came under the fire of Islamic Revolutionary Guards. The *Mujahideen,* however, say that Khomeini regime's version of this incident is similar to the one SAVAK used when it published the news about the political prisoners it killed under torture or through 'unofficial' execution. For example, SAVAK agents confessed, after the Pahlavi regime was overthrown, that

they had executed nine *Fedayeen-e-Khalq* leaders in cold blood in 1974. At that time, however, SAVAK had published its own version of these executions, saying that security guards had been forced to open fire on the nine *Fedayeen* because they were 'trying to escape' from prison.
35. *Ettela'at,* No.16095. 11 March 1980, p.2.
36. Ibid.
37. Ibid.
38. Ibid.
39. Ibid. The demonstrations held in April 1982, against Ayatollah Shariatmadari following the allegation that he was involved in a plot to overthrow Ayatollah Khomeini's regime were irrelevant insofar as the demand for stripping Shariatmadari of the title of Grand Ayatollah was concerned. As is clear by Ayatollah Qomi's above statement, and as confirmed by Ayatollah Rouhani's statement in April 1982, it is not for 'ordinary people' to strip a Grand Ayatollah of his religious authority as Source of Imitation for his followers. Differences between Grand Ayatollahs on political, social, and legal issues have always existed and their mutual tolerance for these differences is regarded as an expression of democracy among orthodox Shias. Even the former Shah, as defender of the Shia faith, showed his respect for this principle by sending the Grand Ayatollah Khomeini, who was openly calling for overthrowing the monarchy, into exile, instead of physically eliminating him. It was for these reasons that Ayatollah Khomeini called for an end to the campaign against Shariatmadari, his rival Ayatollah, after the two had reached a certain form of agreement. Shariatmadari today retains his title and position as a Grand Ayatollah.
40. *Enqelabe Islami,* No.250. 8 May 1980.
41. *Enqelabe Islami,* No.219. 29 March 1980.
42. *Enqelabe Islami,* 27 January 1981.
43. *Enqelabe Islami,* No.460. 28 January 1981.
44. *Enqelabe Islami.* 28 May 1981.
45. *The Pakistan Times,* 16 April 1982.
46. *Newsweek.* 8 March 1982.
47. *Weekly Publication of the Muslim Students Societies In America And Europe,* No.12, 6 November 1981, (in Persian).
48. In December 1981, *Mujahideen's* office in Paris released a tape-recording of the conversation between Khomeini's Revolutionary Guards and the Guard's Central headquarters during street demonstrations on 27 September 1981, in Tehran. In these tapes, the Guard's headquarters ordered a unit to check all hospitals and to transfer the wounded to Evin Prison for execution. The order was also given to the Revolutionary Guards to 'use force if the (hospital) staff raise any objections' about handing over the wounded. Also, it was reported in the clergy controlled *Kayhan* newspaper that a wounded *mujahid* had been removed from hospital and transferred to prison, later ending up before the firing squad. (*Weekly Publication of Moslem Students Society.* Britain,

6 January 1982, p.2).
The above piece of information merely confirms that the official policy of the Islamic State, with respect to its political opponents wounded in demonstrations, is being duly implemented.
49. *The Guardian Weekly*, Vol.125, No.10. 6 September 1981.
50. *Ettela'at,* No.16095, 11 March 1980.
51. Ibid.
52. Ibid.
53. Shariati, A., *Takhasos.*
54. *Time Magazine,* 7 March 1983.

FROM THE MARTYR'S MIND:

DEFENCE SPEECHES, BIOGRAPHIES, AND POETRY OF RESISTANCE

Appendix One

Saeed Mohsen[1] Founding Member of the Mujahideen-e-Khalq Organization

Saeed Mohsen was born in 1939 in a middle class family in Zanjan. After finishing high school in his hometown, he came to Tehran and graduated as a Civil Engineer in 1962 from Tehran University. During his student years he was twice jailed for political activities as a member of the Students Committee of the Liberation Movement.

Saeed was conscripted into the army and had to undergo 18 months of military training after his graduation from university. He learned his military lessons with great interest, for he believed that by using the opportunities that were available, it was possible to start a revolution. Saeed used to often repeat this Quranic Verse: 'We offered the burden of responsibility to the heaven and the earth and the mountains, and they refused. But man accepted to shoulder this trust.' (The Holy Quran, *Ahzab:*71).

From 23 August 1971, when he was arrested to 30 May 1972, when he was executed, he was subjected to violent tortures. But Saeed did not reveal any information. The torch that he lit will become brighter and brighter. Saeed is alive in the hearts of those carrying guns in their hands and fighting against imperialism and dictatorship.

The Defence Speech of Martyred Mujahid Saeed Mohsen Executed by the Pahlavi Regime in May, 1972[2]

> Permission to fight is given to those who are the oppressed, most surely, God will assist them.
> (The Holy Quran, *Haj:* 39)

The war is between truth and falsehood. On one side are the enemies of the people, armed with the latest weapons and technology. On the other side is the will of Iran's toiling masses and the determined hands of workers and peasants bruised from overwork. And today, in a corner of Iran, in this court, we are witness to a scene which constitutes a small fragment of this battle and confrontation. It is a court whose president has no duty except signing an order determined and decided in advance. By signing the papers for our execution, this regime and its social system is perpetuating the greedy grip of masters across the oceans — those 'masters' whose giant oil tankers are plundering away millions of tons of raw material which is the fruit of our people's labour. On this battlefield on one side are the mercenaries tied up with international imperialism, and on the other side are the youth who have staked their lives for people's liberation and are striving to fulfil their religious, moral, and human responsibility. I am certain that in this confrontation, we are the true victors, not you. It is we who shall throw you in the dust with the burst of our machine guns. From every drop of our blood, thousands of armed youth will rise up to destroy your Pharaonic palaces, and your false government.

It is obvious that you and your court are the defenders of a regime which has no other goal but the perpetuation of oppression and suppression, and intensification of exploitation. Our goal, however, is to eliminate the exploitation of man by man in any form, so that a social system is created in which each person can have the opportunity for developing his potential and attaining a higher status of perfection.

You call us criminals and robbers. For..... a robber nothing matters but personal advantage. It is obvious that you, in your system, which is run by robbers and looters who are ravaging the fruits of the labour of old women, workers, peasantry and small girls weaving carpets, should call all pure, socially aware, responsible and selfless youth 'robbers'. In your eyes, the heroes of the nation, the selfless guerillas who have given their lives for no personal advantage but for the cause of God and the people, are classified as hooligans and given a military trial behind closed doors. But tell me, if we are robbers, then are you and all those supporting your system and plundering the people by relying on foreign masters and capitalists, butchering young men and women after torture, honourable citizens?

The last thing that we expect of you is justice. We truly believe that between us and you, nothing rules but the gun. Through our blood, which is our most potent weapon, we will drag you to the Court of True Justice and have you convicted. We have not forgotten that you used to call the Algerian *Mujahideen,* the Palestinian *Fedayeen,* and the revolutionary people of Vietnam and Cuba, miscreants and terrorists.

With all your corrupt glory and power you are afraid of us. Does anyone know about these trials except SAVAK and the military intelligence and a few bayonet-wielding soldiers? No common Iranian is allowed to witness these trials. This is sufficient reason to disqualify your court. I see no need to invoke your law for rejecting this court of trial. Our law is the will of the people expressing itself in our revolutionary struggle which is determined to destroy you.

In the light of Iran's history and given the conditions prevailing in the world and the characteristics of the Pahlavi dictatorship, we have found armed revolution as the only path for true liberation.

70 years ago, our nation, inspired by social and political awakening and as a result of the intensification of despotism in Iran, created the great Constitutional Revolution. The aims of this revolution were twofold:

1) to annihilate a system based on dictatorship;
2) to create a new system heralding equal rights and social justice for the people.

In its initial stage, this movement was successful and led to the defeat of despotism and replaced it with the Constitution which, at the time, was a progressive constitution. However, it was not long before the rage of reaction began showing its loathsome face. People's rights were violated, and the Constitution was trampled upon. Thus began the era of Pahlavi despotism when Reza Khan became king with the support of Britain (in 1925). The first step Reza Khan took was to crush the people's movement and killing or exiling the nationalists. Because of the flagrant violation of the nation's rights, once again the motives that had spurred the Constitution movement, that is, struggle against dictatorship and the creation of a just social system, were reactivated. Even today, these motives constitute the revolutionary motive of the masses, though in a more developed and evolved form. Therefore we believe that the struggle against dictatorship is part and parcel of the Iranian nation's being. If in a society the rights of the people are not violated, do you think people are crazy to take up arms? For us, arms are a means for defending human dignity and human honour. A worker will pick up arms only when his honour—his work and his life—are trampled upon. We have taken up arms for defending the people's life, honour, integrity, and rights. A group of educated intelligentsia are neither sadists nor highway robbers to take up arms. Is it not true that our *Fedayeen-e-Khalq* brothers at Siahkal were the best and the purest among our nation's youth? Despite all your efforts, you have not been able to find among our group of 170 *Mujahideen-e-Khalq* you have arrested, a single individual not possessing the highest moral, human and ethical qualities. We have taken up arms because we see the social honour of our society is being threatened by highway robbers who are freely looting the people with the support of American imperialism. You are putting us on trial by calling us criminals. But this is not the first time that history will be the judge. Since the Uprising of Noah and Spartacus to the Uprising of Hosein, son of Ali, and the progressive contemporary movements, the fighters for truth have always had to face slander and denigration by the oppressors. But tell us, is it your imperialist—backed monarchical system which is robbing the worker and peasant of his earnings, or we? It is our duty to resist with weapons your armed agents who are defenders of criminals and opulent usurpers.

History has shown that during the past 50 years, our nation has been afflicted with a rotten monarchical dictatorship. Since this system does not enjoy the people's support, it has resorted to the strength of arms for its survival. By intimidating the people with the fire of its arms, this regime has enslaved and chained a whole nation. In its history, our nation has tasted the fire of these weapons many times. The cumulative lesson of these confrontations has taught us that there is no way left for our nation except armed struggle. Our nation has realised that the existing ruling system not only lacks the capacity to solve the nation's problems, it is also responsible for the people's misfortunes. Our nation has seen and experienced that the Shah's dictatorship, despite its apparent strength, relies on foreign bayonets for its survival. Thus, this regime cannot last forever. Moreover, the movements in Vietnam, Cuba, Algeria, and Palestine have shown to our people the new path they must adopt. Over the past 50 years, our nation has lost its hope for a reformist solution to its problems. Therefore, it is now armed with the thought and intention of waging an armed struggle for solving its problems. Today, not only our nation, but the whole of the Third World is gripped by the fervour of anti-imperialist armed uprising. The clear goal of this world-revolution is complete destruction of 20th Century exploiters, those who without any hesitation sprayed bullets on the peoples of Vietnam, Palestine, Asia, Africa, and Latin America. This revolution is being irrigated with the blood of the purest sons of Adam. This is why it will have a supremely virtuous outcome. It is our duty that we should offer our insignificant blood for irrigating the sapling of this revolution. It is for this reason that our nation warmly embraces its revolutionaries; for our people see the crystalization of their honour in the blood of their young revolutionaries. It is our belief that just as today the revolution's vanguard accepts death as an evolutionary step, tomorrow, after us, our nation too will confront death with a similar attitude and in a similar confrontation against the imperialist-backed dictatorship.

To sum up, we have shown that it is you who are the criminals, not we. Secondly, the rotten monarchical system has outlived its historical life and is heading towards decay and it is our duty to accelerate its destruction through our will and by offering our lives. Thirdly, the confrontation between ourselves and you is the confrontation of life against death. Either you would remain, or we. On the basis of the principle of universal evolution and historical necessity, the revolutionary movement of the people will be victorious. Whether we live or die, we are victorious. We have purchased victory with our blood. As Hazrat Ali has said, it is death to live as an oppressed, and it is life to die a victorious death. Whatever you do, whatever plans and plots you contrive, our victory is sure, certain, and guaranteed.

'Can you await for us but one of two good things (death or victory in Allah's way)? And we await for you that Allah will afflict you with chastisement from Himself or by our hands. So wait, we too will wait with you.'

(The Holy Quran: *At-Toubah:* 52)

In our struggle and striving, we anticipate attaining either of two virtues, martyrdom or victory. We are also waiting that wrath befalls you, whether from God or through our hands. Wait, we too are waiting. We are waiting for you with the bullets of our guns. So you also order your executioners and torturers to wait for us; so that we find out who is victorious and who is the criminal liar.

From the economic point of view, we believe that growth in production is not possible without mass mobilization. This means that so long as people do not utilize their real energies for production, even mechanizing the system of production cannot meet the needs of the society. Moreover, removing the needs of the society through production cannot in itself lead to the real goal of the society to direct man's energies for the fullest blossoming of his capacities in order to create the ideal conditions for human justice to rule, both materially and spiritually. That is how mankind, with self-knowledge, correct understanding and interpretation of the world, can become the creator of a new world and meet its higher inner needs. To move along this path of perfection requires the complete mobilization of the masses. It is a movement which is brought into effect by human thought. Such a mobilization and movement depends upon inner transformation in the individual and the people and the flowering of revolutionary spirit on the basis of the verse: 'God does not change the condition of a people unless they first change themselves inwardly' (the Quran, *Ar-Rad:* 11). It is not possible for movement and transformation to take place in a society unless it originates from within the people; thus creating a sense of responsibility in relation to other people and future generations. This inner transformation generates commitment and enthusiasm for service to the people which is what the creator desires. It gives real value to human life and liberates the individual from the confining shell of selfishness and narcissism, which today dominates your system. This is how the principle 'all for one, one for all', will be realised. The movement and mobilization of the masses should be in a direction that serves the interests of masses, and not for serving the interests of a particular group or class, for in that case, people would become victims of greater exploitation.

When the enemy, through coercion and force, brings the forces of workers and peasants under his control and employment, and refuses the worker the right to benefit from the fruits of his labour, when the capitalist system showers bullets on protesting workers in order to defend and continue its exploitation of the suffering classes, we are left with no option but to pick up arms, so that we may fight and disarm the robbers plundering people in broad daylight. The rotten traditions, contaminations, and inhuman dependencies can be rent asunder and transformed only through revolutionary action. Only a revolutionary society can transform moral decadence into virtue and deviations into sublime values, thereby consolidating the economic infrastructure of the society.

From the economic viewpoint, the disorganization and chaos in our society are the result of exploitation of one class by another and of man by man. We believe that nothing in the world has real value except human life. Man transfers his life through productive work into goods and products. This means that man loses a part of his existence and dissipates his energy and life, his youth and capacity to work, through investing these in productive work. Thus, what he produces gains value and reaches the customer. The value of a commodity is equivalent to the human work concentrated in it. It is because of man's work that things have value. Unlike you capitalists for whom a commodity is a lifeless thing, for us, human life is reflected in every produced item. If you regard the hand-woven carpet under your feet as a mere commodity with a lifeless pattern, we have witnessed the blood of workers and little girls enmeshed in its fibres and colours. These patterns, from our angle, possess human life. Man concentrates and invests a part of his life and existence in the raw material present in nature. To the extent that he increases the value of the product, he loses his life span. This is how human work and production is part of his being, and none has any right to it. No one has the right to claim it. We can never accept that the fruits of one's labour should be taken by another. As Hazrat Ali has said, the fruits of the labour of a worker are not meant to be swallowed by another. This principle forms the basis of our economic thought, and on the basis of our Islamic ideology and our belief in the authenticity of the individual and society, we consider it the basis of correct exchange. On these grounds, only that system is acceptable to us where man is given the opportunity to utilize his energy for work without being exploited. From this perspective, your system, because of its capitalistic infrastructure, is a reactionary system. We are therefore determined to transform, with the people's help, the cultural form and the economy of this system — that is to say, the monarchical superstructure and the economic infrastructure. From the economic viewpoint, cultural and social relations are dependent upon the same exploitive infrastructure. For bringing about a cultural transformation and for effacing corruption and poverty, the people have no alternative but to rise against the imperialists.

In your system, your leaders plunder the wealth of the nation. For a night of official ceremony and festivities, they spend millions from the national income. They know neither the heat of summer nor the chill of winter. Their hands have not touched any tools of production except delicate scissors for clipping the ribbons on an 'Opening Ceremony', or for holding for a moment an elegant axe for performing a symbolic ceremonial function. In the system that we envisage, following our historical models, we see Ali, the leader of the Islamic State, planting palm trees, irrigating trees and digging wells with his overworked, blistered hands. . . . . (in the social, political and spiritual model that inspires us) the 'highest person', the leader of society, does productive work like a most ordinary and simple worker in society. At the same time, he is burning with concern lest a person goes to sleep with an empty stomach in the remotest corner of his State. When the rights of a non—Muslim subject, a Jewess, who is the responsibility of Ali's government (because she is residing in the Islamic state,) are violated, he becomes so upset, pained and disgusted, that he says: 'If an honourable Muslim dies because of his pain and disgust on this incident, he is not to be reprimanded — indeed, for me this would be a worthy course of action.' One who does not comprehend human pain and suffering does not deserve to live in human society. Compare our *(Mujahideen-e-Khalq's)* model of leadership with those 'leaders' who shed tears and show a glum face when they visit an area impoverished by calamities, and yet, clad in expensive dress and jewellery, they spend the same night in revelries drunk with power and pride. You will say to us, Ali was Ali, you cannot be Ali. That may be true. Ali as a personality is a rare phenomenon in history. But today, Ali's thoughts and ideas which exhort people to rise up against injustice, for creating unity, equality and brotherhood among humankind, are no longer rare or strange for mankind. Indeed, these thoughts represent mankind's ultimate ideals and wishes.

Today's world is giving us the good tidings that the lofty ideals of Ali are being realised. If a revolution has come about in China, if the Cuban society, Vietnam, and the liberation movements around the world are directing human conscience and morals towards the sublime, if today the selfless sacrifice of a human being for others is creating the epic of the 20th Century, assuredly, we see Ali on the summit of the history of human thought. We have risen up for attaining this objective. We have risen to create a world which will destroy the exploitation of man by man in every form. This goal knows no time or place. Be it Iran, Palestine, Africa, Vietnam, Latin America, or any other place, whether today or tomorrow, wherever our blood is shed, our ideals and aspirations will mature and grow. For us, to be martyred beside Palestinians, our *Fedayeen-e-Khalq* brothers, or at the gallows of the dictator has only one meaning. For the attainment of our noble goal for our society, we are confronted by the enemy in the form of American Imperialism and the ruling class of Comprador Capitalists in Iran. This enemy is manifesting himself through the State's intelligence system, and military administration, and it is armed to the teeth with weapons and strategy against us. Our life and death and your life and death are contradictory to one another. For the destruction of our enemy, be it SAVAK or the head of this system, we are constrained to rely on our machine guns. Simply because the armed oppressor and exploiter can be defeated only through arms. The path which our nation has traversed (during the past 70 years) has brought it to the beginning of armed revolution. We have a formidable battle lying ahead of us. A long term battle. We take pride in being simple soldiers in this battle. By selflessly sacrificing our insignificant lives, we have taken a very small part in this important mission. Our insignificant blood is nurturing the blossoms of revolution.

> Victory to the armed struggle of our people.
> Glory and peace to the pure souls of the martyrs of the Nationalist Movement (of Dr. Mossadeq).
> Down with the enemies of the people.

> 'Allah compares truth and falsehood; the scum passes away as a worthless thing but that which profits the people remains on the earth.' (The Holy Quran, *Ar-Rad:* 17)

Saeed Mohsen ended his defence speech by quoting the first 14 verses from *Daybreak* (Chapter 89, the Holy Quran).

Mehdi Rezai: The Red Rose of Revolution

Mehdi Rezai joined the *Mujahideen-e-Khalq* in 1970, when he was only 17. He was killed under torture by SAVAK when he was 19. Once a brilliant student at Tehran University, Mehdi renounced his academic career to devote himself fully to his revolutionary struggle. He carried out several successful and daring hits against symbols of imperialist domination in Tehran.

SAVAK arrested him in 1971 after Mehdi's pistol jammed in a gun battle during which he had eliminated one of the Shah's agents. Torture did not break his will. According to authentic accounts, Mehdi was tortured night after night. His flesh was burnt with a hot plate. His feet were lashed with steel cables. Before dawn, Mehdi would be released by his tormentors to crawl back to his cell. Those political prisoners who were in the same prison as Mehdi and won their freedom during the Islamic Revolution vividly recall that as Mehdi crawled past each cell on his daily return from the torture chamber, he would cry out 'Resist! brothers, resist! The battlefield is here! Here lies the field of struggle between the people and their enemies.'

Mehdi was given a military trial. His defence was recorded and preserved by SAVAK in its archives. SAVAK could never have imagined that a few years later, this speech would become the most revered landmark in the revolution and a challenge to Muslims to take social action against oppression. He opened his speech with *Sura Nisa*, verse 74: 'Why do you not fight for those who are oppressed people in your society—men, women and children who cry out: O Lord! Save us from this land of oppression and send the saintly one who is closest to you to aid us.'

'It is precisely in response to this cry for justice that we have launched our struggle.' Mehdi said in his defence speech. He explained that social and spiritual struggle was inherent in man's quest for perfection and evolutionary growth. 'A human being who is consciously on the journey towards perfection is the most precious phenomenon in creation. The life aim of such a human is not eating and sleeping — it is the realisation of the supreme qualities of the divine in the individual by aligning and identifying oneself with these qualities. The aim is *Leqa Allah* or attaining the highest degree of perfection and divine qualities.'

It was their aim, Mehdi said, to create such social conditions in which all humans were provided the opportunity to strive for the highest stage of perfection and humanness — it was not possible for people to realise their God—given capacities in an oppressive and unjust social system.

'Our aim is the prosperity of the people and the shattering of any kind of oppressive social and economic relations and the edifice of anti-Islamic education. A free society, classless and united in *touhid* is the society of our ideal.' It was preferable for Mehdi to be put on trial in the illegal military court of those who had usurped the people's power, rather than to be condemned in the Court of God for passivity and indifference while the people were being unabashedly exploited and oppressed. It was, therefore, not possible for him to remain silent and inactive in the face of injustice and oppression, Mehdi said, his action being only a response to God's warning: 'Fear not the calamity that will fall on your oppressor, but also the calamity that you will reap for remaining silent.' (The Quran, *Sura Enfaal:* 26).

In the final part of his defence, Mehdi referred to the regime's strategy for discrediting the *Mujahideen* by branding them 'Islamic-Marxists'. Regarding this, Mehdi said that both Islam and Marxism, while differing in many basic principles, supported equality and brotherhood of man, since they were both opposed to the exploitation of man by man. 'Islam is a religion of action, which says that anyone who puts up with injustice in this world will have the same state allotted to him in the next. Islam teaches that peace and bliss will come to the believers only through a struggle with the enemies of God and the people,' Mehdi said, as he sought to reveal the revolutionary essence of Islam.

The *Mujahideen* had given up the comforts of life because they were not the kinds of persons 'who sit still when people are suffering from hardship and deprivation'. Moreover, Hazrat Ali, Mehdi's revolutionary model, had declared: 'God has taken a pledge from those who are aware of the real meaning of inhuman relations and social problems, that they shall not remain silent while the oppressors feed themselves and the oppressed are starving.' With a verse from Saadi, the classical Persian poet, Mehdi ended his defence. 'One honoured dead is worth a hundred wretches free.'

The following poems, *Mother* and *In the Name of God, the Annihilator of oppressors* are attributed to Mehdi. He composed *Mother* in prison. The poem was recorded in 1972 in the haunting voice of Reza, Mehdi's elder brother, and widely circulated. Reza died in a shootout with SAVAK in 1973. The other poem was written by Mehdi in his small notebook which was returned to his family after he was executed. He is known to have often recited it aloud in his cell. Mehdi's mother is alive and although she lost three sons — Mehdi, Reza, Ahmad, and her 18 year old daughter Sadiqeh, she is firmly engaged in the battle for progressive Islam. She is endearingly called 'The Mother' of all progressive *Mujahideen*. In February 1982, Mrs. Rezai lost a fifth child, her daughter Azar Rezai, to Khomeini's firing squad. Azar Rezai was married to Mousa Khiabani, a leader of *Mujahideen-e-Khalq,* also killed in February 1982. It is reported that at the time she was killed, Azar Rezai was pregnant.

Notes

1. Excerpted from *Anan Kay Shahadat ra bargozidand* (Those who chose Martyrdom). *Mujahideen-e-Khalq* Organization, 1975, p. 4-10.
2. Excerpted from *Moda'fiat: Esnad-e-Montash-ere-Sazman-e-Mujahideen-e-Khalq-e-Iran.* (Defence speeches: Published Documents of Peoples Mujahideen Organization 1974, p. 7-30.

MOTHER

> *By Mehdi Rezai, the 19 year old* **Mujahideen** *member tortured to death in 1972.*

O Mother! don't glue
Your tearful gaze to the door
Hoping I'll return someday
The sun of my turbulent life
Will set at noon
In my childhood you planted
In my soul
And in the soil of my thoughts
Seeds of love
For the toiling masses
By feeding me verses from the Quran

You told me: 'The way of God
Is the people's cause
Strive to the limit of your life
On His Way
Fighters for Truth are the dawn
Of liberation
Free yourself from the rule
Of the vain!'

Since I have grown
And looked around
I've found myself surrounded
By children
Gripped with suffering and pain
Their pale faces are veiled
From the pedestrian's eyes
Covered in the dust
Of passing footsteps
I've seen how the ailing child
Of a poor mother
Choked and died in her lap
Tears rolled from
The mother's eyes
With tense teeth she bit
Silence into her lips
I've seen how the plundering mouth
Of the devil is open
Devouring the fruit

Of other men's work
Every night he dines
With a glass of wine
Filled with the blood
Of unseen peasants
I've seen how the despaired
Deprived masses
Are groping for a future
Devoid of light
Thieves are plundering our homes
But our friends are watching
In silence
Those pure verses I had read
A thousand times
Began revealing their secrets
To the heart of my soul
Verses from Sura *Fajar Hadid* and *Saf*
Opened for me windows of hope

Then suddenly
The night was pierced
By the call of Mujahideen's bullet
Heralding dawn
The tempest of Mujahid's
Vital will
Rent asunder a hundred
Spiders' webs

O mother! see how the first
Seed you planted
Has flowered in my soul
And blossomed in all directions
The flame that you kindled
In my breast
Flared up from the barrel
Of my gun!
O mother! accept my final gratitude
For those first rhymes
You sang for me
Those pure verses with their mysteries
Kindled the thrill of *shahadat*
In me!
O countrymen! your path
Was dimmed by the night
I used my blood to kindle the torch
For your light

Soon you shall also step
Upon this path
My privilege it was to be burnt
On this path
Today, the spark of guns
And the sound of bombs
Is making our enemy tremble
Tomorrow when
The Mujahideen's Revolution
Spreads
Enemies of the people
Will be effaced from the world
The ecstatic emotions of Union
With the Friend, tonight
Are summoning me to the dawn
Of a glorious martyrdom
The knower of secrets
Has robbed me of my sleep
Because of my loving anticipation
Of martyrdom

The poem given below was found written in Mehdi Razai's notebook returned to his family after his death in 1972.

In the Name of God, the Annihilator of Oppressors

The old man
Without crying, or lamenting
or feeling small
Always used to tell us
Don't be sad,
My son has been martyred
With his blood he has opened
a path
Towards eternity and immortality
I feel blessed
For I had prepared him
for such a day
This is the path of eternal glory
In the name of God!
Don't be sad.
This is my way! This is my way!
So that I may fight! O my people!
So that I may set myself to
any fire!

From my wound
The sword of vengeance
would sprout

From my eyes
The mouths of cannons
would shout
From the eyes of my people
Fire would rain
O people sharpen
your knife's blade
On the oppressor's neck
Who is your executioner
This is my way! This is my way!
Every drop of my blood
is a red star
On the flag of revolution

I fight with the sword
stemming
From my wounds
of vengeance
And I am ready for any risks
To set myself to any fire.

Defence Speech of Masood Rajavi in the Military Tribunal of Pahlavi Regime in February 1972.[1]

Masood Rajavi joined the *Mujahideen-e-Khalq* in 1966, the year he entered Tehran University as an under-graduate student in the School of Law. From 1967 to 1971, the year when he was arrested by SAVAK, Rajavi worked with Mohammad Hanif-nejad and Ahmed Rezai as a member of the organization's study group for developing the Islamic nucleus of *Mujahideen's* ideology. In 1969, when he was only 21 years old, Rajavi became one of the 12 members of the Central Committee of the organization. The following year, Rajavi and several other members of the *Mujahideen-e-Khalq* left for Palestinian camps for training in guerrilla operations. They took part on the side of the Palestinians against King Hosein's army during the 'Black September' conflict in 1970. In October of the same year, Rajavi returned to Iran. Shortly thereafter, he was captured by SAVAK along with many other members of the *Mujahideen* organization. In February 1972, Rajavi and his comrades were given a military trial and sentenced to death. The *Mujahideen* turned their trial into an indictment of the Pahlavi dictatorship with their defence speeches. In April, 1972, under pressure from various international quarters such as Amnesty International, PLO, and personal pleas from George Pompidou, then President of France, Francois Mitterand, and Jean Paul Sartre, Rajavi's death sentence was commuted to life imprisonment. A major factor in mobilizing French pressure in favour of the *Mujahideen* leaders was Rajavi's elder brother, a practicing physician in Paris. The life sentence, however, did not mean that Rajavi was spared solitary confinement, torture, hospitalization for torture wounds followed by more torture — a routine that had become common against the Shah's 'unrepenting' political prisoners.

Masood Rajavi was among the last of the 126 political prisoners, mainly members of the *Mujahideen-e-Khalq* and *Fedayeen-e-Khalq*, who were released by the Pahlavi regime in January 1979, and whose release the deposed Shah described as the greatest mistake of his career. Also among those released with Rajavi was his would be wife, Ashraf Rabi'i. The two got married in July 1979, in a simple ceremony performed by Ayatollah Taleqani, regarded as the spiritual and ideological father of *Mujahideen-e-Khalq*. The dowry that the Ayatollah handed to the bride consisted of a volume of the Quran and *Nahjul Balagha*, (the book of Hazrat Ali's statements), and also four volumes of Taleqani's commentary on the Quran. It was during Rajavi's wedding that Taleqani, sensing that the intolerance of the emerging religious monopolists would lead to a direct confrontation between the latter and the *Mujahideen*, advised the *Mujahideen* to go underground and engage in ideological struggle for propagating the true Islam. 'It would be a pity and a great loss if they destroy you. You must preserve yourself. They (the religious monopolists) are neither bothered about America, nor are they frightened of communists. They are only scared of you. This is the reason why they are putting so much pressure on you and campaigning against you. Use your pen and your thought as much as you can. If it becomes necessary, go in hiding and operate secretly. It would be a pity if you are all destroyed. We do not have many young men and women who are as aware and rooted in faith as you. If you are liquidated, there will be no one to replace you.'[2]

A few words may also be said about Ashraf Rabi'i, Rajavi's wife. Like the *Mujahideen* leader, Ashraf had also got involved with the *Mujahideen-e-Khalq* organization during her first year as an Engineering student at the prestigious Aryamehr University of Technology which she joined in 1971. Three years later, in 1974, she married Ali Akbar Nuri, a fellow combatant of the *Mujahideen* organization. That same year SAVAK arrested her. In the torture sessions that followed, Ashraf was beaten so severely that she lost the hearing of one ear and suffered a broken nose. Her body was systematically burnt for hours. Her wounds became so bad that her knee bone was exposed through the flesh. SAVAK averted her death by hospitalizing her. However, after partial recovery, Ashraf attempted suicide in her cell by swallowing a number of needles she had managed to take from the hospital, but survived. Finally, eight months after her arrest, Ashraf was given a life sentence by the Military Court. In 1977, Ashraf was taken to the mortuary to identify her husband's corpse, whom SAVAK had killed in a street gunfight. The experience deeply affected Ashraf. During the two years that followed and until her release early in 1979, Ashraf secretly worked for organizing female members of the *Mujahideen* in Qasr prison. She was among those members of the organization who carried on their ideological struggle during their imprisonment on two fronts: leftist opportunism in the name of Marxism and rightist reaction in the name of religion.

In February 1982, three years after her release and 11 years after she had joined the *Mujahideen-e-Khalq,* Ashraf Rabi'i was gunned to death by the Islamic Revolutionary Guards of Khomeini's regime. She leaves behind a one year old son, Mostapha, named in memory of Mostapha Zakeri, the 14 year old *Mujahideen* supporter killed by the 'power monopolists' for selling the *Mujahideen's* newspaper in 1980.

The following is an excerpted speech of Masood Rajavi delivered on 16 February 1972, in the Military tribunal of the Pahlavi regime. Rajavi's speech, along with the defence speeches of other *Mujahideen* martyrs, was widely circulated during the six years preceding the Tehran uprising in February 1979.

'This trial will end tonight or tomorrow night. So perhaps these are the last nights of our lives. If we are not executed, we will be sentenced to life imprisonment. The regime is holding this trial because the people's movement has intensified and international concern for the state of political prisoners in Iran has increased. For example, Jean Paul Sartre has requested for permission to attend this trial. Al-Fateh issued a special bulletin in our support, and radio Iraq has read out the names of a number of the Shah's political prisoners threatened with execution. The Pahlavi regime, therefore, decided it was in its own interest to hold this trial.

'Each of us has been allocated only half an hour for his defence. Since this does not give us sufficient time to present our case in our ideological context, my comrades will continue the text of this defence in the context of political and economic realities and the rationale and history of our organization and revolutionary struggle.

'The cause for our misfortune and the suffering of all the people at this stage in history is international imperialism. Puppet regimes have been installed here and there by imperialism. Were these regimes to rely on themselves and their people, they would not last even for a day. There are two fronts in the world today. On the one side are the impoverished, the deprived and exploited masses, the homeless and the hungry, the struggling Palestinians and revolutionaries. On the other side are the affluent, the greedy owners of oil wells, big industries and war machines. There is no question of a compromise or a human relationship between those two fronts. And it is an honour for us to belong to the first of these two fronts. We are proud of what you call are our crimes. We feel honoured that we are fighting, hand in hand with other revolutionaries, for destroying imperialism and Zionism. Only two options face us today. Either struggle or surrender. Either we must fight like the Vietnamese, Chinese, and Palestinians, or we must submit ourselves to bondage, like the (Shah's) Iran. The odds we are facing in our struggle are heavy. But a human being cannot be cleansed without suffering and trial. When I speak these words, I have in mind the mothers and fathers whose children are in prison. But such is the philosophy of life. Their children will be destroyed physically, but dawn is near. We must endure.

'I and my friends are children of Dr. Mossadeq and followers of his path for national independence and freedom. We have turned our backs on money and position. It was the people who brought Dr. Mossadeq to power to work for nationalization of oil. His was the only legal government our country has had. But Mossadeq was overthrown and the political opponents of the (Shah's) regime were massacred. Following this, the regime flung open the doors for the unrestrained plunder of Iran's wealth. Oil revenues began to be mainly used for purchasing arms and paying the salaries of American advisers.

'Today, the regime has found itself compelled to don a new dress in order to prolong its survival. It is carrying out land reforms and sharing profits with factory workers. But it is playing imperialism's game. Since the *coup*, (against Mossadeq in 1953) corruption in government administration and bribery are on the increase as are the misfortunes and deprivations imposed on the people by the ruling classes. Take a look at the shanty towns around Tehran. If the poor fall sick, they are condemned to die while waiting unattended outside the hospitals. The shanty town dwellers have nothing to lose except their debts. In rural areas, exploitation by landlords has been replaced by exploitation by the government. These are some of the things creating readiness for revolution. Under conditions when all voices of protest are being muffled and people are suppressed, the only way for struggle is armed resistance by the people.

'To serve government propaganda, the regime's Prosecutor is accusing us of wasting the country's foreign exchange in purchasing arms. I wish to ask: are we the one's who have transferred huge amounts of foreign exchange from this country and sold the nation, or you? Who is hoarding foreign exchange in Swiss accounts? Who owns these hotels, night clubs, and casinos? If he (the Shah) has not acquired all these by robbing the nation of its wealth, then we must assume that his father was a thief. Are we the one's who are wasting the country's foreign exchange or those who import luxury goods and cosmetics, dresses from Dior and flowers from the Hague, whose expenditure for a night of revelry is astronomical. Our oil resources are being heartlessly plundered. If the present trend is to continue, Iran's oil reserves would be depleted by 1987. The present oil production stands at 227 million tons a year. Iran is receiving only $1.3 for every $10 of oil that is taken away and sold at high prices in European markets. We are losing at least two billion dollars in this unequal transaction. Mr. Prosecutor, take a look at this amount, and not at the foreign exchange we have used for purchasing a few machine guns. Hundreds of millions of dollars are ending up in the pockets of foreign companies. In a Press statement, the chairman of the Planning Commission has confessed that an amount running into hundreds of millions had been embezzled under various pretexts. We were promised that with the oil income, Iran would become a welfare state. But the masses have become more impoverished. People are denied their legal rights. When the workers of brick and smelting factories went on strike, soldiers opened fire on them. 200 workers were killed. Troops killed Dr. Khan Ali during the teachers' strike, and wounded so many others. The teachers and the factory workers had merely asked for a pay increase. Yet they were fired at, and their killers got promotions. When the regime reacts to the legitimate demands of the people in this manner, is it possible to remain silent and not pick up a gun?

'Our country is suppressed under the tips of bayonets. To resist this general suppression, even the clergy, which had withdrawn for the past 50 years, is entering the scene of struggle against the Pahlavi regime. There was an uprising in Qom. Students of religious schools attacked soldiers and soldiers killed two persons. This led to an uprising by the clergy, the bazaar merchants, and students. The result was the Massacre in June 1963. It was after this massacre that Hanif-nejad, Saeed Mohsen, and Badizadegaan came to the conclusion that it was not possible to secure one's rights through discussion and logical arguments. They referred to the Quran and the *Nahjul Balagha* to begin a new revolutionary movement. Besides the *Mujahideen-e-Khalq*, other revolutionary groups have also emerged and continue to emerge to fight for the defence of human dignity.

'That so many revolutionaries are joining the underground resistance shows that the existing conditions are such that hundreds of our best youth have stepped on the path of armed struggle. This proves that our struggle is not waged for any personal motive or objective. Hundreds of highly qualified doctors and engineers are on this path. Ten years ago, the activity of opposition groups was limited to the clandestine distribution of newsletters and bulletins. But now we are picking up arms. This is only the beginning of our struggle. We are aware that victory cannot be achieved quickly and easily. Hazrat Ali has said: "God does not destroy the exploiters and oppressors of the times Himself. He gives them the opportunity to return to the straight path. When they do not do so, they sink deeper into the swamps of exploitation and decadence. Then He delegates to the people the responsibility to carry out Divine Justice. God does not heal the fractured bones of any nation without suffering and trial."

'The (Pahlavi) regime is endeavouring to lead our youth astray by propagating the moral decadence of Western capitalism. Instead of creating conditions for heightening the social and political consciousness of the young, the regime is encouraging corruption and immorality by setting up "Youth Palaces" (and such filthy publications as *Zan-e-Rooz* [Woman today]). The regime's objective is to prevent the young from getting involved with the real problems concerning them and their society.

'Ruthless suppression is being openly practiced in order to crush the spirit of resistance and instill an attitude of despair and powerlessness among people. Armed guards are being installed in universities. SAVAK's budget is running into hundreds of millions. No one can be taken into employment without first undergoing a screening by SAVAK. The Police and SAVAK have been given unlimited authority for dealing with political dissidents. The director of Qazel Qile prison has instructed his personnel to deal with political dissidents as a butcher deals with the lamb. The regime is not prepared to tolerate opposition or criticism in any form. The workers of Jahan textile industry who were demanding a pay rise were attacked by soldiers. 12 of the factory workers were killed. A few months ago, soldiers attacked Tehran University and Arya Mehr University. Even the professors were mistreated and assaulted.

'There is nothing the regime can do but intensify its oppression. This is a clear indication of its weakness and is a sign of its impending doom. Political prisoners are being subjected to savage torture. Many of them have died under torture. According to article 131 of the Constitution, if an official causes the death of a political prisoner (under interrogation and torture) he is to be dealt with as a murderer. Yet the killers of political prisoners are going about freely and getting promotions. Burning the body of the prisoner with a stove, pulling out the finger nails, whipping and blows to the genitals are the methods most often used. Mohammad Hanif-nejad was beaten so heavily that the bones of his hands, feet, nose, and ears were crushed. Behrooz Dehqani was killed under torture. A baton smeared with acid was thrust into the rectum of Masood Ahmadzadeh. Before he died, Ahmadzadeh had to spend two months of gruelling agony in hospital. You cannot endure listening to our words. We do not expect this inhuman regime to treat us differently. That is why we are fighting to overthrow it. We are looking forward to the day when our people will drag the traitors to the people's court. Down with American imperialism. Hail to those who endure agonies and suffering for the sake of revolution and freedom.'

Mujahideen-e-Khalq's Poetry of Resistance

A glimpse into the inner transformation the *Mujahideen-e-Khalq* experienced and the social commitment this transformation generated in them is available in the poems and revolutionary songs the *Mujahideen* composed during their imprisonment. Many of these poems developed from revolutionary songs the *Mujahideen* sang together in prison to express their solidarity. As a result, even though those who wrote and developed these songs were executed or killed under torture, their message survived in the memory of their prison mates.

During the Shah's dictatorship, the *Mujahideen* sometimes succeeded in smuggling their statements and poems out of prison. In rare instances, a poem would be found scribbled in the notebook of a martyred *mujahid* when his personal effects (shoes, clothes, wrist watch, etc.) were returned to his family after his execution.

When scores of *Mujahideen* who were serving life terms in Pahlavi prisons were released during the Revolution, they flooded the Islamic Revolution with the *Mujahideen's* songs. No longer were these songs and poems representative of the social, spiritual and intellectual struggle of remote 'heroes'. Shared and assimilated by thousands of young revolutionaries, their message became the collective consciousness of a progressive revolutionary generation of Muslims. It represents the birth of a new era, marking the birth of a new consciousness and a new man —one who is aware of himself as the agent of a Super Power on earth— the Super Power who has designed the universe with a purpose. The objective of this guerrilla of God is to endlessly strive for the perfecting of humanity, society, and his own self through a permanent revolution. By consciously choosing to submit to the will of God, His agent proceeds on the path of evolutionary growth towards perfection. In the words of Mehdi Rezai, the 19 year old martyred *mujahid*, 'A human being who is consciously moving in the journey towards perfection is the most precious phenomena in creation.' Death does not exist for him, his immortality is a settled fact. Therefore, he fulfils God's trust by whole heartedly hurling himself into social struggle for removing the hurdles in the path of social and spiritual evolution of man and society. The consummation of his revolutionary life and struggle lies in martyrdom. *Shahadat* for the *mujahid* is the 'acme of life's line, a stature sublime, reserved for His chosen ones.' Dying for the people is the main gateway to God, for the people are children of God.

Reza Razai, Mehdi Razai's brother, was killed by SAVAK in 1973, aged 24. In the poem that follows, Reza talks about 'witnesses' — those who carry the message and knowledge to others, bearing testimony to its truth in their own personality. Clearly, then, the 'witnesses' in the poem are the ideologically aware *Mujahideen* committed to social struggle:

The Search for Witnesses

> *And we bring these days (of trial) — that Allah may know those who believe and take witnesses from among you. (Quran 3:139)*

Our sorrow is not sorrow
Ours is a load of sorrows
Load of thousands of faded
faces
Sorrow of a hundred
expectant eyes
Load of hopes
for a thousand dawnless nights

We should talk of fire
Red fire that brings colour
to faces
I think of nothing
but the dawn of the night
I think of nothing
but the colour
Of gunpowder and copper
on the battle field.

We don't talk of stations
and staying
We don't even talk about going
Our concern is how our ashes
Can become the seeds
for other Mujahideen
Our talk is about burning
Our talk is of effect
Our talk is about
'witnesses'
Just that

Untitled Poem

(by Reza Razai, 1973)

It is not possible to raise
the seed of faith
On dry, hollow words
It needs to be irrigated
with blood

For its growth

If you step into the battlefield
of Faith
then step like a lover
Don't think it is a road
without peril
Either don't think of becoming a Mujahid
Or be like Habib
The Mujahid of the path of Truth
should be prepared to lay
His life
Don't think the dark night
has no dawn
Tomorrow the sun of freedom
will rise.

The Song of Blood

(Composed in prison 1971–72)

When our blood began
flowing on the path of truth
The seeds of revolution
quickened with life
The spark of people's
vengeance
Set fire to the straw house
of the people's enemy
On the revolution's sky
a star was born
The way for the final battle
has been opened
Through his world-view
and the Mujahid's machine gun
Arise and commit yourself
truly,
with the resoluteness
of blood and steel
Arise, for the Hand of God.
Will burst out
from the people's sleeve
Arise, Arise
The true revolution is being raised
by the Mujahideen.

Shahadat

(Written by a **mujahid** *martyr in Mashhad prison, 1976)*

On this dawn of blood
My message to you
is *shahadat*.
The mujahid guerilla knows not
defeat
I'm a *shaheed*
Blessed for me is *shahadat*
Dawn is stretching
Evil withdrawing
Rage is rising to become
God's Hand
And bursts from the sleeve
of Mujahideen
Shahadat is a blessing
Shahadat is liberation
It's the path to a world
Knit in Divine integration
I've staked my life on God's command
I'm liberated from all prisons
But with the people share
Their imprisonment
Lo! the night has paled with
fright!
Arise and look at the new
sun rise
Dawn is bursting
From the Mujahideen's gun.
Shahadat! Shahadat!
A message from Quran
Coming from God
To favour the oppressed and the weak
God has urged Muslims
with the message
The acme of life's line
is *shahadat*.
Blazed in the night of oppression
like a star
I heard this message ......
I'm a Muslim
So long as there is oppression and injustice
I'm a *shaheed*
I'm a *shaheed*

I'm a *shaheed!*

The Highest Jehad

(1972)

Come, let's stake our lives
On Truth
And sacrifice ourselves
For our heroic people.
Our struggle will continue
To be waged
By the masses
Arise!
For the highest *Jehad*
Has become our life's path!
The way of the people
is the way of our *Jehad*
The fiery weapon in the people's hand
Is the message
For the people's final war
Through the workers
struggle and blood
And the peasant's determined rage
The highest *Jehad*
Has become our life's path
Between the people and their oppressors
Nothing exists
except battle or bondage
The path of final liberation
As the way of Mujahideen
Has become our life's path.

Nation of Martyrs

(Composed by a **Mujahid-e-Khalq** *in jail, 1972)*

O Iran! nation of martyrs!
O the eternal garden of lions!
I have awaited long
To become one
Of the Mujahideen
I lay my life at the brink of dawn
For the people of Iran

So that the soil of Iran
Becomes the land of red tulips
Of martyrs
The movement of the impoverished
Uproots and ruins
The oppressor's palaces
This revolt is raging
In every heart in the world

Listen to my last words
Enliven again the old story
Pick up my weapon
When I fall
To burn down
The oppressor's palace
Make my way your career
To liberate the people
Recall every moment
Your people rolled in blood
My last words have been
Allah-o-Akbar!
People's love has been
My guide
My leader, Quran's light

On Fatima Amini

(A 27 year old school teacher, Fatima Amini was the first **Mujahideen** *woman killed under torture in 1976).*
(This poem was written during the Islamic Revolution)

The pure lady of liberation came
Embodying the oppressed people's rage
She stood clothed
In honesty and faith
The light in her eyes
sparked with union
of the day and the night
They (SAVAK) asked her
Who are you?
Where do you live?
'I am a Mujahid'
She replied.
'The people's child'.
I was born in the land

of people's toil
I'm the echo
of people's silent rage
My bedmate is the machine gun
And the hand grenade
My song is the storm
of liberation
Even if you shred me
With your lashes
I'll tell you nothing
My only word
will be the people's song'
Thereafter
Our pure lady of liberation
the tall mountain
of perseverance and faith
was lashed by the whip of the wolves
In silence, with fortitude and pride
She let go of her life
For the way of the people
Under torture of the frenzied

Today the legend
of your fortitude
is the lullaby
of awakened children
Your patience, faith, and ideal
is the sound of every song
the voice of every protest.

The Song After the Revolution

One of the *Mujahideen's* musical scores released almost a year before thousands of their supporters were executed in 1981, anticipated the struggle against religious dictatorship and also the price such a struggle would entail. As the *Mujahideen* see it, the struggle against the idols of dogma and reaction is a 'continuation of the Abrahamic mission for breaking the idols of the time' and destroying the obstacles on man's path towards social and spiritual evolution and freedom. Appropriately entitled *Azadi*, (Freedom), this collection of revolutionary songs declares itself to be 'the furious protest of all the oppressed and manacled peoples of the world who have risen against enslavement and bondage throughout history'. For the *Mujahideen*, the 'Anthem for Freedom' is a 'song of the devoted lovers of freedom who are seeking to liberate themselves through liberation of their society'.

It is a 'tempestuous echo of the continual battle of the oppressed and toiling people of the earth against inhuman social systems'. 'The righteous voice of the *Mujahideen* is ringing in this anthem of freedom—freedom from the claws of imperialism, exploitation of man by man, and reaction.'

Technically and qualitatively, *Azadi* can be rated among the most explosive, original and creative works in the field of poetry and the music of resistance. The words and the music are an ecstatic blend of passionate emotional commitment with ideological direction.

(AZADI) Freedom

(by **Mujahideen-e-Khalq** *1981)*

O freedom! for you
I've endured prisons,
travelled among tempests
and shredded the petals
of my heart
like flowers on battlefields.
I've let my blood flow
in trenches of resistance
for your call to blossom
in people's hearts
and explode
on their lips.

Your name is my name
Your way is my way
O freedom! freedom!
Without you, darkness
drowns the world
and prison is
the victor.

O freedom!
With tears and blood
I make this covenant
not to let you down
Shed your light, O freedom!
When we're gone
on the dust
of our graves.
Drop by drop
my blood drips

on the Divine path
so that freedom flowers
on
the red soil of Iran.

O freedom!
the lantern of our blood
is burning
on your path
to let your sun
split the darkness.
Your rage will strike
like thunder on the night
You're roaring
in people's blood.

Notes

1. *Modafe'at*, (Defence Speeches). Published Documents of People's *Mujahideen* Organization of Iran, 1975, p.29–42.
2. *Taleqani–Paydar-e-Mojahidin* (Taleqani – *Mujahideen's* Father), Muslim Students Association, 1979, p. 21.

Appendix Two

APPEAL BY IRANIAN LAWYERS COMMITTEE

Subject: Suppression of the Iranian Bar Association

The sectarian theocratic regime in Iran has struck yet another blow upon freedom and the right of defence in our country.

After taking over the premises of the Bar Association at the Palace of Justice in Teheran and confiscating its records, library, and funds the regime has arbitrarily arrested some of the distinguished members of the Bar including:

1. Mr. Abdul Hamid ARDALAN, the President of the Bar Council,
2. Dr. Mohammad Taqi DAMGHANI, a long-standing member of the Bar Council,
3. Mr. Jahangir AMIRHOSSEINI, an alternate member of the Bar Council,
4. Ms. Batoul KEYHANI, Secretary of the Bar Association and a barrister in her own right.

To resist persecution and suppression most other members of the Council are either in hiding or have taken refuge outside the country.

The Bar Council in Iran, which is the elected ruling body of the Bar, is comprised of 12 standing members and 6 alternate members. Elections for the Council take place with the participation of all barristers, every two years.

The "Islamic" regime acting outside its authority postponed the election for a new Council, pending an "Islamic" or sectarian purge within the Association. Meanwhile the so-called "Revolutionary Council" allowed the standing Bar Council which was elected in June 1978 to continue its tasks, but in fact and in reality to act as a caretaker.

The right of barristers to take up the defence of those facing "Revolutionary Tribunals" was overruled, even though the "Islamic Constitution" sanctions this basic right.

Executions of at least seven barristers have taken place in the past six months. These included Mr. Manouchehr MASSOUDI, the Legal Counsellor at the Office of the former President Banisadr for his endeavours to save the innocent from such arbitrary actions of Mr. Khomeini's "Revolutionary Tribunals" which concluded his own fate, and also Mr. KHAKSAR, a young radical barrister who accepted to defend the members of the People's Mujahedin Party.

Orders have been issued for the arrest of several barristers who had constantly insisted upon the exercise of the right of defence, including Dr. Abdul Karim LAHIJI, a distinguished civil rights lawyer who has resisted arbitrary arrest by chosing a clandestine way of living.

In view of the above, all professional and humanitarian organizations and personalities as well as the Media are requested to voice their protest against such grave assaults upon human dignity in Iran, and to help to draw the attention of the world towards the gravity of human conditions in a country where a Nazi-like regime suppresses the most basic right of defence, the indispensable independence of the legal profession and commits acts of genocide against religious minorities, Iranian nationalities such as the Kurds, professional groups fighting for human rights, and all those who resist the sectarian domination of a ruling sect. The regime brutally arrests, tortures and executes any person without any charge, prosecution, defence or trial. The arbitrary rulings and lack of recognition of any civilized standards of justice, has led to the execution of more than 8000 innocent persons (by February, 1982) including teenagers (youngest being 13 years of age) and pregnant women.

Under the circumstances, many thousands of innocent people are being detained and put under inhuman conditions (e.g., over sixty prisoners are forced to squat in cells originally made for 12 prisoners at Evin Prison); those who fight for their basic rights are massacred from day to day to the extent that *one execution has taken place every half hour* on most days starting June 1981; no legal and judicial standard determines the limits of permissible penal action by the authorities to the frightful extent that Mr. Musavi-Tabrizi, a mullah appointed by Mr. Khomeini as the "Revolutionary Prosecutor-General", on 18 September 1981, officially declared that all those arrested on the streets at the time of a demonstration "will be tried on the street without the slightest hesitation" where the mere testimony of any two persons, will suffice to establish their crime against the "Islamic state", to be followed by a sentence of death and execution on the spot.

There is, therefore, no doubt that many human lives including that of the Members of the Bar are in serious danger. Whilst the Iranian Regime closes its borders to all foreign observers and journalists, in a general plot to avoid the exposure of its crimes and the great magnitude of its assault upon human dignity and liberty, any move to undo this plot and to expose the truth may help to save many human lives and the lives of those who are forced to face an internecine strife at the height of their struggle and hardship to end human sufferings within a nation which has in the past three decades fought two brutal regimes for its freedom.

On behalf of:

Iranian Lawyers Committee (in exile)

for the Right of Defence and Preservation of Human Dignity in Iran

> H. Matine-Daftary,
> Vice-President,
> Iranian Bar Association

19th February, 1982.

(The Crimes of Khomeini's Regime: A Report On the Violations Of Civil And Political Rights By The Islamic Republic Of Iran. ISF–Iran May 1982)

Postscript

Over the past three years, reports on the 'unimaginable violations' of human rights attributed to the clerical regime in Tehran have been dismissed as nothing but western propaganda by supporters of the regime. However, since the clerical regime unleashed the crackdown against its political opponents on 20 June 1981, the mounting evidence of documents shows that these 'unimaginable violations' are nothing but the realisation of the fantasies of the custodians of the Khomeini regime in practical terms. As early as 15 July 1981, less than a month after the Khomeini regime launched its campaign for eliminating opposition, the National Unity of Women in Iran, in an international appeal, pointed out that the Islamic regime was giving the female members of opposition an extra share in 'inhuman and barbaric behaviour' because of the reactionary views of the regime towards women.[1] Following are some of the examples of physical and psychological harassment cited by the National Unity of Women:

1. Beating girls in public and humiliating them sexually by pulling their breasts, in and out of prison.
2. Kidnapping opposition girls and women suspected of sympathising with the opposition and subjecting them to torture. Rape of imprisoned girls and gang rape.
3. Defloration of young girls by fingers on streets after arrest by Islamic Revolutionary Guards in order to later prove to the prison medical authorities that they are not 'good girls'.
4. Execution of pregnant women. A case involving the killing of a 8-month pregnant woman has been reported.
5. Executing teenagers, as young as 13 years of age.

The international appeal also quotes Ayatollah Mohammadi Gillani's official interview where be declared that the execution of a 9 year old girl was justifiable in Islam because this was the age of puberty for girls; and so from the Islamic point of view, declared Judge Gillani, 'there is no difference for us between a nine year old girl and a forty year old man.'

A more recent example of these 'unimaginable violations' gives concrete evidence to the effect that the blood plasma of political prisoners and anti-regime demonstrators sentenced to death is being removed from their bodies prior to their execution. This blood, it is alleged, is being used for saving the lives of Islamic Guards of the Khomeini regime wounded in street battles against urban guerrillas or on the battle front against Iraq. One of the first authentic accounts pointing out the possibility that the above allegations were not based on Western propaganda but on actual facts, was made available by supporters of *Mujahideen-e-Khalq* last February, and recounted in the magazine of *Fedayeen-e-Khalq* supporters published from Paris.[2] It was reported that the blood of Ali Niaz Baz, a young supporter of the *Mujahideen-e-Khalq*, had been drained from his body by the Islamic regime prior to his execution by the firing squad, as confirmed by the slain *mujahid's* father. The father has reportedly said that shortly before his son was executed, he was given permission to meet him for the last time. When the son was brought to meet him, he could barely stand on his feet, and had to be supported by two Islamic Guards. His complexion, according to the father, was palish white, and cracks showed on his lips. 'They have taken my blood,' were the only words the son managed to mutter to his father before he was taken away to be executed. When the body of the young *mujahid* was returned to the father for burial, he noticed that although there were six bullet holes in his son's body, there was hardly any sign of blood around the bullet wounds. That the Islamic regime has, of recent, started to hang its political prisoners sentenced to death rather than kill them by firing squads, and leave the dead body hanging for several days before returning it to the deceased's family, reveals the regime's attempts at neutralizing the evidence of 'bloodless bullet' holes on the bodies of those executed. However, documents recently published by opposition sources conclusively prove that the Islamic regime has officially instructed revolutionary courts all over Iran to remove the blood of all those victims sentenced to death by the Islamic courts. A document issued by the Chief Prosecutor of the Islamic Republic in October 1981 reveals that as the highest religious authority in the country, Khomeini has given religious sanction for removing the blood of political victims sentenced to death in view of the non-availability and shortage of blood plasma in the country. The full text of the Chief Prosecutor's instructions issued to all Islamic Revolutionary Courts in the country's provinces and districts reads as follows: 'When our brothers, the *Pasdars* (Islamic Revolutionary Guards) get wounded during street gun battles and at the battle front (against Iraq), and are taken to hospitals, they are in dire need of blood transfusion. However, the non-availability of blood plasma and difficulty and delay in obtaining it has led to the deaths of wounded (Revolutionary Guards). In order to help solve this problem, you are requested to give the order that the blood of those persons who are sentenced to death and whose execution is to be carried out immediately, should be transferred, by means of a syringe, and under supervision of trustworthy medical personnel, into suitable containers. The blood thus obtained should be immediately delivered to the nearest blood bank or hospital, so that it can be used for saving the lives of our wounded brothers (the Islamic Revolutionary Guards). It may be pointed out that in order to dispel the possibility of religious objections to the above action, the intricacies of this problem (of blood shortage and the need for removing the blood of those condemned to death) have been referred to the Blessed Presence of the Ruling Jurist, Imam Khomeini, Leader of the Revolution and Founder of the Islamic Republic, who has declared that there is nothing religiously wrong with the carrying out of these steps.'[3] The copy of this document has been reproduced on the facing page.

It will be recalled that one of the constant themes of Khomeini's speeches during the struggle against the Shah's regime was to accuse the Shah of building more and more prisons and 'turning the country into a graveyard' with the bodies of its political opponents (who, it must be mentioned, were mainly members of the *Mujahideen-e-Khalq* and *Fedayeen-e-Khalq* organizations executed by the Pahlavi regime). Before he came to power, Khomeini promised that the Islamic government would convert the prisons into parks and museums. Another document of the Islamic regime confirms the opposition's claim that, far from fulfilling its promise, the Khomeini regime has 'converted the existing parks, stadiums, and gymnasiums and other spacious covered areas like museums and even stables and workshop sheds for apprentices, into prisons for its political prisoners.' An official and secret letter issued by the Prosecutor of the Islamic Regime in Mazandaran, the province in North Iran, to the Director General of the Provincial Commission for Technical Training and Manpower Planning, stresses the 'urgent necessity' for constructing a prison in Behshehr, a northern city, because of the acute shortage of space the local government authorities are facing with respect to the number of political prisoners. The letter then requests the Commission for Technical Training and Manpower Planning to hand over a plot of land under its jurisdiction to the revolutionary authorities for converting it into a detention camp.[4]

Another legal problem from the religious angle that Khomeini's Islamic regime has been facing lately involves the execution of virgin girls. According to opposition sources, many religiously oriented Islamic judges believed that carrying out the death sentence against virgin females was 'Un-Islamic'. It is believed that the troubled conscience of such Islamic judges was pacified when one Islamic authority ruled that the virgin girls sentenced to death could be married off to Islamic Revolutionary Guards for a few hours. After defloration by their temporary husbands, the girls could then be executed 'Islamically' without pangs of religious conscientiousness. However, according to another

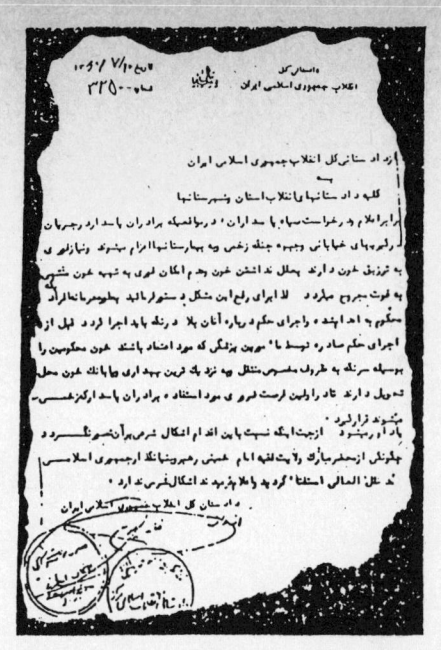

Document issued by the Chief Prosecutor of the Islamic Regime in October 1981, giving religious sanction to removing the blood from the bodies of boys and girls sentenced to death by the Islamic Court before sentence against them is carried out.

religious decree issued by Khomeini, those women and girls who are arrested and imprisoned against charges of 'waging war against God', are automatically regarded as 'spoils of war'.[5] This decree makes it religiously acceptable for the Islamic revolutionary guards and torturers of the girls to rape them. Mounting evidence about the rape of girls prior to their execution, and the coming into the limelight of Hujat-ul-Islam Hadi Ghaffari, a deputy in Khomeini's Islamic Parliament, as a 'professional rapist of the Islamic regime', has prompted the *Mujahideen-e-Khalq* office in Paris to urge the United Nation's Secretary General, Amnesty International, the International Red Cross, and humanitarian organizations worldwide, to directly investigate the situation in Khomeini's jails.[6]

It may be recalled that during the Islamic Revolution, a saying, attributed to Prophet Mohammad and Hazrat Ali, the fourth Caliph, epitomising the people's resolve to overthrow the Pahlavi dictatorship appeared as a revolutionary slogan. It declared: 'An Un-Islamic government may last a while, but a government based on tyranny and oppression shall not survive.' Today, the above slogan is ringing louder than ever before in the annals of Muslim history against a regime that has dealt the gravest blow to Islam in the name of Islam.

Notes

1. *Women and struggle in Iran.* Published by Womens Commission of Iranian Students Assocation. March 1982.
2. *Jahan* (Universe) Journal of Student Supporters of *Fedayeen-e-Khalq* Guerrillas. 3 April 1982.
3. Document No. 3250, dated 1360. 7. 10 (of the Iranian Calendar corresponding to 2 October 1981, issued from the Chief Prosecutor of the Islamic Republic of Iran, and reproduced in *Jahan*, 3 April 1982, p. 18.
4. *Kar*, No. 145, 26 January 1982, p. 15.
5. Weekly Publication of the Moslem Students Society, Britain, No. 3, April 1982.
6. Ibid.

MIDDLE EAST TITLES FROM ZED PRESS

POLITICAL ECONOMY

SAMIR AMIN
The Arab Economy Today
(with a comprehensive bibliography of Amin's works)
Hb

B. BERBEROGLU
Turkey in Crisis:
From State Capitalism to Neo-Colonialism
Hb and Pb

SAMIR AMIN
The Arab Nation:
Nationalism and Class Struggles
Hb and Pb

MAXIME RODINSON
Marxism and the Muslim World
Pb

GHALI SHOUKRI
Egypt: Portrait of a President
Sadat's Road to Jerusalem
Hb and Pb

CONTEMPORARY HISTORY/REVOLUTIONARY STRUGGLES

KAMAL JOUMBLATT
I Speak for Lebanon
Hb and Pb

GERARD CHALIAND (EDITOR), A.R. GHASSEMLOU, KENDAL, M. NAZDAR, A. ROOSEVELT AND I.S. VANLY
People Without a Country: The Kurds and Kurdistan
Hb and Pb

ROSEMARY SAYIGH
Palestinians: From Peasants to Revolutionaries
Hb and Pb

BIZHAN JAZANI
Capitalism and Revolution in Iran
Hb and Pb

ABDALLAH FRANJI
The PLO and Palestine
Hb and Pb

SUROOSH IRFANI
Revolutionary Islam in Iran:
Popular Liberation or Religious Dictatorship?
Hb and Pb

PEOPLE'S PRESS
Our Roots are Still Alive
Pb

ANOUAR ABDEL-MALEK (EDITOR)
Contemporary Arab Political Thought
Hb

MICHAEL JANSEN
The Battle of Beirut:
Why Israel Invaded Lebanon
Hb and Pb

REGINA SHARIF
Non-Jewish Zionism:
Its Roots in Western History
Hb and Pb

HUMAN RIGHTS

JAN METZGER, MARTIN ORTH AND CHRISTIAN STERZING
This Land is Our Land:
The West Bank Under Israeli Occupation
Hb and Pb

GERARD CHALIAND AND YVES TERNON
The Armenians: From Genocide to Terrorism
Hb and Pb

WOMEN

ASMA EL DAREER
Woman, Why do you Weep?
Circumcision and Its Consequences
Hb and Pb

AZAR TABARI AND NAHID YEGANEH
In the Shadow of Islam:
The Women's Movement in Iran
Hb and Pb

RAQIYA HAJI DUALEH ABDALLA
Sisters in Affliction:
Circumcision and Infibulation of Women in Africa
Hb and Pb

RAYMONDA TAWIL
My Home, My Prison
Pb

INGELA BENDT AND JAMES DOWNING
We Shall Return:
Women of Palestine
Hb and Pb

MIRANDA DAVIES (EDITOR)
Third World — Second Sex:
Women's Struggles and National Liberation
Hb and Pb

NAWAL EL SAADAWI
The Hidden Face of Eve:
Women in the Arab World
Hb and Pb

JULIETTE MINCES
The House of Obedience:
Women in Arab Society
Hb and Pb

Zed press titles cover Africa, Asia, Latin America and the Middle East, as well as general issues affecting the Third World's relations with the rest of the world. Our Series embrace: Imperialism, Women, Political Economy, History, Labour, Voices of Struggle, Human Rights and other areas pertinent to the Third World.

You can order Zed titles direct from Zed Press, 57 Caledonian Road, London, N1 9DN, U.K.